Train Robber's Daughter

Train Robber's Daughter

The Melodramatic Life of Eva Evans
1 8 7 6 — 1 9 7 0

Jay O'Connell

RAVEN RIVER PRESS
NORTHRIDGE, CALIFORNIA

RAVEN RIVER PRESS
17630 Osborne St.
Northridge, CA 91325

First Edition

12 11 10 09 08   5 4 3 2 1

Cover design by Jamison Design/J. Spittler

Front cover photographs courtesy the Tulare County Museum and the
Huntington Library, San Marino, California. Additional photography by
Robert Salas

Printed and bound in the United States of America

Library of Congress Control Number: 2007935563
ISBN 978-0-9673370-2-9

In men whom men condemn as ill,
I find so much of goodness still;
In men whom men pronounce divine,
I find so much of sin and blot,
I hesitate to draw a line
Between the two, where God has not.

—JOAQUIN MILLER

Contents

A Curtain Speech   ix

ACT ONE: A FAMILY

Chapter One   Rattlesnake Ranch Wedding   3
Chapter Two   Early Childhood   12
Chapter Three   Concerning John Sontag   24
Chapter Four   Coming of Age   33

ACT TWO: THE TROUBLES

Chapter Five   Robberies and Suspects   49
Chapter Six   Collis Changes All   63
Chapter Seven   A Headline Sensation   77
Chapter Eight   Defiance   92
Chapter Nine   Aid and Support   107
Chapter Ten   Stone Corral   122

ACT THREE: INFAMY

Chapter Eleven   Life in the Theatre   137
Chapter Twelve   Trials and Tribulations   153
Chapter Thirteen Conviction   166
Chapter Fourteen On Tour Again   178
Chapter Fifteen   Hard Times   193

ACT FOUR: MOVING ON

Chapter Sixteen   Oregon Portraits   211
Chapter Seventeen Utopian Dreams   224
Chapter Eighteen   Writing a Legacy   239
Chapter Nineteen   Laguna Beach Passings   252

Source Notes   263
Bibliography   285
Acknowledgments   291
Index   293

A Curtain Speech

Ladies and gentlemen—in the language of Shakespeare: "All the world's a stage and all the men and women merely players." And this is true. We are all actors in the drama of life. We all have our part to play and having played them (either ill or well) death points out our final exit and we vanish from life's stage forever.

R. C. WHITE, *EVANS AND SONTAG COMBINATION* [1]

THE OBITUARY IN THE LOCAL NEWSPAPER where Eva Evans, by then known as Evelyn Kinkela, had lived for nearly four decades was a scant two paragraphs—a half-dozen brief sentences, a mere seventy-two words.

Mrs. Evelyn E. Kinkela died January 10 at the Laguna Beach Rest Home. Burial took place at the Westminster Memorial Park.
Mrs. Kinkela was born in Tulare County, California, May 13, 1876. She has lived in Laguna Beach since 1930. She is survived by her widower, Andrew, at the home address 480 3rd St., and a brother Joseph Evans of Bend, Oregon. The late Ynez Jensen was a sister of Mrs. Kinkela.[2]

She had lived more than ninety-three years, the last four decades of which spent in the same small seaside community. And yet, when she made her exit from life's stage, this was all that was written about her.

Did anyone reading her obituary, buried on the third page, have the slightest idea of the famous people Mrs. Kinkela had known during her long life? Or that Mrs. Kinkela herself had once been famous? Didn't anyone know she had taken part in events once reenacted on stage in front of wildly enthusiastic audiences? That she actually starred on stage as herself? Did no one in her Laguna Beach neighborhood realize that Mrs. Kinkela had lived a life once splashed across the front pages of newspapers? Judging from the thundering lack of details in her obituary, apparently not. She died in quiet obscurity—her final exit barely noticed.

Most people die in quiet obscurity. Most obituaries are painfully brief. But the ominous silence of old age can be deceiving. If we only stopped to listen, we might discover that all those lonely old ladies in the neighborhood, all those cranky old men down the block, have life stories that could fill volumes. And every once in a while, one of those unheard stories is truly extraordinary—a valuable piece of history—a life that demands a thorough biography and not just the obligatory obituary. Such was the case of Mrs. Kinkela, better known as Miss Eva Evans, who was so much more than just a train robber's daughter.

Eva Evans played a key role in the sensational saga of Evans and Sontag, California's most notorious outlaws. It is a classic tale of the Old West. As one historian pointed out, it has all the elements of epic drama: "the greedy railroad barons robbing the farmers of the San Joaquin with their high freight rates; familial love and devotion; farmers accused of train robbery and beset by bounty hunters after blood money; gunfights and ambushes and finally the showdown shootout between a posse and the two outlaws."[3] And although Evans and Sontag didn't retain the household-name status of other American outlaws like Jesse James, Billy the Kid, or Butch and Sundance, the media deluge generated by the train robberies, gun battles and extended manhunt was surpassed by none. Indeed, no two outlaws in California history more grasped the imagination of the public or more dramatically demonstrated the antagonism over big railroad's privileged position than Evans and Sontag.

The circumstances surrounding Evans and Sontag's crimes illustrate numerous themes of late nineteenth-century California history. The antagonism they so dramatically demonstrated—no company was more generously hated in California than the Southern Pacific Railroad, and this prevailing sentiment made their train robberies more palatable to much of the public—was emblematic of the growing rift between big corporations and the general population. The railroad's domination in California also highlighted land issues key to the development of the state. Land issues and animosity clashed at Mussel Slough, and the violent conflict there between the railroad and displaced settlers is a necessary preface to Evans and Sontag and their place in California history.

The way Evans and Sontag seized the public's imagination exemplified an evolving and burgeoning mass media led by William Randolph Hearst. How his newspaper, the *San Francisco Examiner*, covered Evans and Sontag was a case of a young editor cementing a style of journalism that continues to influence society to this day. The newspaper coverage and the ensuing stage melodrama also demonstrated the public's fascination with the cult of celebrity, a cult that seems to burn brighter with each successive generation. It was the media of the day that delineated the mythic profile of these outlaws, making them so much more than mere criminals in the public consciousness and, thus, creating in them archetypal figures—the popular outlaw whose crimes against an evil corporation are cheered by the common man.

Archetypal could be called a "two-dollar word" for cliché, but there was never a story of outlaws and the Old West quite like this one. It involved an otherwise respected member of the community—a family man with seven children. And although the oldest child—his teenage daughter, Eva—was not directly involved in any actual train robberies (as far as we know), she was present at gun battles, served as messenger to her fugitive father, took the witness stand at a famous trial, was a co-conspirator in more than one jailbreak, and finally became a celebrated actress, portraying much of this on stage in San Francisco and throughout the West.

Beyond the outlaw saga of Eva's youth, there was the long adulthood of a woman who had come of age during tumultuous events. How did the headline-grabbing experiences of a teenage girl affect Eva as she navigated through later life? How did her adolescent jaunt through the Old West and the Gilded Age transform the woman of the twentieth century?

Eva's struggle with drug addiction and attempted suicide, her early failed marriages, her brief career as a photographer, her interest in social reform and friendships with famous anarchists and progressive thinkers, her attempt to right her father's story, and her final role as the childless matriarch to the family she survived were all shaded by a turbulent childhood and adolescence. Eva's later life is thus pertinent to the marquee history of Evans and Sontag. It is her entire life, examined in whole, which ultimately completes one of California history's most sensational sagas. Such a rare life demands a biography.

BIOGRAPHIES CAN ONLY BE WRITTEN, however, when adequate sources exist. On this subject a wealth of source material has long been available. Numerous books and articles have already been written about Evans and Sontag, and the contemporary newspaper coverage of their exploits was almost endless. And when considering Eva's story, there is perhaps no better starting point than her autobiographical memoir of nearly 300 pages. Written in the 1930s, she donated it to the Huntington Library in the 1960s. While some historians have questioned the veracity of her narrative[4] (she does alter the facts at times to keep the story in line with previous alibis and elements of her father's defense), a careful reading of the memoir shows that she was, for the most part, quite accurate. This was because, as she once explained, she did not entirely trust her memory, "but went to the State Library in Sacramento and checked [her] story carefully with the daily papers of this period."[5] For the biographer, what this memoir provides are Eva's opinions, feelings and impressions, far more valuable than mere facts, which can always be twisted and disputed.

Two new major sources, however, have recently come to light, illuminating the biographer's path as never before possible. One of these sources surfaced in dramatic fashion. As one newspaper reported:

> History buff Terry Ommen was doing research at the Tulare County Museum...when a couple walked in. As they spoke to the museum curator, Ommen overheard his name.
>
> "The person you need to talk to is right over there," said museum curator Kathy McGowan, pointing to Ommen.
>
> Bob Lilley, who had arrived at the museum from the [California] Central Coast, addressed Ommen: "I have the original copy of the Evans and Sontag play. Are you interested?"
>
> "My mouth dropped open," Ommen said. "[Lilley] said, 'Is that a big deal?' I said 'Yes! It's a huge deal.'"[6]

Terry Ommen, a retired police officer and one of Visalia's leading historians, knew of the Evans and Sontag melodrama. Historians had long considered the script for the play, which Eva herself had starred in, lost to history. What Bob Lilley, the great-great-grandson of the playwright R. C. White, had wasn't just the handwritten original—it was the only known copy. In addition, Lilley had a trunk full of memorabilia that included drafts of a curtain speech, photos, playbills, and handwritten arrangements of the musical underscoring, complete with scribbled margin notes commenting on the nature of audiences in various towns.

The melodrama, which was such a watershed event in young Eva's life, could now be examined in full. Historians before could only imagine what the "blood and thunder" drama was like from Eva's comments in her memoir and newspaper reviews that described the production. For the biographer, this material brought the play and its tour to life, making a key phase in Eva's life now accessible.[7]

Another recent discovery of material involved not only an additional copy of Eva's memoir, but a wealth of manuscripts, correspondence, photographs and scrapbooks that she had kept for posterity. It was that all-too-rare "box in the attic" that all historians dream about; and it was saved by a woman who is herself deserving of a biography. Lillian Kinkela Keil, a former World War II and Korean War flight nurse, was the most decorated woman in U.S. military history. She was also the daughter of Andrew Kinkela, Eva's last husband. When I first contacted Lillian—imagine how thrilled I was to find the actual stepdaughter of Eva—she was swamped with requests for interviews about her own life story and busy attending speaking engagements and memorial dedications. An incredibly active eighty-something-year-old woman, she promised she would get together some of Evelyn's (as she knew Eva) materials for me. She knew she had some letters and stories Eva had written, and maybe even a few photographs, but she wanted to organize them before she showed them to me. Lillian had fond memories of Eva, whom she visited often in the final years before Eva's death, and though she recounted those to me over the phone, I never got the chance to speak to Lillian in person.

Lillian's obituary in the *Los Angeles Times* featured a large headline: "Lillian Kinkela Keil, 88, 'an Airborne Florence Nightingale.'" It included two photos and a couple dozen column inches of copy.[8] It was in striking contrast to her stepmother Evelyn (Eva) Kinkela's tiny obituary thirty-five years earlier. Lillian never got the chance to gather and organize Eva's papers for the biographer who had pestered her, but Lillian's daughter, Adrianne Whitmore, eventually did. Furthermore, she agreed to donate the archive to the Tulare County Museum, where it is now available to historians and scholars.

WITH ALL THAT CONSIDERED, the idea to tell Eva's story was irresistible. But still I felt the need to zero in on what this book was really about—its thematic heart and soul. I realized that what made Eva's story so compelling to me was that it was, above all else and at every turn, a love story. Not the love story the media hyped and Eva herself propagated—a dime novel romance between her and John Sontag. That was the stuff of pulp and greasepaint and while perhaps partly based in reality, it was not the great love story of her life. No, Eva's real story is of the great love and devotion she had for her father. The love they had for each other epitomizes the goodness of humanity. And the good they saw in each other overshadowed the sin and blot that others might condemn.

To more fully understand that love, I still had to answer one key question in my mind: Was Chris Evans really a train robber? He had always denied robbing any trains. And many of those who cultivated his legend were quick to point out that he was never convicted of train robbery. (He was convicted only of murder.) I didn't buy into the media-created Robin Hood myth, nor could I believe the melodrama's portrayal of Evans and Sontag as framed by a villainous spurned lover. I had always felt, like most serious scholars of California outlawry, that Chris was guilty of train robbery. He was a bona fide criminal. To believe otherwise was naïve.

Still, maybe it is more interesting to harbor some doubt—to leave the question open-ended. But how does the answer to that question—or more precisely, Eva's answer to that question—shade *her* character? What doubt, if any, did she have? Did she alibi for her father—one of the primary goals her memoir seems to have had—out of naïve innocence? Or was it the conscious act of a co-conspirator motivated by a loyal love for her father?

Lillian Keil erased all doubt when she related to me something Eva once told her. In explaining to her that I thought Eva's memoir was a carefully constructed alibi and that Eva, like her father, never admitted he had committed any train robberies, Lillian chimed in, "Oh, yes, she did."

"I'm sorry, what did you say?" I replied, a little dumbfounded.

"She admitted it. She told me her father had robbed trains. That was how they got their money."[9]

Here was Eva's blunt admission, in her nineties, of her father's guilt. It was a moment that made Eva Evans suddenly more real—more real because now she was believable. And her acknowledgment of guilt made the undying love for her father all the more real as well. She loved him despite his guilt, and because of that love she protected his image while knowing of and even sharing his sins. She was, until the end, a dutiful daughter.

Perhaps Eva herself provided the best curtain speech when she wrote in the forward of her memoir, "An Outlaw and His Family":

> How does it feel to be the daughter of a man branded as "Outlaw," "Bandit," "Jail-Bird"? I have had people stare at me curiously, the question vivid in their eyes, the more intense because of my own eminently "respectable" exterior. I never answer the unspoken question because the answer would be too startling, entailing the long explanation I purpose to set down in this book. For the answer is:
>
> "I am gloriously proud of my father!"[10]

ACT ONE

A FAMILY

CHAPTER ONE

Rattlesnake Ranch Wedding

In the living room, the large rock fireplace still has every stone in place, and I see in fancy the oak backlog blazing merrily on my mother's wedding night.

—EVA EVANS, *AN OUTLAW AND HIS FAMILY*

THE CRACKLING OF THE FIRE was drowned out by a tangle of voices crowded into the modest ranch house. All the neighbors from near and far were there: the Tyners from Ash Springs; the Bullards from Bull Creek; Si Persian from Sycamore Springs. The Finleys and the Deans had arrived. The Campbells—daughter Laura made the wedding cake—were guests. And, of course, all the Bartons showed up: Florence, Jane, Adelaide, Melissy, Hudson, Jason, Enos, and Orlando. You'd never think the house would hold them all, and sure enough some guests spilled out into the yard, keeping the evening autumn chill at bay with a bonfire.

The Reverend J. P. Jones—some folks described him as a "circuit rider" preacher—called the room to attention. There was an audible hush broken only by the herald of Les Slocum's fiddle. Young Mary Jane Byrd, whom everyone knew as Molly, made a grand entrance on her father's arm. Still two months shy of her sixteenth birthday (although the marriage license said otherwise), she wore a long, black, silk dress with a bustle and pleated ruffles. To Molly, it was the height of elegance, but it took some convincing before her father agreed to let her wear it.[1]

Chris Evans stood proud and erect, ready to receive his bride. Though by no means a tall man, he appeared big and powerful next to his petite wife-to-be. He was clean-shaven for the occasion, save for the reddish moustache in contrast to his light brown hair. Now in his late twenties, it was only recently that Chris Evans could be described as anything but towheaded. But it wasn't his blond hair that was most commented on; it had always been his piercing dark gray eyes. They bespoke the intensity with which Chris approached anything in life, and on that day they reflected the love he felt for the girl beside him.[2]

CHRISTOPHER EVANS WAS BORN in Bells Corners near Ottawa, Ontario, on February 19, 1847. Chris often claimed to be born in Vermont and that his family moved to Canada when he was quite young, but the Canadian Census Report for 1851 states that Christopher Evans was born in Carleton County, Ontario, as were his seven brothers and sisters, including a twin brother, Thomas. His parents, Thomas Galway Evans, a farmer, and Mary Ann Switzer, were both born in Ireland. They apparently migrated to Canada separately and were married in Bells Corners in 1837.[3]

In his own words, Chris Evans' life "until I was seventeen years old was spent in a quiet way, and I was trained by a loving mother who, when I kissed her good-bye, never to see her again in this life, told me to always do what was right, no matter what was the result, and God would take care of me." After he crossed into the United States near Buffalo, New York, Chris joined the Union Army because, as he once wrote, "the great struggle for freedom was going on and I left my home…to liberate the slave."

Chris Evans loved to tell stories about his days as a soldier fighting first the Confederates in the Civil War and later hostile Sioux and Cheyenne on the frontier. Unfortunately, no official record of his service in the United States Armed Services exists, so only his version of the events remains.

> I was sent to Harper's Ferry, where Phil Sheridan was collecting an army to drive General Early from the Shenandoah Valley, and for six weeks was kept busy learning the duties of a soldier.
>
> On the 19th of August, we attacked the Confederate army near Winchester. It was my first battle, and as we marched up to the enemy with drums beating and flags flying I thought it was a grand sight; but before the sun set I looked over a bloody field covered with hundreds of dead and dying comrades, as well as brave Vir-

ginians who fell in defense of their homes, and I vowed then never again to take human life unless in self-defense.[4]

It was a vow recalled by a man who, at the time he wrote the account, was awaiting trial for murder. The jailhouse autobiography, published in the *San Francisco Examiner*, continued with more self-aggrandizing war stories. Chris told of being wounded in the foot by a Confederate gunshot at the Battle of Winchester. He later served at Monrovia station, guarding the Baltimore and Ohio Railroad. He was stationed at Fort Leavenworth after the war, then went to western Kansas to help build Fort Fletcher. He carried the mail to Denver, fighting Cheyennes in the process. He served as a scout, fighting against the Sioux on the Dakota prairies.

A Visalia newspaper once claimed that Chris Evans, while serving under Major Reno, had been close enough to hear the gunshots and screams at the battle of Little Big Horn. But the massacre of Custer occurred years after Chris migrated to California, so this claim was a fiction perpetuated by Chris, or perhaps just as likely, the reporter himself.[5]

The sheer volume of his stories, however, indicates some essence of actual experience. And while the veracity of many of these tales could be challenged, they were an element of the Evans family history. They were a part of how those close to Chris knew and perceived the man. They were an essential ingredient of his recipe for imparting wisdom and life lessons to his children. Chris Evans was wise enough to know that to be effective, even myth must germinate from some kernel of truth. And Chris Evans was an expert mythmaker, both in word and in deed.

CHRIS EVANS CAME TO VISALIA sometime in 1870. As described in family legend, his choice of city was left entirely to chance. In the late 1860s, after Chris tired of fighting Indians and took "French leave" of the Army, he migrated to California with his buddy, Jack Egan, by walking along the Union Pacific line, which was under construction at the time. They arrived in San Francisco in May 1869. Thus, Chris completed his own cross-country journey the same month the golden spike was driven in Utah, completing the transcontinental railroad.

Chris found work on the Western Pacific Railroad at Livermore Pass, where he had, in his own words, "charge of a gang of Chinamen at a tunnel." After that job ended, he and Egan headed out in search of more work. In the hills near Mission San Juan Bautista, they came to a crossroads. With no destination in mind, they "stood a stick up in the middle of the road and agreed to go the direction it fell." It landed in a southeast direction, and they struck out for Visalia.[6]

At that time, Visalia was the only significant town between Los Angeles and Stockton. Founded in 1852, Visalia was a thriving town of nearly a thousand people when the majority of the San Joaquin Valley was open plains populated only by the abundant native wildlife and the ever-growing cattle herds. Formerly known as the Four Creeks country, Visalia was situated in the midst of a broad and fertile plain, with Tulare Lake twenty miles to the west and the foothills of the Sierra Nevada mountains an equal distance to the east. As described in one early history of the region, "its beauty and fertility attracted a large population at an early day, and long before the advent of the Iron Horse." In 1861, a mere nine years after the town was founded, the first city directory was published listing five physicians, four law firms, a half-dozen dry goods dealers, two hotels and four saloons.[7]

Upon his arrival in Visalia, Chris secured work as a laborer and ranch hand from a man known as Pike Bill Owen. Chris was still a young man, barely in his twenties, and later wrote that he spent two of the happiest years of his life working for the Owen family. He claimed Pike Bill's wife was like a mother to him and their children loved him.[8] But not all was happy and peaceful during his first year in Visalia, as evidenced by a notice in the *Visalia Delta* in January 1871.

Chris Evans had become acquainted with a man named Tom Love. They were described as business partners. One day, Love became involved in a heated argument with Newton DeMasters over rent due on a pasture. Tempers flared, and DeMasters drew his revolver. He shot and wounded Love. Chris tried to interfere and DeMasters fired a shot at him. He missed, and there was only one thing for Chris to do. He ran into his house to get his rifle. By the time Chris returned to exact his revenge, several bystanders had gathered and interceded, preventing further bloodshed. Love survived the gunfight, and years later Chris claimed he had nursed his partner back to health. There was no mention of any arrests connected to the altercation.[9]

CHRIS EVANS MET HIS BRIDE, MOLLY, at the very house where Jesse Byrd now prepared to give away his teenage daughter's hand in marriage, a place the Byrds called the Rattlesnake Ranch, near the small setlement of Auckland in Tulare County. Jesse Byrd had made his westward migration with his growing family in the early 1850s. He was from Virginia and his wife, Isabella Meade Saunders, was from Tennessee, where their first son was born. Their next three children, all boys, were born in Texas.

The Gold Rush eventually enticed the Byrds to California, but Jesse never made much money in the Amador County mines. Hearing tales of rich tule lands in the southern San Joaquin Valley in the summer of 1859, the Byrds, with little Molly just a babe in arms, relocated to Tulare County. The family first settled in Farmersville, a few miles southeast of the county seat of Visalia. Jesse began to raise stock. In those days before the "No Fence Law," cattle were still king in the Central Valley; feed was plentiful and the stock could be driven to market. From the early 1850s until about 1870, cattle raising was the only industry in the San Joaquin Valley.[10]

The cattle industry in California can trace its roots back to the Spanish mission period. It was the one great industry of colonial California. Commercial value, however, was limited to the hide and tallow trade; beef only being used for local consumption. The rapid influx of immigrants into California during the Gold Rush was responsible for stimulating the beef industry—all those miners needed meat. The San Joaquin Valley had ample grazing land available for settlement, and so it was natural that the cattle industry would flourish there. In 1853, the counties of the San Joaquin Valley reported that they had 15,621 head of cattle. Seven years later, nearly a quarter-million cattle roamed the valley floor and adjacent foothills.[11]

Cattle and land barons, by buying old Mexican land grants at dirt cheap prices or by acquiring giant tracts of government-subsidized swampland, came to control much of the state. After only two decades of statehood, California found itself a more stubborn oligarchy than at any time during Mexican rule. Nine million acres of its best land were held by a mere 516 men. One man, Henry Miller, amassed over one million acres, ran 100,000 head of cattle, and controlled much of the cattle industry.[12] Still, for those able to acquire some land, work hard, and pray the forces of nature cooperated, the lure of staking their fortunes to raise cattle was irresistible in California's great Central Valley. But the risks were considerable, especially for small-scale ranchers like Jesse Byrd.

In 1865, Byrd's stock was wiped out in a flood, so he took to higher ground, buying a ranch in the foothills about twenty-five miles northeast of Visalia. His spirit never recovered from this financial setback, and he struggled to make the Rattlesnake Ranch thrive. This struggle was exacerbated by his battle with alcohol laced with fits of anger. As Molly later recounted, her father would drive his cattle to Visalia, sell them, then stay there and drink for days. Upon returning home, he would break furniture, threaten the children, and curse his wife. Molly remembered spending more than one night hidden in the orchard. The name Rattlesnake Ranch was appropriately venomous.[13]

TO MAKE ENDS MEET ON THEIR RANCH, the Byrds served meals and provided board to the teamsters who worked hauling lumber from the various mills in the mountains above Auckland. These mills were situated in and around some of the greatest concentrations of giant sequoias anywhere on earth, but it would be several years before any large-scale logging of Sierra redwoods occurred. In the 1870s, logging in the southern Sierra was still a relatively small-scale operation, due in great part to the difficulty accessing the timber lands in the steeper southern part of the mountain range. Nonetheless, a number of small mills were established in the mountains above Auckland such as Smith Comstock's mill, about two miles south of what is today Sequoia Lake; the McKinsey mill, a couple of miles to the west; the Hart mill near the later-named Hartland; the Wisher mill on the flank of Redwood Mountain; and the Barton mill near the head of Dry Creek at a place called Cedar Springs.[14]

Getting this lumber down to the valley was a difficult and costly task. It took talented and steel-nerved drivers to guide teams of horses with heavily-laden wagons down the steep, curvy, and rutted roads. The old-time teamsters of the area—men such as old man Hart, Billy Downing, Wes Loverin and Horace Whitaker—were hardworking men who had a way with horses.[15] One of these teamsters was twenty-seven-year-old Chris Evans. Hauling lumber down from the Barton mill at Cedar Springs, Chris often stopped for meals at the Rattlesnake Ranch. When he first set eyes on young Molly Byrd, it was, he wrote many years later, "a case of love at first sight, never to end in this life."[16]

Molly's watery-blue eyes reflected the anxious anticipation she felt standing next to Chris on her wedding day in front of gathered family and friends. She exuded innocent beauty, her fair coloring a striking contrast to the dark dress she wore. Her square face and thin, slightly down-turned mouth were a youthful mirror of her mother's stern visage.

Isabella Byrd, surrounded by her other children, including her four older boys, looked on as Molly took the oath of marriage. The tears were those of a mother watching a daughter suddenly grown up. The stern set of her jaw had more to do with the fact that her new son-in-law, if she was to believe his stories, fought for the North in the still painfully recent war. After ten years, her Tennessee blood still boiled at the thought.

Immediately after the ceremony, the fiddler was joined by other musicians for some good old Arkansas mountain music, Virginia reels and Irish jigs. Dancing broke out spontaneously. Tireless square dancers stopped only for supper at midnight, then more dancing until sunrise. When Reverend Jones finally set his hand to the marriage certificate, with Houston Campbell and Elijah Perkins serving as witnesses, it was the fourth day of November, 1874.[17]

AFTER THEY WERE MARRIED, CHRIS AND MOLLY spent the first months of their marriage alone together in the mountains. Chris was hired to stay at the Hyde mill all winter to keep the snow off the roofs so the buildings would not collapse. Chris loved the mountains, the snow, and the solitude. Molly loved Chris. Long before the winter snows began to melt, she was pregnant with their first child.[18]

In the spring of 1875, Chris Evans acquired a piece of land about a half mile below the Hyde mill at the edge of one of the region's largest giant sequoia groves. He had traded a place he had previously purchased on Dry Creek for this 160 acres he christened the Redwood Ranch. It quickly became a special place for Chris and his budding family, Molly now large with child. His family further expanded when his twin brother, Tom—along with his wife and baby daughter—arrived from Canada. Before long, Tom learned that his wife also was expecting another child. Chris and Tom worked to make the Redwood Ranch ready for their growing families.

Molly Evans, a product of her times and country upbringing, was quite a shot with a rifle and an excellent rider. She could put a loop over a horse's nose, jump on his bare back, and ride like the wind. But one June day in 1875, she was holding the bridle of a high-spirited horse while Chris saddled it. With the reins wrapped around her hand, when her husband threw the saddle on the horse, it bolted and dragged her along the ground.

The next day, Molly gave birth to a baby boy. Molly and Chris had so wanted a son. They had planned to name the baby Eugene if it were a boy. Eugene only lived a couple hours.

Chris made a redwood coffin for the baby and buried his first-born son under a tall cedar near a creek running through the magnificent forest. That fall, Tom's wife gave birth to a baby girl who lived only a few weeks. She was buried next to her cousin Eugene under the cedar tree.[19]

Chris continued to work as a teamster. During the summer and fall of 1875, Chris, his brother, Tom, and his brother-in-law, Louis Byrd, were all employed hauling freight to and from the Hyde sawmill. One day at the mill, Chris found a piece of doggerel verse that had obviously been left for him to discover. It was a crass rhyme that was pointedly insulting to Molly, inferring she had become pregnant before they were married. (Molly did indeed give birth to their first child only seven to eight months after their wedding day. The family explanation, of course, was that Molly being dragged by a horse undoubtedly caused a tragically premature birth. Had the baby been born full term, it surely would have survived.) And the pain of that recent loss undoubtedly made Chris that much more indignant at the public insult of not only his sixteen-year-old wife, but his dead son.

Chris Evans did not suffer indignity easily. He had reason to suspect the author of the offending verse was an older man named A. D. Bigelow. On November 6, 1875, Chris Evans, Tom Evans and Louis Byrd met up with Bigelow and another man named Hunter on the Camp Badger road. Chris brutally beat Bigelow with a piece of iron while Tom Evans and Louis Byrd held Hunter at gunpoint.

Before long, a deputy sheriff came looking for the Evans brothers and Louis Byrd. Chris and Louis had fled into the mountains, but Tom surrendered to authorities without incident. Chris and Louis eluded authorities—Chris had reportedly said he would never be taken—but finally Jesse Byrd convinced them to surrender themselves by offering to pay for any fines. In early December, they turned themselves in and, later that month, all three stood trial in Visalia.

The jury found Tom Evans and Louis Byrd not guilty, but concluded that Chris Evans was guilty of assault and battery. The judge fined Chris one hundred dollars or a hundred days in jail and remarked that he should not take the law into his own hands. Jesse Byrd paid his son-in-law's fine and the incident was behind them. The following spring, however, Bigelow died. Some of his friends said he never recovered from the thrashing an angry Chris Evans had given him. Chris felt the old man simply got what he deserved.[20]

THE NEXT SPRING, Chris, who loved the mountains, crossed the mighty Sierra on foot, via a pass at the base of Mt. Whitney. He made the trip because he heard good paying jobs were available at the Cerro Gordo mines in Inyo County. Molly stayed behind with her family at the Rattlesnake Ranch. She was in no condition to make the difficult mountain trek. Molly was pregnant again and would have to wait several months for any kind of travel.[21]

CHAPTER TWO

Early Childhood

———◆———

Way down in the meadow where the lily first blows,
Where the wind from the mountains ne'er ruffles the rose;
Lives fond Evelina, the sweet little dove.
The pride of the valley, the girl that I love

—19TH CENTURY POPULAR SONG

WHEN MOLLY GAVE BIRTH to her second child on May 13, 1876, it appeared as if this one, too, would not survive. The tiny baby, a girl this time, weighed scarcely two pounds and was only twelve inches in length. To further complicate matters, Chris was far away from home. The tallest mountain range in the country separated them: Chris working the Cerro Gordo mines, and Molly lying in bed holding their newborn to her breast, praying her baby would somehow survive.

A tune called "Sweet Evelina" was popular in California at that time. "Dear Evelina, sweet Evelina/My love for thee shall never, never die" proclaimed the chorus. Molly named her tiny baby Evelina Isabella after the sleepy-time song and paid tribute to her mother with the choice of middle name. Molly's mother, certain the child would die, thought it would prove a bittersweet honor. She believed no baby that small had ever survived. She even admitted later that she intended, once the baby did die, to put it in a jar of alcohol and send it to a museum—a statement no doubt intended to garner a reaction.

Although Molly's baby was small, she wasn't what one would call skinny. She had dimples in her knees and elbows, and seemed to be otherwise healthy. She ate well, but still could not drink enough milk to keep Molly's breasts from hurting. Molly's mother suggested they look for a newborn puppy to help alleviate the pressure, and one was found at a neighboring ranch. Putting a puppy to the breast was a fairly common means of relieving nursing mothers.

Molly's mother told a story—which became an often-repeated family legend—of similar problems when she nursed Molly's older brother, Louis. It seems there were no puppies to be found in the mining camp near Jackson where Jesse and Isabella Byrd lived when they had little Louis. Just about this time, Jesse was out hunting and shot a bear. When he went over to retrieve his kill, he saw two tiny cubs trying to hide under a log. He caught one and brought it home. "Here, Mother, this is just as good as a pup," he told Isabella, who put the baby bruin to her breast. Thankfully, the hungry cub latched on and was a great relief to her swollen breasts.

She nursed the cub alongside Louis and the two would often play together. But the bear grew faster than the boy, and before long he'd hug Louis and nearly squeeze the breath right out of him. By this time, Isabella no longer had the need to nurse, so they gave the tame bear cub to a miner headed for San Francisco. About a year later, Isabella was in Stockton and saw a crowd gathered on a street corner. She edged her way through the throng to see what they were watching. It was a bear— a thin and neglected-looking animal on the end of a chain—standing on his hind legs and "dancing" around slowly while his keeper played the harmonica. The bear saw Isabella. He suddenly dropped to all fours and pulled at his chain, trying to reach her. She knew it was her bear, just as he obviously knew it was her. She turned and hurried away, tears in her eyes, and regretted sending him into such a miserable existence.[1]

This would become a favorite story of Eva's, as tiny Evelina Isabella came to be called.

IN NOVEMBER, MOLLY AND SIX-MONTH-OLD EVA journeyed by wagon, train and stagecoach to Inyo County. Chris was happy to have his family back with him. His brother, Tom, had earlier come to Inyo, but it wasn't long before he and his homesick family returned to Canada. Chris was surprised to see how small his little daughter was. Perhaps Molly wasn't exaggerating when she claimed she could put her wedding ring on the little girl's arm like a bracelet.[2]

Cerro Gordo was the site of one of the most productive silver and lead mines in the state. The mines produced bullion so fast that transportation became the chief problem. In 1873, the mine owners had organized the Cerro Gordo Freighting Company, but the company's sixteen-to twenty-team wagons could not keep up. The advent of steamships by the company on Owens Lake helped, shaving eight days from the round trips made solely by the wagons. It was on one such steamer that Chris Evans found work.

The *Bessie Brady* was an eighty-five-foot propeller-driven boat with a twenty-horsepower steam engine. With Captain Titchworth at the helm and engineer Chris Evans on board, the steamer made daily round trips from the Swansea smelting operation on the north side of Owens Lake to Cartago Landing at its southern foot, hauling seventy tons of freight. The vessel performed the same service cheaper than teams and wagons hauling a mere one-tenth the weight between the same terminals in five days.[3]

The 1870s were a turbulent time in Inyo County. The area became host to some of California's most notorious Mexican bandits. Tiburcio Vasquez and his forces arrived there in 1874, one time even holding up a stage that carried Mortimer Belshaw, the owner and financier of the Cerro Gordo mine. Belshaw was relieved of his watch, a pair of new boots, and the money in his pocket.[4]

Tensions between the Americans and Mexicans remained throughout the decade. Molly recalled when a Mexican killed a popular law officer in Inyo and rekindled a feud. One day she opened her door to see a dead man hanging in a tree. Molly told Chris she could no longer live in such country and demanded that they leave. By then, fortunes were waning in Cerro Gordo, so he happily acquiesced.[5]

DURING THE FIRST FEW YEARS of Eva's life, Chris Evans moved his family around often. After leaving Inyo County, the family journeyed to San Francisco and then took a boat to Seattle, where Chris hoped to homestead. It was a stormy trip, and Molly was seasick for the entire eight-day voyage. Once in Seattle, the incessantly rainy weather depressed Molly so much that after six weeks she demanded they go back to California. Again, Chris honored his young wife's wishes.[6]

Perhaps one reason Molly was so sick on the journey to Washington was because she was again pregnant. The family returned to Visalia in 1878 where Molly gave birth to another baby boy they named Elmer. Not long after, Jesse Byrd traded his Auckland ranch for one in Adelaide in San Luis Obispo County, some 150 miles to the west near California's Central Coast. Chris decided to move his growing family out to Adelaide as well and was able to get work in a nearby quicksilver mine.[7]

When Eva was just four years old, both she and Elmer contracted diphtheria. A doctor told Molly he didn't believe he could save the little girl, who was still so tiny, but was confident the husky boy would pull through. Miraculously, it began to look as if both would survive. Eva was beginning to wobble around on weak legs, and Elmer was regaining much of his strength. Then one day Elmer had a convulsion and suddenly died.

No one had told little Eva about her brother's death, but as she remembered decades later:

> I must have wondered where the baby was, because when no one was looking I slipped into the bedroom and saw a box on the table in the corner of the room, pulled a chair up to the table and looked into the box, and there was baby brother, looking just as though he were made of white wax. Even if I did not really understand it, it must have been a shock, because it is the first thing I can remember. I was four at the time.[8]

WHILE CHRIS AND HIS FAMILY were living in Adelaide, beyond the Coast Ranges from the Central Valley, an event occurred in Tulare County that would become historically emblematic of the relationship between the entire state of California and the Southern Pacific Railroad. In an indirect way, this event—the tragedy at Mussel Slough—would become an almost necessary preface to any mention of Chris Evans.

While no one could deny the prosperity that the arrival of the railroad made possible in the San Joaquin Valley, frustrated farmers, merchants and land seekers also blamed their troubles—high transportation rates, a slumping economy, and a frustratingly slow agricultural development—on the highly visible railroad monopoly. In the Mussel Slough area, near Hanford in the west of what was then still Tulare County (now Kings County), groups of settlers began moving onto railroad-reserved sections of land in the early 1870s. The reserved land had yet to be patented to the railroads, and these settlers were betting railroad claims would eventually be voided by the courts. The government had reserved this land for the railroad in alternate sections along various proposed rail lines, which, in addition to cash subsidies, provided the capital to build and begin operations of the railroads. (There would also be complaints that many of these proposed rail lines were only that: *proposed* but never realized.)

The settlers tried in vain to file claims on the land. They sent petitions to Congress with no result. In 1878, some Mussel Slough farmers formed the Settlers' Grand League to publicize their position and create solidarity. Seeking to allay growing alarm, the railroad sent out prospectuses, which assured that when the railroad won title the farmers occupying the land would be offered the right to purchase that land at $2.50 per acre "without regard to improvements."

The railroad received legal title to their grants and began to send land appraisers to evaluate their holdings as a step toward sale. The land was first offered, as promised, to those in possession, but at exorbitant prices of $17 to as much as $80 per acre, a value that reflected the improvements made by the settlers, ignoring the option price promised. League members refused to pay. In 1879, the courts upheld the railroad's right to evict the settlers, who were squatters in the eyes of the law.

The situation deteriorated. In May 1880, U. S. Marshal Alonzo Poole, along with a Southern Pacific land grader and Mills D. Hart and Walter J. Crow, two recent purchasers of railroad land, set out to take possession of the disputed lands. While settlers had congregated in Hanford for what some called a picnic but which the *Visalia Delta* described as "a grand indignation meeting of the settlers,"[9] Poole and his contingent visited a ranch and emptied the house of furniture in preparation for the new owner, Mills Hart, to take possession. After arriving at the second property—the Brewer ranch where Walter Crow was to take possession—Poole and his men were met by a contingent of settlers who had gotten wind of his mission. The settlers demanded Poole and the others surrender their weapons. According to the *Delta*'s early account:

> Some fifteen settlers on horseback came up to within fifty or one
> hundred yards of the Marshal, he alighted and advanced, meeting
> them half way, and saluted them in a gentlemanly manner, saying
> that in his official capacity as U.S. Marshal he was compelled to
> perform his duties in this matter, although it was against his de-
> sire. A formal demand to surrender was then made to the Marshal
> by the leader.[10]

There was, in effect, a stand off. The marshal began to read his orders from the court. One of the settlers remarked that they didn't want to hear any of it. At a signal from the leader, each of the horsemen cocked his weapon, some armed with rifles, others with shotguns and revolvers. Poole later recalled the clicking of the locks to have been a startling sound to his sensitive ears. Suddenly a horse reared, knocking Poole into the road. Shooting broke out on both sides; five of the settlers and one of Poole's men were killed. Walter Crow was later found dead in a field two miles to the south with a gunshot wound in his back.[11]

The tragedy at Mussel Slough was an immediate cause celebre. Settlers, frustrated at their inability to acquire land, cast the railroad as pure villain. Nearly twenty years later, Frank Norris summed up their attitude in his historical novel, *The Octopus*. In the book, loosely based on the Mussel Slough affair, he called the railroad:

> The symbol of a vast power, huge, terrible, flinging the echo of its thunder over all the reaches of the valley, leaving blood and destruction in its path; the leviathan, with tentacles and steel clutching into the soil, the soulless Force, the iron-hearted Power, the Monster, the Colossus, the Octopus.[12]

While Norris' account may have been highly fictionalized, it depicted the prevalent attitude toward the railroad with stunning accuracy.

THE EVANS FAMILY WOULD EVENTUALLY return to a vastly changed, and changing, Central Valley. The previous decade had been one of great development there. The arrival of the railroad in 1872 had, for better or worse, affected the life of every resident. Bulk transportation was the catalyst that made cereal-grain farming possible on an unprecedented scale, ushering in the era of the bonanza wheat farms. Irrigation was further bringing opportunities to persistent small farmers who had earlier been derisively labeled "sandlappers."

Furthermore, the passage of the No Fence Law, in 1874, made it mandatory for cattle ranchers to fence in rangeland, putting the onus on them to keep their stock off neighboring farms rather than making the farmer fence in his land to keep cattle off. In an era before the development of cheap barbed wire, it was a blow to the cattle industry, but a boon to the ever-growing number of crop farmers. It hastened the end of the open range.[13]

The new decade also brought many changes for the Evans family. In August 1880, Ynez was born. Unlike Eva, she was a big baby, weighing almost ten pounds. All little Eva could think when she saw her was that she didn't like the fat red-headed baby. She was so fat you couldn't even see her nose when you looked at her sideways. In 1882, Molly Evans gave birth to another girl, Winifred, who weighed even more than Ynez.[14] Perhaps little Eva had gotten used to pudgy babies, because the now six-year-old girl thought this one looked all right.

The family returned to Visalia in the autumn of 1882 to a city that, like the Evans brood, was expanding. The Evans family holdings were also expanding. Chris had earlier purchased property in a recently added tract of city lots in northwestern Visalia for two hundred dollars. He had apparently done well working in the quicksilver mine because upon their return to Visalia, he and his mother-in-law, Isabella Byrd, also purchased forty acres of farmland from J. M. Canty. The property was located about a mile south of the city. They planned to farm it, and in the meantime, built and maintained homes on their city lots on the north side of town.[15]

By this time, Molly's mother had separated from her hard-drinking and abusive husband, who was now living with one of their sons on a ranch not far away. Isabella never talked of the cruel treatment she had endured from Jesse Byrd.

The Evans family's return to Tulare County also meant a return to the Sierra Nevada, the mountains Chris loved so much. He was finally able to bring his daughters to a place that was very special to him: the redwood cabin on the forest homestead where he had earlier buried his firstborn son. The family would stay there in the summer months to escape the valley heat and also so Chris, who often found work in the sawmills, could have his family close by.

In the spring of 1883, Eva saw the Redwood Ranch for the first time. The family drove up in a lumber wagon, Eva riding in the high spring seat atop a tool box that her father had converted to a seat. From that lofty perch, as evening approached and the mountaintops glowed with the last warm light from the setting sun, she saw the little house half concealed by cedar trees; her dad declaring that because it was getting late, they would camp there. He tried the door to the house and it wasn't locked. They walked in, and her father boldly proclaimed, "Nice in here. Why stay outside?"

There was a big living room with built-in bunks, a fireplace with wood stacked beside it, and a good stove in the kitchen with the wood box full.

"What do you think of a fellow that will go off and leave a place like this?" Chris asked seven-year-old Eva. "Let's stay till he comes back." Molly had to suppress a giggle, knowing full well that Chris himself had built and stocked the cabin. It was some time before Chris let his daughter in on his little joke.

Sitting in the cabin at nights, gathered around a roaring fire to chase the mountain chill, Eva and her sisters would listen to their dad tell Indian yarns and the occasional bear story. He often told them of the time when walking across the High Sierra to the Cerro Gordo mines, he was attacked by a grizzly and killed it with his hunting knife. But, for Eva, the Indian stories were the best.[16]

One such story was recounted by historian Wallace Smith in his book, *Prodigal Sons*. Smith relied heavily on interviews with Eva, and one can easily imagine the following account remembered from countless retellings at the behest of a youthful Eva.

Late one evening Chris, on patrol duty in advance of the troops, lay down on his blankets in a small thicket. A Sioux Indian had been trailing him cautiously and, in the early dawn, sneaked up on Evans and swung his tomahawk at the sleeping scout, cutting through three of his ribs. This annoyed Evans very much, who did not like to have his slumber disturbed in such a rude manner. He felt that a remonstrance, a reprimand, or even an argument would not meet the situation. After thinking the matter through, which didn't take him long, he decided that this was a time for action and that steps must be taken to remove his assailant from this mundane sphere. Evans hurriedly assembled his weapons, and employed them in the execution of the techniques learned in the school of the soldier. This led to the demise of the noble red man. Chris wanted his girlfriend in Canada to appreciate his prowess, so he carefully removed the scalp from his late opponent and mailed the Indian's hirsute adornment to her. The stench from the uncured souvenir led postal inspectors to open the package somewhere en route and Evans received a severe reprimand from Washington D.C.[17]

One can almost hear the crackling fire as this yarn was gobbled up by enthralled children. And although this story brags of killing an Indian, Chris always claimed his sympathies were very much with the "Red Man."

CHRIS WAS, IN THE EYES OF HIS ADORING DAUGHTER, very much a man of principle. Eva maintained there was a very strict code in their home. "You must not lie. You must not steal. You must not carry tales. You must respect the rights of others. And you must fight your own battles." It was a code that Chris knew could only be established by example. In the matter of lying, Eva later wrote that she never lied to her father but once to escape a scolding, and she believed that he never lied to her or to the other children. The deception about the Redwood Ranch was a joke, a little game. And there was one other time when he concealed the truth to save her pain, but it was not, in her mind, a lie. She told the story in her memoir as follows:

> I had a black spaniel—Toodles—and sometimes Dad used to take him to the south ranch with him. Coming home one night, with the dog running beside the wagon, a big dog jumped out at him, and in escaping he got under the wheels. When Dad arrived home he said nothing about it, but after we children were in bed, he and Mother went to the back of the vineyard with a lantern and buried him. The next morning I couldn't find my dog, and Dad said, "Yesterday I fired that Swede who has been working on the ranch, and after he left I couldn't find Toodles, so maybe he stole him to get even."
>
> Months went by, and no Toodles: and I spoke often of what I'd do to that Swede if I ever caught him.
>
> The following summer, while I was helping Dad build a fence at the Redwood Ranch, I started in on the Swede again.
>
> Dad said, "I just can't stand your never forgiving that poor man. He didn't steal your dog; Toodles was killed." He recounted the whole incident, telling me where the dog was buried, and I said, "You are just a common liar, and I don't want anything to do with you."
>
> As I turned to leave him, he said "Eva, listen to me. This was not a lie—just an effort to save you pain. I thought you'd forget it in a little while. I'd never lie to you, dear. How could I expect the truth from you if I did?"[18]

Little Eva stayed angry for nearly a week, but then felt all was right between them. She evidently saw the good intentions in her father's withholding of painful facts. "Never again," she claimed, "did I have reason to doubt my father's word."

Just a few days before the Christmas of 1884, another child was born to Chris and Molly. This one a boy they named Joseph. Chris was a devoted father to his growing brood. Eva often enjoyed watching her father walk the floor, reciting Tennyson's *Locksley Hall* in his "wonderful sing-song voice," lulling the baby in his arms to sleep. Chris only completed seven years of "common school" as a child, but read extensively and educated himself far beyond his formal education. He loved poetry and Tennyson was his favorite.[19]

> *Here about the beach I wander'd, nourishing a youth sublime*
> *With the fairy tales of science, and the long result of time;*
> *When the centuries behind me like a fruitful land reposed;*
> *When I clung to all the present for the promise that it closed;*
> *When I dipt into the future far as human eye could see,*
> *Saw the vision of the world and all the wonder that would be.*

How apt that he would recite the dramatic monologue which, according to Tennyson himself, represented "young life, its good side, its deficiencies, and its yearnings" to his various progeny.

It was about this time, according to her memory, that Eva began school. Books had always been important to Chris, and so it is odd to think that he would have waited until then to send his oldest daughter off to school. Proximity wasn't the problem, as the public school in Visalia was about a half-mile from the Evans house. Originally called the Little White School, Visalia's first public school was organized in 1857 and the whitewashed board-and-batten building was replaced by a commodious two-story building in 1872.

Nonetheless, it wasn't until she was nine years old that Eva experienced her first day of school. Considering the prevailing schooling habits of the time, this wasn't so out of the ordinary. Student attendance was inconsistent at best; in fact, it was common for many children to stay out of school part of the year. For example, in 1875, the total enrollment at the Visalia school was 441 children, but the average daily attendance was just about half that number.[20] The need to work at family farms and businesses and, for many families, the regular relocation to summer mountain homes contributed to sporadic attendance. The Evans family usually left for the Redwood Ranch in early April and often would not return until after the first snowfall in October. Consequently, the Evans children averaged only about six months of school a year. "What I liked was missing the final examinations; a written review of the work of the entire term, on which depended one's promotion to the next grade," Eva once recalled, adding that "Not one of us ever failed to be promoted; how we got by, I don't know."

Eva's size may also have been a factor in keeping her away from school so long. This is best illustrated by a memory she had of her debut at school. On that first day, the janitor, "an older man with a thin lined face but twinkling blue eyes," came up to Eva on the school grounds during recess and said, "Ain't you awful young to be comin' to school?"

"I'm nine years old; I'm not young," Eva replied.

"You're awful little; whose girl are you?"

"My father's name is Christopher Evans," she snapped back, and walked off with her head held high in the air. She had evidently heard enough about her size for one day. The janitor, Mr. McKeon, later became one of Eva's most valued friends.[21]

Chris Evans, who was well-read and prided himself on his literary prowess, spent time teaching his children himself. This was how, even with her late start and sporadic attendance, Eva still managed to progress through the grades; that and her oversized sense of pride and determination.

LIKE ANY FATHER, CHRIS' GREATEST RESPONSIBILITY was providing for his growing family. He had always been able to find work doing a variety of tasks such as teamstering, logging and mining, but these jobs were mostly up in the mountains. Down in the valley he found various jobs, from clearing land of oak trees, to operating a gang plow and Fresno scraper, to working the twenty-two-mule-drawn harvesting combines during the wheat harvesting season. But many of these jobs, too, were seasonal and took him great distances from his family. He was also at the mercy of employers, a mere wage earner. Like many men, Chris longed to work for himself. He was now in possession, along with his mother-in-law, of forty acres just south of town. Making it sound grander than perhaps it was, they referred to the property as the "South Ranch." Farming was the opportunity that would finally put his fortunes in his own hands. In 1885, Chris decided to plant the entire tract to beans, the emerging popular cash crop in the San Joaquin Valley.

As Wallace Smith explained in *Prodigal Sons*, Chris was cautious about his horticultural venture. He checked with the depot agent at Tulare about shipping rates before signing a contract with an Oakland firm to sell his entire crop at an agreed-upon price. Doing his homework, he knew that a decent crop would turn a handsome profit.

When he brought his crop in to the depot in Tulare, the shipping agent informed him that the rate was considerably higher than when he had checked earlier. Having signed an ironclad contract with the buyer in Oakland, Chris was forced to ship his beans at a loss. He had no other options.[22]

Farmers were at the mercy of the Southern Pacific Railroad, which held a monopoly on transporting goods in the San Joaquin Valley. Of course, the owners of the railroad could argue that they made commerce possible in the valley, so the farmers owed their very existence to them. Still, in the eyes of many, the huge corporation hardly seemed to be playing fair. If Chris harbored resentment toward the Southern Pacific over his failed business venture—and by all accounts he harbored a great deal—he was far from alone. He had plenty of company, from the displaced settlers of Mussel Slough to other frustrated farmers paying exorbitant freight charges.

Soon, another man would join this brotherhood, and there is nothing like a common enemy to bring people together.

CHAPTER THREE

Concerning John Sontag

———————◆————————

*It was in late September of that year, 1887, after we came down
from the mountains, that a tragically important event occurred. It
seemed simple enough at the time—Dad met a young man named John
Sontag, an ex-employee of the Southern Pacific Railroad.*

—EVA EVANS, *AN OUTLAW AND HIS FAMILY*

WHEN JOHN SONTAG WAS INJURED working on the railroad,
it was, statistically speaking, a common occurrence. Nev-
ertheless, it did warrant this brief mention in the *Fresno
Weekly Expositor* for August 31, 1887: "John Sontag, the brakeman on
the railroad who was so severely injured while coupling cars the other
night, is resting quite comfortable. Dr. Rowell expresses his opinion
that only one rib has been broken and backbone severely wrenched.
Good nursing and Father Time will pull him through." Injuries among
railroad workers were, by modern standards, disturbingly frequent. The
United States Census Report on transportation for 1880 reported over
8,000 rail accidents that year alone. By far the most dangerous job in
railroading was that of brakeman. The need to couple cars and ride their
tops to operate hand brakes made it incredibly risky.[1]

John Sontag, who was fairly new to the railroad trade, had been
accidentally thrown while coupling train cars in Fresno. An engineer
mistook his signal of "go ahead" for "back" and, as John stooped over
to uncouple the two flat cars loaded with iron rails, he was dropped between them. The train was moving at a slow rate and halted just as the
wheels ran up to his body, but he was gored by the protruding payload.
Another six inches and the grinders would have crushed him to death.[2]

As it turned out, he escaped with his life but suffered crushed ribs,
a pierced lung and a broken leg. The actual extent of his injuries, and

their lasting effect, is hard to determine. It was later claimed that the accident had shoved his heart over to the right side and the injuries, once healed, left a hole in his back large enough to accommodate a doubled up fist.[3]

HE WAS BORN JOHN CONTANT on May 27, 1861, to Jacob and Maria Contant of Mankato, Minnesota. Jacob was from Holland and the former Maria Bohn was born in Germany, both were devout Catholics. John and his younger brother, George, born in 1864, attended Catholic school. John served as an altar boy. His mother hoped that one day he would become a priest, but John did not share his mother's interest in that vocation.

In 1866, John's father was killed in an accident while helping construct the local schoolhouse. The next year Maria married Mathias Josef Sontag who, like Maria, was a native of Germany. Mathias eventually got into the hotel business, buying the Mankato House, the city's first hotel, and then later building the Sontag Hotel. Maria and Mathias were active members of the St. Peter and Paul's Catholic Church. As major donors, their names were emblazoned on one of the church windows.[4]

By 1880, the Sontag family (John and George adopted their stepfather's last name) had greatly expanded. Mathias and Maria now had three daughters: Anna, age fourteen; Mary, age nine; and four-year-old Josephine. The Census report for that year lists eighteen-year-old John Sontag's occupation as laborer. He still lived at home, but it wasn't long after that John Sontag, perhaps to spare friction with his mother who was so intent on him entering the priesthood, said goodbye to his family and journeyed to California. (It should be noted that both his brother, George, and Eva later wrote that John left home in 1878, when just sixteen years of age. Either someone misled the Census taker or John perpetuated a myth, playing up a more youthful flight from the family nest.)[5]

When John first arrived in Southern California, he was able to find plenty of work repairing damages caused by the recent flooding of the Los Angeles River. (Again, there is some discrepancy, as Los Angeles was abnormally dry in the late 1870s and early 1880s. There was, however, a big flood in the winter of 1883-1884 that caused considerable damage. This either means Los Angeles wasn't his first stop after leaving home, or he left home at a much later age than he cared to admit.) But after that work dried up, he drifted north to the San Joaquin Valley.[6]

In 1887, John was living in the railroad town of Tulare where he obtained a job as brakeman for the Southern Pacific, working the main line between that town and Fresno. That the main line didn't pass through Visalia, the county seat and most substantial town in that part of the valley, was just one more bone of contention Visalians had for the railroad.

Just as the establishment of the Butterfield Overland Mail station had provided a boon to the emerging "cow town" back in the late 1850s, city officials assumed the arrival of the railroad would provide a similar, if not more dramatic, boost to their emerging agricultural economy. But the railroad had issues of right-of-way and land grants to contend with, and it was more cost-effective for them to run the line farther west, thus creating their own railroad towns. One such town, just a few miles south of Visalia, they christened Tulare. The intention of the railroad in thus naming it was unmistakable; the plat map of this new city named after the county (which had been named for Tulare Lake at the county's western edge) was even marked "County Seat" and certain blocks were set aside for county buildings.[7]

Spur lines to both Goshen, eight miles to the west, and Tulare city, six miles south, were eventually financed and built, and a rivalry between Visalia and Tulare for the county seat was never able to swing in Tulare's favor, but another layer of animosity toward the Southern Pacific had been established.

LYING IN HIS BED in the Southern Pacific hospital in Sacramento following his accident in the summer of 1887, John Sontag had little concern for the politics behind so much collective animosity toward his employer. His only concern was getting better. It was a concern the railroad did not share.

The railroads, like most industries of the mid-nineteenth century, did little to assume responsibility for injured workers. While they did provide company hospitals, these facilities were generally filled to capacity and always short on beds and treatment. Furthermore, as declared by historian C. B. Glasscock, "many of the hospital jobs were filled via political appointments, or as rewards for past favors, as the railroad constituted the strongest political power in the state. More often than not, hospital attendants were chosen for their vote-getting potential more than anything else."

John was blunt with hospital personnel who treated him. When, after several weeks, the surgeon asked him how his broken leg felt, he boldly stated that he was just as bad as when the railroad had brought him in, adding that there was not a single nurse or orderly in the "whole damn place that's worth hell." These venomous words were imagined by Glasscock, using invective dialogue to illustrate a bitter and outspoken John Sontag. He continued the imagined exchange that led to John's early dismissal.

"You're a well man now," Glasscock had the doctor spitting back. "You lie here and bellyache while sick men are lined up in the corridors waiting for your bed. A lot of you lazy bums in here never had a clean bed or decent treatment in your lives until the railroad began to take care of you. Get up and walk. You've loafed long enough."[8]

In John's own words (or at least those a newspaper once quoted him as saying), when he left the hospital and went to the office of the Southern Pacific to ask for light work until he recuperated completely, they treated him "as though I was asking them to make me a present of their road and rolling stock." John was offered his old job of brakeman, but when he pointed out he was still hobbled and couldn't physically perform that job, they told him that was the only choice. Take it or leave it. John had no real choice, and that, he claimed, was "the last I had to do with the Southern Pacific."[9]

The Southern Pacific Railroad had, in John's mind, failed to fix his broken leg, consented to let him starve due to lack of employment, and succeeded only in making one more bitter enemy. Upon dismissal from the hospital in Sacramento, John Sontag returned to the railroad town of Tulare "in strong rebellious frame of mind, and aroused at the railroad's action towards me."[10]

THAT SAME YEAR, the Southern Pacific acquired another enemy. And this enemy was capable of arousing an entire readership that would grow by leaps and bounds. In early 1887, George Hearst, long a political opponent of Leland Stanford (one of the "Big Four" owners of the Southern Pacific Railroad and former governor of and later senator for California), gave his struggling San Francisco newspaper to his son.

Will Hearst had spent several aimless years at Harvard, excelling only in throwing parties and spending his father's money. Never graduating, he left Boston and moved to New York. He had decided he "didn't want to go into any business that would take a long, dull preparation."[11]

Journalism and publishing seemed, to Hearst, a viable option. He drifted about in New York for a year, getting practical experience in the newspaper business. There he observed what Joseph Pulitzer had done with the *New York World*. He sensed that Pulitzer's success was based upon one simple theory: "Attract readers, readers, readers." Hearst studied Pulitzer's methods of attracting those readers: striking features, bold illustrations, and sensational campaigns.

Over the course of almost two years, Hearst wrote his father several letters pleading for a chance to take over the *San Francisco Examiner*. In one letter, he set forth the changes he would make. Most of these proposed changes were admittedly in imitation of the *New York World*. Hearst suggested that his *Examiner* be as original as possible and avoid the common practice of the day of publishing clips from other newspapers, but would, he wrote:

> ...clip only when absolutely necessary and...imitate only some such leading journal as the *New York World*, which is undoubtedly the best paper of that class to which the *Examine*r belongs—that class which appeals to the people and which depends for its success upon enterprise, energy and a certain startling originality and not upon the wisdom of its political opinions or the lofty style of its editorials: and to accomplish this we must have—as the *World* has—active, intelligent and energetic young men; we must have men who come out West in the hopeful buoyancy of youth for the purposes of making their fortunes and not a worthless scum that has been carried there by the eddies of repeated failures.[12]

After the relentless lobbying, George Hearst could not help but acquiesce to his son's enthusiasm. On March 4, 1887, William Randolph Hearst took over the *San Francisco Examiner*. Pouring his energy (and his father's considerable money) into expanding and improving the paper, before long it offered serious competition to San Francisco's leading daily: the *Chronicle*. Hearst complained that the *Chronicle* was "fighting tremendously hard, and it does not hesitate to adopt any idea we bring out...If they see anything good, they grab it."[13] Hearst lived to scoop the *Chronicle* and did everything he could to attract readers, readers, readers!

Hearst loved a good fight. It was with the *Examiner* that William Randolph Hearst found his fighting voice, and with that voice he would carry on his father's anti-Republican, anti-railroad, and pro-labor leanings with a sensational verve. Of course, to John Sontag, the battles of a wealthy newspaper editor in San Francisco were of little concern. Even if John never heard of William Randolph Hearst, Hearst would someday hear of him. John would never have imagined he'd someday be the one to help Hearst scoop the *Chronicle* and attract readers, readers, readers!

Following his discharge from the railroad hospital in Sacramento, the embittered brakeman from Minnesota returned to Tulare. There, a group of his former co-workers paid his expenses at a hotel near the depot where several of the railroad workers lived. He was reduced to accepting charity and was still crippled by his injuries. Whether organized labor gained a friend or the railroad made an enemy was irrelevant. John Sontag needed a friend and a job.

CHRIS EVANS WORKED at various grain warehouses throughout the southern San Joaquin Valley in the autumn of 1887. Employed by the Grangers' Bank of California, who loaned farmers money for seed and machinery, his job was to check in the wheat brought in for shipment from farmers who owed the bank money, thus ensuring the bank was paid first from the farmers' profits.[14] It was an environment rife with venting against the railroad. Wheat growers, who were begrudgingly repaying loans to the bank, would complain about unjust freight charges for shipping their wheat. Or they might explain how when they ordered machinery from Back East, it had been shipped to a northern terminal and additional charges and delays were incurred in getting it to them—delays that cost them their crop, ruined by standing beyond maturity.

Despite a farmer's proclivity for complaint, the 1880s in the San Joaquin Valley was a time of unmatched wheat productivity. It was the era of the bonanza wheat farms. Grain farming was one of the first agricultural enterprises in the valley. It could be successfully dry-farmed most seasons, and the arrival of the railroad a decade earlier provided a boon, opening up vast markets. Additionally, the California varieties of wheat were able to withstand long shipment by boat, which allowed for export to Europe.

In 1886, Tulare County produced nearly six million bushels of wheat, roughly one-third of the state's entire production.[15] Still, small farmers continued to struggle. A great deal of this wheat production was from the so-called "Bonanza Farms," made possible (and profitable) by the monopolization of the land by a relative few. Not really farming at all, but more like a variation of mining, exploitative farmers would decimate the soil, planting the fields year after year without rotation of crops, giving the land neither rest nor fertilization. Once a section was exhausted they would simply move on to virgin soil elsewhere on their vast landholdings. The same feverish frenzy that characterized mining in Gold Rush California also characterized wheat farming.[16]

In 1887, wheat production in the San Joaquin Valley was nearing its statistical peak. The following year, the town of Traver, located on the main rail line some ten miles northwest of Visalia, shipped more wheat than any town in the world ever had.[17] The grain warehouses where Chris Evans had charge were located at shipping points just south of the depot in Traver. These were in the railroad towns of Tulare, Pixley, and Alila, near the county's southern boundary. Chris didn't like spending so much time away from his family in Visalia, but a job was a job and he needed money to provide for his growing family. Molly had given birth to another son, named Louis Napoleon after Molly's older brother (and one-time playmate to a bear). His brood now included three girls and two boys. His oldest, Eva, was eleven years old and could now be called on to help Molly with the other children. But there was much to be done and it was a constant struggle for Chris, alternating between the demand to earn money and his need to take care of things at home.

One day in September, Chris was walking by a hotel in Tulare. It was a hotel frequented by railroad workers; the hotel where John Sontag was staying. A number of men were sitting out front talking when Chris passed by and stopped to talk to one of the men he knew. As Chris later related to his family, after greetings were exchanged and John Sontag was introduced to him, one of the men told Chris: "We've been telling Sontag here about the Mussel Slough tragedy. He was badly injured in an accident and the company won't do anything for him. We just want him to know he ain't the only one that's suffered from the injustice of the railroad." Chris was then asked to relate the story of Mussel Slough to John Sontag, who was apparently unaware of the incident.

Chris told how one of his wife's uncles had been cheated out of his land and years of hard work, although he explained that this uncle wasn't there the day the men were killed. Chris then told Sontag that several settlers were slain at Mussel Slough by "that dirty renegade, Crow, blackhearted as his name." Chris claimed to have known him, and although he was a settler, he was "getting railroad pay long before anyone knew it."

Chris then reportedly offered Sontag and the others the following synopsis of the situation that led to the killings at Mussel Slough:

> The railroad was given alternate sections of land for building the road. Naturally, they wanted to enhance the value of these holdings; so, in order to induce settlement, they offered the land at two and a half to three dollars an acre, and it would be some time before buyers would have to pay even that, because the railroad had not yet received their patent for the land from the government.
>
> Men came in with their families, built houses and barns, and began tilling the soil. Most of them went to the rich tule lands near Tulare Lake, not far from the present town of Hanford. When they offered payment for this land, they were told it would be twenty-five and thirty dollars an acre. They refused to pay it, and ejectment proceedings were started. [18]

In the eyes of Chris Evans, and indeed all those listening to his story that day, the railroad had succeeded in robbing the settlers of Mussel Slough not only of their land, but the result of their hard work. That Walter Crow was shot in the back after the dispossession and ensuing battle was undoubtedly viewed as just by these bitter men.

It is hard to imagine that anyone who spent any time at all in Tulare County during that period would not be familiar with the recent events at Mussel Slough—especially someone who had been employed by the very railroad involved. But this, according to Evans family legend, was the conversation that marked the meeting of Chris Evans and John Sontag. Perhaps Chris was taking credit for providing John with some kind of social awakening, as if he needed further ammunition for his bitterness against the railroad.

Chris took an immediate liking to the down-on-his-luck former brakeman. Chris went on to explain to John that his work with the bank gave him little time to do anything at home, so he needed someone to help around the house and take care of his horses. Chris offered to give John a job and place to live until he could get back on his feet. Chris then warned him that he had but one concern: "I have to be particular who I have, on account of the children. I don't want a man that will swear at my horses, or before my children."[19]

And so John came away from the encounter with the two things he so desperately needed: a friend and a job. Chris further promised that if things worked out and, if by spring, he was strong enough, he could stay on and help him with the teams he kept for hauling lumber from the mills in the mountains. He told John of his ranch near the mills and predicted that the mountain air would help him regain his strength.

THE CHILDREN IN THE EVANS FAMILY liked John immediately. He also got along with Molly and, perhaps more importantly, Grannie Byrd, who lived next door to Chris and his family. It also helped that John had such a knack with horses. It was evident from the way he treated the animals that he cared deeply for them; his method of working horses was steeped in gentle kindness and respect. He was not the type to abuse or break the spirit of an animal.

It wasn't long before John seemed like one of the Evans family. And there was one person in the family who took a particular liking to him. Before Chris brought John home to meet his family, he had mentioned his children and, in particular, his oldest, Eva.

"You'll like her," he told the twenty-six-year-old John Sontag. "She's a cute little trick; talks like a little old woman. But she's not much help to her mother. Hates the inside of a house."[20]

John couldn't help but be impressed by Eva, whose small size made the mature words coming out of her mouth all the more incongruous. Her head cocked upward to look taller people in the eye, her expression was colored by slightly upturned indentations at the edges of her mouth. In an older girl, this might be taken as a knowing smile, an indication of sly trouble from a girl becoming wise to her womanly wiles. But it's more likely John saw Eva for what she still was: a precocious little yellow-haired girl eager to impress with boyish bravado.

For eleven-year-old Eva, the arrival of John Sontag was a life-changing event.

CHAPTER FOUR

Coming of Age

A T TWELVE YEARS OF AGE, EVA—who had always hated housework—was old enough to do outside chores such as helping
John Sontag in the barn, cleaning the stables, and tending to
the horses. She was also old enough to read newspapers, and when, in
1889, local headlines splashed words like "robbery" and "murder," it
would catch her tomboyish attention.

On February 23, 1889, the *Tulare Daily Evening Register* reported
that the "city was thrown into a state of considerable excitement last
night by the report that train No. 17, Jas Symington conductor, had been
held up by masked men at Pixley and robbed." Newspapers throughout
the state reported the robbery, with multiple-column accounts offered
in the Tulare and Visalia newspapers.

While it is unknown if Eva read the news accounts, if she had she
would have learned that shortly after the train pulled out of the Pixley
station, two masked men appeared in the engine's cab and ordered, at
gunpoint, the engineer and fireman to bring the train to a stop. Once the
train came to a stop two miles south at Deer Creek, the masked assail-
ants marched the engineer and fireman back to the express car.

Deputy Constable Ed Bentley of Merced, who happened to be a passenger on the train, left his car and began walking up toward the engine
to see why the train had stopped. Some reports claimed this was at the
behest of conductor Symington.

Meanwhile, the Wells Fargo express messenger refused to open the
car door that he had locked from the inside. One of the robbers threw a
dynamite charge under the express car, which startled the express messenger inside but did not succeed in opening the door.

At the sound of the commotion, Bentley, who had walked up along the other side of the train, stooped to look under the railroad car. One of the robbers heard him on the other side, and Bentley probably never saw the barrel of the shotgun until the blast that sent him flying back on the ground. He was seriously wounded. The bandits were heard firing additional shots into the night. The reason was not immediately apparent.

The desperadoes then ordered the engineer and fireman "on peril of their lives, to have the express messenger open the door. In order to save the lives of the men, the messenger did as requested and he was also brought within the range of the deadly weapons and directed to open the express box."[1]

The robbers rifled the express car, but initial reports did not mention the amount they obtained. Later estimates claimed their haul ranged anywhere from a few hundred dollars in coins up to $5,000. Some rumors ran as high as $50,000. The bandits backed away, covering the trainmen with their guns, and disappeared into the night.

Bentley was scooped up and put on the train, which quickly returned to Pixley so he could receive medical care. At some point, a passenger alerted train personnel that he'd seen another man shot. Authorities went back to the scene and there found Charles Gabert's body. He was a passenger from Kern County who had also walked up to see what was going on. He lay dead next to the tracks. Bentley would survive eight days before succumbing to the severity of his wounds.[2]

The *Visalia Delta* opined that the robbery was a daring one and noted that while "it is thought by some that the perpetrators were novices because of their shooting Gabert and Bentley," the robbers had "planned the deed well and were not new in crime."[3] One can only guess what opinion, if any, Eva had formed of their deeds.

THE PIXLEY TRAIN ROBBERY became the main topic of conversation for many days throughout the valley. All kinds of rumors—new ones everyday—were circulated. A reward of $2,000 for each bandit was offered, and the *Delta* concluded that while their whereabouts were unknown, "it is hoped most sincerely that their cunning will not cheat the gallows."[4] Weeks passed, and with no suspects named (much less in custody), it appeared the perpetrators of the Pixley train robbery had indeed cheated the gallows.

News of the robbery and the unsuccessful investigation would have likely been discussed at the Evans house. After all, it was a big news story, and one can imagine the young Evans boys aching to hear all the gory details from the newspaper accounts. Perhaps this prompted John Sontag to tell a story of his own brush with a famous gang of outlaws.

One Sunday in early September 1876, eight strange men rode into John's hometown of Mankato, Minnesota. Four of these men registered at his stepfather's hotel. All the men rode magnificent thoroughbred horses, exhibited considerable sartorial splendor, and carried bundles behind their saddles. They looked to many like cattle buyers, and their arrival in town was not without notice. One Mankato resident, upon seeing one of the gang, told friends that he had just seen Jesse James.

Most just laughed, scoffing at the claim that this was Jesse James. What would Jesse James be doing this far north in Minnesota?

James, along with a band of former rebels-turned-bandits that included his brother, Frank, and cousin, Cole Younger, had been robbing banks and trains throughout their home state of Missouri and neighboring states for nearly a decade. They had become so celebrated in the anti-Union press, most significantly through John Edwards' columns and Jesse's published letters in the *Kansas City Times*, that people undoubtedly imagined Jesse James sightings all the time. He was the most famous criminal in America at the time, and he had already become the archetypal outlaw hero.

Although viewed by some as a modern-day Robin Hood, there were plenty of others who still considered him a cold-blooded killer. Of course, with little more than a decade having passed since the end of a bitter Civil War, the nation was still divided on many issues. While his actions were blatantly those of a common criminal, to those in political sympathy with the former Confederate guerrilla—a "bushwhacker" who rode with Quantrill and Bloody Bill Anderson terrorizing Union loyalists and abolitionists in Missouri during the War of Secession— Jesse James was perceived as a hero. If the perception had been that he merely robbed banks and trains for personal gain, it is less likely he would have been lionized and more likely he'd be lynched. But James' career was proof that if one can politicize crime, there will always be a portion of the population who will support it or, if not actually support it, at least forgive it or label it as something other than crime.[5]

Whether John viewed Jesse James as an outlaw hero or brutal criminal is unknown, but he vividly recalled the legend's visit to Mankato. The Monday after their auspicious arrival, Mankato's conspicuous visitors convened and rode to the local bank. A building next door was under construction and several workers watched the visiting group intently from the construction site. Noticing the local citizenry's interest, the gang rode away.

When the gang returned an hour later, an even larger group of local townspeople had gathered near the bank, including fourteen-year-old John Sontag, and watched them intently. The visitors could clearly see they were being observed and noticed that one man even pointed at them.

Convinced their plans to rob the bank had been discovered, they quietly left town. Yes, it actually was the James/Younger gang, presumably having come to Mankato intending to rob a bank. Instead, they headed for Northfield, forty miles away. It was later learned that what the Mankato locals were staring and pointing at was not the gang of potential bank robbers, but their magnificent horses. Mankato was a town whose men appreciated good horse-flesh.

As it turned out, Northfield became the site of the James/Younger gang's most famous robbery; or in this case, attempted robbery. It was in Northfield that they met their Waterloo. All except Frank and Jesse were either killed or wounded and later captured.

After the "Northfield Raid," Mankato buzzed with excitement and Jesse James fever ran rampant. The surviving members of the gang, including Jesse James himself, approached the Mankato area again, this time on the run from posses.

Citizens of Mankato and posse members, who came into town each day after an exhausting search, gathered at local saloons and hotels. At the Sontag Hotel, adolescent boys John and George Sontag would overhear accounts each day by "those who had been out on the front," mingled with fabrications woven by the local grapevine. Jesse James eluded capture, and his legend, already cemented in the national consciousness, became all the more real and exciting to the impressionable Sontag boys in Mankato. The legendary outlaw had, time and time again, proven wrong the old saying: "Crime does not pay." [6]

It is, of course, pure conjecture to imagine John, prompted by news reports of a deadly train robbery in Pixley, telling this story to the Evans children. This scenario is all the more ironic when we consider that the Pixley train robbers were, in fact, John Sontag and Chris Evans. Just how much the Evans family knew of Chris and John's involvement in that robbery is impossible to know. It is probably safe to assume that the younger children knew nothing of what was going on. Chris was the father of five children, with one more on the way. But did his pregnant wife know he and John had robbed that train at Pixley? Did his oldest daughter, twelve-year-old Eva, realize her father and John Sontag were responsible for the deaths of two men?

Before the year was out, Molly gave birth to another son. This one they named John Christopher, and one has to ponder the significance in that choice of names. John and Chris were inextricably linked. John was like one of the family. And as the 1880s drew to an end, Eva, although still small for her age, was blossoming. She developed the curves of womanhood and a maturity of attitude beyond her thirteen years.

IN JANUARY 1890, the *Visalia Delta* announced in headline "Another Train Robbed," reporting that the No. 19 train from San Francisco had been stopped just south of Goshen "by two masked and well-armed men and the express car robbed in much the same manner as was done near Pixley on the 22nd of February of last year."[7]

Like that previous robbery, the engineer and fireman were, at gunpoint, ordered to stop the train and marched back to the express car. Express companies, such as Wells Fargo, that transported bonds, money and other valuables for banks and other clients, paid the railroads for the contract to operate an express car on their route. This car was manned and operated by the company's express messenger, or agent, as he was sometimes called. It was backbreaking and dangerous work, and the pay was modest. An express messenger had to lay his life on the line for shipments that might exceed a half-million dollars. Despite the amounts carried, messengers were often blasé about their responsibilities. One historian of the express industry wrote that "an outsider in those silver-dollar days would have been startled at seeing two or three hundred canvas bags containing a thousand silver dollars each, stacked in the end of a car like so much salt; but to the messenger it was a humdrum, common experience."[8]

The express messenger in this latest robbery, much like the one in the Pixley raid, was convinced to open the car under threat of death to the trainmen. News reports did not mention if he was blasé or not.

And tragically, like the prior holdup, a curious passenger happened upon the robbery in progress and, like the two victims before him, was killed. This time it was a vagrant by the name of Jonas Christiansen, who had been riding stowaway. The *Fresno Weekly Republican* described his fate:

> During the time the men were being taken to the express car a tramp, who was beating his way, crawled out from between the

cars on the other side of the train, and the larger of the two robbers, who seemed to be the director of affairs, caught sight of him,
and evidently thought it was some one coming up to ascertain the
cause of the delay. In the twinkling of an eye he threw his shotgun around and fired under the train, following the shot with the
remark: "I got that fellow."

The engineer, when later interviewed by the newspaper, commented
that the way the robber used his gun was "something wonderful," explaining that when the masked bandit noticed the tramp he dropped
down and wielded his gun between the engineer's legs and shot under
the car before the engineer even saw a movement made.[9]

And just as with the Pixley robbery, the bandits vanished. In spite
of concentrated efforts by local officers and Wells Fargo and Southern
Pacific detectives to locate and capture them, the identities and whereabouts of the bandits remained unknown. Witnesses had given descriptions of the masked men, which matched those of the Pixley robbers;
but because the men wore long black masks completely concealing not
only their facial features, but the contour of the head and shoulders,
specifics were limited to basic size. One bandit was tall, around six feet
and fairly thin; the other was shorter, maybe five feet seven inches and
perhaps 150 pounds. Had Eva read these descriptions in the paper, she
would realize they applied to numerous people; but she'd also know
they applied to John and her father.

NOT LONG AFTER THE GOSHEN ROBBERY, Chris went to Modesto to
see a man named Thomas Wallace, who owned and operated one of the
largest livery stables in the San Joaquin Valley, having heard through
the grapevine that Wallace wanted to retire. Chris had always loved
horses and relished the chance to operate a business that would allow
him to stay home instead of constantly working for others at distant
sites. And John Sontag, who had such an easy way with horses, would
be the perfect partner. He decided to see if he could make a deal with
Wallace for the stables. It seemed the ideal business opportunity. Chris
made the deal that spring and was set to take possession the following
September.

Eva later claimed that her father acquired the money to lease the
stables by mortgaging his South Ranch property to Sol Sweet, a Visalia
businessman who owned a mercantile in town. The family had long
known Sol, and Eva remembered from the time she was a little girl go-

ing to Sol's store and shopping for the family. She never used money, but would take "the book" and charge everything they needed.[10]

Considering the timing of this business venture—one that would take considerable capital and would also remove Chris and his family from the area—one can't help but see it as circumstantial evidence for the prosecution. Supposing, of course, there ever was a prosecution—or even a suspect. But Chris Evans was apparently not suspected and so the timing of his venture, at the time, passed unnoticed.

Early in September 1890, Chris relocated his family to Modesto, a growing town along the Southern Pacific line some 130 miles north of Visalia. Chris chartered a box car and packed all the family's household goods—including about 200 jars of fruit preserves Molly had made from the orchard next to their house—along with his horses and tack for shipment north. Chris found a house to rent for the family right around the corner from the stable.[11]

The stable itself was a mammoth two-story structure, measuring 100 by 120 feet. Notices ran in the local Modesto paper announcing the firm of "Sontag and Evans, successors to Thomas Wallace." Their advertisement bragged that the facilities for keeping transient stock were unsurpassed by any establishment in the state. As new proprietors, Chris and John seemed intent on making improvements; their ad also pointed out they had just completed the largest feed stable in that section of the state and were now prepared to furnish teamsters and the transient-traveling public with all kinds of stock feed.[12]

New business partners Sontag and Evans purchased Wallace's inventory of equipment, stock and feed and added to this the horses Chris already owned and brought with him to Modesto as well as John's tack and equipment. The structure itself, however, they merely leased. This still would have required considerable capital. As anyone who has started their own business can attest, the initial outlay can be overwhelming, and there always seems the need to spend more money.

SHORTLY AFTER THEIR RELOCATION to Modesto, Chris found it necessary to make a trip to Stockton to buy buggy ropes and harnesses. He decided to bring Eva, now fourteen years old. She had always enjoyed helping her father. Eva adored spending time with her dad. As a young girl, she would follow him around outside while he worked, whether he was cutting wood or plowing the orchard or tending the horses. Molly could scarcely keep her rambunctious daughter in the house. When Chris got work operating a gang plow, he built a deep box seat for his tiny daughter who would sit up high, next to her father, on the big horse-drawn plow. "I didn't mind the bumps," she later recalled. "I could smell the sweet earth, watch the horses straining at their tugs, look up at the blue sky, and listen to the meadow larks."[13]

During cherished summers at the Redwood Ranch, she always helped her father with chores. One time, while helping build a fence from redwood posts—she held the posts straight while he shoveled the dirt—he made her promise that in the event of his death, she "would have his body placed inside the great redwood tree in the lower end of the meadow." Chris even explained to his young daughter how to accomplish the somewhat morbid request by having a section removed just large enough to stand his body up inside, uncoffined, and then have the slab of wood replaced and sealed.[14] The two obviously had a special bond and Eva was, as the saying goes, undoubtedly her Daddy's girl.

And so it was natural he would ask her along on the supply trip to Stockton. But this became much more than just a shopping excursion. After the business was attended to, Chris decided he would take his oldest—and although he might never admit it out loud, his favorite—on a little vacation to San Francisco, which was just a short journey by boat through the Delta from Stockton. In a way, coming as it did with Eva on the verge of womanhood, the trip was a rite of passage; a chance for the naïve girl from the country to experience, for the first time, a big cosmopolitan city. Perhaps it was also an opportunity for Chris to discuss with his daughter her growing bond with John Sontag. Any father would have concerns over where, via the sheer forces of nature, their relationship would naturally be heading.

Regardless of her father's motives, it was a trip she would always remember. She vividly described it decades later:

> So we took the boat to San Francisco. At supper time that evening, we found ourselves in front of a brilliantly lighted place with a sign over the sidewalk made of lights that read "Café." We went in, expecting to see people eating, but it looked like the lobby of a hotel. A man motioned us to an iron grilled door, and another man opened it, and we stepped in to a little room, and the floor of it moved up—not slowly, either. Did I admit to my father I was frightened? I did not.
>
> We went up two floors, and when the door opened, another man ushered us into a room where there was a table beautifully set for two. Off this room, I saw a curtained doorway. I looked in and

there was a bed in this room, and I said, "Look, Dad? This is a hotel; you can sleep here, too."

He took one look, seized my hand, and said, "Daughter, this is no place for us."

We didn't wait for the elevator; we hurried down the stairs.[15]

As Eva learned years later, the establishment they happened into was the notorious Poodle Dog Café. While not officially a brothel, as her description might hint, the French restaurant with its private upstairs dining chambers certainly saw its share of illicit affairs. As one chronicler of San Francisco's Gilded Age remarked, "When *bons vivants* and men about town wanted to dine, the Poodle Dog was their destination. In its first-floor dining room husbands could and did eat in public propriety with their wives; in its well-appointed and cozy third-floor nooks, they could and did dine with their mistresses in an atmosphere suggestive of naughty but tender abandon."[16]

So well-known was the Poodle Dog's reputation for perfumed iniquity in its upstairs dining rooms that music halls began to joke about people who ventured higher than the first floor of a French restaurant. Perhaps the maitre'd, seeing Chris Evans and his pretty young companion (young enough to be his daughter, he surely thought!), assumed she was his mistress and so showed the furtive couple to a place where they could have some privacy.

They found a more suitable place to dine, but when they later visited Chinatown, a Chinese man came up to Chris and said, "You likee see China Mary? One lookee, two bitee." Chris quickly decided Chinatown was no place for them either.[17]

The next morning, he took Eva to the Cliff House. Perched just above the water at Seal Rocks, the spectacularly situated eatery was a favorite rendezvous for Sunday drivers of stylish horse rigs. While it, too, at times enjoyed a racy reputation as the scene of wild parties, one can safely assume it was respectively sedate the morning Chris and Eva dined there. That afternoon, they returned home to Modesto. It was in Modesto now that Chris had every hope and dream of making the best possible life for his family.

THAT HIS HOPES AND DREAMS were now, quite literally, hitched to his horses suited Chris just fine. He had always considered horses the kings of the animal world, and Eva once theorized that he preferred their society to that of the average human being. There were three particular horses Eva felt sure of which this was true: an iron gray mare he called Lucy, and two of her progeny, a fine black stallion named Paddy O'Neil and his sister, Patsy. As a colt, Paddy had been treated as a pet, once even taking advantage of his status as a member of the family to enter the house and raid the pantry, much to the chagrin of Molly.

Nonetheless, Paddy was a *working* member of the family, and one day in December, Chris rented him out to a man who needed a horse and buggy for what he claimed would be a leisurely overnight trip. Either the man was being deceitful or his plans changed, because he returned later the same evening, and as soon as he drove in through the Sontag and Evans stable doors, Chris knew Paddy had been mercilessly driven beyond endurance. As Eva later recalled:

> My father did everything that could be done to save his life, but just before midnight he died. (Dad had called me to help him.) When Paddy's labored breathing stopped, and the beautiful head was lying still in the straw, Dad laid his head on Paddy's shoulder and cried.
>
> The next morning he hunted up the man who had killed the horse, and beat him so that he had to be sent to a hospital. When my father was consumed with a righteous wrath, his soft voice changed to one that cut like a whip, and the blaze from his eyes just scorched. I think the reason he could just pulverize much larger men was because they were half scared to death before he ever hit them.[18]

Eva never mentioned if any charges were brought against Chris for this reprisal beating.

The tragedy of Paddy O'Neil notwithstanding, as the year came to a close, the Evans family now had genuine reason to be optimistic. Their first Christmas in Modesto was likely a happy one. Molly was again pregnant. Chris and John were now established in a legitimate business, earning money doing work they both loved. Whether Molly saw this as an alternative to a life of crime is unknown (as we don't know how much she knew), but she would have certainly seen it as an opportunity for many positive things—for income, fulfillment, and a chance to have her husband home more often. Eva would have shared many of these feelings, but may have had more insight into the reality of the situation, given her close relationship with her father and with John. One has to recognize the possibility that Eva knew far more about the train robberies than anyone else in the family.

Eva, having succumbed to the forces of nature, had discovered her feelings for John by then. As she later wrote:

> It was the most natural thing in the world that I grew to love him. He was gentle and kind, and very handsome; six feet tall, with wide shoulders and narrow hips, wine-brown eyes, dark brown hair, clear olive skin with high color in his lips and cheeks.
>
> By the time I was fourteen, it was understood that we were to be married when I was seventeen. But my father would not allow me to go places with John—not even "buggy riding," as other girls did in those days. Nor did I go out with other boys. My father was my escort; he would take me to a party, and then be waiting at the door when it was time to go home.[19]

Eva's complaints of an overprotective father don't diminish the sense that the Evans family was happy and full of hope in Modesto, with time and distance all but obliterating any dark thoughts of train robbery.

THE PEACEFUL OPTIMISM the Evans family felt was shattered in the early morning hours of January 7, 1891. In the dead of night, around two a.m., Eva was awakened by the glare of light on her bedroom window. She put on shoes, grabbed a coat and rushed outside. Her father was just coming out of the house himself and together they ran to the corner; toward the source of the awful glare. The livery barn's roof was a solid sheet of flame.

There was little Chris could do when he arrived on the scene. According to Eva, her father was able to break open the office window and help the night man, William Hall, out to safety. Shortly thereafter, the fire department arrived. As reported in the *Modesto Daily Evening News*, the "hose and hook and ladder companies were soon at the scene, the former playing a stream on the outskirts of the fire and the hook and ladder tearing down the corral fence to prevent the spread of flames."

Suddenly, according to Eva, Chris remembered Jacob Claypool, and he implored the firemen to concentrate on the end of the building that contained a loft bedroom. Chris often let the sixteen-year-old boy, who worked driving a freight wagon to the La Grange mining district and boarded his team in the barn, sleep in the upstairs room forward of the hayloft. But there wasn't a thing the firemen, or anyone, could do.

> After the fire had burned down somewhat [the *Evening News* continued], the charred remains of young Claypool were seen near the front of the building, removing all hope as to his having escaped. A stream was played on that portion of the fire so as to recover the remains as soon as possible and when taken out charred pieces of blanket were found about the body, showing that the boy perished while in bed and had undoubtedly been asphyxiated and died without consciousness or pain.[20]

Just as they were taking out the charred remains of Jacob Claypool, Molly arrived upon the scene. When she saw the grisly body, she began screaming hysterically. She was taken home and for days after was so ill it was thought she might lose her baby.

While the sight of the burned boy's body undoubtedly affected Eva, there were other things that night that haunted her. More than forty years later she wrote:

> When Mother was taken care of, Dad and I went back to the barn and watched the walls fall in. Long since, the horses had ceased to scream—twenty-two of them—most of them ours. Patsy O'Neil and her mother, Lucy, the beautiful Palominos. Only two teams were left. John was away on a business trip to La Grange with the bays, and a man had hired the grays for a trip to Oakland. These four horses, a carriage and a buckboard, were all that were left.
>
> Long after everyone had gone, Dad still sat there on the curb, with me beside him. Finally his shoulders were shaken with sobs. I didn't say anything. What was there to say?[21]

It was the second time in as many months that Eva watched her father cry, but this time was about far more than the death of his horses. He cried over the demise of his dreams; hope was extinguished in that fire. Eva may not have realized it at the time, sitting there on that cold January morning watching her powerful father rendered helpless with sobs, but she later recognized that he was never again the same man.

Eva, too, had changed. In the previous three years she had experienced the physical changes of a girl passing through puberty. She had entered into a courtship and looked forward to marriage. She may or may not have realized that the two men in her life—her father and her fiancé—had committed crimes of robbery and murder. She witnessed horrible deaths connected to the fiery destruction of her family's business. She saw her father wracked with sobs of bitter disappointment.

Her innocent allure transformed so utterly, Eva still radiated beauty, but now it was a more complicated womanly appeal. Her precocious smile became shaded with pain, the upturned ends of her mouth partly a grimace against life's terrible hardships. For Eva, it had been a gradual process—her coming of age—but the fire that morning acted as a kiln that in a watershed moment hardened her.

ACT TWO

THE TROUBLES

CHAPTER FIVE

Robberies and Suspects

FOLLOWING THE TRAGIC FIRE at the Sontag & Evans Livery Stable, the district attorney conducted an investigation that concluded there was no evidence of foul play. Insurance settlements were made, although because neither Thomas Wallace (who still owned the structure) nor Chris and John were fully covered, the amount of the insurance award fell short of covering the loss; and most of it, according to Eva, went to paying outstanding bills.[1]

Nonetheless, all concerned had little choice but to rebuild. Chris Evans had relocated his family to Modesto. He had staked his future on the business, but the fire had left the family in a financial crisis and re-establishing the livery stable seemed his best hope. Six weeks after the fire, Chris sold his Visalia farm property to Adolph Levis.[2] This offers perhaps the best testimony as to the family's dire need for money.

Rebuilding the stables and business proved difficult. At one point during construction of the barn, another fire broke out. The Modesto paper reported that "owing to the greenness of the lumber and the dampness of the wood from the late rain, the fire went out without doing much damage." This fire, unlike the one that earlier destroyed the building, reeked of foul play. Several sacks saturated with coal oil were found in and near the stables. The attempted arson, according to John, indicated that "someone was trying to get rid of the competition."[3]

TRAIN ROBBERS STRUCK AGAIN in February of that year. Chris and John were busy trying to rebuild their livery business in Modesto, so if Eva read in the newspaper about a train being held up by masked ban-

dits way down at the southern end of Tulare County, she would have realized that *this* time, at least, her father and fiancé were not involved.

The holdup at Alila (present-day Earlimart, near the Tulare-Kern
County line) was announced in one newspaper headline as "An Ineffectual Attempt at Robbery." Within a few days, the papers reported
that authorities were hot on the trail of suspects. Would Eva, assuming
she knew of her father's earlier crimes, have allowed herself a tinge of
pride that these new train robbers were such inferior practitioners of the
trade? Or was she just relieved, hopeful that these new bandits might be
suspected of the other train robberies as well?

The robbery at Alila was in many ways similar to those at Pixley
and Goshen. At about 7:50 p.m. on February 6, 1891, the Southern Pacific southbound train No. 17 left the Alila depot. Shortly after leaving
the station, two masked men armed with revolvers entered the locomotive's cab and ordered the engineer to stop the train, then marched the
engineer and fireman back to the express car. But instead of opening
the doors, the express messenger blew out the lamps, opened a window
and fired several shots at the bandits, who had, similar to the earlier
jobs, shielded themselves with the engineer and fireman. In the ensuing
gun battle, the express messenger was slightly injured and George Radcliffe, the fireman, was mortally wounded. The bandits, surprised by
the determined resistance, aborted the robbery and fled into the night.

Although the express messenger, Charles Haswell, was credited
with successfully defending his car against the assault of robbers, he
was also universally censured for endangering the trainmen, and indeed
it was suspected that his shots killed Radcliffe, who died the next day.[4]

Eugene Kay, the recently-elected sheriff of Tulare County, received
a telegram reporting the attempted robbery. Kay, Deputy Sheriff George
Witty, and former sheriff Dan Overall took a special train from Visalia
to the robbery scene. In remembering the case decades later, Kay recalled, "I believe I made the best time that had ever been made from the
Sheriff's Office in Visalia to Alila."[5]

Once onsite, witnesses gave the lawmen descriptions of the bandits,
and a spur strap and pieces of a saddle were found nearby where the
outlaws were thought to have camped. Two sets of horse tracks led
from the scene southwest toward the Coast Ranges.

What went unreported was that Sheriff Kay already suspected two
Visalia residents of the earlier robberies at Pixley and Goshen. But with
information from one of his deputies that those suspects couldn't possibly have been in Alila, and the fact that the tracks, unlike the earlier

robberies, led to the southwest, Kay theorized that this robbery attempt "might have been the work of anyone."[6]

Sheriff Kay and his posse followed the fresh trail to the ranch of Bill Dalton, near Paso Robles. Grat, Bill, Bob and Emmett Dalton were accused of the bungled Alila train robbery. By early March, Eva would have read in the newspapers that two of the Dalton brothers were in custody and Sheriff Kay had left on a cross-country pursuit of two more of the brothers. What Eva may or may not have known was that her father was well acquainted with Grat Dalton.

THE DALTON BROTHERS were originally from Missouri, a state that produced some of the most notorious outlaws in the country. It had been the home of the James and Younger gang, and indeed, the Daltons were neighbors, acquaintances (and in the case of the Youngers, first cousins) of the infamous outlaws.

Lewis Dalton married Adeline Lee Younger in 1841 in Jackson County, Missouri. The couple later moved to Coffeyville, Kansas, for a short while, then to Cass County in Missouri. They raised a dozen children, including Littleton, Gratton, William, Bob, and Emmett. The Dalton boys were considerably younger than their infamous cousins, Jim and Cole Younger. As Littleton Dalton once reflected late in life, "No, the Dalton Gang never ran with the Youngers, and the Youngers had nothing to do with the Dalton boys going bad. Laziness, bad company, bad habits, and bad whisky did that, regardless of any stories you may hear."[7] Nonetheless, one can't help but ponder the Dalton's link between the Youngers and, hence, Frank and Jesse James, the most famous train robbers who ever lived.

Gratton Dalton had served as a U. S. deputy marshal in Oklahoma when, in the words of one historian, "that Territory required unflinching resolution and dauntless courage." He left that position under some suspicion of impropriety and ended up in New Mexico where "he and a brother had an unfortunate altercation with gamblers which proved injurious to the reputation of the Daltons."[8]

When Grat (Gratton) and Bob arrived in the San Joaquin Valley, their older brother, Lit (Littleton), was residing on a ranch near Clovis. Another brother, Bill, owned a ranch in Paso Robles. Their father, who owned race horses, came to California and followed the county fair race circuit in the Central Valley. Grat loved the race circuit; he was an enthusiastic gambler and shrewd horse trader. A cousin of his was a wheat grower near Kingsburg, and it may have been through him that Grat obtained work at one of the grain warehouses along the Southern Pacific line.

Chris Evans and Grat Dalton worked together for a time at the Pixley grain warehouse. Lit Dalton later theorized that perhaps it was at that warehouse that his brother and "the later train bandit, Chris Evans...weighed the chances of a successful train robbery in the San Joaquin."[9] Maybe it had started out as idle venting against the hated railroad, or maybe the subject came up when Grat bragged about his famous relatives. But it is certainly easy, knowing the events that later transpired, to picture Chris and Grat—during a lunch break, per-haps— plotting fanciful crimes that would reap untold riches before returning to their mundane labor.

A few days after Grat Dalton was arrested for the botched robbery at Alila, he was released for lack of evidence and went to San Francisco. A Southern Pacific railroad detective named Will Smith reviewed the case and was certain that the evidence against Grat was sufficient to initiate a felony charge against him. Smith arrested Grat in San Francisco and transported him back to the Tulare County jail in Visalia, where he was charged with attempted train robbery. Bill Dalton was later arrested in Paso Robles for his part in the crime, but Bob and Emmett Dalton escaped to Oklahoma. Although Sheriff Kay spent three months on a 6,000-mile manhunt, he was never able to capture the fugitive Dalton brothers and returned to Visalia in May to prepare for the trial against Grat Dalton.[10]

SHORTLY BEFORE EVA TURNED FIFTEEN on May 13, 1891, John left California to visit his family in Minnesota. He had left Modesto ear-lier that spring, heading down to Fresno while Chris and his family remained in Modesto. John arrived in Mankato the day after Eva's birthday. Later that same month, Carlton Evans was born. He would be the last of Chris and Molly's children and, being the youngest, would always be thought of as Baby Carl.

Deprived of John's company, Eva spent a difficult summer in Modesto. The family moved to another part of town, and one can only guess at the reasons. Perhaps they found a better house to rent or may-be had to find a cheaper place. It is unknown how Chris was earning money. With John now in Minnesota, it is clear the Sontag and Evans livery business had temporarily disbanded. By June, Chris had given up all interest in the livery stable business. What he was doing for money is anybody's guess.

There are sources who put Chris Evans in Visalia during late June and early July, attending the trial of Grat Dalton. It was Littleton Dalton who told historian Frank Latta that "Chris Evans attended Grat's trial every day court was in session."[11] A contemporary report in the *Tulare County Times* supported this assertion. The heavily reported trial commenced June 15, and it wasn't until July 8, 1891, that a jury pronounced Grat Dalton guilty. The *Visalia Delta* stated that after the verdict was read "the female relatives of the family wept bitterly, but the defendant did not...betray any emotion."[12] No mention was made of what reaction Chris Evans may have had.

In July, during the hot San Joaquin Valley summer when temperatures commonly soared above one hundred degrees, the Evans children all came down with scarlet fever. Things would have been insufferable in the Evans household. But in August, as soon as the children got over their illness, Chris announced he was taking them all on a trip to the seaside. It was a memorable vacation, which Eva described in her memoir forty years later.

> So, early on an August morning, 1891, we set out...The morning we started on the trip, Dad had said: "This vacation belongs to you children. If we have only been an hour on the road, and you find a place you like, we will stop until you are ready to go on."
>
> So the next day when we drove into Martinez, and the other children had their first glimpse of salt water, there was an instant decision made to camp there. We camped in a grove of eucalyptus trees on the brow of a hill overlooking the blue straits of...the upper arm of the Bay of San Francisco.
>
> From here we went to Oakland and across the bay to San Francisco. While there, Dad made me drive the grays through the city traffic; he said it was good for the morale of both girl and horses.
>
> Leaving San Francisco, we went down the peninsula to San Jose, through the Santa Cruz Mountains, and had several happy days among the Redwoods of the Big Basin. But we were not so much impressed by the size of the trees. They looked more like cedars compared to our own Sequoia Gigantea. On to Santa Cruz, where we remained three weeks, and enjoyed surf bathing for the first time in our lives. Leaving here, we circled Monterey Bay to

Monterey, where we stayed a week; then back to Modesto through Pacheco Pass.

I tell of this trip because it was the last really happy time we ever had with our father.[13]

Although Eva didn't give a date for their return to Modesto, the vacation she described would have lasted well into September. Perhaps she had another motive for describing the trip in such calendar-consuming detail.

Meanwhile (according to later testimony by his younger brother, George), John Sontag only stayed a short while in Minnesota before returning to California. George claimed that sometime in August his brother received a letter from Chris asking him to come back. Telling his family only that he had to go away, John one night simply disappeared. Ten days after his abrupt departure, George read about another train robbery in California.[14]

THE *SAN FRANCISCO CHRONICLE* DEVOTED more than half of its front page to the train robbery near Ceres, just seven miles south of Modesto. The September 4, 1891, issue described how the robbers had placed an obstruction on the track and when Engineer Neff slowed the train to a stop, the robbers scrambled on the engine and compelled him and Fireman Wallace to extinguish the headlight, then made them get down and go to the express car and ordered it opened. "In many respects," the paper noted, "the crime bears a strong resemblance to the robberies of Southern Pacific trains at Pixley, Goshen and Alila, all of which occurred in the lower San Joaquin Valley within the last two and a half years."

Two days later, a meeting of the entire detective force in pursuit of the robbers was held at the El Capitan Hotel in downtown Merced. Sheriff Thomas Cunningham of San Joaquin County, noting that a coat apparently left behind by one of the bandits had a cleaner's mark from a Visalia laundry, said to Sheriff Kay: "Gene, it looks to me to be another one on your Tulare County boys we suspected."[15]

The Tulare County boys they suspected were none other than Chris Evans and John Sontag. Why Sheriff Kay suspected Chris Evans of the earlier robberies could be traced back to none other than Grat Dalton. It should also be pointed out that the theory was developed with the assistance of one of Kay's "most valued deputies," Oliver Perry Byrd, brother of Molly Evans.

In the Goshen robbery, $2,000 in new two-dollar bills were taken. At that time, a two-dollar bill was a rare article sure to create much comment when presented as legal tender. When Kay took office, he had been briefed on the Goshen heist and the earlier Pixley robbery by his predecessor, Dan Overall. Additionally, he questioned his deputies Billy Russell and Perry Byrd in detail about the robberies. As Sheriff Kay recounted in Frank Latta's *Dalton Gang Days*:

> It may be news to many people that one of the few persons ever caught passing those two-dollar bills was Grat Dalton. Don't misunderstand me. Grat didn't perform the Goshen robbery, nor did he share in the spoils. But he passed some of the bills not long after that robbery was performed.
>
> I didn't know Grat, except by sight, but Grat knew all about me. I stopped him on the street and said, "Say, I hear you have some two-dollar bills. I haven't seen one since I left Missouri. Let me look at one." He pulled out two or three and showed them to me. They were perfectly new and had consecutive serial numbers. I said, "Where in the world did you get them?" He started to say something about a horse. I have forgotten his exact words. Then he suddenly became suspicious and shut up like a clam. We investigated the horse clue. I knew he must have sold, or hired out a horse. At the livery stable we found that Grat had sold a horse to Chris Evans.
>
> Now, all of the officers knew that two-dollar bills had been taken in the Goshen robbery, but Perry Byrd and I were the only officers who suspected that Chris Evans and John Sontag had robbed that train. I sent [Deputy George Witty] to check up on the horse deal. When Witty returned, he took me to one side and said to me, "Gene, I found where Grat got the money, but it don't mean a thing. Chris Evans says that he bought Grat's horse to use in his Modesto livery stable and Chris got the bills when he cashed a check at Sol Sweet's store." In Witty's mind, that settled it. Chris Evans' word was as good as a bond.[16]

Kay followed up with Sol Sweet, who admitted cashing the check, but told the sheriff he had paid Chris in gold pieces.

And so, following the Ceres robbery, Kay paid a visit to the former Visalia residents now considered suspects by various law officers: Chris Evans and John Sontag. Kay claimed they were in Modesto at the time, thus contradicting Eva's later assertion that Chris was on vacation with his family. A comment in her memoir about John being back in Minnesota until after the Evans family returned to Visalia later that fall was also at odds with Kay's account.

Nonetheless, after questioning Chris and John in Modesto, Kay became convinced of their innocence. As he recalled years later, "all investigation I was able to make indicated that they had been at home during the Ceres attempt." It is unknown what alibi was offered to Sheriff Kay, but it was apparently a good one. Perhaps there was a family member, young and innocent enough to believe, able to convince the sheriff that Chris and John were indeed home the night of the Ceres robbery. "As they were clearly innocent of the Alila job, I at that time was even becoming skeptical of their connection with either the Pixley or Goshen robberies," Kay remembered. "I didn't know what to think," he admitted. Kay didn't have any suspects for the Ceres job.

Railroad Detective Will Smith, on the other hand, was adamant that the Daltons did it. He clamored for the arrest of the Daltons, loudly proclaiming that nobody but the Daltons had been holding up trains in the San Joaquin. Smith went so far as to claim he had watertight evidence against them. Will Smith was a highly experienced detective, but was considered a loose cannon by some. He'd been employed by the Southern Pacific since 1888, and his personality didn't make him very popular with many of the public law officers. Sheriff Kay begrudgingly told the arrogant railroad detective: "All right, Smith, you swear to the complaints and, if the boys are still in existence, I'll serve the warrants."[17]

In a few days, Kay arrested Bill Dalton and Riley Dean, but they soon established a clear alibi, although Bill continued to be held in the Tulare County jail for his part in the Alila affair.

Although Sheriff Kay claimed Chris Evans was in Modesto shortly after the Ceres robbery attempt, still another source puts him in Visalia on September 4, the day after. It was on that day, according to county records, he and John Sontag paid a visit to the Tulare County Recorder's office to record, in front of a notary public, a number of property transactions. Among the recordings the two made that day was a transaction that had allegedly occurred twenty months earlier, on January 2, 1890. At that time, Chris sold his city lots to John Sontag in consideration of

$1,100 in gold coin. John recorded that he, in turn, had sold the same lots on April 18, 1891 (when he was a resident of Stanislaus County), to Eva Evans for a mere five dollars in gold coin.[18]

That same day Chris deeded and transferred title on the Redwood Ranch to Molly "in consideration of love, affection, for better maintenance, support, protection and livelihood." And so, the day after the botched Ceres train robbery, Chris Evans (who had earlier sold his south Visalia farm property) and John Sontag became, at least from a legal standpoint, devoid of all property. Even though Chris and John now owned no property, it was all still in the family, albeit in Molly and Eva's names. Could this shuffling of ownership (and even the impending union of Eva and John) have been motivated by more than just romantic love? Were they merely trying to avoid creditors? Or did they have other more sinister reasons for trying to cover their assets?

GRAT DALTON ESCAPED FROM the Visalia jail on September 27, 1891. He had told some of his cellmates he had a friend who was helping from the outside. Pieces of hacksaw blades, which had been smuggled in, were later found in the cell toilet. When Dalton, along with two other prisoners, sawed through bars and bolted from their cell, later rumors claimed Grat found a Winchester rifle and ammunition hidden in the weeds. While the two men who escaped with Dalton were captured, Grat eventually made it back to the Oklahoma Territory where he rejoined his brothers, Bob and Emmett.[19]

Sheriff Kay took a lot of heat for the highly publicized jailbreak. He knew Grat had received help from the outside. Some suspected his brothers, but all reports indicated they were still in the Oklahoma Territory. It was a year before Sheriff Kay was confident that he knew who furnished the hacksaw blades and planted the Winchester rifle and ammunition. Perry Byrd, one of Kay's most trusted deputies—a man Kay never knew to furnish "a single bit of false information"—told Sheriff Kay it was his brother-in-law, Chris Evans, who had sprung Grat Dalton from the Visalia jail.[20]

Eva would later refute the rumor that her father had assisted in the escape. In a 1940 letter to historian Wallace Smith, she wrote that while her father would have enjoyed aiding and abetting Grat, "because I can remember that he thought it was a good joke that Dalton escaped so easily from their new jail," he could not have done so because he "just happened not to be there." Eva also stated that newspaper reports claiming her father had attended Grat Dalton's trial in early July, when her father was still in Modesto, were both "untrue and unjust."[21]

The Evans family returned to Visalia in late October or November. Eva distinctly recalled it was that late in the year because she remembered not wanting to start school as soon as they returned, but had wanted to wait until after the Christmas holidays.[22] Eva would have been in high school at the time. During the time the Evans family had resided in Modesto, a new school building had been built in Visalia. Costing $30,000, a three-story brick building with a belfry towering impressively upward replaced the old wooden structure. This new building had fourteen classrooms, an office and a large assembly hall with a stage. The third floor of the school was used for the newly-established Visalia High School, which had just been organized that September. Regardless of the brand-new facilities, Eva was still "looking for an excuse to stay out of school."[23]

As winter approached, the excitement concerning the Ceres robbery had pretty much blown over. With the tragedy of the Modesto stable fire behind them and the fuss over San Joaquin train robberies on the wane, perhaps better times were ahead for the Evans family. But, as Eva sadly remembered, her father seemed unable to pick up the broken threads. "He looked worn and worried."[24]

JOHN DID NOT STAY IN CALIFORNIA for long after the Ceres robbery. According to his brother, George, he returned to Mankato the following week.[25] It is hard to imagine a man leaving his fiancée behind in California a second time in less than six months without good reason. But perhaps John saw opportunity with his younger brother back in Minnesota.

John Sontag's younger brother had a troubled past. At fifteen, George Sontag was caught stealing cigars from an employer and sent to reform school. After a few months, he escaped, then ended up in jail. Upon his release he left Mankato and moved to Racine, Wisconsin. After four years of railroading, he moved to Omaha, Nebraska. It was there he was again arrested, this time for embezzling from an employer. In 1884, he was sentenced to two years in the Nebraska State Prison. A year later he escaped, but on advice from his mother he later turned himself in. After finishing his term as a model prisoner, he got married and started a family. They moved around, living in LaCrosse, Wisconsin, and later Chicago where George worked various railroading jobs. Finally, in 1891, he returned to Mankato and started painting houses.[26]

It is not difficult to imagine the older brother, an experienced train robber, talking his younger brother, a two-time convicted thief, into their next joint venture. By November, the Sontag brothers had decided to try their hand at train robbery without Chris Evans.

The work of masked men who held up a train near Racine, Wisconsin, made the front page of the *San Francisco Chronicle* on November 12, 1891. The details were so similar to the recent California train robberies, the newspaper reports could have recycled earlier accounts by just changing the dates, locations, and names of the train men. The one significant difference from the previous two robberies at Alila and Ceres was the successful acquisition of several thousand dollars. The robbers would have gotten more, but as George Sontag later recalled:

> I made a search of the car and found three small safes. The messenger told me they were time locks, and could not be opened. I told him to get them out, as we could open any kind of a safe. They were too heavy, so I threw in a stick of dynamite and blew the safes out of the car, badly damaging the latter.
>
> John started with the bunch for the engine, I hollering to him to wait while I blew the safes open. He answered back: "Here comes a special [train] from Racine." Racine was only seven miles away.
>
> We took what money we had [already] secured, $9,800, and left the scene.
>
> The road was slushy, and we had a hard time getting to a cabin where we could break our guns and put them in their cases. We then proceeded to town. Arriving there we went home, our mother sleeping through the night and never dreaming that the sensation she saw in the papers next morning was caused by her two sons.[27]

Thousands of miles away, Eva would read the sensational account of the robbery and probably have a better idea than Mrs. Sontag of just who the bandits might be.

A few days after they returned to Mankato from their successful train heist near Racine, John asked George to go out to California with him, "just to look around." George claimed he made the trip West mainly to meet Chris, whom he had heard so much about.[28] Besides, they now had more than a little traveling money ($9,800 was a fortune in those days), and God knows California would be warmer than Minnesota during the dead of winter.

George temporarily left his wife, family, and house-painting business behind to investigate the opportunities available in California. He and John arrived in Visalia in December 1891. It is unknown what Eva's first impression was of George. She was probably just focused on John, happy to have him back with the family. Her seventeenth birthday was only six months away, and she had to have been thinking of marriage.

George, on the other hand, was not too impressed with Chris Evans. He later described him as "a somewhat religious man of medium build with reddish hair and slow movements, who looked more like a farmer than a train robber." Even though George was skeptical of Evans, his brother had given him nothing but the best accounts of both his bravery and good judgment. George evidently put stock in his older brother's opinion.

In the late winter and early spring of 1892, Chris and the Sontag brothers spent some time in the Sierra Nevada. In February, Chris filed a mining claim in the Sampson's Flat district of Fresno County. George later remembered not so much prospecting for gold or silver, but searching for "potential hiding places, places of concealment to where they could escape quickly when they needed them."[29]

If the three were indeed laying the groundwork for yet another train robbery, it would all have to wait. That spring, John had an accident with a runaway team and broke his ankle and would have to stay close to home to recuperate. George suffered eye problems and went to San Francisco to see a specialist, then received word that his wife had just had a baby, so he returned to Mankato. In June, Chris told his family he was going to Sampson's Flat to work his mine with his good friend, Clark Moore. It is unknown if Eva, when she said goodbye to her father that June, knew that instead of going to the mountains, Chris went to San Francisco and purchased a ticket to Mankato under an assumed name.[30]

Eva was no doubt grateful to have John stay behind. Perhaps she even cherished the idea of having her fiancé around without her father's protective presence. So little is known of their actual relationship during what had to be a strained courtship. Eva herself was oddly silent on the details in her memoir. It gives one pause to consider that there never really was a passionate romance, but the engagement was merely a convenient inevitability. Nonetheless, it is pleasant to think of the warm nights of early summer beckoning the young couple—Eva taking care of her handsome lover, still recuperating from his broken leg. With her watchful father away, they might finally have had the chance to "go buggy riding" unchaperoned. Eva was now sixteen years old, and how could she not have been yearning for just that? She was also an attractive young woman—ample temptation for the thirty-year-old John.

EVA NEVER MENTIONED her father's trip to Minnesota in her memoir for good reason. On July 2, near Kasota, Minnesota, Chris and George botched a train robbery.

Chris arrived in Mankato on June 28, 1892, under the assumed name of Charles Naughton. The two men quickly decided to rob the "Omaha," as the Chicago, St. Paul, Minneapolis and Omaha Railroad was commonly called. After checking train schedules and scouting a location, they put their plan in action, boarding the train at St. Peter on a dark, rainy night.

The details of the Kasota robbery again have the ring of familiarity: two masked men scrambling into the locomotive from the tender, ordering the engineer to stop the train, walking the trainmen back to the express car, demanding the express agent open the car and then the safe, firing shots to intimidate anyone thinking of interfering. But this time, the express messenger was cleverly able to hide the money during the confusion of the robbery. One of the bandits searched the express car and safe, but did not find any money.

Although express company and railroad officials maintained that no money was taken, their intense desire to capture the highwaymen led to rumors and a general belief that surely they must have scored some loot. George, himself, later claimed to have doubts that Chris hadn't gotten any money from the safe. He was understandably angry—and no doubt skeptical—that the messenger was able, under his partner's very eyes, to take a package containing thousands of dollars and succeed in hiding it. "In the face of later events," George would later admit, "I would not hesitate to say that I was a young fool, innocent in the game, and let an older hand stall me out of my share in the haul."[31]

Again, as in the previous robberies, law enforcement officers and detectives swarmed the area in search of the outlaws. Rewards were offered by the express company. But unlike the earlier holdups, this time authorities had suspects worth watching.

A detective for the American Express Company, J. W. Hartshorn, noticed similarities between the Racine and Kasota robberies. He also began to grow suspicious of George Contant, a house painter who resided in nearby Mankato with his wife and young children, who seemed to have ample money despite little work painting houses. Hartshorn also felt that George fit the description of one of the bandits in both robberies.

Hartshorn also suspected a man named Charles Naughton, who was staying at the Sontag Hotel in Mankato. Any newcomer would have naturally aroused suspicion, and Naughton had arrived in town just a few days before the Kasota robbery. After Hartshorn had "Naughton" interviewed, Chris and George let it be known they were going fishing at nearby Lake Washington. Instead, they fled town. When Hartshorn learned they had gone to Minneapolis instead, his suspicions were confirmed.

Chris Evans, traveling as Charles Naughton, and George Contant (unlike John, he had resumed use of his birth name) were shadowed as they made separate journeys to California. Pinkerton detectives in Portland were told to trail them after they made train connections in Oregon. George was trailed all the way into Fresno. At the time, authorities did not realize Charles Naughton was Chris Evans, and the latter made it back to Visalia unnoticed.[32]

With her father back home and John's leg on the mend, Eva looked forward to things getting back to normal. As the dog days of August approached, she eagerly anticipated escaping the valley heat up at the Redwood Ranch, where the family had spent so many happy summers. Little did she imagine that she would never spend another day with her father at that special place in the mountains.

CHAPTER SIX

Collis Changes All

And then came the one that indirectly brought about our
tragedy. Midnight, August 3, 1892, at Collis, Fresno County,
Train No. 17 was attacked for the third time.

—EVA EVANS, *AN OUTLAW AND HIS FAMILY*

T HERE WAS IMMEDIATE TENSION when John met his brother upon his arrival in Fresno. George told of the botched Kasota job and how he thought he'd been trailed from Minnesota. When George hinted that he didn't trust Chris Evans, John immediately became angry. He accused his younger brother of having "cold feet." John goaded him into considering doing another job with Chris. "I could see," George would later write, "that he trusted Evans more than he did me."[1]

When Chris showed up in Fresno the next day, George was still feeling wounded from the fraternal slight and in a confrontational mood. According to George, he asked Chris "what kind of play he had made in Minneapolis to arouse the police against us and get the detectives on our trail. He denied any move that might have been responsible." George claimed that from that point on, Chris Evans' attitude toward him was such that he could see that, no matter how cordial and friendly he had been to his brother John, "his relations toward me would not be so warm that I could go without an overcoat." [2]

Amid these personal tensions, Chris Evans and the Sontag brothers—all three now veteran train robbers—were compelled to plan another robbery. A sense of urgency was precipitated by the failure of two of the previous three jobs. The men needed money and figured one big score could solve all their problems. With recent indications that they were now considered suspects, they were becoming that most dangerous breed of criminals: desperate men who felt they had nothing to lose.

Despite the growing friction, they agreed that George and Chris would perform the next job. John's leg was still too weak to take part in the actual robbery, but he still had plenty of planning and preparation work to perform. Perhaps one factor in tempting the trio back to the robbery well was the news that the Dalton brothers, now reunited in the Indian Territory, had recently made off with over $18,000 in a single train robbery near Adair, Oklahoma.[3]

With plans cemented, the three went their separate ways to prepare. Chris and George agreed to meet up in the mountains while John returned to Visalia. Train schedules and express shipment routines needed to be checked and confirmed. Locations needed to be scouted. Dynamite needed to be acquired, which was stolen from Sweet's store in Visalia.[4] Guns, ammunition, disguises and other such tools of the trade had to be gathered and prepared. Amidst all this surreptitious activity, did John have any time for his courtship with Eva? And was his focus on other matters a source of frustration for Eva, especially since her father had been absent so much in recent months? Eva was, after all, a girl who craved the attention of men.

On August 2, 1892, John rented a team and buggy from Frank Bequette's stable in Visalia. He told Bequette that he planned on driving the rig up to the mountains where Chris and his brother were working a mining claim. Back at the Evans house, John loaded the buggy with two shotguns, three pistols and six dynamite bombs, several dozen rounds of cartridges for the shotguns and pistols, overalls and masks. Chris and George, meanwhile, had met up in the mountains and then parted ways once again with plans to meet up at an appointed time and place. George headed to Visalia where he rejoined John. Chris made his way to Fresno.[5]

With all that was going on, it is no surprise that, as Eva later recalled, their "family movements were not running in the orderly manner they had before we moved to Modesto." She made this comment explaining that they would normally leave for the Redwood Ranch in the spring.[6] But with all the comings and goings of Chris and John, they still hadn't readied to make the move to the mountains, and the oppressive heat of late July and early August only added to family tensions.

How much Molly knew of their plans is a matter of pure conjecture. If cognizant of what was brewing, would she have pleaded with her husband not to proceed? Or did she knowingly remain silent and compliant? Perhaps Chris only told her that he had business to attend to—members of the family would all later claim Chris had been at Sampson's Flat working his mine during this time—and as soon as he finished they could all go to the Redwood Ranch to escape the valley heat.

With Chris gone much of this time, John made most of the preparations. How much he told his future wife, Eva, is not known; but she would have had to notice he was busy preparing for something. What Eva knew, or said, or felt as John left Visalia with the rented team and wagon bound for Fresno is anybody's guess. She didn't discuss it in her memoir.

AFTER THE SOUTHERN PACIFIC constructed a new line between Tracy and Fresno, a new railroad town was established about fifteen miles west of Fresno. It was christened Collis, in honor of the president of the railroad: Collis P. Huntington. The town, which originally consisted of nothing more than a water tank, a pump, and its lonesome caretaker, would later be renamed Kerman.[7]

It was there, at the Collis station on the night of August 3, 1892, that two masked men boarded the engine's tender car as the evening express train from San Francisco was pulling out. Almost every newspaper in the state printed the details of what followed. The *Los Angeles Times* offered this typical example:

> They covered the engineer and fireman with double-barreled shotguns and announced that they had to obey their orders under penalty of death. When the train passed Rollinda station [six miles east of Collis], the engineer was ordered to stop. The robbers ordered the engineer to get off the train and walk a short distance along the track while they proceeded to bombard the two doors of the express car by exploding dynamite cartridges, about eight in all, which tore the doors into splinters and smashed the floor.
>
> They entered the express car and, covering George Roberts with a double-barreled shotgun, ordered him to open the Wells Fargo safe. Roberts set about doing this, but was so excited and nervous that he forgot the combination, and so informed his captors, who thereupon struck him a heavy blow on the head with a gun and threatened to kill him if he did not immediately open the

safe. With trembling hands he did so and they took out the sacks of coin.[8]

After removing several money bags from the safes, the bandits directed the train's fireman, Bill Lewis, to help carry the sacks a few hundred yards down the track. The train's engineer saw the robbers proceed to where some horses were waiting, but he could not tell how many. The bandits then mounted horses and rode rapidly away. None of the witnesses saw that they quickly met up with a third accomplice who waited with a buggy farther off. The three train robbers then proceeded toward Fresno.

Lewis and the engineer, Al Phipps, were able to make temporary repairs to the locomotive (which the robbers had attempted to disable with an additional dynamite blast) and drove into Fresno, where officers were notified of the robbery. Express messenger George Roberts had been badly shaken in the blast that shattered the express car, but would quickly recover. Early reports stated that the robbers had gotten away with as much as $30,000 to $50,000, but these estimates were later revised downward. According to one report in the *San Francisco Examiner,* "three bags of silver, containing about $1,000 each, were taken, and some rolls of gold coin were taken, but no very great amount. It is thought to not exceed $5,000."[9]

Once safely away from the scene of the robbery, John picked up one of these bags. He told his partners he wanted to see what was inside. George cut a hole in one of the sacks and pulled out a coin, which felt strange in his hand. Lighting a match, they discovered they had Peruvian "adobe" dollars. George ripped opened another bag and found it, too, had the worthless (to them) Peruvian coins. George would later recall his brother's comment: "Well, kid," John said to his younger brother, "there's sure bad luck following you."[10] The job wasn't a complete bust, as the other bags held several hundred dollars of good money.

George rode in the buggy only as far as Fresno. Chris and John then swung back to Visalia, arriving home in the wee hours of the morning. In Fresno, George was able to buy a ticket and take the No. 17—the very train they had robbed just a few hours earlier—down to Goshen Junction and from there catch the local into Visalia.

Thus it was that on August 3, 1892, Collis was added to the roster of otherwise insignificant San Joaquin Valley towns along the Southern Pacific road—Pixley, Goshen, Alila, Ceres—that gained temporary fame as venues for the biggest headline-grabbers in the state. But this robbery, Eva would later claim, was different. Loath to admit that Pixley and Goshen and Ceres had contributed to their troubles, she blamed the Collis robbery for all the family tragedy that would follow. As she wrote forty years later, "It was two days later that repercussions from this affair entered our home to blast our lives."[11]

GETTING READY TO HEAD to the mountains, there was much to do around the Evans household. John and Chris had returned the morning before from, as they claimed, the mountains and John returned the rented team and rig to Bequette's livery stable. The horses had been worked hard and for some reason had their shoes removed. George also arrived in Visalia that morning on the train from Goshen. After the train arrived in the early morning hours, bringing with it news of the robbery near Collis only hours earlier, Visalia was in a "fever of excitement." One passenger even brought pieces of the shattered express car door into Visalia and they were placed on exhibition at the Palace Hotel. People swarmed to the hotel to view the relics of a robbery.[12]

The next day, the Evans family planned to leave for the Redwood Ranch. John busied himself cleaning guns. Eva noted that her father had asked John to put the shotguns—loaded with small shot so they could hunt quail and rabbits once they got in the mountains—in a bedroom closet just off the living room. His reasoning was so the children wouldn't "find them and perhaps knock one over."[13]

At some point, George showed up at the house. Eva was not very glad to see him. As she explained in her memoir years later, there was much to do and she resented the interruption. Oddly enough, George ended up showing Eva how to shoot a pistol. As Eva remembered, somehow the subject of guns came up and George expressed surprise that she had never fired a revolver. "What kind of a frontier woman are you?" George teased the girl.

She replied she could well shoot a rifle, but George pointed out a rifle wouldn't protect her. "You can't run around carrying a rifle. Come on; I'll show you how to handle a revolver."[14] Here again, Eva was focusing on guns when telling the story of a watershed day in her life. Was this all part of a carefully crafted outline of circumstances to show the innocence of her father and fiancé? Even if so, it is telling that Eva would remember George suggesting she needed protection.

Recounting her lesson with a revolver, Eva stated "the gun was so heavy I couldn't make much of a showing with it, so we returned to the house and I laid it down on a dresser in my room, which stood just inside the door. As was proven later, there were two bullets in it."[15] Eva's memory had carefully placed firearms at strategic and readily accessible places throughout the Evans home.

Meanwhile, detectives for Wells Fargo and the Southern Pacific, as well as sheriffs and deputies from more than one San Joaquin Valley county, were converging on Visalia. Representatives of the express company and railroad agreed to offer rewards and immediately following the robbery, several lawmen met in Fresno to discuss the details of the case. Both longstanding and newfound suspicions were now pointing to residents of Visalia as the Collis robbers. Authorities learned that two Visalians, who had long been under surveillance because of Sheriff Kay's suspicions, were not at home the night of the Collis robbery. It was then ascertained that one of them, John Sontag, had hired a team and buggy the day before and returned it the day after. Furthermore, those same large horses had been spotted near Fresno. (Even though the liveryman had been told they were being hired for a trip to the mountains.)

The migration to Visalia by concerned authorities included, amongst others, Detectives James B. Hume and John Thacker from Wells Fargo, W. E. Hickey and Will Smith for the Southern Pacific, and Sheriff Thomas Cunningham from Stockton. Undersheriff Fred Hall and Deputy George Witty headed local Tulare County efforts for an absent Sheriff Kay, who at the time was occupied trailing a horse thief into Santa Cruz County.[16]

Efforts were then made to confirm suspicions. One historian's account, which unfortunately was not annotated and so impossible to trace, described an interesting chance meeting on the street:

> When Detective Will Smith, of the Southern Pacific, met Evans casually on the street of Visalia the second morning after the hold-up at Collis, he greeted him pleasantly and stopped to pass the time of day and comment on the robbery. It was hot, as only an August day in the San Joaquin can be hot. Evans was in his shirt sleeves. It was evident that he was not armed, and Smith strolled down the street with him, trying, as subtly as a railroad detective could try, to pump him about the robbery without arousing his suspicions. One bit of information, and one bit only, did he get. That was the fact that John and George were at the Evans house on the outskirts of town.[17]

George, it turned out, was much more talkative than Chris Evans. As Eva pointed out, after the morning target practice, John and George headed downtown and George ended up in a local saloon and, as the Irish would say, once in his bottles apparently found his tongue. A local bartender then informed Deputy Witty that George seemed to know a lot more about the robbery than a casual observer should have.[18]

As Detective Smith later told an *Examiner* reporter: "Between eleven and twelve o'clock, Deputy Sheriff Witty and myself went to Evans' house and asked for George Sontag. We wanted him to come down to the Sheriff's office a make a statement, as we had heard that he was on the train that was robbed near Collis. John Sontag, George's brother, was in the house at the time. George accompanied me downtown and made a statement, which was taken down in shorthand. His story proved that he knew a great deal about the robbery, so he was placed under arrest and charged with the crime."[19] It was at this point that Smith made an error in judgment. Confident that he could finesse the situation, Smith decided to return to the Evans house and bring in John Sontag. Smith also planned on picking up a trunk of George's belongings at the Evans house and so secured the services of H. N. Denny, an express man, to follow him and Witty to the Evans home with a wagon. Newspapers would later opine that if Smith had only waited for Sheriff Cunningham and Detective Thacker and included them, the return visit to the Evans house would have been more successful.[20] In hindsight, it was clear Smith underestimated the situation.

In considering Eva's account of the day, the timeline becomes a bit confusing. She claimed that after going downtown with his brother, "John left George when he started drinking, because John seldom took a drink. Someone must have told him before he came home that George had been arrested. We knew that he had gone away in the morning, but did not know that he had returned."[21] Eva was very careful to make it clear she did not know John had returned. But did she know George had returned only to leave with the officers? He was, after all, picked up by Smith and Witty around eleven-thirty in the morning at the Evans house. Or was Eva's memory confused about which day the shooting lesson took place? The target practice and John and George's trip downtown could have occurred a day earlier, which would have been the day immediately after the robbery. This would also make more sense in a timeline that had George drinking enough to loosen his tongue, arouse suspicion in a bartender, and see that suspicion relayed to Deputy Witty.

Or was Eva's narrative just a carefully plotted fiction to explain away the convenient presence of loaded shotguns and a pistol readily at hand in the Evans home?

Eva's description of a fateful encounter later that hot August day explained the significance of those guns.

> When John and George had left our house, I had returned to my interrupted tasks. I was sitting at the sewing machine, trying to finish a sunbonnet, when I suddenly remembered that Mother had said I was to pick the figs. It was while I was doing this that John had come over from Grannie's and had gone into the bedroom without any of us seeing him.
>
> It was so hot that every window and door was open. The front door of the living room was directly in line with the one that led to the hall, so that when I entered the back door to return to my sunbonnet work, I saw two men at the front door. I did not know who they were, but it turned out that one was Witty, a local officer, and the other was Smith, a Southern Pacific detective.
>
> "Where's Sontag?" said one of the men, meeting my startled gaze.

They were asking a question to which they thought they already knew the answer. Upon arrival at the Evans house, as they were hitching their horses (which actually belonged to Sheriff Kay), they noticed John Sontag entering the rear of the house.

Whether Eva really thought John was still downtown, as her memoir claimed, or in his room over at Grannie Byrd's house next door, or if she realized he was actually in the house at the time, no one will ever know. But startled at the sudden intrusion and rightly concerned that officers of the law were asking about her husband-to-be, she blurted out the only thing she could. "I don't know," she told them.[22]

WILL SMITH'S RESPONSE, Eva would claim for decades to come, was "You're a damned little liar. I saw him come into this house not five minutes ago."[23]

Will Smith had a slightly different memory of his conversation with young Eva Evans. He simply recalled asking the girl "where Mr. Sontag was, and she said he was not in."[24] Most later accounts of the exchange have adhered to Eva's version, the reasons probably having more to do with dramatic impact than veracity. But Eva's version, while possibly embellished or even blatantly contrived, conveniently rings true to Will Smith's caustic personality.

A native of Scotland, Smith had been deputy sheriff in Yuma, Arizona; a guard at the territorial prison; and a U.S. customs inspector. A Southern Pacific Railroad company detective since 1888, the unmarried Smith was headquartered in Los Angeles, his working territory all of Southern California and Arizona. Overbearing and abrasive to the extent that other officers hesitated to work with him, Smith's public image was less than admirable. Sheriff Kay said of Smith many years later that he was absolutely unreliable and thought he had tried to undermine his work from the moment he took office. He felt the railroad detective had "jumped the gun" on more than one occasion.[25]

Keeping Smith's personality in mind, it is easy to believe he would have been less than civil to the young Eva. And Eva's insulting and profane version of the confrontation offers more than just an example of Smith's caustic arrogance; it provides a defendable reason for Chris Evans to be upset with the men who appeared at his door. What father wouldn't be angered at this insult to his daughter under his own roof? But regardless of whether or not this insult was offered, the fact remains that Chris Evans and John Sontag were suddenly facing authorities in what they felt was an increasingly desperate situation. These lawmen had already arrested George. Did he run off at the mouth? Had he cracked under the pressure? Tensions were naturally high, and tempers were at a hair-trigger setting.

At this point, according to Eva, she fled to the barn to get her father. "Daddy, there are two men in the house," she excitedly told him. "They asked for John, and I said I didn't know where he was, and the man said I was a damned liar." Eva wrote that her father's eyes flashed, but he said little as he headed for the house, Eva following because, as she explained, she wanted to see him "wipe out the insult."[26]

Smith's version did not mention Eva leaving to get her father, but neither did he say she didn't. Instead, the account, as written in the *Examiner,* stated:

> Just then Chris Evans entered the house from the back door. The front portion of the house consisted of a sitting-room on the right and a bedroom on the left side. In place of a door to the bedroom there was a portiere. There was another bedroom back of the sitting room. Evans was in the latter bedroom. He said that Sontag

had gone up town. I told him Sontag had just entered the house. I stepped up to the front bedroom and pulled aside the portiere and there stood Sontag with a double-barreled shotgun. I jumped to one side and attempted to unbutton my coat to reach my six-shooter when I saw that Chris Evans had me covered with another shotgun.[27]

Exactly who fired the first shot is a disputed fact. Even Eva would eventually change her story. She swore under oath a year-and-a-half later that Smith had stepped in quick and drew his revolver and fired. But when writing her memoirs forty years later, she would remember it was Witty who "pulled out a revolver and fired it before he could aim it at anyone, but I heard the bullet whistle past my head as it went out through the open door."[28] Even after decades had passed, she was careful to explain away the lack of any corroborating bullet found in the house.

One detail that all accounts seem to agree on is that Smith and Witty quickly turned and ran. The *San Francisco Chronicle* noted that "the two officers, seeing that the robbers had the drop on them, turned to run, one going to the right and the other to the left. Evans pursued Witty and Sontag went after Smith." Smith recalled looking over his shoulder "just as Evans fired at Witty." He then stopped and fired two shots at Evans, and at that point claimed Sontag stopped and fired at him. Smith openly admitted that he and Witty had run "out through the front door. Witty ran through the gateway and I went over the fence." As their pistols were no match for shotguns, it was the only smart thing to do. Nonetheless, Smith received a peppering of birdshot to his backside.[29]

Eva described how her father pursued Witty. Standing just behind John, she watched her father fire two shots from the revolver he had just picked up from the dresser in Eva's room. One of the shots hit Witty in the shoulder, spinning him around and knocking his gun from his hand. He was only about fifteen feet from the front porch, and although wounded, he was able to regain his balance and run through the gate and across the street. Chris, now with an empty revolver according to Eva's accounting, ran after Witty and out of her view.[30]

Witty made it to the front yard of a neighbor, J. W. Howell, who offered the following account in the *San Francisco Examiner*:

Witty ran to the rear of my house and then went clear round to the back yard, still followed by Evans. The murderous pursuer snapped his pistol at Witty, but it missed fire. He cocked it again and then pulled the trigger and Witty was shot in the neck. He fell to the ground, and blood spurted out of his nose and mouth and from the bullet wound. It was a terrible sight.

Witty, lying prostrate on the ground, piteously begged Evans not to shoot again. Evans came right up to him and aimed his pistol at the wounded deputy.

Witty said, "For God's sake, don't shoot. I am dying." I told Evans not to shoot and, after looking at his helpless victim lying on the ground and covered with blood, he turned around and went back to his house.[31]

When Chris returned to his house, he approached his sixteen-year-old daughter, Eva, who would never forget the look on his face; his eyes were more ablaze than she had ever seen them. She was stunned at what he said. For the first time in her life, she heard her father use rough language. "I got that son of a bitch!" Chris then got control of his terrific anger and calmly asked his daughter to go look for his coat.[32]

She found her father's coat hanging in the fig tree, and by the time she got back with it, John had untethered the horses the lawmen had left behind. (Smith made a rapid departure in Denny's express wagon that was standing by to transport George's trunk. The wounds to his backside were minor and would offer more emotional embarrassment than physical pain.)

Before chaos erupted—before Molly and the other children came in from the back orchard; before people came pouring into the place, asking questions about the shooting; before Grannie Byrd came over to try to consol a hysterically sobbing Molly; before officers came to ask Eva what had happened and what had caused the shooting—John and Chris quickly drove away with Sheriff Kay's team of horses.

OFFICERS SCATTERED IN EVERY DIRECTION after the shooting at the Evans house and subsequent flight of the suspects. A large number of men started out in carriages, on horseback, and on foot. At least forty men were on the roads north of town searching for Chris and John. Word had been sent to Sheriff Kay, who immediately boarded a train in Santa Cruz and headed back to Visalia, his horse-thieving prisoner in tow.[33]

It was, in the words of the *San Francisco Examiner*, a "fated suggestion" for lawmen to stake out the house and barn of Chris Evans the night of the shootout and ensuing departure from town. "At first the idea was pooh-poohed," the newspaper account stated. "But the wisdom of the older heads prevailed, and ex-sheriff Dan Overall of Visalia was asked to find some men to take the watch." Among the men he hired was Oscar A. Beaver, a special deputy sheriff from the nearby town of Lemoore. There were some who claimed these special deputies were recruited with the promise of "ten dollars and an oyster dinner."[34]

It wasn't until one o'clock in the morning that Overall had organized his posse to watch the Evans place. Beaver, armed with a shotgun and revolver, was stationed on the bank of a small ditch just east of the Evans barn. Constable Charles Hall was posted on the northwest corner of the block behind the Evans home. Wells Fargo detective John Thacker held a commanding view of the front of the house from the south side of the block. Overall and W. H. Fox took positions near the Byrd house, just south of the Evans home. What they didn't know was that Chris and John had already slipped back to the Evans home in Sheriff Kay's buggy, which was parked with the horses in the barn. Overall, who didn't believe Evans and Sontag would dare to return to the house, was so sure that the stakeout was an exercise in futility that neither he nor Fox were even armed.[35]

Molly and Eva also doubted their men would be so audacious as to return to the scene of the trouble. But earlier that night, Eva and her mother, lying in the dark, quietly talking after getting all the children to sleep after such an eventful day, were shocked when someone stepped onto the front porch. They were only slightly relieved when, hearing a familiar voice, they realized it wasn't more officers, but Chris and John.

Eva—so worried that the house might be surrounded—asked John why in the world they had come back. The reason, he told her, was George. Figuring he would be transported to Fresno on the night train, they planned to rescue him. "We'll hide behind the wood piled along the track, and they will be so surprised that we will take him without killing anyone." A more likely motivation for the risky return was a need for supplies. The rescue of their compatriot would have been, of course, a more noble reason for risking capture, and Eva naturally emphasized—if not synthesized—such positive character attributes in her father and her lover.

According to Eva, Chris and John did in fact leave for a while that night, ostensibly to rescue George, and while they were gone she and her mother gathered supplies and fed and watered the team. They were unaware that officers, by now, had indeed surrounded the house. After getting food and supplies ready, Eva and her mother stood out on the porch waiting for their men to return. Under the sweet smell of a large jasmine vine, mother and daughter talked in hushed tones so as not to awaken the children. "I told her what Dad had said that afternoon when he returned from shooting Witty," Eva remembered. Her mother then told her, "Your father's crazy; there is no other way to account for what has happened." While it is hard to imagine Eva didn't know exactly what was going on, there is something credible and tender in the way she presented her mother's naiveté. Eva continued her account of what followed:

> It was a bright moonlit night; at that time there were no trees between our house and the road to town. Just then [Mother] looked out and said "Here they come; Oh, God! Look at them. Right out in the middle of the road, with guns slung across their backs!"
>
> As soon as Dad reached us, he said, "George was not brought to the train. Mamma, is our supper ready?"
>
> They ate hurriedly, with only the moon to light the table through the open doors and windows, and then we carried the rest of the supplies to the barn.
>
> Dad had opened the barn doors, and was just ready to back out the team, when I saw a man rise out of the ditch. Dad and John were in front of the team.
>
> I caught John's arm and said, "A man! Look!"[36]

At that point, according to newspaper accounts, a shot was fired. Who exactly fired it and why, one news report admitted, might never be known. It was immediately answered with a fusillade. The *San Francisco Examiner* offered the following account worthy of the most lurid dime novel:

> "Bang! bang! bang!" roared the shotguns, and the whistling crack of the rifle added its menace to the din. Then came a dreadful cry.
>
> "Help! help! help! Murder! murder! Boys, help me; I'm dying."[37]

According to Eva, it was Oscar Beaver who fired the first shot. The initial volley from his rifle was fired right into the team. "The horses screamed, and John and Dad pulled them down into a heap," Eva recalled. "I drew Mother to the ground, so that we were shielded by the horses." It was only at that point, she claimed, that John and Chris discharged their weapons.[38]

As the papers explained, after the wounding of Beaver, the other members of the stakeout posse did not dare approach for fear of drawing fire from the robbers entrenched in the barn. Overall called again and again, "Oscar, is that you?" but received no response, save groans from the general location he believed Beaver to be. It would be folly to attempt a rescue of the wounded man, lying out in the open moonlight within easy range of the bandits' guns.[39]

Meanwhile, in the barn, Chris and John waited, expecting other lawmen to attack. There was no word nor movement; nothing but the sound of the wounded horses. Even though they were Sheriff Kay's horses, both Chris and John were deeply pained by the suffering of the animals, one of which eventually died. The only other sounds were the groans of a dying Oscar Beaver, lying on the bank of an irrigation ditch. Eva was still holding Molly down, but realized it wasn't necessary. Her mother had fainted.

During the confused inaction of the frightened lawmen—they were finally able to carry away the bullet-riddled Beaver and then continued a cautious surveillance of the barn—Chris and John were easily able to make away unnoticed on foot. As Eva described their departure, neither her father nor John said a word to her, "but went straight out across the open common in the bright moonlight to the oak trees about a quarter of a mile away. They were afoot, without food or extra clothing, and John was still lame from a broken ankle."[40]

Thus it was, for the second time in less than twenty-four hours, that young Eva Evans watched the two most important men in her life leave. She was left alone to deal with an emotionally distraught mother, the inevitable onslaught of officers, her frightened and confused younger siblings, and the gnawing fear that her men had little hope to escape. Were she able to imagine the tumultuousness that lay ahead, she too would have likely fainted.

CHAPTER SEVEN

A Headline Sensation

It did not take long for Hearst to find the formula he was looking for. Within weeks of taking over the paper, he began to run crime stories on his front pages, and he continued to add them.

—DAVID NASAW, *THE CHIEF*

THE ENTIRE FRONT PAGE of the *San Francisco Examiner* on Sunday, August 7, 1892, was devoted to the story that Eva Evans was living. The coverage consisted of a detailed recap of the previous few days' events, filling all seven columns of the front page and spilling over onto four columns of page two. Several illustrations enlivened the front page, including pictures of the blasted express car from the Collis robbery; a view of the Evans' house, "from which he began shooting at Witty"; and, as the caption declared, the "Barn to which the robbers returned for the money and from which they shot Oscar Beaver."

While every grisly detail was covered in the thousands of words that followed, the story was neatly summed up in its headlines. "BAFFLED BY BANDITS" topped narrative titles set in bold fonts of descending size: "Train Robbers, Hemmed In by Detectives, Shoot One of Them and Escape; FIGHTING IN THE DARK; Sontag and Evans, After the Desperate Encounter with Witty and Smith, Return to Visalia; DOUBLED ON THEIR TRACKS; Discovered in Evans' Barn and Surrounded, They Fatally Wound Oscar Beaver and Again Elude Capture; CREEPING AWAY IN THE NIGHT; The Guards, Disconcerted by the Fate of Their Comrade, Relax Their Vigilance, and the Outlaws, Taking Advantage of the Situation, Cut Across the Country on Foot Towards the Mountains; Their Departure Not Discovered Till Morning."[1]

While Eva would undoubtedly disagree with some of the details of the lurid account, even she would have to admit the headlines accurately summed up the story. But in the days immediately following the sensational shootouts—two gun battles in less than twenty-four hours, both right in front of sixteen-year-old Eva—she probably didn't have the time nor inclination to read the papers. Her life was, as she described, "thrown into a hectic, unreal world."[2]

ONE LOCAL NEWSPAPER COMMENTED on the large number of persons who, over the weekend, had come to the Evans place to gawk at the scene of the gun battles. It was noted that until Sunday, two bloody spots where Beaver fell could be seen and the stable front where the horses had been shot was spattered with blood. "The interior of the barn was visited by many persons," the paper reported, "until the family, growing tired of so many callers, wired the door."[3]

While the intrusion of so many curiosity-seekers was bothersome to Eva and her mother, the invasion of brazen officers was downright traumatic. Eva later recalled the "strange men coming to our home at all hours of the day, asking questions about Dad and John—were they at home on a certain date? Had our father given us any newly coined money to spend? What were we living on, now that our credit had been stopped by Sweet & Co.?" These were questions Eva somehow felt "nobody in the world had any right to ask," even though John and her father were suspects not only in several train robberies, but in the shootings of several law officers, one of whom had died. Eva would later admit only to feeling more "bewildered than frightened."[4]

It wasn't long before the officers came looking for evidence of the spoils of robbery. Newspapers reported that Wells Fargo detectives, accompanied by a deputy sheriff, visited the Evans place to see what could be found. One paper noted that, in addition to a freshly-dug hole officers had previously noticed, "they discovered another hole large enough and about the shape to receive a Wells-Fargo box. It is an old hole and is believed to have been dug to bury the box secured at the time of the Goshen robbery."[5]

Empty holes with freshly turned dirt were only circumstantial evidence, and the officers' frustration grew as their investigation intensified. According to Eva, the search moved to inside the house. In her memoir she remembered:

The second day after the trouble several men, headed by a deputy sheriff, came to the house, looking for money. Until we went to Modesto we had never had either beauty or comfort in furniture; but there, Dad bought Mother a "parlor set"—a sofa and two chairs—upholstered in brocaded mohair in dark blue and gold. We all thought them beautiful, and tried to take such good care of them, and we shipped them back to Visalia. When these men came, they stuck sharp knives into them and ripped them open, looking for money. They cut our mattresses, too. The little children cried. Mother and I told them what we thought of them, but it didn't stop them.[6]

The papers did not report these abuses, but then neither did they report one amazing stroke of humanity amidst the otherwise callous climate. Sheriff Kay came to the Evans house the next day. He'd heard of the harsh treatment from his deputy and offered his apologies to Molly. Remarkably, he even gave her some money to pay for the damaged furniture. Eva would forever after respect Sheriff Kay, and he always returned that respect to Eva and her entire family, regardless of the circumstances of duty that put him at odds with Chris Evans.

Besides the need to question the family and search the property, officers swarmed the Evans place at the slightest rumor of activity. One evening, twelve-year-old Arthur Patnot rushed breathlessly into town claiming a neighbor saw Evans and Sontag return home in a spring wagon and drive into the barn. That neighbor, L. D. Whitt, lived just across the road from the Evans place and asked the boy to go into town and inform authorities while he stood by and watched the barn. "The news created the greatest excitement," the *San Francisco Examiner* reported, "and men ran in every direction, and everybody that could secure arms rushed out to the scene."

With the Evans home surrounded, Sheriff Kay asked Frank Byrd, Molly's brother, to go to the house and tell the women and children to leave, as they would be in danger if a fight ensued. Byrd refused, fearing he'd be shot if he were not recognized. Time passed while officers discussed how to get the family safely out. Finally, at about eleven o'clock at night, Sheriff Kay knocked on the door, awakened Mrs. Evans and simply asked her if Chris was home. She said he was not and accompanied the sheriff to the barn with a lighted candle. There was no sign of the wagon or the men. By this time, the over-zealous neighbor Whitt admitted "he only heard the barn door shut, but saw nothing."[7]

FILLED WITH INDESCRIBABLE SUSPENSE was how Eva recalled the days following the troubles. All she and her mother knew for sure was that their men had not been found. They did not know where they were—if they were safe or hungry or hurt or anything. With posses swarming the area, all the women could do was worry. "In the meantime," Eva complained, "the ceaseless persecution of the family went on."[8]

Several posses formed with little coordination between them. The sheriff from Fresno County, where the Collis robbery occurred, had formed one posse. Local Tulare County officers headed other posses. After returning from an initial foray, Sheriff Kay and over a dozen men equipped themselves for a week's pursuit and headed out again. He told reporters he was confident the robbers would be captured, although he cautioned it might be "several days hence."

Still another squad was under the control of the railroad and express company detectives, including detectives Hume, Thacker and the increasingly-ridiculed Will Smith. The arrogant Smith was having trouble organizing recruits. The press had printed a statement by Denny, the express driver who accompanied Smith away from the scene of the initial shootout, accusing him of cowardice. Smith was now being referred to, in print, as "The Sprinting Detective." Further reports, such as one in the *Fresno Expositor*, claimed that "no one would volunteer to go under his leadership, as people have lost all confidence in his methods." Nonetheless, the experienced detective was finally able to muster a posse and headed for the mountains.[9]

The hunt had become, at least according to the *Examiner*, a political contest. The paper noted that if Sheriff Kay should find and bring in the men, he would undoubtedly win re-election. But if the former sheriff, Dan Overall, captured the men, there would probably be a "change in the political aspect of Tulare County." The paper further opined that "with the political parties making their fight on the Sheriff's office," the bandits had picked a particularly bad time for a train robbery.[10]

As the days passed, the papers began reporting the return to Visalia of these various posses. While most of the men had been admonished to keep silent on their activities and progress, they brought with them from their searches little more than rumor and speculations.

The rumor earlier spread by the Evanses' neighbor Whitt was, it turned out, prophetic. Eva later recounted that only days after the troubles, Chris paid his first visit to the family. According to Eva's account, she was awakened one night by the sound of her father's voice, audible from the next room where he talked in hushed tones with Molly. Eva jumped out of bed and "in a moment was in his arms." Chris assured his daughter that everything was all right and that no one was going to kill him.

This is what he said to Mother and me that night [Eva wrote in her memoir]:

"Do you remember what I told you in the few minutes we had to talk when we were here last? That John had said, 'It's the S. P. after me.' You know what that means, don't you? If they mark a man and go after him, he's doomed. They own the courts and the judges. It's less trouble to convict an innocent man than it is to hunt down the guilty one.

"Do you recall that several years ago a box of gold watches and rings was found on the steps of the South Methodist Church? Some robber wag's idea of a joke. Maybe he was behind in his dues to the church, and ironically paid with something he did dare not use. These watches and rings were traced to that Goshen train robbery, and one of the local officers told me that ever since then there has been a detective in Visalia, looking for other clues, hoping to pin this crime on a Visalia citizen.

"You know by the papers what George did the morning of the day the trouble started. He went down town and got drunk, went from one saloon to another, bragging about what he knew about the Collis hold-up. He told contradictory stories that were carried to the Sheriff's office, and he was arrested. John was told of this before he returned home that day.

"Do you recall that it was reported, after every one of the several train robberies in the San Joaquin Valley, a tall and a short man committed the crime? Everyone knows what the railroad people did to John, and how he hates them. If George was guilty, here was the short man. Then his brother John must be the tall one; so they came after John.

"When I came into the house that day, I only thought of what they said to you. Then I recognized Witty as a local officer, but I didn't know who the other fellow was. They turned to flee the instant after Witty fired, because just then John stepped into the room with both shot-guns. When Witty pulled his gun, I believe he meant to cover me and search the house for John. That shot was a clear case of 'buck-ague'—he was so nervous that he shot without meaning to. The fight was on; I knew I could not stop John, and without even waiting to see if you had been shot, I pulled that revolver, and, as they ran, gave my attention to Witty, the man who might have killed you.

"I don't blame John for not giving himself into their hands. With only one lung, and his heart in the shape it is, prison would be death in a short time. I wouldn't let them take him; he has suffered enough at their hands. You know what happened after that; now there is no turning back.

"I have never robbed a train. If I had, you would not be penniless now. But I've killed one man, and wounded another. Regret or remorse would be useless."[11]

Here was a point-by-point defense and explanation of circumstances that confirmed her father's innocence. What choice did the sixteen-year-old Eva, who adored her father, have but to believe in what her father said? But believing *in* what he said was different than simply believing *what* he said.

Eva Evans, in the twilight years of her life, admitted to those close to her what she never admitted in writing: her father had indeed robbed those trains.[12] This simple fact does not, however, make her memoir ring false. Like her father, she believed not necessarily in his innocence; but in *asserting*, with all her heart, his innocence. She had no other choice.

Regardless of what Eva and her family may have believed or later asserted, to most people at the time, the guilt of Chris Evans and John Sontag was a foregone conclusion. What remained unknown was just who would be able to track down and capture the fugitives.

ON AUGUST 11, 1892, the *San Francisco Examiner* noted with a tinge of purple to its prose the arrival of "Arizona thief-catchers—big square-jawed, clear-eyed fellows, slow of speech and much given to similes from the cow ranges"—on the morning train. "Their six-shooters thump against the back of the chairs in the hotel." One of these men was Vernon Coke "Vic" Wilson. He was accompanied by Frank Burke, a deputy sheriff from Yuma County, Arizona, and two Yuma Indian trackers. These men had been retained by the railroad for the express purpose of capturing Evans and Sontag.

Vic Wilson was well qualified for the assignment. A former Texas Ranger, he was born in Virginia in 1857. After two years in the Rangers—during his service he was wounded in a gun battle with a Texas outlaw whom he shot and killed—Wilson went to work for the railroads in 1878, serving as a conductor, baggage man and brakeman. In 1883, he returned to law enforcement when President Cleveland appointed him Chief of Mounted Customs Inspectors for a southwestern district. Headquartered in Tombstone, Arizona, Wilson held the post for four years. After getting married and having a child, he temporarily left law enforcement and took up farming; but in 1890 he was hired by the Southern Pacific Railroad as "Special Agent" for Arizona and New Mexico.[13]

As the days passed and the various posses returned to Visalia empty-handed, the *Examiner* offered a possible excuse. "In the light of recent events," the paper theorized, "it would seem that Evans and Sontag, the train-robbers, have a legion of friends in the mountains. They are aided and sheltered by the people in the hills, and as long as they are in the mountains they will be safer than any other part of the United States." But in the same article, it was pointed out that "the officers and people of this city have a great deal of confidence in the ability of the Arizona scouts, who arrived in this city on Wednesday, to capture the bandits."[14]

Thus, Hearst's newspaper was setting the scene and delineating the characters of an ongoing dramatic saga that the dynamic publisher saw as an incredibly fortuitous—for his newspaper, at least—turn of events. For Eva, it was simply more bad news.

George Sontag, meanwhile, languished in the Visalia jail. On the evening of August 13, the jailer sitting in the front of the building heard a horrible racket going on in the cells. He called in officers to inspect the inmate quarters, checking George's cell first. It was quickly discovered that a large hole had been made in the ceiling through the lattice work. Four rivets had been severed and four lattice bars had been bent back, making a good start to a path of egress. A knife with a serrated edge was found in the water pipe, and a piece of wood was under Sontag's pillow.

All George earned for his efforts was a shackled leg and the promise he'd be more closely guarded. According to one newspaper, "Sontag had little to say when the means of his exit from the cell was discovered, but disgust and disappointment were depicted on his countenance." It was never discovered who smuggled the knife to John Sontag's brother.[15]

As August drew to a close, the harassment of the Evans family resulted in more bad news. Wells Fargo detectives James Hume and John Thacker showed up at their house at dawn on August 30. They had come to search for the swag and brought with them the recently-arrived Arizona trackers: Frank Burke and Vic Wilson. The search party was armed with shovels and large metal rods with pointed ends. It would have been a rude awakening for the Evans family, but they were forty-five miles away in Fresno.[16]

That same morning, the preliminary grand jury examination of George Sontag was held in a Fresno court. (George would be tried in Fresno because the Collis robbery occurred in that county.) Eva and Molly Evans sat in the anteroom of that court, waiting to testify, while back in Visalia, detectives uncovered two sacks of coin in the Evans yard. Even if they had been home, there was little Eva or Molly could have done to stop detectives who, thrusting their metal rods into the earth, discovered swag buried under a peach tree about halfway between the Evans house and the barn.

Detective Thacker had always been convinced that money from the Collis robbery was secreted in the Evans yard somewhere. The *Visalia Delta* noted that Thacker "says he has noticed that when officers have visited the place, Mrs. Evans and daughter invariably went to one particular place in the yard and conversed." Despite Thacker's self-professed powers of observation, it took several hours of systematic probing until the incriminating evidence was finally uncovered.[17]

The sacks of coin were not immediately examined on the site, but brought back to the Fresno Wells Fargo office. An official for the company was later quoted in the *San Francisco Chronicle*: "What the amount [of the uncovered money] is I am not prepared to state, but I can say this, that the silver unearthed consists chiefly of Peruvian, Chilean, Guatemalan, Venezuelan and Ecuadorian silver dollars. These were, of course, no use to them in their flight, for they would give them dead away." This official added that his company's "main rejoicing is that the money found on Evans premises is of the very class of coin we lost, which establishes beyond any doubt the guilt of the men whom Hume, Thacker and Smith have all along declared to be the bandits."[18]

Later that very same afternoon, the grand jury brought an indictment against George Sontag on a charge of train robbery.[19]

EVA WAS BY NOW keeping close tabs on what was printed in the various newspapers. For one thing, her father was interested in reading the news reports. In his recent nighttime visit home, Chris told Eva that a friend from the mountains, Bill Downing, had offered to serve as messenger on his weekly trips to the valley hauling lumber. "You can save the newspapers and give them to him," he instructed her. "Also have a letter ready, with anything I need to know." [20]

Visalia's two primary newspapers were the *Delta,* with George W. Stewart as editor, and the *Times,* run by Ben Maddox. Both published daily and weekly editions, with the *Visalia Daily Times* calling its weekly version the *Tulare County Times.* While these newspapers, as well as several papers in Fresno, offered ample coverage to what was perhaps the biggest local story in memory, neither could compare to the big San Francisco dailies, especially William Randolph Hearst's *Examiner.* Crime stories always appealed to Hearst's keen sense of the sensational, and although he didn't coin the term, his paper certainly exemplified the latter-day news mantra of "If it bleeds, it leads." Readily available and widely read in Visalia, the *Examiner* offered the most in-depth and sensational coverage. Hearst had the resources to throw at the story and sent several reporters, photographers, sketch artists, and support staff to Visalia. Hearst's rival, Michael de Young, was determined that his *San Francisco Chronicle* not be outdone by the *Examiner*, so the *Chronicle* devoted nearly as much column space to Evans and Sontag as the *Examiner*. Still, the *Examiner's* coverage was unsurpassed. The local papers simply could not compete.

One article that was particularly memorable to Eva, because it showed a "feeble attempt to analyze" her father and contained so much inaccurate information, appeared as a human interest feature in the Sunday edition of the *Examiner* in mid August. As Eva theorized, because no one could understand Chris Evans, the best the reporter could do was to saddle him with a dual personality—the headline referring to him as "Visalia's Jekyll and Hyde."[21]

The fanciful profile opened with an account of a woodsman, mortally injured in a logging accident, receiving last rites from Chris Evans, a fellow logger. Those around stared in wonderment to hear the Latin words solemnly delivered. "He sent the others away, heard the poor ax man's confession, shrived him and with the administration of extreme unction, poor Mike's soul passed out among the pines." Word spread of his deed, and one day the boss asked Chris Evans where he learned to play the padre. "I studied to be a priest in Canada," the paper had him saying, and that, the anecdote concluded, was all Chris Evans ever said about it. Thus, the tone was set for the story of how the "man who started out to be a priest became a train robber....for the strange transformation from Evans the Farmer to Evans the Outlaw....a dual life that deceived everyone."[22]

In that same article appeared the first reference in print that Eva and John were engaged to be married.

> Everybody knew how it was between John and Eva. She was the oldest child—a slender but strong slip of a girl with clear eyes and a resolute little mouth. The tall, quiet young man was waiting for her. The neighbors knew it and they waited, too, for a merry wedding of Chris Evans' girl, for who in town but liked the steady farmer!

When Eva said this article was full of so much inaccurate information, was she thinking only of the information about her father? A romance between her and John made great copy. It also made the reading public more sympathetic to them. While it is pure speculation, it would be remiss not to acknowledge the possibility that this article marked the actual birth of a fictive romance.

Eva, herself, continued to be fodder for the press. In September, the *Visalia Daily Times* ran a short article mentioning that Eva, a sixteen-year-old student at Visalia's public school, had reportedly received a letter from her fugitive father and was reading it to some of her female classmates. This could have been the pure fancy of an overzealous reporter because, according to Eva, she didn't even start back to school that fall. With all that was going on, she was more needed at home.[23]

Whether she was thrilled or horrified at seeing her own name in print, one thing was certain: it wouldn't be the last time she would do so. Newspaper editors from near and far had discovered that the Evans family made good copy. And to keep readers interested, the stories were beginning to adopt a more sympathetic tone.

This shift can also be seen in editorials. While continuing to denounce their crimes and urge their capture, this condemnation was increasingly tempered with comments on the otherwise upstanding character of the outlaws and criticisms of the lawmen hunting them. An editorial in the *Examiner* noted that "large and ferocious thief-catchers from Arizona have been imported to Visalia to deal with Rancher Evans." Describing them as "formidable characters" that had brought their "sombreros, curling mustaches, pointed goatees and sawed-off rifles along," they offered quite a contrast to Evans, "a plain granger, with hands made horny by honest toil in the intervals between train robberies." The editorial, echoing the Jekyll and Hyde profile, went on to state that Chris Evans "appears to always have been a good and quiet citizen, punctilious in paying his debts and respected by all who knew him, or rather thought they knew him."[24]

One *Examiner* columnist, the entertainingly-caustic Ambrose Bierce, offered the following criticism of law enforcement in his "Prattle" column:

> Messrs. Sontag and Evans, the Visalian train-robbers, are justly entitled to the gratitude of Man the laugher: they have done much to promote the gayety of nations. The revelations of cowardice and inefficiency which they have supplied detectives and law officers with opportunity to make would mitigate the facial austerity of a marble young sheep in a cemetery….Of the now dissolving cloud of detectives, deputy-sheriffs and private reward-seekers, if any ever have lead in his paunch it will be because he swallowed it. [25]

As THE VARIOUS POSSES continually returned empty-handed to Visalia and the hunt for the bandits languished, newspapers were reduced to writing about rumored sightings of Evans and Sontag.

On August 21, 1892, the *San Francisco Examiner* wrote that the duo had been spotted in Big Pine in Inyo County. The following day, several papers printed the news that they were seen in Oro Grande, on the Mojave River forty-five miles north of San Bernardino, apparently headed for the Colorado River. On August 23, the *Los Angeles Times* reported that "the Collis train-robbers have escaped over the Sierras and are now in Nevada." Another report in the *Los Angeles Times* a couple of weeks later proclaimed, in headline, the "Daring Pair—Evans and Sontag Once More Heard From—They Pay a Visit to Pixley and Get Their Horses Shod." A later report in the *Visalia Daily Times* put the local outlaws 150 miles to the north, in Tuolumne.[26]

One historian with an intimate understanding of the region summed up the situation as the manhunt entered its second month. In *Train Robbers and Tragedies: The Complete Story of Christopher Evans, California Outlaw*, Harold L. Edwards wrote:

> In spite of the conflicting reports regarding the outlaws' where-abouts, the officers, detectives, and fortune-hunters believed the outlaws were in the Sierra Nevada Mountains of Tulare or Fresno Counties, and they concentrated their efforts in those districts. However, the fugitives seemed to have vanished. They were actually moving through the rough country on foot and off traveled roads. They hid in makeshift camps deep in brushy thickets and often traveled at night. They sat for hours in the daytime on the summit of Stokes Mountain, watching the southern approaches to their retreat for the approach of officers. Stokes Mountain, sixteen miles northeast of Visalia, was an ideal vantage point. It extended about four miles westward from the mountain range like a fin-ger pointing into the San Joaquin Valley. From its highest point, a viewer had a 180 degree view of the valley floor. And, on a clear day, Evans had an extensive viewing range, especially using binoculars. By rapid movement and alert vigilance, the fugitives managed to avoid the movements of the posses.[27]

Knowing her father and John were close to home, Eva would have welcomed the rumors of their far-flung sightings. She would have known the reports were mistaken—reporters were obviously eager for news and would believe any farmer who claimed to have seen the fugitives—because the family was never completely out of contact with Chris for very long. Eva claimed her father, soon after his earlier visit, sent a messenger to the family, instructing them to hitch "Big Jim," their big sorrel horse, to a cart and send him to an appointed location via a friend. Eva claimed she would often hear the sound of that big-footed horse go past the house in the middle of the night.

"I know now what it meant," Eva explained forty years later. Her father was checking on the family—looking for prowlers. When Eva thanked her father for doing so, despite the obvious risk, he told his daughter, "Oh, it was not a hardship; it broke the monotony. By starting at dusk we could be back in camp before dawn and sleep all day." Even though he knew "it worried your mama to have us come in," Chris was apparently glad to be near his family "anyway for a little while."[28]

One rumored sighting, this one closer to home, was via a very reliable, upstanding source and so carried much validity. If true—and there is little, if any, reason to doubt its veracity—it was also one of their boldest, most daring moves: a daylight visit to County Supervisor Samuel Ellis' house in the hills northeast of Visalia.

While Eva undoubtedly read about the visit in the papers, she claimed also to have heard about it directly from her father. According to Eva, the visit was prompted by her father seeing that his old friend, Sam Ellis, was part of a posse searching for him. "He hated having men he had thought his friends hunting him," Eva declared, so one day Chris decided he and John would pay him a visit and teach him a lesson.

News of the visit made all the papers. The headline in the *San Francisco Chronicle* most succinctly summed up public opinion: "BANDITS WITH NERVE," it proclaimed. According to Ellis' own statements, around noon his children saw a man, or men, lying in the rocks of a gulch about 300 yards from the house. Ellis' sister then went out to investigate and saw a man standing behind a bush. Unable to see his face, she went to him and said pleasantly, "Good morning." The man returned the salutation, and she recognized the voice of Chris Evans. She invited him to the house. According to the account in the *Delta,* after they walked a few steps another voice was heard saying "Chris, you forgot your gun."

Sontag then came forward with two shotguns and handed one to Evans. Then all started to the house. Once in the house, they were invited to sit down for dinner. Evans said they would take seats, "but not give up their guns, as they were pursuing a leaden policy." [29]

When Sam Ellis finally came in and saw who his house guests were, the *Chronicle* reported his first words were: "Hello, Chris! How do you do?" It was a tense moment. As described in the paper, "Evans took two or three steps toward Ellis, said he would shake hands, even though he ought not to. Chris then said: 'You have been hunting me, but you must not hunt Chris Evans any more. The officers may do so, for it is their business, but my friends must stop it.'"

The various newspaper accounts went on to describe how Evans told his side of the story: that he thought he was shooting at Detective Smith when he was pursuing Witty. That they thought they had killed Sheriff Cunningham rather than Oscar Beaver. Ellis went on to say that "Evans told my wife that he had not robbed the train, and said that the coin recently dug up was put there by the detectives." It was clear that

Chris Evans was using Supervisor Ellis as a conduit to plead his defense to the public.[30]

As sundown approached, Chris and John drove away from the Ellis ranch, misappropriating the supervisor's cart and horse and heading toward Visalia. According to Eva, Sam Ellis promptly reported the visit to officers. Sheriff Kay came out and followed the cart tracks toward Visalia, but eventually they were obliterated and lost on the well-traveled road.

Samuel Ellis never again joined in the manhunt.[31]

EVA'S OLD FRIEND, the school janitor, Mr. McKeon, met Eva on Main Street one day in early September. Eva had undoubtedly read about the Arizona manhunters who had arrived in Visalia. On this day she got her first glimpse of them. Mr. McKeon pointed them out. "Them's the killers brought in from Arizony to go after yer Pa," Eva remembers her old friend saying.[32]

The following confrontation, which Eva described in her memoir, was used in virtually every subsequent written account that followed. Writers simply could not resist the heightened drama of it, and whether it happened exactly as described or not, it was certainly true to the emotions Eva was feeling at the time.

Eva walked across the street toward the men. Before she reached them, the marshal mentioned that Chris Evans' daughter was approaching. As Eva got near, one of the men—Vic Wilson—loudly proclaimed for all gathered that he had twenty-seven notches on his gun, and he was headed to the mountains the next day. "Evans and Sontag will make twenty-nine."

Eva later wrote that "he looked directly at me and I did not take my eyes from his face as I walked slowly past. A killer's face; cold, light eyes; dark skin; thin, sharp nose; hard mouth. I was boiling with rage, and all the way home I tried to think of some way to avenge the insult." While the moment was certainly dramatic, according to sworn court testimony by Eva herself, she actually learned of Wilson's pledge to add the notches secondhand, from a worker at the Palace Hotel named Jack Camlin. It seems even Eva was a writer with a weakness for dramatic license.[33]

Although the story of Wilson's pledge became often repeated, it does not reflect what is known of his personality. Wilson (the nephew of former Texas governor Richard Coke) was not a braggart. He was considered a gentleman. And even Eva's description of his physical appearance indicates she could have had him confused with the darker-skinned, half-Hispanic Frank Burke.[34] But the point of Eva's story (which would later become central to a claim of self-defense) was that these manhunters intended to kill her father. Whether one of them bragged about notches on his gun or not was irrelevant to what she felt she had to do.

Eva claimed she then sent, via family friend and messenger Bill Downing, a letter of warning to her father. The wording of the supposed letter has been disputed by historians. Carl Glasscock, in his 1929 *Bandits and the Southern Pacific*, claimed that after hearing Wilson's remark, Eva "walked on, quickening her step at the corner and hurrying home. Eva immediately sat down and wrote a note to her father." According to Glasscock, she said of Wilson: "He's a bad man, Pa. He's a killer. Don't let him get you. I only hope you get him first."[35]

More than two decades later, Wallace Smith, utilizing a copy of Eva's memoir, offered an even more startling version of Eva's message. "I'll be much obliged if you will kill him," Eva wrote to her father, and added an enclosed note. "And when you do, here is a note to pin on him: 'Send on some more killers with notches on their guns. Signed Eva Evans.'"[36]

Carl Glasscock, Wallace Smith and Eva Evans, all with a grand sense of drama, had set the stage. Wells Fargo and the Southern Pacific, interested backers in the real-life melodrama, upped the stakes when they offered a reward of $10,000 for the capture of Evans and Sontag.[37] The newspapers were beginning to depict the outlaws as almost sympathetic characters, and the lawmen were increasingly portrayed as less-than-admirable—either bumbling or diabolical or both—in the press. Little did Eva realize that these were merely the opening acts of a blood-and-thunder melodrama she was living.

Chapter Eight

Defiance

I would to Heaven I could see Detective Smith, Warren Hill, John Broder, Detective Thacker and the three Apache Indian trailers in one bunch. I wouldn't leave one of them alive. They deserved to be born dead.
—Chris Evans, *San Francisco Examiner*, October 7, 1892

A FTER STRUTTING AROUND THE STREETS of Visalia for a few days (as Eva put it), Vic Wilson and another "bad man" (Eva's choice of words) from Arizona, Frank Burke, headed for the hills of eastern Fresno County. Having already made several unsuccessful forays into the mountains in the month since arriving in Visalia, they now traveled with a posse organized by Constable Warren Hill of Sanger. It included John Broder of Visalia, Al Witty of Modesto, Andrew McGinnis of San Francisco, the two Indian trackers who came out from Arizona with Burke, and Detective Will Smith.[1]

After his earlier ill-fated confrontation, Smith had suffered criticism and ridicule from the press. He undoubtedly heard the rumors that Chris Evans pledged to shoot him down. According to Supervisor Ellis' account of his recent encounter in the newspaper, Evans and Sontag "had a vindictive feeling against Detective Smith, and their actions and words inferred they would shoot him on sight."[2] One could assert that the manhunt had become personal for the Southern Pacific detective.

Other posse members had personal connections to the case as well. Al Witty was the brother of Deputy George Witty, who had been wounded in that initial confrontation at the Evans home. And Andy McGinnis had been friends with Chris Evans in Modesto. As Eva later recalled, he was a bill collector and when the Evans family left Modesto, her father told McGinnis if he collected on some of the bad debts from his livery business, he could keep the money.[3] McGinnis was living in San Francisco when the report of reward money brought him to Fresno, hoping to collect on a different kind of debt.

A few days after the posse set out, newspapers announced a deadly shoot-out at Jim Young's mountain cabin near Sampson's Flat. One Visalia paper reported that "the pursuit after Evans and Sontag, the Collis train robbers, has again resulted disastrously, and in a fight between the officers and the bandits yesterday morning two brave officers, V. C. Wilson of Tucson and Andrew McGinnis of San Francisco, formerly of Modesto, were killed." The big city newspapers splashed lurid headlines. The *Los Angeles Times* proclaimed that "BULLETS FLEW—A Deadly Fusillade Poured into the Posse by the Outlaws—Two of the Pursuers Shot Dead—The Rest Scattered. " And in San Francisco, the *Chronicle* announced "TWO MORE VICTIMS—Deadly Work of Evans and Sontag—The Leader and a Deputy Killed." These were alarming headlines, especially for the Evans family.[4]

While this news would have undoubtedly frightened Eva—especially some of the reports that either Chris or John or both had been wounded in the battle—she must have also felt a twinge of delight. Vic Wilson would never add another notch to his gun. Her father had avenged the insult. "Send some more killers with notches on their guns," she might proudly have repeated to herself.

NUMEROUS EYEWITNESS ACCOUNTS of the shoot-out at Young's cabin exist and most tell essentially the same story. From the posse's point of view, Burke recounted how, after the posse found a recent campsite and some old suspenders in eastern Fresno County, they "started for Sampson's Flat to watch the trails for the outlaws."

> We started to go to Young's house to get some potatoes and to leave a note for John Broder, who was expected back the next day. Wilson, McGinnis, myself and Witty had dismounted and started down the hill to the house on the south side. Wilson and McGinnis led off and I was about twenty yards behind, with Witty behind me. I started off to a watermelon patch...suddenly, when the men were about five steps from the house, we saw two men run out and shoot.[5]

Eva's memoir provides an explanation of why her father and John Sontag were in Jim Young's cabin and recounts the events from a point of view entirely different from the posse's. The details are consistent with the other accounts.

Eva explained that her father and John didn't have an adequate hideout in the Sampson's Flat area and, knowing the area was filled with bounty hunters, felt it unwise to build a fire in the open. So they decided to go to Jim Young's cabin to cook some food. She described the small cabin, which stood in a clearing with the edge of the woods behind and a barricade fence made of fallen trees in front. It had just one room, with a ladder leading to a sleeping loft in the attic. There was, she pointed out, just one window and one door.

> While Dad and John were cooking breakfast, [Eva continued,] Ed Mainwaring, a young Englishman who owned a nearby claim, came in to borrow some tools. He had seen the smoke and thought Jim Young was at home. He was our friend, and was not surprised to find the men in the cabin. John was getting breakfast, and Dad was sitting by the window reading a paper. Ed lingered, talking to John.
>
> It all seemed peaceful and safe enough. They did not know that Warren Hill's posse was approaching. The trail had been picked up in this way: I had sent my father some new suspenders, and the old ones, once a bright red, had been left behind where they slept the night before they went to Young's cabin. The Indians found this camp and said it had just been vacated, so the trail was warm. When the posse approached the cabin, they expected to question whoever was at home concerning the outlaws. They did not expect Evans and Sontag.

What none of the accounts from the various posse men can explain is why the officers approached the cabin so unsuspecting of any danger. There is often a fine line between bravery and recklessness, and no one will ever know what the two men leading the approach were thinking.

> Suddenly my father looked up from his paper and saw a number of men clambering over the log barricade. Just behind were other men on horseback. Dad called to John: "We're trapped. Here comes a posse." To Ed Mainwaring he said: "Take that bucket and walk towards the spring as if you were going for water. Don't

look in their direction, and don't hurry. Take it easy, and we won't shoot till you are out of range."

The two men in the lead, Vic Wilson and Andy McGinnis, came on toward the cabin. When they were about seventy-five feet away, John said, "Good God, Chris! One of those men is Andy McGinnis!"

As they drew nearer, Dad said. "Yes, and the other one is the man Eva wrote about. I'll get him from the window. You go to the door and stop McGinnis."[6]

The most dramatic version of what happened next comes from Chris Evans himself, and his account undoubtedly provided the basis for Eva's version. Chris told how they waited "until the first two men came within fifteen or twenty feet of the door, then we thrust our shotguns through the window panes and blazed away, one barrel each." He recounted that both men fell and as he swung open the door and came outside through the gun smoke, he heard McGinnis cry out to Sontag: "For God's sake, don't John." Evans then claimed they dashed by the fallen men and opened fire on the rest of the posse. Witty fell and bellowed "like a calf." Burke tumbled over the barricade fence and out of sight. And "Sprinter Smith," as Chris called Will Smith, "with a wild cry, wheeled his horse, clapped spurs to its flanks, dropped his head against the horse's neck and flew back up the trail."

Warren Hill managed to make his escape, even though his horse was shot out from under him. The Indians took refuge behind a rock pile and fired back wildly. Chris exhibited his sense of humor when he explained: "Pretty soon I made it so hot for them that they thought distance would lend enchantment to the view and dashed away down the road."[7]

All of this happened in a heartbeat, but the battle was not over. Eva stated in her memoir that although Burke later claimed that he wounded Evans and that there were three men in the cabin and one of them shot at him from the attic, "here is what really happened":

When Dad stepped out of the cabin, McGinnis was trying to get to his feet, and when Dad advanced upon him he commenced to beg for his life, saying "Don't kill me Chris, I'm hard hit—I'm out of it."

"I ought to kill you, you dirty dog, but if your life's worth anything to you, keep it," Dad said, and, as he turned away, a bullet from Burke's rifle drilled John through the arm. Then came a roar very close beside Dad, and he staggered and almost fell to the ground. A bullet had clipped his skull, cutting off the edge of his eyebrow. He said for an instant the world went dark. When he could see, he turned toward the sound...[8]

"I whirled around," Chris later told the *San Francisco Examiner*, "throwing in a cartridge as I did, and saw McGinnis trying to shoot me again. I shot him in the left temple; the gun dropped from his hands; he quivered one instant, and Andy McGinnis climbed the Golden Stairs."[9]

It is clear from Chris and Eva's language that the killing of both these men—Vic Wilson, who so offended Eva that she urged his demise, and Andy McGinnis, a former friend-turned-bounty hunter—was laden with personal vendetta.

A FEW DAYS FOLLOWING THE SHOOT-OUT at Young's cabin, Molly and Eva would have shuddered at the headlines in the papers. "BLOOD IN THEIR PATH," announced the *San Francisco Chronicle,* with further banners surmising "Either Evans or Sontag Wounded" and that "Officers Sure of a Speedy Capture." Additional headlines noted that the reward would now be paid whether the "Bandits Are Taken Dead or Alive." (That cliché phrase never appeared on the wanted poster for Evans and Sontag.) The *San Francisco Examiner* noted two days later that the hills were full of "Man-Hunters—A Small Army Now Out After Evans and Sontag." The women back home could only take solace that headlines also proclaimed "Not a Trace of the Bandits" was found.[10]

Despite the uncertainty in the papers, Molly and Eva may have soon realized that both their men had been wounded at Young's cabin. While Chris only suffered a minor graze to his brow, the shot to John's arm was more serious. The bullet had gone through the arm. As Eva later learned, following the shoot-out, her father and John "walked away to a creek, where they stopped, and Dad dressed John's arm. Dad ran a silk handkerchief through the hole, and then tied a tourniquet above the wound. But John had already lost much blood, and there were twelve miles to go over rough trails before they reached the Downing home on Dry Creek." John was nursed back to health by Jane Downing for ten days. Because Bill Downing served as a messenger between Chris and John and the family back in Visalia, Eva would have soon learned of the extent of John's injuries. She may even have visited him, although she makes no mention of doing so in her memoir.

She does, however, note that when she next saw her father, the first thing she said was "You did not pin that note on Wilson. Why?" Her father explained that they didn't have time with the posse still sniping at them, that he did not know how badly hurt John was and, finally, he "did not want the world to know what a bloodthirsty little devil you are." He made the last remark with a gleam in his eye.[11]

That Eva, and the world, was eventually able to read her father's account of the shoot-out was due to the work of one cunning newspaper reporter for the *San Francisco Examiner*. There were numerous reporters covering the story—and the sensational shoot-out at Young's cabin attracted even more reporters—from both local papers and the big city dailies. Jo P. Carroll, described in one paper as a "well-known writer…serving as war correspondent for several papers," and Charles Michelson of the *San Francisco Examiner* were among journalists who rode with posses.[12] But it was another reporter who befriended Eva and managed to get the real scoop.

EVA FIRST MET PETEY BIGELOW at George Sontag's arraignment. News of George's appearance in a Fresno courthouse to face indictment for train robbery couldn't compete with Michelson's firsthand accounts of the posse's pursuit, now being carried out with renewed vigor after the recent bloodshed. Indeed, the court appearance rated barely one column inch compared to several full columns of sensational details of the manhunt, including an illustration of "The Scene of Evans and Sontag's Latest Slaughter."[13]

When the charming and affable Bigelow showed up at George Sontag's arraignment, it wasn't just to file a story about the expected indictment and an announcement that the actual trial would begin a month later. He undoubtedly sensed an opportunity. That opportunity was in the person of Eva Evans.

Henry D. "Petey" Bigelow was called "one of the brightest and most versatile writers" in the California press on the one hand and "flagrantly uncertain and unreliable, but an able writer and hence pardonable" on the other. One historian of California journalism described Bigelow as a tall, slight man who wore "suits made specially for him by Poole's of London, an elegant derby, a big silk cravat, small Vandyke and large mustache." Bigelow augmented his outfit with a flower in his buttonhole and carried a light cane that he would swing to punctuate his walk. "When distinguished actresses, actors, musicians, authors or travelers appeared in San Francisco," it was once written, "Petey was on intimate terms with them in a matter of hours. He took them to dinner, sent flowers, showed them the town, and kissed the ladies good-bye. There was a box at his disposal in the leading theatres, and each florist in town had him on his free list."[14]

A man of unfailing and irrepressible good humor, Bigelow eventually, in the words of one colleague, found it "impossible to work under the severe order and discipline necessary to journalism and so gradually drifted out of the higher walks of the profession."[15] But in 1892, when he was still in his early thirties, Bigelow was at the top of his game. And thanks in part to meeting Eva and her mother, he would summit the pinnacle of his career.

An editorial in the October 8, 1892, issue of William Randolph Hearst's *Examiner* summed up Bigelow's accomplishment with a self-aggrandizing flair:

> What Sheriffs with their posses and innumerable detectives, stimulated by great money rewards and animated by a desire for vengeance, have so far failed utterly to do what an *Examiner* reporter has done—found Evans and Sontag, the Collis train-robbers and the slayers of Beaver, Wilson and McGinnis. It is true that there is a decided difference between a quest which is peaceable in its intent and one that is conducted with a cocked Winchester, but that does not detract from the glory which Reporter Bigelow has won for himself and his profession. The history of interviewing records no feat which transcends his in courage, ingenuity and success. Nothing like it has ever been done on the Pacific Coast.

Although Bigelow later testified in court that he had gone into the mountains only to interview people about how they had been treated by the detectives and officers and that his meeting with Evans and Sontag at John Coffee's cabin was purely accidental, his earlier written statements, as well as Eva's written account, show that arrangements were made and carried out by the Evans family and friends such as Clark Moore. Eva wrote that Bigelow simply "came to us and asked us to arrange an interview for him with Dad and John. I was able to do this, and the result of that visit to the fugitives appeared as a full-page article in the *Examiner* of October 7, 1892."[16]

In the article, Bigelow claimed he "sent a message to [Evans] more than a fortnight ago asking for a personal interview," but with whom he sent the message he didn't say. It would have been a little more than two weeks since Bigelow met Eva Evans at George's arraignment hearing, so it is feasible that the Evans family had helped arrange the interview. [17]

Bigelow's article provided Chris Evans with a public voice, and not surprisingly, he took the opportunity to provide his version of the recent events filled with declarations of innocence and detailed alibis. While Evans never denied killing any men, he noted that all were in self-defense. And because he vehemently denied ever robbing any trains, those that unjustly hunted him were the cause of the unfortunate violence.

There was, Bigelow ironically observed, "not a bit of defiance in either Evans or Sontag." He called them "cool, determined men." Bigelow did, however, note the anger Evans expressed concerning the manner in which his wife had been treated by the authorities.

> When I described the espionage to which Mrs. Evans had been subjected at Visalia, Evans ground his teeth with rage, just as the old Berserkers of Iceland did a thousand years ago. He exclaimed at one point:
>
> "I would to Heaven I could see Detective Smith, Warren Hill, John Broder, Detective Thacker and the three Apache Indian trailers in one bunch. I wouldn't leave one of them alive. They deserved to be born dead."
>
> Against Smith, their enmity is extreme. Evans explained that their contempt and desire for vengeance would not be nearly so great if Smith had stood up to them like a man. [18]

What Bigelow presented to the world was, contrary to his own words, the very picture of defiance.

TWO OTHER ITEMS IN THE NEWSPAPERS that same week would have caught Eva's eye, for she knew her father would have been greatly interested.

Under the headline "Died in Their Boots," the *San Francisco Examiner*, just the day before Bigelow's interview appeared, reported that the Daltons had been gunned down in Kansas. In an attempt to rob two Coffeyville banks simultaneously, the gang of brothers met armed resistance from a number of officers and citizens. Both Bob and Grat Dalton were killed in the battle, and Emmett Dalton was seriously wounded. Throughout the summer of 1892, the Dalton brothers, who had reunited in Oklahoma following their troubles in California the year before, pulled off a series of successful train robberies. As the *Examiner* proclaimed, "the Dalton gang, most famous of all highwaymen, most daring of all train robbers, most cruel of all murderers, surpassing in reckless deeds the notorious James and Younger brothers, is no more."[19]

While Eva may have fretted that this was a possible outcome for her father and John, she might have been more upset that the *Examiner* claimed the Daltons were the "most daring of all train robbers."

Although the death of his acquaintance and possible accomplice, Grat Dalton, would have saddened Chris, the death of a man he never met would have been just as momentous for him. On October 5, 1892, the same day the Daltons met their demise at Coffeyville, England's greatest poet, Lord Alfred Tennyson succumbed to illness. He was Chris Evans' favorite writer. How it would sadden him to read of the dying poet, lying with a volume of Shakespeare on his bed, his hand holding it open to "Cymbeline" and the song beginning "Fear no more the heat of the sun." Tennyson's waning sight fastened on the full, red harvest moon sweeping up over the wooded Surry hills, while the watchers stood hidden and dumb in the shadows of his unlighted room.[20]

Eva could recall her father so often reciting the poet's words, walking the floor of a room dimly lit by a single candle, crooning to the baby in his arms:

> *Many a night I saw the Pleiads rising thro the mellow shade,*
> *Glitter like a swarm of fireflies tangled in a silver braid.*
> *Here about the beach I wander'd, nourishing a youth sublime*
> *With the fairy tales of science, and the long result of Time;*

Tennyson was dead, but his words—words that echoed in Eva's earliest childhood memories—were immortal.

EVA AND HER MOTHER ATTENDED George's trial, which commenced in late October in Fresno. Eva remembered that they sat with the defendant during the proceedings so that they could "not only listen to, but could look at the witnesses." Eva, though only sixteen years old, was wise enough to realize that this was more than just George's trial. "To me it seemed," she later wrote, "that the Southern Pacific was much more concerned about building up a case against my father and John than against George...I was not surprised that Chris Evans and John Sontag, though far away in the mountains, were being tried at the same time."[21]

The newspapers did not let the presence of Eva and her mother at the trial go unnoticed. The *Los Angeles Times* reported that when "Sontag came into court he took his seat beside Mrs. Evans and daughter and freely conversed with them." While Molly was dressed in a plain gown of dark material, the *Times* felt compelled to describe Eva as "quite attractive in a neat blue gown with a jaunty sailor hat. Her mother seemed in excellent spirits and seemed to be considerably amused at times about some matters which they were conversing upon." Indeed, as the *Examiner* noted, all three came into court smiling and chatting, as if they had not a care in the world.[22] As the trial progressed, George's false bravado was sorely tested. A parade of prosecution witnesses had provided a solid, albeit circumstantial, case against George. As a reporter for the *Examiner* (presumably Bigelow, as he was known to be attending the trial) stated: "Bit by bit the prosecution in the Sontag case is getting evidence on record which, if it does not prove conclusively that the defendant is guilty, shows without doubt that someone about Evans' domicile had an intimate acquaintanceship with the robbery."

Of course, an acquaintanceship and guilt are two different things; and George listened to the testimony "smilingly and confident." He reportedly was heard to say, "Wait till it comes my turn and I'll make everything clear."[23]

The following day the reporter for the *Examiner* offered an appropriately binding metaphor. "Today was one of the most interesting in the Sontag trial. The prosecution completed the links in the chain with which they expect to hold the defendant, and the latter began his efforts to break through it. After four hours' work he hadn't even strained the chain."[24]

By defense attorney W. C. Caldwell's own admission, they had "no startling disclosures to make, but only a plain declaration of the defendant's whereabouts since he came to California." This would, the defense maintained, provide George's alibi and prove his innocence.

At this point, Eva and Molly became more than mere spectators. "Mrs. Evans and Daughter Testify," advertised newspaper headlines; but the substance of what they said was less than compelling. Eva's brief appearance on the stand consisted of her denial that she had ever seen a cloth mask—she was shown a mask and a piece of similar cloth found in the Evans barn—left behind by the robbers and said she did not believe there was any such material about her home. She was not even cross-examined.

Molly Evans followed. She too examined the mask and said she had never seen it nor had any such cloth ever been in her house. She also testified that the day after the Collis robbery, George had come to her house and had breakfast, then Chris and John arrived in a buggy. She said that two days before both Sontag brothers left the house saying they were going to the mountains. There was very little cross-examination, and so the testimonies of Chris Evans' wife and daughter garnered little notice.

George took the stand in his own defense and denied any involvement in the Collis robbery. At one point in his lengthy testimony, when asked why he didn't speak of the train robbery the next morning, George said he felt kind of suspicious. "I'll tell you the truth about it," George admitted. "By the actions of Chris Evans in going down from the mountains with me and by the way John Sontag drove away from there and my meeting him in Fresno, I thought it best not to say a word before the women, and I did not. I wanted to wait till I got them aside and have them speak to me first."[25] As Eva and Molly sat and listened to what George was saying, they had to wonder if he was getting ready to sacrifice Chris and John to save his own hide.

"And you suspected they had something to do with the robbery?" the prosecution asked. "Yes," George replied. "To tell the truth I did at that time."[26] By this time, it little mattered to jurors what George Sontag had left to say.

Following closing arguments, the case went to the jury. It was already after nine o'clock in the evening, but deliberations did not last long. After being out only fifteen minutes, the jury brought in a verdict of guilty. After being led out of the court, George told an *Examiner* reporter that while he knew the case pieced together by detectives looked strong, he had hoped for a hung jury. He then added that "regarding what I testified about my suspicions of Evans and my brother on account of their strange actions about the time of the robbery, I want to say now that I found I was mistaken some time ago, and I think them innocent."

As WINTER SET IN, there began a lull in the manhunt. Although there were still reports of rumored sightings throughout November and December, news reports began to thin as the cold and wet weather took hold. Manhunters still searched the mountains, but weather and the fatal mistakes of earlier posses proved a deterrent. And now months into their ordeal, Chris and John had ensconced themselves in what were proving to be impenetrable hideouts. But before winter had completely shut them in, Eva acted, in her own words, as "messenger boy" for her father and John.[27]

According to Eva, she made daring midnight rides to their mountain hideouts carrying "a message or some needed article." As these trips were clandestine, there exists only her account as a source, and it is natural to question the veracity of her claims. But whether or not she made these dangerous journeys in reality or in her mind, they nonetheless existed on some level and became a real part of her legacy. Although she may have exaggerated the particulars, given her personality and outdoor skills, there is no reason to doubt she didn't take some risks in making at least one visit to her father and John in the mountains.

Eva credited her grandmother's bay mare, Kitty B., with making these undetected flights to the mountains possible. Few remembered, she pointed out, that the horse had been raced as a three-year-old at the county fair. Eva recalled how in the dead of night, she would lead Kitty B. out of her grandmother's barn, saddle her with the custom-made Visalia Saddle that was the pride of her heart—"hand carved leather and the most beautiful creak; you must love saddle-leather to know what I mean"—and walk out from beneath the branches of the huge cottonwood that grew beside the barn.

Dressed in a boy's overalls, Eva would ride out of town bound for the hills. Eva explained she felt comfortable in boy's clothing—it's what she usually wore summers at the Redwood Ranch—and knew if people saw her they'd simply think she was some farmboy returning from town in time for his chores.

"I would not ride too fast," Eva recalled, "until I had passed through the oak tree belt and had reached the open country where it was easy to see if anyone followed. Then I would slack the reins, lean forward on Kitty B.'s neck and say 'Go!'"[28] A dramatist might imagine Eva's long blond hair cascading out from her hat as she rode like the wind through the moonlit night. And rode toward the men she loved.

Eva described two of the camps where Chris and John stayed. These were both near Bill Downing's place. The Downing family had turned out to be their most dependable friends and messengers, and so Chris wanted to stay near them. The first camp, located about three miles from the Downing ranch, was only about 300 feet off the road to the Redwood Ranch and not far from the old Hyde mill, where Chris and Molly spent their honeymoon. Christened "Camp Manzanita," it consisted of a makeshift cabin built up against a large flat rock. Eva described how they papered the walls with newspapers containing stories about themselves. Later visitors to the hideout would comment that many of these newspapers were adorned with illustrations by John.[29] Surrounding the cabin on all sides was a dense growth of manzanita. And while the twisted red branches of the bushes concealed this hideout, it was too close to the road for comfort. With posses continuing to scour the country, Chris and John decided to find an even more secure hideout.

Chris had long known of a cave about a half-mile from the Downing house, located in the steep canyon of Dry Creek, which fit its name for only part of the year. In the spring, when the creek was high, the cave could only be entered by climbing through the cascading waters flowing right by its entrance. Eva, quite accurately, described it as "a long, deep fissure, in a cliff, with an opening about three feet high and seven feet long."[30] Chris and John closed the opening—except for door space—with rocks, some of which they dug out of the cave to make it deeper. They also left "loopholes for guns." Into this secret place—it was inaccessible on horseback, so Eva would have had to scramble down on foot if she ever visited the cave—they put a coal-oil stove, food, supplies, and ammunition. This was, as they came to call it, Fort Defiance.

IT WAS A HARD WINTER for the family at home. In November, Molly was given final notice by Sweet & Co., who carried their mortgage, of foreclosure on their house. Their store credit had earlier been withdrawn at Sweet's mercantile, and Molly had been relying on her mother and the Byrds for support. Now they were forced to move into Grannie Byrd's two-story house across the street.[31]

Molly could take no solace in church. She had been a member of the South Methodist Church, but after the troubles, she was "read out" of the church for her husband's crimes. Not long after that, Eva later pointed out with more than a tinge of vengeful irony, the minister, Reverend Reams, ran off with the fifteen-year-old organist, deserting his wife and children.

At school, the Evans children faced the taunts of their schoolmates. Molly would urge eight-year-old Joe and Louis, who was barely of school age, to just walk away, but Eva would tell them not to take anything from anybody.

"If the reader has any sympathy for anyone," Eva admonished decades later, "it should be for Molly Evans." Eva saw her mother tortured by her anxiety for her husband's safety, her struggle for money and to care for her seven children, and the fear of what would be. Eva admitted that she, on the other hand, felt "buoyed up by the excitement of the chase."[32] As winter deepened, Chris and John's existence in the mountains became more and more unbearable. With the "excitement of the chase" at a lull, and the cold, wet weather gnawing at them in their rudimentary shelter, Chris decided to take the risk of a trip home to see the family. It has been claimed that they made as many as eight successful trips home. As historian Wallace Smith pointed out, one such trip was during the Christmas holidays, and Evans and Sontag stayed with the family for two weeks. Smith noted that it was puzzling how they could spend so much time at the house in town with a $10,000 reward on their heads "and remain undetected. Either the people of the community liked the hunted men, feared them, or were just stupid."[33] Carl Glasscock—he described the Christmas visit in his 1929 book, *Bandits and the Southern Pacific,* twenty years prior to the Smith account— commented that it seemed "almost impossible that seven children, ranging in age from the baby to Eva, the eldest, herself only sixteen, excited as only children can become excited by Christmas preparations, could have kept the secret of their father's presence in the house."[34]

In her account of the visit, Eva addressed those concerns. Contrary to later reports, she stated, "Chris Evans did not romp with his small children that Christmas of 1892—though Mother did let him play with Baby Carl, because he could not 'talk plain' and no one would have noticed if he prattled of his father." Eva explained that Ynez and Winifred were old enough to keep the secret. Eva also pointed out that Grannie Byrd's house was surrounded by a high picket fence and the porch was covered with vines, so that one could come out of the parlor and go to the upper rooms without being seen. "When the men came home just before Christmas," Eva wrote, "they went into the unused bedroom, and when the children were not around we carried their meals in to them. That is how we could have Christmas together. They stayed two weeks."[35]

Even before the troubles, John had stayed at Grannie Byrd's house, where he had the upper bedroom. It had a clear view of the road to town and during the Christmas visit, John would go to his old room and nervously watch for any men looking for them. Molly was understandably anxious having Chris and John in the house, but Eva was happy and excited. She remembered her father was his jolly and lovable self, telling stories and making plans for their future. "One listening at the keyhole would have heard only a happy father with his wife and daughters," Eva later reminisced, "not an outlaw with a price upon his head." John, on the other hand, felt a sense of doom. Eva recalled that whenever they were alone, he "talked constantly of the hopelessness of it all." He would talk of his plans for escape and could not understand why Chris would choose to jeopardize the family so. Perhaps John simply couldn't understand the irrepressible love Chris had for Molly and the children—a love that would overwhelm caution.[36]

Eva's description of John paints him as morose and pessimistic—hardly the kind of man with whom she would enjoy spending time. This is especially noticeable when compared to the way she describes her father on the very same page, using words like "jolly" and "lovable" and "a happy father." At no time during her account of that Christmas visit is there any sense that she had a passionate love for John. Reading the passage out of context, one would never suspect she and John Sontag were engaged to be married.

"The happy days," as Eva described the all-too-brief weeks at Christmas, "came to an end; the men returned to be hunted."[37] That she was saddened to see her father leave is undeniable—it tore deeply at her heart. But of John, her feelings are unclear. Popular myth later painted a passionate romance between the two. But is it also possible she felt some indifference or even resentment? She may have even secretly hoped that John would escape on his own—let him leave for Mexico or some such place never to be seen again. She would then join her father and hide out with him in the mountains. How different would that be from the best days of her childhood with him at the Redwood Ranch, before the troubles? Before John came.

Eva wasn't so much in love with John Sontag as she wanted to *be* John Sontag—to take his place beside her father.

CHAPTER NINE

Aid and Support

E VIDENCE THAT EVA HAD achieved public notoriety of her own appeared in a Stockton newspaper in February 1893. In a published letter to the editor, a resident of the railroad town of Lathrop claimed he had "reliable information" concerning a secret marriage between Petey Bigelow and Eva Evans. "They passed through here this evening en route to Sacramento and will go to the Golden Eagle hotel," the concerned citizen noted. He added that "the bride is quite pleasant looking, with a remarkable growth of flaxen hair. She seemed to be quite pleased with her surroundings while seated in the car awaiting the start to Sacramento hurriedly."[1]

Molly denied the rumor in an interview she granted to a Fresno newspaper, calling the story false in every particular. "Mr. Bigelow is a married man," Molly pointed out, "and has two children. I have his wife's picture with me now. She is a sweet English lady." Molly then lamented the malicious attacks to which she and Eva were subjected. "I don't see why they are always starting those stories about us. They may say whatever they please now about my husband and Mr. Sontag, but I and my daughter should not be held responsible for anything they may have done."[2]

The rumor, as far-fetched as it sounded, was not completely unfounded. Eva very likely was seen in the company of the charming big-city reporter, as she indeed accompanied him to Sacramento and then to San Francisco, where they even attended a night at the Tivoli Opera House.

Eva explained that Bigelow, now convinced of her father's innocence, became a champion of their cause. When it was reported that

California governor George Markham was being pressured to call out the state militia, Bigelow suggested that Eva go with him to Sacramento to lobby the legislature and the governor against such a drastic measure. "I felt frightened at facing such august personages, but if Petey thought it would do any good, I was glad to go," Eva later remembered. "It was a remarkable two-weeks' adventure for the little girl who had never been in a large city except under her father's protection."[3]

In Sacramento, Markham personally assured Bigelow that he had no intention of calling out the militia. There was no need for Eva to plead for sympathy, and she was relieved that she did not have to talk to the governor.

Bigelow then took Eva to his home in San Francisco, where she met his wife and children. She also met his sister, Constance Bigelow. She, too, was a reporter and became so enamored with the saga of Evans and Sontag that she later insisted on being taken to the scene of their activities. (Before long, her byline would appear in *Examiner* articles on the fugitives' ordeal.)[4]

Bigelow brought Eva to the *Examiner* 's Market Street headquarters, where she was able to meet some of the most famous and colorful newspapermen (and women) working on the West Coast. William Randolph Hearst, still not yet thirty years old, had staffed his *Examiner* with the best reporters, editors and business executives that money could buy. According to one Hearst biographer, someone walking into the *Examiner* building would find the best newspaper staff in the West. It included Arthur McEwan, "the war horse of the editorial page, with a pen of acid"; there was "the caustic but admirable Ambrose Bierce, one of the most brilliant satirists and essayists of the epoch"; and Winifred Sweet, "wholesome as a May morning, first of the famous sob-sisters," who wrote scathing exposés promoting social causes. There were a number of writers described as "masters of clear, incisive English and reporters to the finger tips," and Bigelow's close friend and good-natured rival, Eddie Brophy, the wild Irish boy from Dublin University.[5]

Outside the *Examiner* offices, Eva was exposed to a grand city. San Francisco was known as "The Paris of America," and the 1890s were called the Champagne Days because, like sparkling wine, the spirit of San Francisco bubbled with exuberance. As one writer observed: "Champagne was in the bubbly air of the city and in the veins of its gay young blades whose pranks were the gossip of two continents." It was a city where men drank deeply and lived well. And it was a time of great actors and strange characters, eager artists and earnest young poets. Strolling in San Francisco's streets, one might meet the actors John Drew and Maurice Barrymore; the artists Charles Rollo Peters and William Keith; or writers belonging to the newly-termed Bohemian set like the boyish Jack London and the burning novelist, Frank Norris, who called San Francisco the "city where nobody thinks."[6] Although Eva had visited San Francisco before, even finding herself one evening in the notorious Poodle Dog Café with her father, this eye-opening tour of the city with the flamboyant Bigelow as her guide included a very memorable first for her.

Eva was thrilled to accompany Bigelow to the Tivoli Opera House. Originally a beer hall, the white wooden building on Eddy Street near Market Street hosted light and grand opera and was a cherished part of life to the throngs who attended almost religiously. Down in the un-cushioned two-bit seats, friendly German waiters would serve foaming glasses of beer to the patrons.[7] Eva and Bigelow, however, shared a lux-ury box, prime partitioned seats with a commanding view of the stage below. Eva ached with anticipation as the orchestra, seated in a dim pit before the stage, made streaks of sound tuning their instruments. Anticipation heightened as hissing gaslights in the auditorium silenced to darkness. The grand front curtain opened with a swish, the stage coming alive with vibrant color and the eye-popping glare of burning limelight. The rich opulence of the costumes, the sensual warmth of gaslight, the glowing color of richly painted backdrops all enveloped an awed Eva, seduced by her introduction to the theatre.

Before the performance was over, they were joined by Edward Bro-phy, who Eva hadn't yet met. Bigelow introduced them and gave Eva the jovial warning to watch out for Brophy. "He's Irish; don't let him make love to you." Bigelow then left Eva in the custody of his charm-ing and handsome friend, explaining that he had to go drop off some-thing at the *Examiner* office.

Of course, Bigelow knew he had nothing to worry about. Brophy was a perfect gentleman with Eva, but he did offer the young lady this advice concerning his friend—Henry "Petey" Bigelow. "You'll want to look out—he'll feed you to the presses some day."[8] With her attention fixed on the performance below, one has to wonder if she even heard Brophy's warning.

CHRIS EVANS' GOOD FRIEND, CLARK MOORE, was arrested immedi-ately after George Sontag's trial and faced arraignment in December on three indictments. The charges were of being an accessory after the fact of murder for harboring Evans and Sontag. These were for the murders of Oscar Beaver the previous August and Vic Wilson and Andy McGinnis in September. After a number of continuances, the case of the people versus Clark Moore was brought to trial in early March.[9] The heavily publicized trial in the Fresno Superior Court attracted a large crowd, and once again brought Petey Bigelow to Fresno.

Through witnesses' testimonies, the prosecution sought to show when, where and in what manner Moore furnished aid and comfort to the outlaws and that he refused to betray them into the hands of the officers. But as the prosecution wound up their case, headlines in the San Francisco papers summed up the general consensus. "Moore Not Gloomy," they declared, because the "Evidence Against Him Very Weak."[10] The defense would now present their case, which primarily stated that Moore had never met Evans and Sontag except by accident.

Molly Evans and, presumably, Eva were in the courtroom when Bigelow took the stand. As Bigelow's own paper reported, the San Francisco journalist had gone to the hills "to interview the people as to how they had been treated by the detectives and officers." That, he claimed, was his principal purpose, although he admitted he wanted to find Evans and Sontag if he could. After meeting Clark Moore in Fresno, Bigelow asked him if he would serve as his guide in the mountains. "The meeting of the robbers at Coffee's [cabin] was not previously arranged," he asserted, explaining he had asked Moore if they could stop there for dinner. They were surprised to find Evans and Sontag inside. Bigelow flatly denied he had arranged the interview through the family or any other person. "Clark Moore," Bigelow testified, "never told where Evans and Sontag were, but said he did not know and did not believe he could find them."[11]

Sitting there listening to the sworn testimony, Eva had to realize this contradicted Bigelow's written account of the meeting. Perhaps the prosecution never read Bigelow's articles, in which he described how "the rendezvous had been designated" and that he had "sent a message...and offered to be at any rendezvous he might name" and that it was "ten days before an answer came, and as it was favorable I set out with the one man in the region whose name was like magic—Clark Moore." Eva was glad her friend Petey Bigelow did all he could to protect her father's great friend: Clark Moore."[12]

Clark Moore had many friends. After only three hours of deliberation, the jury returned with its verdict for acquittal. "There were general congratulations among the witnesses, a hundred strong from the adjoining counties," the *Examiner* reported, "and Clark Moore was given a supper by his many friends." There can be little doubt that Eva Evans and Petey Bigelow were at that party.

As SPRING BROUGHT WARMER WEATHER, things heated up in the pursuit of Evans and Sontag. Bullets flew and headlines popped in April, but the battle was forced not by the posses scouring the mountains, but by the brazen boldness of the outlaws in returning once again to Visalia.

On April 6, a Fresno newspaper reported that Evans and Sontag were spotted deep in the mountains above Sampson's Flat and although officers pursued their trail, they had little hope of finding them. "The last trace of Evans and Sontag was had as they were making their way into the almost inaccessible mountains toward the headwaters of the Kings River." According to local gossip, however, the outlaws had visited their home in Visalia several times during the winter, and one Visalia paper predicted an encounter between them and the officers could be expected at any time.[13]

Two weeks later, Sheriff Kay received word that Evans and Sontag were comfortably ensconced in their Visalia home. According to several newspapers, Kay garnered this intelligence from schoolchildren after, as one reporter explained: "Bandit Evans' little boy told some of his classmates that Papa is at home." The *Examiner* maintained that the schoolboy story was merely "a ruse to shield the man who betrayed the bandits, for he declared that his life would not be worth owning should his name ever become known."[14]

Wanting to avoid a confrontation that would endanger Molly and the children, Sheriff Kay devised a plan. As evening approached, Kay and a posse of eight men left town and rendezvoused at the Visalia Creamery, about a mile from the Evans home (which was actually Grannie Byrd's house across the road from the house Molly lost to foreclosure) just outside of town. After dark, they headed for the Byrd/Evans house. Kay posted four men on one of the two roads leading out of town about three-quarters of a mile from the house, and four others guarded a position on the other road a block from the Evans home. Kay and a deputy stationed themselves just south of the Evans barn, from which point every movement about the house could be watched. Kay set up a system reminiscent of Paul Revere to signal his men: he would fire one pistol shot if he saw the outlaws heading out on the road east; if they took the other road, he would fire two shots. Now all the lawmen had to do was wait for Chris Evans and John Sontag to walk into their trap.

As midnight approached, a man came out to the yard and circled around toward the barn. Soon thereafter, voices were heard and the barn door was thrown open. One of the outlaws drove out in a cart with a single horse, the other walked behind.

Evans and Sontag started toward the mountains on the east road, and when they got a short distance from the barn Kay fired a lone signal shot. The fugitives immediately wheeled in the other direction. The outlaw on foot jumped into the cart. The whip was put to the horse and they drove rapidly away. Kay fired four shots at them and ran toward the barn with his shotgun, thinking they were coming back to the barn.

During the long wait, some of the posted men had compromised their sentry positions. They had been lulled to inattentiveness. Hearing the gunfire, they all opened fire but at the long range and darkness of night, the brief shower of pistol balls and small shot was ineffective. The outlaws did not even bother to return fire and easily escaped. Chris Evans was reportedly heard yelling, "Here we are: give us hell, God damn you!" as he and Sontag flew out of town.[15]

How frightening this must have been for the family, who had just said goodbye to their men, only to hear a chilling fusillade outside in the night immediately after their departure. Eva rushed to the back of the orchard to see what was happening. Though she couldn't see much in the dark, she got close enough to hear "the clatter of that horse's hooves down the…road." Suddenly it stopped, and Eva thought to herself, "They've both been killed."[16]

When Eva overheard the posse men heading back to town, cursing and swearing at each other accusations of blame for the botched ambush, she felt some sense of relief. Molly's reaction to the close call can be summed up by the following newspaper report:

> Mrs. Evans, the wife of the robber, was prostrated with the events of last night, and when the shots were fired she fainted away several times, only to recover and then lapse into a semi-conscious state. Considerable trouble was experienced in reviving her, and she was confined to her bed during the day. She was unable to tell about her hunted husband's perilous visit, and says no one was home except her children, her husband and Mr. Sontag.[17]

While Molly's delicate constitution in the face of such turmoil was no doubt genuine, her inability to talk about what happened frustrated reporters and lawmen.

At daylight the following morning, Eva was seen walking along the road on which her father and John left town. A reporter for the *San Francisco Chronicle* theorized she was looking to see if she could find traces of blood.[18] To her great relief, she found none. The news would buoy her mother. Chris and John had evidently made a safe getaway once again. But even Eva would have to ask herself how many more times they could literally dodge bullets.

Not surprising, Sheriff Kay was subject to ample criticism following his failed ambush. Newspaper editorials suggested that perhaps Kay "does not really want to catch them" and that his conduct demanded explanation and "the Grand Jury of Tulare County should require him to make it."[19] And while the Evans family could expect the papers to chastise the sheriff, Eva was troubled that her friend Petey Bigelow joined in the criticism. He commented in an editorial that in dealing with Evans and Sontag, "the amateur Sheriffs of Tulare have tacticians who bewilder their brains."[20]

But what really saddened and angered Eva were Bigelow's comments about her father. Bigelow called Chris Evans reckless. "To my mind," he stated, "he was always reckless. His companion, John Sontag, is his only restraint." How could her good friend Petey say such things about her father? She had been warned, of course. Bigelow was a reporter; he would feed anyone to the presses.

BACK IN THE MOUNTAINS, EVANS AND SONTAG continued to make headlines throughout the spring of 1893. One of the episodes that prompted headlines served to further the Robin Hood image Evans and Sontag were beginning to enjoy.

Eva, who, according to historian Wallace Smith, served as "the Intelligence Corps for the little army of two men," got word to her father that Will Smith, the railroad detective he had publicly vowed to kill on sight, had purchased a ticket and planned to take the stagecoach to Sequoia Mills in the mountains.[21]

On May 1, the papers reported that Evans and Sontag held up the stage on the road to Sequoia Mills near Camp Badger. "They searched the passengers, but, finding they were poor men, they returned what they took from them," the *San Francisco Examiner* reported, adding that Evans proclaimed, "We are not robbing workingmen, but want to find some of the men who are hunting us." In an editorial a couple days later, the *Examiner* further contributed to a growing myth with a prescient suggestion:

> The latest exploit of Evans and Sontag has a Robin Hood flavor about it that really ought to inspire Smith and De Koven [theatre producers] to crib some music and put these picturesque rascals into an opera. For people that like highwaymen we should think that Evans and Sontag would be just the kind of highwaymen they would like. They have not the gloomy ferocity of the James boys, nor yet the harmless flippancy of Black Bart. They are sure enough desperadoes, with real guns that go off on occasion, but at the same time they have not that tigerish lust for blood.[22]

They may have drawn blood, however, later that month. When Deputy Marshal Samuel Black was shot near Camp Badger, the papers immediately attributed the ambush to Evans and Sontag. The lead paragraph in the *Visalia Delta* proclaimed that "the blood-thirsty bandits, with a $10,000 reward hanging over their heads, added another victim to their already long list."[23] Everyone assumed it was Evans and Sontag who shot Black. He had been hunting the bandits since the previous October, and it was reported that a resident of the mountains had delivered a message to Black, purportedly from Evans and Sontag, just a few days earlier, warning he would be killed if he did not leave the country.

Black was shot as he and Tom Burns returned to Black's cabin from the Camp Badger Saloon. They returned fire. Burns ran back to the saloon for help. Black's determined resistance caused the attackers to retreat into the brush and the fight was over. Black was shot several times in the thigh, legs and groin. His wounds were not fatal, and Black later claimed he was not discouraged over the result of the encounter, but rather "expressed his determination to make the bandits suffer for every pain he has felt."[24]

This story was, however, disputed by some. Eva later insisted that Black had "a way with women," and it was, according to Eva, a jealous husband who waited in the darkness to shoot Black down.[25] The *Examiner* printed the claim by another Visalian who had just returned from Sequoia Mills that Black was "suspected of being too familiar with a woman at Camp Badger, whose husband worked at Sequoia Mills. The shooting resulted in some way from this, but more he had not been able to learn."[26] This report was, according to one Visalia newspaper, "generally discredited, and lacked confirmation."[27] Few besides Eva promoted the jealous husband theory. The public had little doubt that it was Evans and Sontag who shot Deputy Marshal Black.

Under the headline "A Poet's Version," the *Examiner* ran still more copy about the shooting. This dispatch, from the paper's latest correspondent on the scene, summarized the "many stories and opinions" circulating through Sequoia Mills and Camp Badger after the shooting: "Some say there was no fight, that Black and Burns did the shooting for effect. I think not. Some say Evans and Sontag made the attack. Others say they are not in the country. I inspected everything a few hours after the fight, and think it was them that made the assault." The reporter cited the threat Black had received from the bandits as evidence in support of his opinion, although he noted there was "no sympathy for the hurt man-hunter anywhere in the mountains, and much derision for his companion who ran away at the first shot."[28] The byline on the article belonged to one of the most famous poets of the day: Joaquin Miller.

When Joaquin Miller arrived in Visalia, he was an internationally known figure, and his presence caused quite a sensation. With his trademark red flannel shirt, high-topped boots, wide brimmed hat and long white beard, the eccentric author cut a striking figure. Born Cincinnatus Hiner Miller, the flamboyant poet adopted the moniker of Joaquin in honor of the legendary early California desperado Joaquin Murrieta, whom he had once defended in print. Ina Coolbrith (who just happened to be one of Eva's favorite poets) suggested the pen name that came to fit him like the fringed buckskin jacket he was fond of wearing. After the success of his book *Songs of the Sierras* in 1871, he became known as the "Poet of the Sierra."[29] As Miller's artistic persona was so intrinsically linked to an infamous outlaw and the California Sierra, it was doubly appropriate that Miller should come to the mountains in search of Evans and Sontag. Surely W. R. Hearst appreciated the sense of ironic flair Miller brought to the assignment.

It was no secret that Miller intended to obtain an interview with the elusive bandits. The *Tulare County Times* reported, upon Miller's arrival in Visalia, that he planned to head to Sequoia Mills and Sampson's Flat "in the interest of the *San Francisco Examiner*," and the *Los Angeles Times* noted, when it reported on the shooting of Black, that "Mrs. Evans is said to be in the mountains on a visit to her husband, and to obtain an interview with him for Joaquin Miller."[30] The paper's implication that Miller had the cooperation of the Evans family would turn out to be true, but no one imagined the extent of that cooperation or how long Joaquin Miller and the Evans family would remain friends and allies.

MEANWHILE, IN FOLSOM PRISON, GEORGE started to make new friends, including a fellow lifer named Frank Williams, who had been convicted on three counts of stage robbery and was known to associates as "Smiling Williams" because, as George explained, "under all circumstances his countenance was wreathed with a smile that bespoke satisfaction, but under which he did many things that were dangerous." It didn't take George long to become convinced that Williams was "on the square, and a good fellow to tie to."[31] Williams was drawn to George, who was something of a celebrity when he entered Folsom. No one had received more press than George's brother, John, and his partner, Chris Evans. And besides, train robbers were at the top of the pecking order in prison hierarchy. George asked around about Williams and became satisfied he was someone in whom he could confide. Knowing Williams ached for his liberty as much as George did, they "talked this matter up."[32]

Williams introduced George to a young convict named William Fredericks. Like George, he was of German descent; and like Williams, he had been convicted of stage robbery. But unlike them both, he was scheduled to be released soon.[33] Fredericks became their confidant and agreed to help in a plan that had formulated in the desperate minds of men facing life terms.

One key to their plan was guns, and before Fredericks was paroled, George told the young German where he might be able to obtain firearms and who might offer help. He was told to ask for a Mrs. Bolivar. It was a code name based on an inside joke George and his brother John shared. And there was only one other person who knew they used the name Simon Bolivar, the South American revolutionary leader known as "the Liberator," for Chris Evans. Eva Evans once asked about the nickname, and John explained that Bolivar was a man who fought other people's battles. Chris chimed in that it was just one of John's romantic notions to call him by that name.[34] So George knew if Fredericks showed up at the Evans home and asked for Mrs. Bolivar, he would be immediately known as a comrade. Eva would know George had sent him.

On the day of his discharge Fredericks was sent to Warden Charles Aull's office. Aull had posted German-speaking guards near George Sontag's cell and so knew that something was brewing. He told Fredericks they had "positive knowledge that he intended to act in conjunction with John Sontag and Chris Evans for the purpose of bringing arms and ammunition within the prison for the purpose of liberating George Sontag" and warned that "if he attempted anything of the kind he would surely be killed." Fredericks treated the advice in a contemptuous manner. [35] Undeterred, the young convict headed south for Visalia.

JOAQUIN MILLER'S "BARD AND THE BANDIT" appeared in the Sunday edition of the *San Francisco Examiner* in early June. He placed his "interview" at the base of the General Grant Tree, in a spectacular grove of giant sequoias. Like the Bigelow interview eight months earlier, there would be expressions of doubt as to the veracity of his meeting. In this case, however, there was evidence to support a theory of, if not fraud, at least excessive poetic license. In Eva's memoir, she wrote that when the *Examiner* sent Miller to talk to her family and, if possible, arrange a meeting with Evans and Sontag, they "decided to fake an interview." Eva explained that she had a photo of the famous General Grant tree and Joaquin decided to set his meeting with Chris Evans at the foot of the massive tree. Knowing her father's love of the Big Trees, this was an appropriate venue for the fictional meeting, and, as Eva pointed out, it would have the added benefit of serving as a decoy, sending the manhunters "scurrying into that neck of the woods."

Miller's interview with the bandit could not compare with Bigelow's earlier scoop. One historian of California journalism called it "a crashing flop as an interview with a bad man. There were almost no quotations in it, and either Chris was giving none or Miller was too confused in the presence of the great man to take notes, or perhaps he had to hold his arms above his head all the time."[36] Indeed, to call it an interview was a misnomer. The only direct quote from the subject was when the bandit asked the bard if he would take a little package home to Mrs. Evans. There were, however, some interesting assertions. In explaining how the troubles began for Evans and Sontag, Miller wrote:

Well, the oldest child is sixteen, pretty, refined, educated to a high degree for a laboring man's daughter. To say that two men loved her would be quite enough. Bear in mind that what I am about to say did not come from her lips or from those of any of her family, still I think it true that a detective and one of the alleged brigands both loved her. The detective was a hatchet-faced, unmannerly man; Sontag was handsome. Now, here you can read between the lines. I know nothing, I say nothing, of any loves or hates. The trouble began before the alleged robberies of the train. After the train robbery the detective, who seems to have known the humble premises very well, came hastily to the house and said, "Where is your father?"[37]

Joaquin Miller had written what sounded like something out of a tawdry melodrama. Was he actually implying that Will Smith had accused Evans and Sontag because he fancied himself a romantic rival and felt jilted by Eva? And while Eva had to have been flattered by Joaquin's description of her, she must have cringed at the implication of romance between her and Smith. Not only was Eva's personal life becoming more and more fodder for the press, but increasingly it was subject to speculation and outright fiction.

Miller's article also offered an overtly sympathetic view of the family at home. "I found three generations in one little old house, the seven tow-headed babies ranging from the cradle to the altar, the pale mother of the seven and the mother's mother," he wrote. He described the bullet holes in the boards of the house and the "signs of honest poverty." He noted that one little boy was "shaking with ague" and commented that "in fact the whole family seems to have the fever—not that Visalia is sickly, but their nerves have been strung to such a tension this past season that I wonder that they live at all." While visiting with Molly the evening before he set out for the mountains, Miller claimed that "out of the long talk of hours…I gathered only this one thing notable: she was particularly anxious that her husband should hear that the children were getting on at school, and that they were all well—all exceedingly well—and the pale mother's lips quivered with the lie she told."

Just a few days after Miller's article appeared in the *Examiner*, headlines proclaimed another apparent visit to Visalia by the bandits. Sheriff Kay, after receiving word that the outlaws were at home (an earlier rumor stated they had snuck into town disguised in women's clothing, but Kay disregarded that one), took several officers to the Byrd/Evans house and surrounded it. This caused a general excitement, and according to the newspapers "people gathered on the street in groups to hear the reports of the guns of the bandits and officers in deadly conflict."

After questioning Mrs. Byrd and Molly in the house, Kay became satisfied they were not at home and sent word to the officers that the bandits had again escaped.[38]

The next day, the newspapers claimed it had all been a false alarm. The "fearless bandits of the Sierra foothills were not in Visalia after all" and the "excitement of the past two days resulted from the fright of a small boy who went to steal apricots from the orchard that Christopher Evans once called his." Again reporters found opportunity to write about Eva. The day after the excitement, a reporter noted that Eva sat on the rear stoop of her home cleaning a gun. "She was plying the oily rags with vigor and beside her lay a number of cartridges. It would surprise no one if occasion came to see this girl bring her gun to her shoulder in defense of her father."[39]

IRONICALLY, THE SAME DAY THAT RUMORS brought Kay and his posse to the Byrd/Evans house, another prominent lawman rode into town. Back on May 31, Wells Fargo detective John Thacker had sent a telegram to U.S. Marshal George Gard in Los Angeles to arrange a meeting in Fresno. George E. Gard was an experienced lawman, having served as a police officer, detective, and ultimately, chief of police for Los Angeles. He was later elected sheriff of Los Angeles County before his appointment in 1890 to the federal post of U.S. marshal for the southern district of California. A Civil War veteran who had learned his trade in the rough and tumble streets of 1870s Los Angeles, Gard was never considered an office-bound lawman.[40]

Thacker was disgusted at the efforts of local law enforcement. He felt that with a proper strategy—one that recognized the fact that Chris and John traveled at night and often made forays into Visalia from the mountains—a small posse under the command of an outside authority could ensure the outlaws would be apprehended. At the meeting in Fresno, Gard agreed with Thacker that "if we could get a party in the mountains unobserved, we could capture the outlaws."

Marshal Gard then returned to Los Angeles and obtained federal warrants against Evans and Sontag. The charges were for destroying government property—the U.S. mail—in the commission of the Collis train robbery. With warrants in hand, as Gard later recalled, he "decided that if I could get away I would serve them in person. The bandits had run about long enough, and it was a duty I owed to the people to try and assist in their capture."[41]

Within a couple of days of Gard's arrival in Visalia, Thacker had put together a small, hand-picked posse in Fresno, and Gard joined up with them. According to Gard, they concentrated their efforts on an area of Stokes Mountain, near an old stone corral, "keeping a watch on the only road that leads into Wilcox Canyon, the bandits' stamping ground."[42]

There was, perhaps, good reason for confining their search to this area. According to family lore, Molly was on the verge of a nervous breakdown that early June and the family decided that Chris and John needed to come home for a family conference. Molly refused to let Eva serve as messenger boy, as she had done in the past. Instead, a man was sent whom Molly trusted. When this trusted friend casually asked Chris which road he would take home, Chris told him: "Over the trail through Wilcox Canyon that comes out at Stone Corral."[43]

On June 10, Gard and three of his posse spent the night in the abandoned cabin of Billy Bacon at the foot of Stokes Mountain, within sight of the old landmark known as Stone Corral.[44]

MOLLY'S EMOTIONAL STATE at this time was best described in Joaquin Miller's recent article, which appeared a week earlier. Miller, so much more the poet than a journalist, concluded the article with his presentation of the package Chris Evans had asked him to deliver to his wife.

> I laid it down on the stand by the lamp, and the old grandmother and the sick mother untied the strings hastily, and with such trembling hands as I want to see no more, and then helpless, heartbroken sobs!
> What! Only two pretty snow plants—two rich red snow plants! That was all. But the wife caught them up and kissed them and caressed them to her heart, and kissed them again and again, and left the grime and mountain sand and soil that was still clinging to them on her face, to be washed away with tears as she hastened to leave the room.[45]

Was it the gift and the longing to see Chris that moved Molly to tears; or did she somehow sense something symbolic in these rare, blood-red plants, which with the melting of the snow rise from the duff of dead and dying leaves and needles like phallic staffs proclaiming a rebirth tainted violent red? Surely Joaquin Miller appreciated the poetic symbolism. One can only wonder if Eva shared the poet's view and if she further worried that the symbolism was loaded with prophecy.

CHAPTER TEN

Stone Corral

The beginning of the end has approached, and the record of crime that has darkened the pages of Tulare County will soon be ended.
—*SAN FRANCISCO EXAMINER*, JUNE 12, 1893

INITIAL REPORTS OF A GUN BATTLE with Gard's posse claimed that the "Bandit King" was seen to fall. "Chris Evans Shot" proclaimed the headline in the *San Francisco Chronicle*. Because the shootout had occurred at dusk and lasted into the night, first reports were sketchy at best. Officers thought that Evans was fatally wounded, but that John Sontag had escaped. They would have to wait until morning's light to sort everything out. Word of the climactic battle reached Visalia well before dawn when a wounded officer, Fred Jackson, was brought into town for medical attention. Little was clear except that at a place called Stone Corral one of the bandits was shot and lay dying out in the darkness and the other, despite being wounded, had apparently managed to escape.[1]

When this news hit town, it spread like wildfire. According to one Visalia newspaper, although few people were on the street at midnight when Deputy Rapelje arrived with the wounded Jackson, "news of the battle was soon known, and a large number of people came down town to hear the latest particulars." The paper further noted that Perry Byrd, brother-in-law of Chris Evans and night watchman in the city, "was an interested listener of the graphic reports of the bloody encounter with the train robbers." Molly and Eva were thus undoubtedly alerted to the turn of events they had so long dreaded.[2]

By the time the first published news accounts hit the streets of Visalia, a clearer picture of what actually happened at Stone Corral had come into focus. Nonetheless, the night passed with Eva thinking her father was either dead or dying. When officers brought the captured and wounded outlaw into town at around ten o'clock the following morning, a large crowd had gathered. The wagon carried not Chris Evans, but John Sontag, and as it pulled up in front of the jail, "persons came running from all parts of the town to get a glimpse of the pale features of the man whom all California had learned to fear."[3] Soon after Sontag was taken into the jail, Molly and Eva arrived in a covered carriage. There had to be a sense of relief from both women, but also a continuing dread, even though Sontag told reporters that Chris had not been shot and had escaped and would never be caught.

THE NAME STONE CORRAL dated back to the early 1850s, when a settler constructed a circular enclosure out of large rocks on the lower slope of Stokes Mountain to pen his hogs. Sometime later, rancher Billy Bacon built a small cabin just below the stone hog pens. By 1893, both the corral and cabin stood abandoned. Were it not for the events of June 11, 1893, the name would have been long forgotten. Instead, those two words—Stone Corral—would cause Eva to shudder the rest of her life whenever she thought about what happened there.

Marshal Gard and his posse—Deputy Sheriff Hiram Rapelje of Fresno; Fred Jackson, an officer from Nevada; and Tom Burns, an operative of the Morse Detective Agency—moved into Billy Bacon's abandoned cabin at the foot of Stokes Mountain on June 10 and began watching for the outlaws. According to Rapelje's account in the *Delta,* the posse had spent the previous week in the mountains "looking for signs of the desperadoes or obtaining information regarding their whereabouts."[4] Neither he nor Gard mentioned receiving a tip from anyone, but they had picked this particular cabin to lay in wait because it was near the road from Wilcox Canyon and they'd be able to "see everybody that passed along."

During Sunday, June 11, the posse rested in the cabin. While two men slept, the other two kept watch from inside the cabin where they couldn't be seen from outside. Meanwhile, up on Stokes Mountain that day, Chris and John sat and watched the surrounding country, scanning the cabin on the flat below with binoculars, but as the lawmen's horses were tied on the opposite side of the house, the fugitives saw nothing amiss.[5]

According to Marshal Gard's account, just before sundown Rapelje saw two men come down the hill and called out to Jackson. Jackson looked through a telescope and saw that one man had two guns and the other only one, although they later discovered he had another under his clothes. Gard and Burns had been napping and were quickly alerted.

Unsuspectingly, Chris and John walked toward the cabin; Evans was in the lead. Several accounts would later note that the situation was similar to that at Young's cabin, only in reverse. Gard stated that "when Evans and Sontag had reached a position about one hundred yards from the cabin, Rapelje looked around the corner. Chris saw him and fired the first shot and then fell to the ground after his fire had been returned. The fight lasted about an hour, and about 140 shots were fired."[6]

A shot fired by Jackson found Evans and knocked him down. Rapelje fired at Sontag, who also dropped to the ground. The wounded fugitives sought cover behind a pile of straw and manure as the gun battle continued. Jackson went around the house for a better shot and took a bullet in the leg.

As darkness fell and neither side could see, the shooting abated. Lying in a pile of manure, a mere hundred yards from their would-be captors, Sontag was seriously wounded. Local newspapers credited the fugitives with the following purple-tinged dialogue:

"Are you much hurt, John?" Chris asked.

"Yes, I am shot to pieces. I can't stand this, old Pard; kill me."

According to John, he begged his friend to kill him. "Shoot me through the head before you go," he pleaded, but Chris refused to do the deed. John later tried to do it himself, but being barely able to grip his gun, his efforts to put himself out of his misery proved ineffectual.[7]

After the firing had ceased, one of the outlaws was seen to crawl from behind the straw pile on his stomach and Rapelje commenced firing at him. According to the deputy, the man then rose to his feet and ran toward the hills, Rapelje pursuing and shooting at him. It was so dark that the retreating form could not be distinguished, and he was soon out of sight. The shooting had completely stopped and the officers procured a wagon from a nearby ranch so they could transport the wounded Jackson to Visalia for medical attention. The *Delta* reported:

> After Officer Jackson had been placed in comfortable quarters in the Palace Hotel, and medical aid summoned, Mr. Rapelje notified the county officers of the fight and asked that a posse be organized and sent immediately to the scene of the conflict. The posse was

soon organized, and well armed they left this city in carriages, accompanied by a *Delta* reporter.

The first gray streaks of dawn had just begun to appear when the officers left this city to relieve the officers at Stone Corral. The twenty miles was covered in a short space of time, the sun having just appeared above the eastern horizon when they reached the scene of the past night's fight.

Rapelje returned to Stone Corral accompanied by deputies George Witty and Sam Stingley. Visalia City Marshal William English went along with them, followed by newspaper reporters Jo P. Carroll and Harry Stuart in a buggy. Visalia photographer E. M. Davidson rode in the buggy with the reporters. At dawn, they joined Gard and Burns at the cabin. The *Delta* offered a colorful description of what followed:

> The officers approached the manure pile, which the bandits had used as a breast-work during the fight. Peeping out of the straw two heavy brogan shoes were discovered, and it was known then that one of the robbers had been discovered. The officers removed the straw from over the body of the wounded bandit, and the features of outlaw John Sontag were seen. His face was covered with blood and dirt, and his hat was lying near. Close by were found two shotguns and a Winchester rifle.
>
> When discovered, Sontag was almost in a comatose condition. The air was unusually cold and Sontag suffered intensely. It was found that Sontag had been shot in the shoulder and arm, the shot passing through and entering the right lung. He had bled profusely, and his clothes were saturated with blood. His face had an ashy hue, his lips were parched, and his eyes had a wild, glassy stare. Efforts were made at once to revive him. He opened his eyes and gave a wistful look about him. He moaned in anguish, and gave evidence of intense suffering.[8]

At that point, Marshal Gard promptly arrested the wounded outlaw. After the arrest, the photographer Davidson had all those present at the scene, including Luke Hall who resided on a nearby farm, visibly arm themselves and stand in a loose line behind the prostrate Sontag. It was only after photos were taken that John was transported to the Visalia jail where he received medical attention. He later claimed he "did not mind going through the ordeal of being photographed" and even expressed his appreciation when the officers "propped his head against a box and covered him with buggy robes and an overcoat."[9]

That evening, after Eva and Molly had visited John at the Visalia jail and learned that Chris had made his escape and remained at large, Petey Bigelow paid a visit to the Evans home, where he found Molly "in the throes of hysteria." Bigelow described Eva sitting in a large old-fashioned rocking chair, swathed in a quilt made by her grandmother. "She was pale and trembling, and her sisters, Ynez and Winifred, were bathing her head. The two sisters were rejoicing in a sort of uncanny mirth over the escape of their father from the officers." The girls told Bigelow they were sure he was all right and that he would never be caught.

Eva then told Bigelow of her visit with John. "We talked in whispers," Eva told her reporter friend. "Last night I felt all this was coming and when I went into the jail this morning I walked up to John's bed and said: 'Are you in pain, dear?' He said 'No' and, alluding to a favorite card game, added he had been 'euchred at last.'"

Eva explained to Bigelow that she had always been fond of John, since she was a little child, although no mention was made of an impending marriage. Eva admitted that "when I kissed him good-bye today, I knew I should never see him again."[10]

EVA STILL HAD HOPE of seeing her father alive again, and indeed, that evening word reached Visalia of his whereabouts. He was seriously wounded, but alive. By midnight, Undersheriff William Hall was en route to the Perkins ranch in Wilcox Canyon to capture Chris Evans.

During the shootout at Stone Corral, Deputy Rapelje had fired repeatedly at a fleeing figure. A trail of blood indicated he had wounded Chris Evans. But the next morning, lawmen were unable to trace the end of this gruesome path. They could not find the wounded bandit.

Several of Rapelje's bullets had indeed found their mark. One bullet plowed across the small of Chris' back, making a superficial wound about nine inches long. Another struck his right wrist. The most serious and painful injury was a bullet wound that broke both bones of his left wrist, rendering his arm useless. Chris was also shot in the right eyebrow, partially blinding him. Later reports, perhaps exaggerated, claimed the injured eyeball dangled from the ocular nerve.[11] It was in this gruesome state, during the dark of night, that Chris struggled his way toward the Perkins house in Wilcox Canyon. His most desperate need seemed to be water, and just after dawn he finally stumbled upon the well pump out in front of the Perkins house.

Eva's father was well familiar with the widowed Mrs. Perkins' place. Molly's brother, Perry, was married to the oldest Perkins girl. Thus, they were related by marriage. As Eva later explained, "We always treated the Perkins family like relatives, and it was to our house they came on their trips to town. While my father and John were being hunted, they often went to the Perkins home, so it was a natural thing for him to try and reach this refuge in his quest for water."[12]

When Mrs. Perkins discovered blood on the well pump, she sent for her son Elijah (who lived a short distance away) to come and investigate. He soon found Chris in an upstairs room, accessible from stairs outside the house, lying wounded on the bed. He was a horrible, bloody sight, and Perkins proclaimed, "Well, Chris, you are in a pretty bad fix, ain't you?" To which Chris replied, "Yes, and I want you to dress my wounds."[13] Elijah Perkins and his mother spent the rest of the day tending to Chris Evans' wounds and trying to convince their friend to give himself up. Eva claimed her father remained defiant and told Elijah that he would soon recover and that Eva could come take care of him.[14] Elijah claimed Chris soon gave up that idea, realizing Eva would be followed. He also saw the folly of being taken to his home in town, so Elijah concluded that the only thing to do was to go to Visalia and notify law officers.[15] The *San Francisco Examiner* summed up Elijah Perkins' situation.

> Why Perkins gave away the secret of Evans' whereabouts is somewhat involved in doubt. His friends would like it to be understood that he was acting with the knowledge and consent of Evans, but this Evans denies. The impression has been put out that Perkins was requested by Evans to disclose his whereabouts in order that Perkins might secure the reward offered for his capture and give it to Mrs. Evans. At any rate, Perkins managed to get an appointment at about 10 o'clock with Deputy Sheriff Hall and then and there informed him that Evans was lying seriously wounded at the house of his mother. Before Perkins gave the information he made a dicker with Hall for a sum of money to be paid to him.

The *Examiner* article also noted that "Perkins' narration of the visit of Evans to his mother's house and of his subsequent disclosures to the Sheriff do not quite seem to tally with the idea that he was acting for

Evans, and the knowledge that he dickered for money, if it cannot be shown that he acted with the bandit's consent, will be apt to prejudice him very considerably."[16] One thing no one accused Elijah Perkins of was handling the situation intelligently. But that little mattered to Deputy Sheriff Hall, who quickly headed for the Perkins place to capture the wanted fugitive.

Chris Evans was arrested without resistance the next morning. The only struggle was between competing lawmen who showed up at the Perkins place, for it seems word had leaked to other officers. There was some argument over jurisdiction and who had a right to take the prisoner. Of course, it was all about the reward money.

As Eva described the scene, a posse of Fresno County officers, including Sheriff Jay Scott, Deputy Hi Rapelje (whose shots had wounded both Sontag and Evans) and some "free-lance blood-money hunters," arrived at the back door of the Perkins house just minutes after Undersheriff Hall had gone in at the front door.

> By the time they reached the attic room, my father had already surrendered to Billy Hall. When the killers demanded their prey, Billy Hall said, "This house is in Tulare County. Chris Evans is my prisoner."
>
> And there, over the body of what they thought was a dying man, they were on the point of killing each other. Guns had been drawn when Dad said, "Gentlemen, fight it out later. I'm suffering terribly. Get me to a doctor."[17]

Eva would never forgive Elijah Perkins for his role in her father's capture, although he wasn't considered as much a Judas as another "trusted friend" and relative. Eva would reveal the identity of this suspected traitor in sworn testimony six months later. When questioned as to why there was ill-feeling between her family and her cousin's family, Eva replied, "Because Perry Byrd betrayed [Chris Evans] and caused him to be shot down like a dog." While it was common knowledge that Molly's brother Perry served as a deputy for Sheriff Kay—indeed, Kay once called him one of his most valued deputies, and Perry had been involved in the hunt for Dalton following his escape from jail—there is no direct evidence that Marshal Gard had been in contact with him.[18] But if Gard did have reason to concentrate his search on the trail leading out of Wilcox Canyon at the landmark called Stone Corral, inside information from an informant would have been the likeliest path to that reasoning. And a better connected candidate than Perry Byrd to both local law officers and the Evans family did not exist.

Elijah Perkins, on the other hand, was perhaps considered by the Evans family as nothing more than a buffoon and a loose-lipped opportunist. Nonetheless, the family would exact their revenge in a very public forum before the year was out, and Eva felt God exacted his revenge when Perkins was later killed in a freak accident. "Just his feet were sticking out from beneath a huge rock that for centuries had been balanced on a tiny pedestal," she wrote, her words oozing karmic satisfaction.[19]

But for now, Eva faced an emotional crisis. If she was broken up about John Sontag hovering near death in his jail-cell bed, she was now completely devastated knowing her father lay wounded in the Visalia jail. Her only consolation was that at least, for now, he was alive and she could be with him.

EVA, MEANWHILE, WAS PLAYING A ROLE in the plot brewing up at Folsom Prison. She had received a letter late in May from George saying that a friend of his named Johnson would call on her, and that any favors she could show him would be appreciated. It was several weeks before a young man showed up at the Evans house inquiring about a "Mrs. Bolivar." Eva had been expecting him, but with the recent tragic events she had undoubtedly put it out of her mind. She agreed to meet the mysterious stranger later that evening out under a tree in the orchard.

William Fredericks, using the alias Johnson, told Eva that he had heard what happened to John Sontag and her father. He explained it took him over a week to get down to Visalia, as he'd been kicked off of trains several times. He only had the five dollars they gave him when he left prison and didn't dare beg for fear of being arrested. "Here is what George wants you to do," he then told Eva. "Get them some guns."[20]

While she at first resisted the request, Fredericks continued to plead with her. They met several times. He "talked a long time about how terrible life was in prison, especially for the men who had to break stones under a broiling sun; of how unhealthy it was, so many of the men suffering from malaria." Eva had to be thinking about her father's impending fate.

Eva finally agreed to help him, and her thoughts turned to Si Lovern, a local saloon keeper. She explained to Fredericks that Si had come to see her family after the men were captured and said "You remember them bums that hung around my place that were supposed to be huntin' yer Pa? Well, they pawned their guns for one last drink and lit out of town."[21] And so it was that Si Lovern had a back room full of guns. Eva suggested Fredericks somehow acquire them, and before long Si's saloon was broken into (although the burglary may have been a story to cover Si's possible—even likely—cooperation.)

Eva did not try and deflect her part in this when she wrote many years later how after Fredericks stole the guns, he hid them in Grannie Byrd's barn. She admitted getting an old blanket and quilt to roll them up and made a pack like tramps carry. Not stopping there, Eva even admitted that she gave Fredericks all the money she had—about three dollars—and added Witty's revolver, which she had kept, to his bundle of stolen rifles from the saloon.

Eva got to know this "strange lad" over the many days they plotted together. He told Eva many stories about himself and his family background. At twenty-five, Fredericks was nearly eight years older than Eva, although she pointed out that her new-found criminal accomplice looked much younger than his actual age. He was, in Eva's estimation, "really nice" and Eva became very fond of him. She had a weakness for handsome, dangerous men, and it would become more and more apparent to Eva that men had a certain weakness for her.

It was near the summer solstice when Fredericks finally left. Helping him adjust the pack on his back, Eva wished him good luck and a safe journey. "Worry over the outcome of the prison break was now added to my heartache and anxiety over my father and John," she later wrote.[22]

DESPITE HER DIRE PREDICTION, Eva's initial visit with John after the shootout at Stone Corral was not the last time she would ever see him. A few days later, both John and Chris drifted between life and death in different jail cells. Doctors had amputated her father's arm two days after the battle. "Maybe it was necessary, but I have never believed that it was," she bitterly recalled. No one was permitted to see him until after the amputation, and then Molly was allowed to visit with her husband. "As mother was leaving," Eva later wrote, "they handed her a bundle saying 'Your husband's clothes.' When she opened it at home she nearly fainted. They were stiff with dried blood." Eva took the clothes and buried them behind their old house nearby, in the vineyard where her father had buried her little dog Toodles so many years earlier. Stabbing the spade into the dry summer dirt, Eva cursed the men who shed her father's blood. Cursed them to the end of their days.[23]

Thinking of what had happened to her father, Eva bristled with anger. Seeing what had happened to John, she felt more subdued emotions laced with pity. Decades later, Eva wrote in her memoir:

> As I stood beside him, John took my hand in his and I laid my other hand on his forehead where the bullet had grazed it. His beard had been removed and his face was framed in a bandage that covered the hole in either cheek where his bullet had gone in and out. The agony that held him until the end already gripped him. As he lifted his eyes to mine it was all I could do to keep from crying out. There was more there than a broken body. I saw a broken heart.
>
> I murmured some meaningless words. I could not say what was in my heart. There were no words for that. I just tried to tell him with my hands, and then there was a voice saying: "Your time is up, Miss Evans. I'll take you to your father."[24]

The *Visalia Delta* described Eva's subsequent meeting with her father. "She entered the cell, and without a word, kneeled at the side of the cot, placed her arms around the head of the wounded outlaw, and showered kisses upon his face."[25] When Eva was told it was time to leave, she pleaded to stay all night in the cell with him. According to Eva, this request was granted, but in the morning her father admonished her not to carry on so. "I'm not dead yet," Chris told his daughter.

Despite this quiet reassurance, Eva was distraught. Upon leaving the jail, she nearly broke down. A friend who had been waiting outside the jail for news led the hysterical girl to his buggy. As they drove, Eva talked wildly. The friend took her home where Molly put her daughter to bed. They had to hold Eva down until she finally slipped into a troubled sleep. "It was thirty-six hours before my brain cleared," Eva later recounted, "and I could never remember walking out of that cell or anything that I said during that time."

The very day after her mind cleared, Father Farrelly, the priest who had been so kind to the family, came to her and told her John had asked for the last Sacrament. "Eva," he told her, "John is going to die."[26]

BY LATE JUNE, CHRIS AND JOHN were transferred to the Fresno jail for two reasons. One, the charges they faced—the murders of Wilson and McGinnis—occurred in Fresno County. Secondly, the Visalia jail didn't have a particularly good record of keeping prisoners; and with Chris regaining his health, they had to be concerned about escape attempts. The *Examiner* also noted that "faint whispers of lynching were also heard at Visalia," but the paper admitted that any such reports had no influence in bringing about their transfer to Fresno.[27]

Before June was over, it wasn't an escape by Chris Evans that made headlines, but George's attempt to break out of Folsom Prison that was splashed all over the front page of every newspaper in California. "Escaped to Death" one headline blared.[28] And although George still clung to life despite his wounds, others were not so lucky.

On June 27, Fredericks had returned to Folsom and left the weapons Eva had helped him obtain in the prison quarry. He then caught a freight train going east out of Folsom. When a brakeman attempted to eject him near Colfax, Fredericks shot and seriously wounded him. Fredericks on that day became a hunted man. Meanwhile, on June 28, 1893, his co-conspirators were working in the rock quarry at Folsom Prison. Newspapers called what happened next "the bloodiest episode in the history" of Folsom Prison.[29]

George Sontag and Frank "Smiling" Williams had by now involved other men in their escape plan: convicted burglars Anthony Dalton (no relation to Grat and the Dalton brothers) and Hiram Wilson, stage robber "Buckshot" Smith, and convicted murderer Charles Abbott.[30] While these men were working in the quarry, George was nearby unloading boulders from railroad cars. George walked to the quarry and approached a guard. The plan was set in motion. Utilizing the secreted weapons and using a guard as a human shield, the men made their escape attempt. But the guards fought back by opening fire.

The escapees dodged into a shallow depression behind some boulders and returned fire. A hot gun battle ensued, lasting about forty-five minutes. The guards' concentrated fusillade poured into the depression and ricocheted wildly off the boulders.

Unable to withstand the barrage of bullets, the besieged convicts raised a hat on the end of a rifle barrel as a token of surrender. The guards cautiously approached the convicts and found Williams, Dalton, and Wilson riddled with bullets and dead. Abbott survived, but had a broken leg and two additional wounds. George was seriously wounded.

Although several were mere graze wounds, he had suffered a broken thigh, and bullets had shattered his shinbone. A round was also lodged in his lower abdomen. Upon surrendering to prison authorities, George reportedly said, "I have played my game and lost."[31]

EVA MADE A TRIP TO FRESNO to visit John one last time, but he was barely conscious. She wrote that the door of his cell was unlocked and she walked over to his cot. "His beautiful eyes were dull with suffering; he was dying of peritonitis." John took her hand and laid it on the beat of his throat, then closed his eyes. She waited for him to speak or open his eyes. "When he did neither, I leaned over and kissed the closed eyes, then the spot where my hand had lain."[32] It was the last time she would ever see him.

According to the *San Francisco Examiner*, Chris Evans was baptized into the Catholic faith that evening. "There was a solemn scene in the Evans-Sontag cell when Chris Evans was baptized into the Roman Catholic Church. Chris said that he had promised John Sontag to die in the true faith and that he was happy now that he had resumed the religion of his father. Father Farrelly of Visalia stood as his godfather and old Mrs. Sontag was godmother. Eva Evans was in tears and held her father's hand. She expects to follow him into the Roman Catholic fold in a few days."[33]

With Deputy Hi Rapelje on watch at the jail, John's mother sat with her barely conscious son, whispering in German and patting his forehead. Outside, hundreds flocked to the jail, eager to get a glimpse of the infamous bandit before (or after) he died. Rapelje would, at intervals, look into the cell. Mrs. Sontag was painfully aware that it was Rapelje's bullet that was killing her son, but had little time to reflect on the irony of his current position as jailer waiting for the inevitable, the conclusion of his own shot. Molly, still in Fresno, tried to comfort Mrs. Sontag, but her sympathy only made the tears flow faster. Eva had returned to Visalia, where she was needed to help care for the children.

Throughout the morning and into the afternoon, John lay unconscious. His breathing came harder, and there were longer intervals between the gasps. At one thirty it ended. Mrs. Sontag stooped over and kissed him and let her head lie on her son's face while she cried. Rapelje stepped in at the door in the course of his regular routine; he saw and understood and went away without speaking.

Considering his younger brother's penchant for escape attempts, the *Examiner* ran an ironically apt headline—Death Unbolted His Cell—announcing the death of John Sontag. Eva had earlier knelt beside his bed, and unable to think of a prayer, remembered saying, over and over, "Give him freedom, dear God; give him freedom."[34] John was now free. Her prayers were answered.

According to George, after John died, their mother overheard Eva make the following remark: "Thank God, one of them is dead. If the other one dies, we are all right."[35]

Eva never acknowledged making the callous remark Mrs. Sontag claimed to overhear. Although without admitting it was in response to the supposed comment, Eva later offered evidence of how Mrs. Sontag might have misconstrued her feelings. "I had prayed that John would be granted his desire for death," Eva wrote, "and I felt now that death would be better for George than to be crippled and in prison for life."[36]

George's point in bringing up the comment was that his death, coupled with his brother's, would have eliminated any eyewitnesses to the robberies committed by Chris Evans. For this reason, according to George, the Evans family would have been "all right" upon his death. Eva also acknowledged, albeit indirectly, the danger to the family of George surviving. "George Sontag did not die," she bluntly wrote. "If he had, perhaps this story would have a different ending."[37]

ACT THREE

INFAMY

CHAPTER ELEVEN

Life in the Theatre

*Of course, it was the rankest melodrama. I can smile now,
looking back on the blood and thunder of it. But I was not
conscious then of the cheapness of the play. I was earning
money for my father!*

—EVA EVANS, AN OUTLAW AND HIS FAMILY

LESS THAN A MONTH after John Sontag's dramatic death, the idea to realize his saga on stage was born. For nearly a year, Evans and Sontag had dominated the headlines. Newspapers devoted entire front pages to their various gunfights, especially the climactic battle at Stone Corral. Amidst the violence, the romance between Eva and John found its way into newsprint. Accounts told of Eva's bedside visit to John's jail cell, complete with a sad kiss farewell to her lover's feverish forehead. Reporters described John's final moments, how his labored breathing subsided as his grieving mother sobbed. Heart-wrenching and tragic, the scenes depicted in the press only served to whet the public's appetite for more.

The media feeding frenzy was not, however, limited to the exhaustive newspaper coverage. A photograph of a wounded John Sontag propped up in front of Marshal Gard's posse became a popular cabinet card. Only three days after John's death, an article in a Visalia newspaper noted that the very cabin from Stone Corral had already been dismantled and shipped to San Francisco for use as scenery in a melodrama entitled *The Train Wreckers*. While the story of the play had nothing to do with Evans and Sontag, the novel use of the cabin, the play's promoter promised, would be "well advertised and undoubtedly prove a great attraction itself."[1]

With all the various ways people were seeking to capitalize on events that, for Eva, were tragic and devastating to her family, it wasn't surprising that a dramatist would sooner or later conceive of bringing their story to life in the theatre.

On July 29, 1893, the *San Francisco Examiner* gave a detailed account of the planned theatrical under the headline "The Sontag Tragedy":

> Mrs. Christopher Evans, wife of the notorious bandit [the *Examiner* reported], and Miss Eva Evans, his much-exploited daughter, are going on the stage. They will appear in a tragical melodrama entitled "The Sontag Tragedy," setting forth facts and incidents connected with the Collis train robbery and the various bloody battles engaged in by the robbers before they were shot into subjection and death.

This was the first announcement that the wife of "the notorious bandit, and Miss Eva Evans, his much-exploited daughter," were going to appear on the stage.

The man behind the proposed staging—who made arrangements to cast the two Evans women and who would author the play—was R. C. White. In his mid-fifties, Richard Cullen White was born in New York of Scotch-Irish parents.[2] He had established an acting career in San Francisco, a stage-struck city that since its earliest days had supported numerous theatres.

"How San Francisco loved the theatre," Evelyn Wells wrote in *Champagne Days of San Francisco*, her book about life in that city during "the gay nineties, its most irrepressible era." Wells described the many theatres in the city. There was, of course, the Tivoli, which Eva had attended with Petey Bigelow only a few months earlier. But there were many others, including Walter Morosco's Grand Opera House on Mission Street, where police were always on guard in the back alley after performances to protect actors, for the impressionable city took Morosco's thrilling melodramas to heart and crowds, gathered at the stage exit to cheer the hero and hiss the villain, would sometimes throw stones at the more reprehensible villains.

San Francisco also supported the Old California Theatre on Bush Street, the Alcazar on O'Farrell Street, and the Stockwell Theatre, which later reopened as the Columbia. Over at the Orpheum, which always sold out days in advance, the most popular vaudeville performers trod its narrow stages. This theatre was lovingly known as the "old Orph."

And then there was the Baldwin Theatre, said to be the finest theatre outside of New York. Part of the Baldwin Hotel on Powell and Market Streets, many of the greatest actors played the Baldwin: Fanny Davenport, Maurice Barrymore, Lillian Russell, Julia Marlowe, Edwin Booth, and Madame Modjeska.[3]

San Francisco in the 1890s was truly an actor's town, and one actor "generally known among the local players" was R. C. White. He had achieved, the San Francisco Examiner explained, some small fame (and smaller fortune) a few years earlier with his dramatization of Rider Haggard's popular novel, She.[4] If the Examiner hinted that White's production of She hadn't made much money, the number of column inches devoted to his latest venture was evidence that, this time, White had a winner of an idea—a real money-maker. If some battered old boards from a cabin where the shootout occurred could help sell tickets, think of how the wife and daughter of California's most notorious outlaw (not to mention Sontag's grieving fiancée) would fill theatres.

A CRYING NEED FOR MONEY was how Eva once described their current situation, explaining they needed "money to hire lawyers to fight Dad's battles. Mother and I thought about it constantly, and prayed over it. How could we earn the money?" R. C. White provided the answer to their prayers.

Exactly where and when his offer—an offer that launched Eva's theatrical career—was made is hard to say. Eva, many years later, wrote that White had come to see her and Molly in August to ask them to participate in the play. She must have been mistaken because newspapers were already reporting the news in July.

White, himself, explained in the San Francisco Examiner that he broached the subject with Molly in San Francisco in early July. Molly, according to newspaper reports, was in the city seeking legal representation for her husband, who was facing criminal charges back in Fresno. The Fresno Republican, on July 11, 1893, noted that while Mrs. Evans had traveled to San Francisco to engage attorney Pat Reddy, Eva had returned home to Visalia. Thus Eva was evidently not present when the theatrical producer made his initial overture.

In any event, as White explained, Molly was hesitant to agree to participate until she checked with her husband. Chris, who had just been arraigned for the murder of Wilson and McGinnis in a Fresno court, was, in the purple prose of the San Francisco Examiner, "languishing, maimed and moody, in the Fresno jail awaiting trial for his life with charges enough hanging over him to crush a dozen men." So White penned a letter to Chris Evans that Molly delivered to him.[5]

White undoubtedly outlined the financial deal he was offering in his missive to Chris. Again, there are some discrepancies as to the exact details. White told the *Examiner* that the family would receive "one-half of the net profits," but Eva's memoir claims it was "twenty-five percent of the net receipts." Whatever the arrangement, the need for money to pay attorney's fees was overwhelming motivation for Chris to agree to the deal.[6]

On July 23, Chris penned the following response to White: "I take pleasure in introducing to you James Evans, a dear friend of mine. I have commissioned him to act for me and mine. I am perfectly willing for my wife to join your company and I wish you success. I remain yours, Chris Evans."

Just who was this "dear friend" with the same last name? The *San Francisco Examiner* explained he was a cousin of Chris Evans; and once Chris gave White his seal of approval, James furnished "a synopsis of the events which the tragedy is to bring out." In addition to supplying the "facts on which the play is to be based," Jim Evans would reportedly be cast in a minor part.[7]

There is a degree of mystery surrounding Jim Evans. The length and degree of his association with the Evans family (or if he was indeed related) is subject to conjecture. Obviously, Chris considered him close enough to serve as an intermediary between himself and White. But oddly, Eva never made any mention of him in her memoir. Later reports claimed Jim Evans worked in a Fresno hotel where detectives made their headquarters during the manhunt for Chris and John. "No one suspected his relationship to Chris Evans," the *San Francisco Call* asserted, "and so he heard many of the plans and immediately informed the family in Visalia." The newspaper went on to say it was Jim Evans who had supplied Eva with the boy's clothes she wore when she rode "to Fort Defiance to see her father and John Sontag."[8]

Another clue to his relationship with the Evans family is found in correspondence during Chris' later trial. In a letter to prosecuting attorney W. D. Tupper (which eventually was given to detective Will Smith), an informant claimed "Big Jim Evans" had assisted in the train robberies. This informant, presumably Perry Byrd, added that Grannie Byrd "says that she always new [*sic*] that him & Eva would git the hole [*sic*] kinfolks in trouble."[9] If this comment is true, it hints that there might even have been a romantic link between Eva and Jim Evans.

Although Chris Evans' letter to White, which was published in the *Examiner*, states he was willing to have his wife participate in the play, he made no mention of his daughter. Perhaps that request came later, as one can imagine White waiting until the family was comfortable with the whole idea before springing the request to have seventeen-year-old Eva star in the play. And how easily would Chris agree to allow his daughter to appear on stage? Chris, from his jail cell, might have had moral concerns about his daughter becoming an actor. The acting profession in the late nineteenth century carried with it a rather negative stigma. Many were still of the opinion that it corrupted its performers as well as its audience. One prominent minister called the acting profession "intellectual prostitution" because players threw away their considerable abilities to chase a fleeting prize.

Another common criticism was that acting deadened moral sensitivities. "How can they mingle together as they do," one critic asked, "and make public exhibition of themselves as they do, in such position as they must sometimes take, affecting such sentiments and passions, without moral contamination?"[10]

Additionally, acting was a difficult way to make a living. Advice against an acting career was particularly strong for females. To quote one actress of the time, who when asked by a young woman for advice on becoming an actor replied that it was easy to get a job if one had been through divorce court or part of a scandal, but for an innocent and principled girl, it was almost impossible.[11] Chris Evans would have certainly liked to think Eva both innocent and principled, but she was also in the midst of a great scandal. Just how carefully he considered the downside of allowing Eva's participation is unknown.

Molly's apprehension centered on a fear that people would laugh at her utter failure as an actor. Eva, on the other hand, saw the opportunity as positive and thrilling. While she understood her mother's nervousness, Eva eagerly jumped at the opportunity.

"Is there any girl who has recited 'Curfew Shall Not Ring Tonight' but thinks she is destined to be an actress?" the schoolgirl pondered. "Hadn't I recited 'Osler Joe' so well that I shocked my small world as much as Mrs. James Brown Potter did hers?" the future star proudly thought.[12]

And so it was agreed: seventeen-year-old Eva Evans, along with her mother, Molly, would star in R. C. White's drama of real life.

NEGATIVE REACTION TO THE PLAY surfaced almost immediately after its announcement. The *Bakersfield Echo* editorialized that the portion of the "Evans gang not in jail were going on stage to act in a so-called play." The paper accused the *San Francisco Examiner*, which from the start "has championed the cause of the outlaws and done all it could to create sympathy for them," of being "a partner in the theatrical enterprise, as it gives columns of space to it which in any other cause would be charged for at about a dollar a line." The *San Jose Mercury* predicted that the play would be met with a "dead cold frost."[13]

The fact that the *Examiner* devoted so much space to announcing the play wasn't so much evidence that Hearst had a stake in the production as that he had a stake in keeping the Evans and Sontag story alive. It helped sell newspapers, and that was his greatest concern.

In early September, Molly and Eva, along with the other children, journeyed to San Francisco. White rented the family a flat not far from his own home at the edge of the Mission District. The residential neighborhood, lying south of Market Street between the business district and Mission Dolores, was one of the oldest in San Francisco. With ample and affordable housing, it attracted an ethnically diverse population of working people, but still contained many lovely homes.[14] From their apartment house, it wasn't much more than a mile, most of which could be traveled by street car, to the National Theatre at the corner of Jones and Eddy Streets. Formerly known as the Wigwam, where boxing matches were often on the marquee, the National Theatre didn't boast the reputation of the Tivoli, the grandeur of the Grand Opera House or the Baldwin, or the popularity of the Orpheum. Still, it was an impressive facility to the country-born Eva and would be the site of her theatrical debut.

William Randolph Hearst continued to devote a generous number of column inches to the production with Molly and Eva now on board. Two lengthy articles appeared during the final weeks of rehearsal. Perhaps the Bakersfield paper was right—R. C. White could not have bought such great publicity.

Sex and romance sells—both White and Hearst realized that—and much was made in print of the costume Eva would wear in the scene where she rides to the mountains to see Chris and John. The lead headline heralded: "Eva Evans in Pantaloons." The sub-headline explained how "The New Dramatic Star Will Appear in Boys Clothes, Which She Says She Just Loves."[15] During Victorian times, the opportunity to see a young woman's posterior curves clearly delineated by trousers was titillating. Proof that Eva's appearance in pants added sex appeal was evidenced in a later newspaper column—a reporter for the *Sacramento Bee* admitted he "went to the Evans and Sontag play with the sweet thought that I would there see how a beautiful maiden with the bloom of virginal innocence…would look clad in trousers and astraddle of a horse."[16]

R. C. White had his work cut out for him, transforming this country diamond-in-the-rough into the gilded city's latest sex-symbol. One gets a sense from an interview in the *Examiner* that Eva was having a grand old time.

> Miss Evans was asked to pose in one or two of her dramatic positions for the instruction of an *Examiner* sketch artist.
>
> "But we don't know how," she demurred. "I'm not very dramatic, and, though we've both got our lines, Mr. White will have to show us how to act."
>
> "Take your inspiration from the lines," said White. "Strike a position, so, at the point where you dismount from your horse in Dark Canyon, and look up to the rocks of Fort Defiance. You remember where you say 'Father! John! Where are you?'"
>
> "But I haven't any boy's clothes to pose in."
>
> Here Miss Evans rose and dropped at once into the position indicated by Mr. White, and retained a steady pose while being sketched. White looked at her with pride.
>
> "She'll do," he said laconically.[17]

The *Examiner* also emphasized, in headline form, the "Romance of John Sontag and Eva Evans in the Melodrama 'The Visalia Outlaws.'" The article admitted that "even the playwright cannot make a merry ending out of the grim tragedy of the lives of Chris Evans and John Sontag, but in the melodrama arranged for the stage, R. C. White has made a love story." White claimed his play accurately followed the story of Evans and Sontag as told in the *Examiner.* "I have here all the *Examiner* pictures," White explained, "and will stage the piece according to them. It isn't sensationally melodramatic, but a life story. I haven't made heroes of Evans and Sontag, but have tried to take them as they took themselves."[18] White was thus already denying aspects of his play he knew would draw criticism and controversy.

Objections to the drama, however, provided even more free publicity. The first noted objection came from Will Smith. In the earliest announcement, White declared that he would change the name of any character "portrayed in an unenviable light."[19] The railroad detective— the villain of the drama—was called Wily Smooth. As the *Examiner* wrote and as everyone knew, "Wily Smooth was, of course, Will Smith, the detective of the Southern Pacific Company."[20]

"I have been told," White informed the *Examiner* in a subsequent interview, "that Smith may try to prevent the appearance of this character, but of course we shall say that Wily Smooth is purely a fictitious character and not a picture of Will Smith." White later reiterated that "the character of Wily Smooth…is not meant as a reflection on any particular individual, it being simply a creation to illustrate the abominations of hired gunfighters," and added that when private individuals or corporations hire men to kill their enemies, they outrage the law and should be held to answer for the crime.[21]

While Chris Evans and John Sontag were the heroes of the piece and Will Smith became the villain, Eva Evans was unquestionably the heroine. The fact that she would portray herself added a layer of attraction, and the press naturally focused on Eva. "She's getting ready to be a real star," Molly told an *Examiner* reporter, who noted that Molly looked at her flaxen-haired daughter with much pride.

The newspaper then recounted Eva's real-life adventures riding to the mountains:

"How long a ride was it?

"About forty miles; but I made it in a night, easily enough, and none of those detectives knew anything about it, either."[22]

Eva's considerable riding ability would be on display in the play, dashing in on horseback to warn her father and lover of impending danger. "It wouldn't do for me to ride Big Jim, the horse I did ride on that trip," Eva explained to the *Examiner* reporter. "He'd clear the footlights and be halfway up the theatre in a second."[23] Looking back years later, Eva recalled:

One thing that made the play worth while to me was the beautiful black horse, stage trained, that I was to ride. I rode him every day that week to Golden Gate Park so that we would get to know each other. A runway had been built so that I could bring him on at a gallop, dismount well down towards the footlights, and take the spot against his shoulder just as the actors who took the parts

Eva's paternal grandmother, Mary Ann Switzer Evans, photo circa 1870 taken in Ottawa, Canada.

Tulare County Museum, Kinkela/Keil Collection

Eva's maternal grandmother, Isabella Saunders "Grannie" Byrd, photo taken circa 1890.

Courtesy of Arleen Anderson

This photograph was taken of Molly Byrd Evans in 1893, when she was thirty-four years old.

Illustration made from a photograph taken of Chris Evans in 1878.

John Sontag, a former railroad employee, was in his mid thirties when he came to live with the Evans family.

Eva Evans at seventeen years of age.

William Randolph Hearst took over the *San Francisco Examiner* in 1887, when he was still in his twenties.

The Huntington Library, San Marino, California

Henry "Petey" Bigelow, the colorful *San Francisco Examiner* reporter, scooped everyone when he interviewed Evans and Sontag.

The Huntington Library, San Marino, California

JOAQUIN MILLER, THE POET WHO INTERVIEWED EVANS, THE OUTLAW, FOR THE "EXAMINER."
[*Sketched by an "Examiner" staff artist.*]

San Francisco Examiner

Joaquin Miller, the eccentric poet, relied on his skills at fiction when he supplied Hearst with another interview of Chris Evans.

William Randolph Hearst's *San Francisco Examiner* covered the
Evans and Sontag story in depth, devoting the entire front page to
their exploits on several occasions.

Sheriff Eugene Kay of Visalia wasn't the most effective lawman, but his caution and caring in dealing with the Evans family earned Eva's lifelong respect.

Will Smith, the detective for the Southern Pacific Railroad, was reviled by Eva and her father and became the model for melodrama villian Wily Smooth.

Chris Evans, days after his capture and the amputation of his left arm.

A seriously wounded John Sontag the morning after the gun battle at Stone Corral with members of the posse and reporters posed behind him.

Eva, dressed in boy's pantaloons for the play *Evans and Sontag: The Visalia Bandits*, which opened at the National Theatre in San Francisco in September 1893.

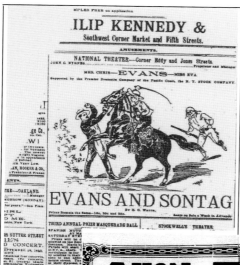

Advertisement appearing in the *San Francisco Examiner* for R. C. White's production of the blood and thunder melodrama: *Evans and Sontag.*

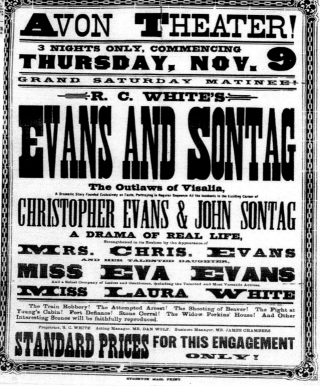

This lithograph poster advertised the "Drama of Real Life," which was "Strengthened in its Realism by the Appearance" of Mrs. Chris Evans and Miss Eva Evans.

Eva Evans in a photograph taken in 1893 to publicize the melodrama.

In 1894 the entire Evans brood appeared on stage in the melodrama. Eva is at center. Standing in rear are Winifred (right) and Ynez (left). The boys in front are (left to right) Joseph Francis, John Christopher, Patrick Carlton (baby Carl), and Louis Napoleon.

Eva Evans, a photographer, sits for a portrait circa 1900.

On an Oregon outing during Joaquin Miller's visit, (left to right) Dolly Davis, Joaquin Miller, Ynez Evans Mason, Eva Evans Cribbs, Norris Jensen, Perry McCullough, with the boatman standing behind the group. The photo was taken in 1908.

Winifred, who worked so tirelessly for her father's parole, with her second husband, Albert Gutierrez, and her son, William Burrell.

Tulare County Museum, Kinkela/Keil Collection

This portrait of Ynez and Joaquin Miller was likely taken by Eva at the Mason & Cribbs photography studio she and her sister owned and operated in Marshfield, Oregon.

Tulare County Museum, Kinkela/Keil Collection

Perry and Eva Evans McCullough in San Francisco in 1915.

Chris Evans, photographed by Eva at her house in Los Angeles in 1914.

Eva Evans McCullough, in 1933, visiting the Redwood Ranch summer home her father had built.

Evelyn (Eva Evans) McCullough and Ynez (Evans) Jensen in Laguna Beach in the early 1960s.

Andy Kinkela and his new wife, Evelyn.

Courtesy of Adrianne Whitmore

The Train Robber's Daughter.

of my father and John rushed from their hiding place to greet me. I think the applause that first night must have lasted five minutes. [24]

News coverage made mention of Eva's training in elocution and "considerable experience in speaking pieces at school entertainments." The *Examiner* reporter indulged her and quoted extensively as she recited a piece she liked "the best of any."

"Oh, it's a beautiful thing. I found it in a Fresno paper, and they told me they'd cut it from an Eastern exchange. But I think Joaquin Miller wrote it. It sounds like him. You know, John's grave is out in those drifting sands near Fresno, and there's one lone tree over it. The poem begins:

> *"In his narrow grave the bandit*
> *Lies in calm, untroubled rest;*
> *Dreary spread the plains about him*
> *Towards the mountains of the west."*

As opening night loomed, Eva and her mother were questioned about how they might hold up.

"Are you nervous over your debut?" the reporter asked. "Do you expect to be frightened?"

Molly, the reporter observed, didn't have half the self-confidence of her daughter—she said she didn't know how it would feel to "take a stage fright. I might get one and run off the stage leaving everything."

"Pooh!" Eva chimed in. "That's nothing to frighten anybody, I should think."

"Ah, but I get the greatest scare of my life every time I appear in a new role," interposed White, who the paper noted was a veteran actor as well as the dramatist.

But Eva simply responded, "Bah! Don't tell us that, or you might persuade us to get frightened for nothing. It can't be anything [compared] to going through the scenes in reality, as we have done."[25]

"LIKE THE ROAR OF BATTLE" was the headline in the *San Francisco Examiner* on September 19, 1893, describing the noise made on opening night.

At 7:30 o'clock last evening the street outside the National Theatre on the corner of Eddy and Jones looked as it used to when the building was known as the Wigwam and there was a big glove contest on.

It was the opening night of the new melodrama, "Evans and Sontag, or the Visalia Bandits," and the fact that the wife and daughter of Chris Evans were to take leading parts was sufficient to pack the theatre until it seemed as if the walls would bulge out and split at the corners. By the time the curtain rose it would have been a physical impossibility to squeeze another human being into the place.

San Francisco's three leading dailies all devoted considerable space to reviewing the play, and it wasn't surprising that the *Examiner*'s three full columns complete with illustrations was the most enthusiastic. The *Call* proclaimed that the play went on without "interruption or drag" and that Eva made a "successful debut." The *Chronicle* called it a "wild and woolly night with Evans and Sontag at the National Theatre" and proclaimed it was a "great night for outlaws and the management of the theatre." The *Chronicle,* like its rival the *Examiner,* also commented on the noise produced from both the players and the audience with the headline "Shots and Shouts."[26]

The audience that first night was as eclectic as it was enthusiastic. It included "many faces that are usually only visible at the Baldwin first nights" or the "three-dollar seats of the Grand Opera House." Also present were many regular patrons of the "blank-cartridge school of acting" and people who do not enter a theatre but once a year. As the *Examiner* described, they all came "prepared to enjoy the play, and it was all they could do to keep their enthusiasm under control. When the curtain finally rose...the gallery and half the orchestra rose to their feet and let out a pent-up howl of anticipation that started the shingles."[27]

The actual play they saw performed that night was at best a fanciful interpretation of events in Eva's life and at worst exploitative and blatantly deceptive propaganda. In the tradition of "blood and thunder" melodrama, it was also described as "three or four solid hours of gunpowder and red fire." One columnist claimed it was "as easily understood from the outside of the theatre as from the front row of the orchestra, for it consists almost entirely of repeated volleys of blank cartridges, followed by howls of approval from the gallery, and both of these are plainly audible three blocks away."[28] Even Eva, many years later, would admit "it was the rankest melodrama." But at the time—the self-described country girl, appearing on stage in San Francisco at the same time Mrs. John Drew was playing the Baldwin—Eva wasn't conscious of the cheapness of the play.[29]

The play opened with John Sontag's mother conversing with Lije Perkins, a character whose business, the *Chronicle* noted, seemed "to be to eat and tell people he is from Wilcox Canyon. He did this in great profusion all night and worked in about all the dialects affected by low comedians." In trying to clarify his comment to the German-accented Mrs. Sontag that John and Eva will "make a spankin' team when they're hitched up together in the matrimonial buckboard," the following exchange, written by White to include their respective dialects, occurred:

LIJE:

Why, you see, Mrs. Sontag, I was usin' a figger of speech. I mean, when they are welded together by the parson, they'll be the dandiest pair of steppers in the county, an' they'll knock the socks off'n any married pair between here and Wilcox Canyon.

MRS. SONTAG:

Yan, Ich dink dot vis so; bud whad fir dey knock ouf their socks, Lije?

LIJE:

You don't understand me. You see, when I say socks, I mean spots. They'll knock the spots out'n 'em.

MRS. SONTAG:

Oh, when you say socks, you mean shpots? What shpots? Ich dond could understood.

LIJE:

Why, goldurn it! I mean that Eva Evans and John Sontag are ripsorters for gait and good looks and when they come in double harness, they'll knock seven kinds of tar out of all Visalia and subjacent surroundings.[30]

That Elijah Perkins was portrayed as such a buffoon had to be a source of gratification for Eva, who undoubtedly held a grudge over his part in bringing the lawmen to the house to arrest Chris. The Evans family, who supplied many of "the facts" on which the play was based, had exacted their revenge.

For Chris Evans, the play also laid the groundwork of his defense, for in the second scene the audience was shown who actually robbed the train at Collis. As the *Examiner* review noted, "Four inhabitants of Mussel Slough in brigand's boots and red cloth masks who deplore their wrongs…hold up a canvas train by tearing a hole in the side and burning a pan of red fire." The *Chronicle* reviewer commented that "it was the shortest robbery on record."[31]

With the innocence of the play's title characters established, the cause of their persecution was then explained. White's production accomplished this with the entrance of his villain: Wily Smooth. In the first act, Eva—alone on stage—wondered aloud why she had such gloomy forebodings. "There is nothing to fear, we have no enemies," she tried to assure herself. And just then, Wily Smooth entered.

SMOOTH:
I startled you. I am very sorry. I was passing and seeing you alone, I thought you would not object to one paying my respects.

EVA:
Certainly not, if that is your only object, Mr. Smooth.

SMOOTH:
What other object could I have? You know my feelings towards you and how persistently you have repulsed me; yet I follow after you like a dog in hopes of a bone.

EVA:
I have never encouraged you to follow me; on the contrary, your attentions are distasteful to me; I have tried in every way to avoid you.

SMOOTH:
I know it, but I contrive to see you occasionally for all that.

EVA:
You intrude yourself upon one. I have no desire to offend you, Mr. Smooth, but I am forced to tell you, once and for all, that our unwelcome visits must be discontinued.

SMOOTH: (angrily)

And I am forced to tell you, just as emphatically, they shall not!
I'll win you by fair means if I can. If not, I'll resort to any means
to accomplish my purpose.

With John Sontag's subsequent entrance, a rivalry is established,
but before John can give Smooth "a lesson on manhood," the cowardly
detective sneaks off.

When Smooth, following the Collis robbery, explains to Deputy
Jud Wilty (the only other character whose name was changed, obviously from George Witty) that he suspects George Sontag, whom he
had shadowed from Minnesota, Wilty asks if he also suspects Chris
Evans and John Sontag.

SMOOTH:

Yes, but I don't want to be too hard on Chris, on account of his
daughter. Confound the girl, she hates me, I know she does and
yet I can't help liking her.

WILTY:

Your liking is thrown away in that quarter; she has no heart for
anyone but John Sontag.

SMOOTH:

Yes, but if John Sontag is implicated in the Collis train robbery,
her heart may turn in another direction, perhaps mine.

And so the scene was set for Smooth's next declaration of love to the
innocent young Eva, who would hear nothing of it.

SMOOTH:

Surely, an avowal of love is interesting to any young girl.

EVA:

Not to me, especially when made by you.

SMOOTH:

Why not?

EVA:

Because you are a man hunter, a hired assassin, a blood hound,
that hunts to death men who never injured you.

SMOOTH:

Hard words, Miss Eva. I'm afraid you have imbibed a hatred for law and order from those who should have taught you to respect it.

EVA:

I have imbibed a hatred for those who, under the protection of the law, hold themselves ready to take men's lives for money. I have imbibed a hatred for the blood-sucking corporation that destroyed the homes and happiness of the people of Mussel Slough. And I have imbibed a loathing for you, and the rest of the sneaking detectives who are ready to commit any crime at the dictation of your masters.

At this point, the audience "greeted each verbal upper cut with approval and made it evident that they were thoroughly in harmony with her anti-railroad sentiments."[32]

SMOOTH:

You should learn to curb your bitter tongue. You are too young and too pretty to give way to vituperation. Come now, be more reasonable. You know how much I love you.

EVA:

Do not touch me! If I thought I could draw your love to me, I should hate myself. Now that you know my opinion of you, go! And cease prowling around this house or it may be the worse for you.

SMOOTH:

If I refuse, what then? What will you do?

EVA:

Protect myself! Or failing that, there are others who will protect me.

SMOOTH:

By others you mean John Sontag, I presume.

EVA:

Yes, John Sontag! And my father!

SMOOTH:
A pair of clods, a couple of hayseeds, who haven't the courage to protect themselves.

EVA:
'Tis true, they're not swaggering gunfighters like you, but hard-working, peaceable men who live by honest labor. But have a care. Go to your kind and leave us in peace or you may regret your intrusion on the clods and hayseeds. [EVA EXITS.]

SMOOTH:
And the clods and hayseeds may regret your treatment of me, my lady. She, evidently, is not aware that George Sontag is laid by the heels. And it'll not be long before Chris and John will keep him company. When suspects once get in the toils of the railroad, they're as good as doomed. [HE TAKES OUT OF POCKET A SACK OF COIN. LOOKS CAUTIOUSLY AROUND.] I found this sack of mutilated and foreign coins at the scene of the robbery. I will bury it in the orchard yonder where it will be found later and thereby fasten the guilt of the robbery on Chris Evans and the Sontags. When they return from the mountains, I'll be on hand with a posse to arrest them. Now then, to bury the sack.

Although the remainder of the play depicted events as they were generally known to the public—the ensuing manhunt, the various gun battles, the capture of Chris and the death of John—the case for self-defense in Chris Evans' upcoming murder trial had thus been presented on the stage of the National Theatre and in the court of public opinion. Just who was being exploited—the Evans family or the sentiments of a public eager to cast the railroad as villain and honest working men as persecuted heroes—is open to debate.

EVA REMAINED THE FOCUS of much of the press coverage after the play opened. Most of the reviews in the San Francisco papers were complimentary of her performance, although they were perhaps more generous in consideration of her youth and lack of experience on the stage. Her greatest booster, the *Examiner*, exemplified a desire that the papers (as well as the public) had to see her do well when they wrote that "Eva Evans is a self-possessed little body, and after her excusable nervousness wore off she put a great deal of spirit into her lines and seemed to enter into her part with real enjoyment and a good deal of appropriation." The reviewer then went on to describe a transformation that seemed to occur as the play progressed:

> That applause that had been fairly hurled at [Eva] since the beginning of the play seemed to spur her on and she played [the scene where she rides to the mountains in boy's clothes] with a real dramatic ability. When it is remembered that she is only sixteen [*sic*] and up to a week or so ago was totally ignorant of anything connected with the stage, her work was really surprising. Mrs. Evans was very nervous and spoke her lines and no more, but Eva really acted and had the audience with her from the opening scene.
>
> Behind the scenes, Eva Evans all but ran the piece. She was as excited and happy as a girl at her first ball, and she was genuinely triumphant over her success. She could not keep still a minute and was all over the place at once, talking, laughing and even dancing with delight. Mrs. Evans moved around in a sort of daze, pleased at her daughter's success and happy at the prospect of earning the money she needs so badly. She has gone through much, however, in the past year and things nowadays hardly rouse her from her listless hopelessness, and she only smiled a sad little smile when Eva hopped off her horse after the fifth act and flung her arms around her.
>
> "I'm not a bit nervous now," said Eva last night about the middle of the play, "but I tell you it made me sick when the curtain rose and I thought of going on before all those people."
>
> "I don't know much about acting yet, but I really like it very much indeed. I think I would gladly become an actress—that is if there were money in it."
>
> Then she fled into her dressing room and audibly requested some one to help find her trousers.[33]

Miss Eva Evans, the train robber's daughter, had become a star.

CHAPTER TWELVE

Trials and Tribulations

W HEN THE NEWS BROKE that George Sontag, from a hospital bed in Folsom Prison, had confessed to the Collis robbery and implicated Chris and John, Molly and Eva were in the middle of a performance at the National Theatre. According to the *San Francisco Examiner*, Eva had just finished one of her denunciations of Wily Smooth when word of the confession made its way backstage. Fearing they would become too upset to continue the performance, R. C. White made sure no one told Eva or her mother. But the rest of the cast and crew heard the startling news and "looked on the two as if a great calamity were hanging over them." Immediately after the performance, a full account of George's damning confession was read to them. Someone had smelling salts standing by just in case. "They listened to the long story," the *Examiner* noted, "and both broke out with a laugh."[1]

A BITTER AND BROKEN MAN, George Contant (newspapers still referred to him as Sontag, but he had reassumed his original surname) felt his only remaining hope was to make a clean breast of everything and, in so doing, work out some kind of a deal. He later claimed he had learned that prison directors had passed a resolution condemning him, once he was well enough to be moved from the prison hospital, to five years solitary confinement in the dungeon. This undoubtedly motivated his cooperation with authorities.[2]

One day in late September, George sent for Warden Charles Aull and told him he wished to confess, adding that he preferred to tell everything to Wells Fargo Detective J. B. Hume and a representative of the Southern Pacific Railroad. George hoped that by making his confession directly to the companies that had been robbed and who offered rewards for the capture of Evans and Sontag, he might be assured of favors. George assumed Wells Fargo and the Southern Pacific had influence with the governor. He asked for several conditions: he wanted his wife and two sons moved from Mankato to Sacramento so that they could visit him; he wanted them furnished with a house and provided money for groceries; and he requested that after a fair and decent interval, he be granted a full pardon. And finally, he insisted that under no circumstances would he talk to detective Will Smith.

The following day, J. B. Wright—a division superintendent of the Southern Pacific Railroad—along with Detective Hume, Warden Aull, and a prison stenographer went to the prison hospital room where George made a lengthy and detailed confession. Wright told reporters that "no inducements were held out to Sontag to confess," but he was assured his statements would not be used against him. Wright did suppose that "the inducement that prompted him above all to confess was the thought of his wife and children, and as he referred to them he raised his hand to wipe his moistened eyes." And although authorities would admit to no deal making, they did point out that they were "favorably impressed at the manner in which Sontag talked" and "thought that they will not object to the convict being granted Executive clemency."[3] A copy of his confession was sent to Governor Markham.

There was more than just self-preservation behind George's decision. He had always felt some animosity toward the Evans family, and those feelings had been recently exacerbated. There was an issue concerning some money Mrs. Sontag had earlier sent for John, which Molly allegedly received but was never able to forward to John. She was unable to, or wouldn't, give the money back to Mrs. Sontag when she came out and, according to George, Molly "didn't want to make the acquaintance of my mother at all." This rude treatment rankled George. He told Detective Hume that "these people slighted her in such a manner that I really cannot express myself as to how I feel about it."[4]

But it was Eva's alleged declaration, right after John's death, thanking God that one of them was dead, and saying "If the other one dies, we are all right," that gnawed at George more than anything.

"Many were the hours I studied over that sentence," George would later write, "before it dawned upon me what she meant." George realized the Evans family was going to try and prove that Chris was not mixed up in any robberies and would claim he was a persecuted man only because he happened to be associated with the Sontag brothers. With John dead, if George too died then they could claim, with no witnesses to prove to the contrary, that Chris was never involved in any robberies. It was with that epiphany, George claimed, that he made his decision to confess.[5] And it was at the conclusion of that confession that he was asked if he would take the stand and testify against Chris Evans.

George's confession was an extensive one. The stenographer could barely keep up with the narrative of nearly ten thousand words. George recounted all the train robberies in which he and his brother, John, and Chris Evans were implicated: Pixley, Goshen, Ceres and Collis in California as well as robberies in Wisconsin and Minnesota. George also detailed the secret planning and arrangements made for his recent jail break, implicating William Fredericks and even, to some degree, Eva. The *Examiner* noted that the confession "mentions a preacher through whom he and Eva Evans corresponded." Officials explained that Sontag gave this preacher letters addressed to Eva that she received. She in turn wrote several letters to Sontag that were handed to him by the preacher. "Parts of the letters, which were written in cipher, were in regard to the weapons used in the battle," the paper stated.[6]

Predictably, Chris Evans flatly denied the allegations in George's confession, labeling it a "string of lies." He took the obvious position that George, in prison with a life term, had everything to gain and nothing to lose. "He wants his freedom," Chris observed, "and hopes by this means to get mercy and freedom through stories false as to me and, so far as I know, false as to John Sontag."[7]

Upon first hearing about the confession, Molly blurted out that she didn't believe George had ever said such things. But upon consideration of the situation, Eva turned more serious and commented that she believed he had indeed said it. "Poor George," she told a reporter. "I guess he has got down to a point where he would lie, even about himself, if he thought it would do any good. He wants a pardon and hopes to get it by this means." Eva then went on to deny she had written any letters to George and knew nothing about supplying him with any guns. (Even though, via her memoir forty years later, she detailed her role in aiding Fredericks to procure those guns.)[8]

Meanwhile, there was little time for Molly and Eva to fret about the impact George's confession might have upon their situation. The play was winding up its initial run at the National Theatre and preparations were under way to take the show on the road.

THE EVANS AND SONTAG COMBINATION was the name of the company R. C. White established to take his theatrical sensation on the road. "Combination" was the term then used for theatrical companies that performed a single play for the season on a prearranged tour. Touring combinations flourished in the last two decades of the nineteenth century; their proliferation largely made possible by the railroads.[9]

The touring schedule of most combinations was grueling. Shows usually played no more than two or three nights in any given town. What made these prodigious schedules feasible were, of course, the railroads. Most railroads offered special rates to traveling companies, such as a two-cent-per-mile reduction plus a free baggage car for scenery pieces, costumes, and other necessities, if enough tickets were sold. The majority of companies traveled in coaches right alongside other passengers—it was only the big stars like Sarah Bernhardt or Helena Modjeska who traveled in lavishly appointed private Pullmans. For actors in combinations, the acting profession meant basically living on a train, broken up only by the endless procession of towns, hotels, and theatres.[10]

For Eva, this exhausting schedule was compounded by the physical demands of her starring role. White knew the expectations of seeing Eva in pantaloons astride a horse helped bring in the crowds, but working with the animal was sometimes problematic. In some of the smaller theatres, they had to forego the horse and Eva would run on after a stagehand created the sounds of hoof beats and the stomping of a horse off-stage. But at least the men in the audience got to see the beautiful young Eva in pants.

At the Hazzard Pavilion in Los Angeles, a platform constructed to make a runway for the horse collapsed, Eva and her steed crashing down with it. Neither was seriously injured, although Eva suffered scratches and bruises.

In Oakland, White searched to find a trained horse. Eva requested he find one with some life in him, complaining she was "tired of old saw horses." White eventually obtained a beautiful bay, which Eva thought she could handle. Apparently the horse was not stage trained and Eva was not prepared for what happened:

> When he was about half-way downstage, he became terrified by the footlights and started backing crossways toward the wings. The canvas trees that were set in front of each entrance had scal-

loped pieces of wood back of the foliage. He smashed into one of these, and then collapsed with me. I felt a pain across my back like fire, but I got him to his feet without getting out of the saddle.

When the curtain fell, someone lifted me out of the saddle and I started to cry, saying "I'm sorry I couldn't finish the scene." Someone said, "Why, you did finish the scene! Snow and Hess (the actors that played Dad and John) rushed across the stage to help you with the horse, but you had him up by the time they reached you, and started right in on your lines. Don't you hear the applause? Half the audience are on their feet."[11]

Eva was not aware that she had spoken a word.

A few hours after that performance, she realized she was injured, but did not know how serious for some time. After finishing the week in Oakland, a doctor told her that three of her vertebrae had been pushed aside and were inflamed. After a week of bed rest, the doctor gave her morphine to dull the pain and the show went on. That injury, and the subsequent treatment, would haunt the young actress for years to come.

WHILE THE PLAY DID WELL in the Bay Area—where Evans and Sontag had received so much sympathetic coverage—the San Joaquin Valley was another story. The public there was far less sympathetic; they were, however, just as curious. Many of the valley papers had roundly criticized the production since its announcement, but, as the *Visalia Delta* noted, the two performances at the Barton Opera House in Fresno "drew a bigger audience than Sarah Bernhardt, the great French tragedienne." The reporter could not resist editorializing, however, that "there is no accounting for tastes."[12]

After playing Fresno, the Evans and Sontag Combination headed south, playing at the Armory Hall in Bakersfield before proceeding to Los Angeles, where they performed for three nights at the Park Theatre. The company then headed east to San Bernardino. A theatrical journal noted that the play was "denounced from the pulpit at San Bernardino, with the startling result that the house was packed for two nights, when it was expected that the opposition would hurt business." The article concluded that "clergymen are sometimes handy for advertising purposes."[13]

The company then returned to the San Joaquin Valley where they faced regional opposition. They were unable to secure a venue in Visalia. As the *San Francisco Examiner* explained, the town where the bandits lived and where they killed and wounded several respected officers of the law declared they would not permit the performance at all. Eva, who had earlier commented on how much she looked forward to playing her hometown, now admitted that performing there would be uncomfortable and it would "not be worthwhile to play Visalia."[14]

Things wouldn't be any more comfortable in Hanford. Because the melodrama, in explaining Evans and Sontag's innocence, attributed the train robbery at Collis to four masked men who represented the settlers of Mussel Slough, the people of nearby Hanford were said to be even "fiercer against the play than in Visalia." In an editorial published by the *Hanford Journal*, the paper called the Evans and Sontag play a "libel on our old citizens, a libel on the officers of the law, and is put upon the stage to raise money and create sympathy for the boldest and most red-handed bandit California has ever produced." The paper suggested "it should be suppressed, if not by law, then by popular protest."[15] Indeed, as reported in the *Fresno Morning Republican*, the local theatre in Hanford refused to do business with the Evans and Sontag Combination, and White had to secure a barn for the performance.[16]

The notices for the Hanford performance contained the harshest criticisms yet. One Hanford paper began its review with the following poem, entitled "To Eva":

> *Eva, dear, thou art remembered*
> *In this land of Mussel Slough;*
> *In our hearts thou hast engendered*
> *Memories of a blonde hoodoo.*
> *Once before we saw thee, Eva,*
> *'Twas the Fourth of last July;*
> *Saw thee in the gallery, Eva,*
> *Ere you played the "Alibi."*
>
> *Eva! Then had'st dreamy visions*
> *Of the world thou wouldst surprise,*
> *And its smoky intermissions*
> *Pass'd before your heaven-blue eyes?*
> *Didst thou ever dream then, Eva,*
> *'Pon this stage, in tragic rants,*

Thous shouldst ever swagger, Eva,
In a pair of "boy's size" pants?

Eva, tho' thy head is swelling,
Girded with a silver band,
And your voice with pathos welling,
Pray don't overlook your hand.
And remember some day, Eva,
Thou'lt exhaust thy stock of blood;
Then, oh then! You'll tumble, Eva,
With a dull and sickening thud.

The review that followed admitted that while it initially looked as if it was going to be a poor house, hordes of people swarmed in from the country and filled the auditorium. The drama was synopsized with phrases like "pathetic scenes were indulged in," and "the escape was wretchedly carried out." When commenting on the stars—the local celebrities everyone came to see—the reviewer got downright personal. Although he maintained that "the less said about Mrs. Chris Evans, the better," he was compelled to say more, observing that she was "never built for an actress and would make a bigger success at any time peeling potatoes than tearing off yards of prose."

Eva, the reviewer kindly suggested, "should employ some one who understands how to make-up." His attack of her personal appearance continued, noting that "her 'salt grass' speeches delivered in an 'alkali' voice, are delivered with an unnatural blinking of the eyes," which he theorized were caused by "the dabs of black on her eyelids and underneath her eyes, which bear evidence of being smeared on by some artist in stove polish." He concluded that her rouge was evidently smeared on "with the palm of the hand."[17]

Nonetheless, business was brisk in Hanford. The SRO (standing room only) sign had to be hung out and, as the *Tulare Times* wryly observed, even though "nobody claims to have seen it," the house was "filled to overflowing."[18] Eva was learning a lesson that R. C. White well understood: in show business, the only bad press was no press.

AT THIS POINT, IT IS WORTH REMEMBERING the member of the Evans and Sontag Combination who served as original liaison between White and the Evans family—James Evans. What small role he may have portrayed on stage in the touring melodrama is unknown, but he soon became Eva's real-life leading man. Eva and Jim Evans stopped off in Fresno after the Hanford shows and got married. Although Eva never mentioned it in her memoir—indeed, there is no evidence in her lengthy narrative that Jim Evans even existed—according to divorce papers later filed in Tulare County, the couple "inter-married at the City of Fresno...on or about the ninth day of November, 1893."[19] If Jim Evans wasn't related to the Evans family before, he was now.

The couple then headed up to Stockton, rejoining the Evans and Sontag Combination for three shows at the Avon Theatre. According to one news report, the so-called contract marriage (reporters apparently did not realize they'd been legally married) was first learned of when the tour was in Stockton, because Eva informed the company she was staying behind at the hotel with Jim Evans, her "husband." It was, in effect, their honeymoon.

Eva's relationship with the tall and lean Jim Evans greatly disturbed Molly, at least according to newspaper reports when the rumor of their union finally circulated. The papers didn't report the marriage until late November, calling it a contract marriage and claiming it had been entered into three months earlier. One newspaper explained that Eva and Jim had entered into the "contract marriage" because Eva was underage, and they would officially wed when she turned eighteen. A later report claimed Molly was so angry about the union that she demanded they have it annulled.[20]

It is impossible to know the exact circumstances of this marriage because the only sources are speculative newspaper rumors and, more concretely, divorce papers later filed in Tulare County. If news reports dating its genesis back to August or September were accurate, this means Eva and Jim started some sort of romantic relationship just about the time they began working together on the play. This would have been only a few weeks after John's death and doesn't speak of a significant period of mourning for her supposed beloved. Also, there is the issue of Jim's possible blood relation and the matter of intermarriage. (Although cousins could legally marry in California, and the practice remains, to this day, more common than many might guess.)[21] Whether they had an actual church wedding or a secret civil ceremony is also unknown, but considering the time it took before the news circulated, the latter is most likely.

It is also possible that the marriage was really a sham, set up for financially or socially advantageous reasons that time has obscured. But

Eva's utter silence on the subject suggests that whatever the circumstances surrounding the marriage, she regretted it and wished it had never happened.

News of her marriage had potential to be worse press than no press. The *Fresno Expositor* predicted it would hurt the play, explaining that "in spite of all sentiment and fact, there was much sympathy for Eva, struggling to make money to defend her father. It was the considering of her in that light that brought most of the success. That romance is largely brushed away now, and the best part of the play has lost its spirit." The paper went on to say that while it is a commendable ambition in a young woman to wish to be happily married, "Eva Evans displayed poor financiering when she let her marriage become public."[22]

Another reporter, who admittedly was thrilled at seeing the "beautiful maiden with the bloom of virginal innocence...clad in trousers and astraddle of a horse," now felt betrayed to learn "she was even then married, and that the bloom had been mussed, and that my sweet thought was a misfit." He complained that if he hadn't, as a reviewer, been admitted to the theatre for free, he would demand his four bits back. "Doesn't she know that no man would warp his eye and impair his eyesight just to see a married woman's trousers on both sides of a horse!"[23]

Despite the threat of Eva's married derriere warping men's virtuous eyesight, the show continued to play to large audiences. The Evans and Sontag Combination headed north to Sacramento in early December. There it would be briefly postponed, as Eva was called upon to appear on an entirely different sort of stage for a command performance.

EVA EVANS WAS SUMMONED to Fresno shortly after the Evans and Sontag Combination arrived in Sacramento. As one local newspaper reported, the manager "received a telegram from Fresno, commanding the presence in that city of Eva Evans, who is wanted to testify in the trial of her father." An understudy—presumably the playwright's own daughter, Laura White—performed the role for two nights at the Armory Hall in Sacramento. A short review in the *Sacramento Bee* noted that the "sensational melodrama" played before good-sized houses, even though Eva Evans was unable to appear.[24] The real show now worth writing about was in a Fresno courthouse, 175 miles away.

By the time Eva headed down to Fresno, the trial was well underway, but she could have followed it in excruciating detail in the daily papers of any city in California. Her mother had already left the tour to be with Chris and attended the trial from almost its inception.

Jury selection had begun November 21, 1893, and the papers reported on this process for several days until finally, on November 29, headlines proclaimed: "Twelve Jurors Secured."[25] It was difficult finding jurors who were unbiased, considering factors such as the extensive press coverage; prevalent animosity for either the alleged train robbers (although "alleged" wasn't a word even known by the press) or the railroad corporation; and the large circle of acquaintances Chris and John had in the area. The Evans family secretly felt that their only hope lay in a hung jury—they only needed one sympathetic juror.[26]

The prosecution equally feared such a possibility and challenged many prospective jurors during voir dire. They had detectives and informants helping them sniff out possible problem jurors. In a letter to detective Will Smith, an informant told that he had a talk with "Chris and Clark Moore and Ed Coffey. Told me that they had one jurreyman [*sic*] on the jury [*sic*] that would hang the jurry for ever before he would convict Chris. His name is Pixford." The letter was signed only "your friend," but was presumably from Perry Byrd. Newspaper reports show a T. W. Pickford summoned on the special venire, but when the final twelve men were chosen, Mr. Pickford was not on the jury.[27]

Having investigators and informants supporting the legal team was, of course, by no means illicit; any good legal team investigates witnesses and profiles prospective jurors. In fact, there is reference in Smith's correspondence that the Evans family was involved in similar behind-the-scenes work. One letter addressed to Will Smith, dated November 27, 1893, on Palace Hotel stationery, describes a shady character working for the defense. "He has a lot of names of witnesses and he is interviewing them to find out what they know. He goes by the name here Frank Morey, but his right name is E. Morrell and says that he stops round the Grand Central Hotel in Fresnoe [*sic*]. Mrs. E has hired him to work for her. He was in jail for knocking a Salvation Army man down in Fresnoe so you can find him."[28]

When prosecuting attorney W. D. Tupper made his opening remarks, he indicated that the people would show that, as motive for the killing of officers Vic Wilson and Andy McGinnis, "on the 3rd of August, 1892, these men [Chris Evans and John Sontag] and George Sontag robbed the train near Collis." Despite objections raised by defense attorney Samuel J. Hinds that the train robbery was irrelevant to the murder charges on which his client had been indicted, Judge M. K. Harris permitted the statement.[29] Here was an early indication of the issue on which the trial would hinge. Although Chris had not been charged with train robbery, his murder trial became a de facto trial for just such an offense. The prosecution maintained that because Chris and John were guilty of train robbery, the law officers had every right—indeed, it was their lawful duty—to capture them. Thus a plea of self-defense could not apply.

The list of witnesses for the prosecution included anyone with information pertaining to the train robbery or the movements of Chris Evans and the Sontags. George Roberts, the Wells Fargo messenger on the train testified. Al Phipps, the train's engineer, recounted his story of the robbery. Frank Bequette testified that he rented a team and buggy to John Sontag. James Arness, a Fresno livery man, testified that Sontag put up the team at his place the night before the robbery. P. H. Patterson swore that George had stayed at his lodging house in Fresno for several days. A. D. Davis testified that Evans stayed at his Traver ranch just prior to the robbery. A detective, Thomas Bury, testified that he saw George and Chris together in Fresno. Edward Politz recounted how he had shipped two sacks of silver coin, one containing Peruvian money, via Wells Fargo.

It shouldn't have come as any surprise who the prosecution would call next, but it was. This witness had been clandestinely transported by train from Folsom the previous night. Instead of being brought to the jail, he had been quartered in the depot under special guard. The *San Francisco Call* provided the following account of what happened next.

> "Call George Sontag," said Attorney Tupper, one of the attorneys for the people. There was a buzz and ripple of excitement all over the courtroom, and Evans looked up with a smile which seemed to say "Let him come."
>
> Evans soon turned pale, and just then George Sontag came hobbling in on crutches, with a large overcoat on, and looking nearly as he did when on his trial here a year ago.
>
> Attorney Hinds began objections at once and the asking of questions was delayed. Sontag sat toying with his short mustache and did not seem quite at ease. He looked by quick glances about the courtroom, but if his eyes met those of Evans neither gave any

visible indication. Evans soon recovered his usual color, leaned back in his chair and waited for the attorneys to get through with their objections.

The examination of Sontag was very long, he being questioned minutely on every point connected with his relations with Evans and the train robbery.[30]

George was a useful witness—his dates, names, and places were thoroughly accurate. His testimony was said to be even more complete than that of his confession and, for Chris, even more damning. Even Eva admitted that "under the gentle questioning" of the prosecuting attorney, the "story flowed smoothly." She maintained, however, that he wavered under cross-examination. Although some of the headlines in the San Francisco dailies agreed—he squirmed on the stand according to the *Call*—Hinds' continued assertion that because George lied before in his own trial, he would lie again had little effect in diminishing the damaging impact of his testimony against Chris.[31]

The *Fresno Morning Republican*, observing that George didn't appear coached in any way, explained that "in his own trial he had told many lies in his effort to save himself….and having failed he was now telling how he robbed the train." The paper also noted that George said he first told the truth about this matter during his confession "on his hospital couch at Folsom." Pressed by Hinds' cross-examination, George admitted he would lie again if he thought he could get liberty by it, but "he stated that he thought his veracity was on a par with the best."[32]

After a number of witnesses had detailed the events at Young's cabin and the killing of Wilson and McGinnis, the prosecution concluded its case. The defense then moved to strike out all evidence connecting Evans with the Collis robbery, arguing that the unsupported confession of George Sontag was all that had been produced implicating Chris Evans. The motion was denied.

On December 7, 1893, defense attorney Hinds offered an opening statement before calling his witnesses. He explained to the jury that "George and John Sontag were the guilty parties and were sheltering under Evans' good name." In support of this, a large number of witnesses would be called to the stand, all of them substantial citizens, who would speak of Evans' good reputation. Hinds indicated that the defense for the incidents at Young's cabin would be that Evans and Sontag were cornered, and having been told again and again that no quarter would be given them, felt they had to fight or die. Everyone knew this would be the essence of his defense, but Hinds also explained he would show why the prosecution did not ask Will Smith to testify concerning the "scrimmage at Evans' house, where he called one of the children a liar."[33] This seemingly minor detail was key, as it would show motive for Chris' first battle with lawmen and his subsequent flight—the actions of a wholly innocent man defending his beloved daughter's virtue.

WHEN THE MIDNIGHT TRAIN from Sacramento arrived in Fresno that night, Eva Evans was on board. Her sister, Winifred, had come up from Visalia earlier that day. As reported in the *San Francisco Examiner*, the sisters would testify the next day "that Will Smith and Witty called them names and came to the house with pistols in their hands. The idea is of course to justify the first shooting that occurred at the house in Visalia."[34] And so the stage was set for the fledgling actress. She would choose her wardrobe carefully, take great care in her personal appearance, and carry herself with grace and confidence. She had undoubtedly practiced her lines. The audience for this performance would include twelve men who would decide the fate of her beloved father. This would be the performance of her life.

CHAPTER THIRTEEN

Conviction

———◆———

*In the afternoon Eva Evans went on the stand. She showed the
result of her theatrical training, from the kiss that touched her
father's cheek to the last word she gave the lawyers.*

———SAN FRANCISCO EXAMINER, DECEMBER 9, 1893

T HE ARRIVAL IN COURT OF THE EVANS FAMILY on the day Eva
was to testify was a theatrical moment to rival any in the stage
play. After having arrived in Fresno the evening before, Eva
accompanied her mother to the train station to meet the rest of the children, who rode up from Visalia with their Grannie Byrd. The family
then made their way to the courthouse. As the *San Francisco Examiner*
described it, there was "a whole busload of tow-headed boys and blue-
eyed girls. They drifted into the courtroom by pairs and threes, joked
with their father and were told to keep still by their mother, and alto-
gether seemed quite at home."[1] The presence of his seven children was
no doubt a calculated move by the defense to remind jurors that Chris
Evans was a devoted family man. With his oldest daughter—the one
with whom he shared the deepest bond—about to testify on his behalf,
pride filled Chris Evans' heart.

Chris undoubtedly noticed the change in Eva's appearance. She had
matured. No longer was she, as one reporter observed, "the slender,
tussled-headed young girl doing chores at the Evans home or going
shopping in Visalia in a home-spun dress." She was, according to the
Examiner, "an actress now and she shows it in her dress, in her voice
and in her manner. She has caught the stage laugh and the stage carriage and is more professional than many who have been half a lifetime

behind the footlights." Eva presented her testimony in, as one Fresno paper put it, "accents slightly Thespian." Another local newspaper noted that she "told her story in an easy manner, as though familiar with it."[2] These comments hint that her testimony was viewed as a carefully constructed, well-rehearsed alibi designed to support her father's case. Two things were key to his defense: that his explosive reaction to Smith and Witty at his home and subsequent flight was caused by *their* brash actions and not by any consciousness of guilt, and that once on the run, he had legitimate reason to fear his life was in danger from blood-hunters intent on killing him first and asking questions later.

Two episodes related by Eva would support this defense with all the colorful dramatics worthy of a blood and thunder melodrama. As in any first-hand account, the ratio of fact to fiction must be taken on faith. It is, however, ironic to imply that Eva may have altered the truth in relating these incidents, for it was an accusation of lying that launched the action of the real-life drama.

A "DAMNED LITTLE LIAR" was the phrase that would become part of the popular lexicon surrounding the saga of Evans and Sontag, although Eva never claimed in court that Smith had used that exact phrase. (She did, however, use the phase in her memoir written decades later.) The *San Francisco Examiner* offered a detailed account of her testimony:

Eva Evans, in a stylish brown coat, came in, kissed her father on both cheeks, fluttered over to her mother for a second and then mounted to the witness stand.

"Do you know a man named Will Smith?" asked [G. G.] Goucher [attorney for the defense team].

"I have met Mr. Smith," said she, precisely, with a lift of her eyebrows.

"Tell how and where you met him."

She faced the jury, adjusted her hat, which was a shade askew, and told how Smith and Witty had come to the door of Evans' house while she and a younger sister were there. "Where is Sontag?" I heard one of the gentleman say. I stopped sewing, arose and walked towards the door. I told the gentlemen that I did not know where Mr. Sontag was. I thought he was about the place and said I would see if I could find him."

"What reply did they make?"[3]

The *Examiner*'s account, understandably, streamlined the dialogue, but when compared to actual court transcripts, it proves accurate. Rather than simply ask what reply Eva made, court transcripts show the tedious manner of lawyerly courtroom questioning:

Q: Did you address that remark to either of the gentlemen in particular, or was it a general answer to the two.
A: Just a general answer.
Q: Do you know which one it was spoke?
A: No sir, I had never met the gentlemen before.
Q: Well, I know, not as to whether you knew the man.
A: Oh, it was Mr. Smith that addressed the remark to me.
Q: What was said then, next, if anything, after you replied in that way?
A: "You are a lier [*sic*]. I saw Mr. Sontag enter this house not five minutes ago."[4]

After careful questioning regarding the layout of the house and the determination that no further conversation took place between Eva and the two men, she explained to the court how she walked "out the door leading through the hall and onto the back porch. There I met my father and I told him there was some gentlemen, a couple of men in the house, that wanted to see Sontag and that when I told them I didn't know where he was, that he called me a lier [*sic*] and he says 'all right, I will go and see what they want.'"

Eva claimed her father picked up a revolver from the bedroom before entering the front room to ask the two men what they wanted. They repeated the question of "Where is Sontag?"

A: And he says "I don't think Sontag is here. I think he went up town a few moments ago," and he says "he did not. I saw him cross from Mrs. Byrd's house here an instant ago."
Q: Very well.
A: And then Mr. Smith stepped forward and in a minute the shooting began. There was not any more said.
Q: Well, did you see anybody else besides the parties already named?

A: Mr. Sontag then stepped out of that bedroom door and as he did Mr. Smith drew his gun and fired and then the shooting began on the outside of the house.

Q: Mr. Smith, you say, drew his gun and fired. You mean a pistol, or a revolver?

A: Revolver.[5]

And so while Eva never made mention of any cursing, she did assert that Smith had called her a liar, that she told her father of this insult, and that when tempers flared it was Smith who drew his gun and fired first.

Eva's testimony was then interrupted when she was asked if she had seen a letter written to her father by Mrs. Evans, telling him that it was unsafe to surrender. The question "called forth the hottest controversy between the attorneys since the trial began." The prosecution objected to the content of the letter as hearsay, and after heated discussion the judge decided to "hold the matter under abeyance until tomorrow morning."[6] Eva was dismissed and would have to continue her testimony another day.

As the newspapers reported, eleven-year-old Winifred Evans was then called to the stand and basically echoed her older sister's testimony. The most interesting aspect of her testimony, however, centered on the one word Eva had left out and made it look, for a moment, as if she was going to contradict her sister's version of events. The following is a direct quote of the court transcript:

Q: Have you stated all the words that Smith said up to the time your father appeared?

A: Yes sir.

Q: Up to the time your father came?

A: Yes sir.

Q: Didn't he say that you were—you will have to excuse the word, the use of this word, because I want to use it now—didn't he say to Eva that she was a damned lier [sic]?

A: No sir.

Q: Are you positive on that subject, are you sure about that?

A: Yes sir.

Q: Just repeat his words again, what did he say?

A: "You are a lier, I saw him come into this room not five minutes ago."[7]

Obviously someone at sometime had claimed Smith used the word "damn." (Why else would the lawyer use it in his questioning?) But on this day, the Evans girls were content to tell the world Smith had simply called Eva a liar; and that, the defense hoped, was damning enough.

THE NEXT DAY EVA was recalled to the stand and offered a colorful story that supported the central theme of Chris Evans' defense. Eva testified that she had gone to see her father in the mountains and that she told him she had "talked with a number of citizens, a great number, neighbors and friends, and that they had heard that the posse, every man, was all armed, and they intended to make a fighting arrest, or if they resisted in any way, to kill them and they would not even give them a show, that they thought they were desperate men and they intended when they met them not to take any chance."[8]

Despite objections from the prosecution, the court allowed Eva to relate second-hand knowledge of a boastful claim made by Vic Wilson. The defense pointed out it should be allowed "because she heard it and believed it and related it to her father as part of the reason why he should not come back to Visalia." Judge M. K. Harris concurred, telling Eva to proceed with her story.

> A: Jack Camlin told me that he overheard Vic Wilson—
> Q: Jack who?
> A: Jack Camlin. He told me that he overheard Mr. Wilson telling a crowd of men that he had 27 notches on his gun and that he had killed 27 men, and that Evans and Sontag would make 29, and that he intended, that he had come up from Arizona with the purpose of getting these men, and that one or the other, Vic Wilson or Evans and Sontag, would be brought out of the mountains dead, and that if they had any money to bet, that they had better bet it on Chris Evans being brought out on a stretcher.[9]

This colorful illustration of a kill-or-be-killed attitude by lawmen fit perfectly with the Evans defense, and the melodramatic nature of Eva's tale was natural fodder for the newspapers. Ironically, neither this nor the "damned little liar" episode from Eva's testimonies were part of R. C. White's lurid stage depiction of events, although each would later become central set-pieces for the lasting legend of Evans and Sontag in numerous books and articles.

With Eva's initial testimony complete, it came time for the prosecution to question the teenage daughter of Chris Evans. Several newspapers noted that "the cross-examination of Eva failed to shake her testimony."[10] This is not to say the prosecution wasn't relentless in their questioning. Prosecution attorney W. D. Tupper harped on every detail ad nauseum, but Eva never wavered in her answers. The extent of his questioning is best illustrated by the page count of the trial transcript. The cross-examination comprised nearly seventy-five pages of typewritten transcript, while Eva's defense testimony tallied of a mere thirty pages. This supports Eva's later memory when she recalled that while her initial testimony was brief, the cross examination was "long and cruel."[11]

Eva was challenged on one point that illustrated the growing rift between her and the Byrd family. She was asked about a conversation she had with Mrs. Perry Byrd and her cousin, Edith. "Did you not say that at the time Witty and Smith came to your house and the shooting commenced, you were over at your Grandmother Byrd's house?" Eva simply replied she had not. Then Tupper asked Eva if her cousin Edith had asked, "Why were you so persistent in saying that Smith insulted you?" and that Eva answered "because she couldn't think of anything better to say against Smith."[12] This implies that Eva had lied and shows that, at the very least, Edith Byrd was talking against her cousin Eva. But Eva was unshaken. She insisted she remembered only that Edith and her mother were away for a month after the troubles and that no such conversation took place.

When Eva was recalled later that day for further direct, she offered an explanation for the rift with her uncle's family. It was, she stated, because Perry Byrd had betrayed her father and caused him to be shot down like a dog at Stone Corral. "Is that the reason you are not friendly?" defense attorney Goucher asked. "Yes sir, for that reason," Eva confirmed.[13] The defense hoped this would diffuse any damaging information originating from the Byrd side of the family.

As the trial drew to a close, George Sontag was recalled to the stand by the prosecution. When asked if Eva had ever related to him the events at her house when Witty and Smith came looking for John Sontag, he recounted a conversation he'd had with Eva where she told the story of that fateful day, but said nothing about either Smith or Witty firing a shot to start the fight. (During earlier cross-examination of Eva, she was hounded about what she told George of these events, and she continually insisted she didn't remember what she may or may not have told him.)[14] While the prosecution tried with both Edith Byrd and George Sontag to discredit Eva's testimony, they were unable to conclusively do so. Even though the prosecution brought conflicting versions of Eva's story to light, they were never able to shake her from anything but her well-rehearsed, well-prepared account. Through her sheer conviction and the subsequent repetition by the newspapers, it became popularly accepted that Smith had called Eva a liar (whether he cursed or not), thus inflaming the temper of Chris Evans. And who didn't believe the irresistible account of Vic Wilson bragging about notches on his gun? But were these points enough to earn acquittal? All Eva could do now was pray.

LATE IN THE AFTERNOON of December 13, 1893, the jury was given the case in the people versus Chris Evans. Several hours later, the jury asked for a copy of the judge's instructions and they continued their deliberations, finally retiring for the night at nearly eleven o'clock. At this point, defense attorney S. J. Hinds told a reporter he believed one juror was holding out for a favorable verdict and "would stay there to the end of his days before he would convict."[15] In fact, the jury had reached, on their third ballot, a unanimous guilty verdict, but it took several more ballots before they could agree on the degree of offense. What started out at eight for first-degree murder, one for second-degree, and three for manslaughter eventually landed at a unanimous conviction of first-degree murder. It took three more surveys to determine their recommendation for sentencing.[16] Perhaps a compromise in arriving at the first degree conviction motivated the two jurors who held out for the death penalty to agree to life in prison. Or perhaps, as one newspaper supposed, the consideration that prevented the death penalty "was the fact that, having lost his right eye and left hand, he would be disqualified to engage in the pursuit of train robbery even should some governor be found hereafter who would pardon him."[17] One thing was for sure: it had been a long night for the jurors, but it would be a longer one still for the Evans family, who would have to wait until the following morning to hear the verdict in court.

"I was not at the trial when the verdict was brought in," wrote Eva in her memoir four decades later. As she remembered it, she had returned to join the touring combination at R. C. White's behest because her understudy was not up to snuff. "She could not ride, and Mr. White had already had protests over the substitution." Eva claimed she was in Santa Rosa with the tour when the verdict was read. Shortly after their arrival there, she vividly recalled, the Sister Superior of an orphanage for girls sent word that on the following morning a Mass, with the little girls singing the responses, would be said for her father's acquittal. "I was listening to children's voices when the foreman of the jury announced they had found him guilty as charged, and fixed his penalty at life imprisonment."[18] Eva seldom got her dates confused in her memoir, but did in this instance. A newspaper report showed that the Evans and Sontag melodrama was scheduled at the Ridgeway Hall in Santa Rosa on December 2, 1893.[19] This was nearly two weeks before the verdict was read, and so while Eva may have indeed listened to Catholic school girls sing a Mass for her father, it was not at the same instant that the verdict was announced in Fresno. According to several newspapers, Eva was indeed in the courtroom to hear the decision read. "Eva wept bitterly in silence," it was reported.[20] Perhaps the memory was too painful to admit, and so Eva replaced it, either consciously or not, with the lilting voices of children singing in a Santa Rosa church.

Chris Evans, despite the wishes of so many, would not be sent to the gallows. At least Eva had consolation in that. She later wrote:

I had been so obsessed by the threat of death by hanging for him, that I had given little thought to the fact that he might be sent to prison for life. And here it was in all its stark reality. A broken man, with a bullet in his head, but not really old. He was forty-seven, and if he regained his tremendous strength he might live for years, shut away from the mountains he loved. But he would be alive! I could see him—hear his voice! He could go on helping us to direct our lives. No one could ever say to the children, "Your father was hung."[21]

EVA REJOINED THE MELODRAMA tour immediately after the trial. R. C. White was happy to have his star attraction back on board, for her absence was not good for ticket sales. Some newspapers were already proclaiming the show had run its course, and when the touring combination shut down for Christmas, many wondered if it would ever resume. For Eva, the hiatus was a well-needed vacation and gave her the chance to be with her family during this difficult period. It certainly wasn't a happy Christmas for the Evans family.

Chris was particularly distraught to learn he had no hope of appeal before being sent to the state prison at Folsom. As was later reported, when his attorney gave him this news, he "looked straight into the eyes of the lawyer and said, with terrible deliberation, 'I will not go to the penitentiary. I will not do it. My family shall not have that disgrace.'"[22]

Molly had never held up well during stress, and this period proved to be no exception. It was reported, upon her first visit with Chris in his jail cell following the trial, that "Mrs. Evans' grief broke forth in tears" and she almost immediately fainted. A doctor was summoned, and "for some time she went from one fainting fit into another. It took some time to overcome her hysteria and subdue her grief."[23]

Eva was, in many ways, the rock of the family. But who did she lean on for strength? With her mother hysterical and her father doomed to life in prison, did Eva find solace in her own marriage? It is easy to forget that she married James Evans only a few short months earlier. That it was a genuine marriage is questionable. A comment in a Fresno paper sheds some light on the state of their relationship. "Eva's contract husband, Jim Evans, is said to be in San Francisco, and has been away from Visalia for several days."[24] That he wasn't with her during this particularly difficult time offers some clue on the state of the marriage.

A clue to Chris Evans' state of mind can be found in Eva's reaction to a request he made. She wrote in her memoir:

> I learned now that there was no hope of an appeal, no chance for a retrial. I had never seen Dad with such a desperate look in his eyes. As soon as we were alone, he said, "Eva, I can't go to prison for life. I want you to get me a gun."
>
> "Dad! You don't mean to kill yourself?"
>
> "Nothing of the sort. I'm going to get out!"
>
> "You can't; I've heard that there are extra guards all around the jail."
>
> "Listen, dear; I have a plan." When he had finished, he said, "You have always been a good soldier. Now take orders. Get me a gun."
>
> "I'll try, Dad."
>
> "That's my girl."[25]

Did Chris Evans really expect his teenage daughter to help break him out of the Fresno county jail by herself?

"A YOUNG WAITER NAMED ED MORRELL had spoken of the admiration he had for my father," Eva once wrote. "I went to him and said, 'If you think so much of my father, would you be willing to help him?'"[26] While there isn't anything patently untrue about this statement, it is purposely misleading. Ed Morrell was not just some waiter with whom Eva happened to be acquainted. He was well-known to the Evans family and had been their confederate for many months. Furthermore, it is not too far-fetched to speculate romantic attraction between Eva and the handsome, young Ed Morrell.

Morrell was born Martin Delaney in 1868 of Irish ancestry and ran away from the Pennsylvania coal fields at an early age. After coming to California, he got work at a Riverside hotel using the alias of Ed Martin, where he stole some money from a room and quickly left town. He was later arrested and convicted of grand larceny in San Bernardino. He was sentenced to two-and-a-half years in prison and sent to San Quentin. There he befriended an old convict, the notorious stage robber Milton Harvey Lee. Morrell agreed to help Lee once he was paroled.[27]

Morrell was released in March 1893 and headed for the San Joaquin Valley. Once in Fresno, he looked up Lee's ex-wife, now married to a man named Hutchinson, who had adopted Lee's two daughters, Grace and Rose. Grace, the older of the two girls, had married her stepbrother, Jim Hutchinson. Jim and his younger brothers had, themselves, all seen the inside of the local jail on various occasions. Ed Morrell had hooked up with a family that couldn't be a good influence on the recently paroled convict.

According to Grace Hutchinson, Morrell once stole a horse from her and when he returned he was full of Evans and Sontag stories. After Morrell disappeared again, he came back and led Grace to believe he'd had something to do with George Sontag's escape. He had some bullet wounds and stories of being cornered at a sawmill in Nevada City by lawmen chasing him and William Fredericks. And just as she had helped Fredericks obtain guns for George Sontag's escape attempt, Eva was now helping Ed Morrell supply arms for a proposed jailbreak.

Morrell and Fredericks may have had more than one thing in common. Ed Morrell can be seen as the most recent in a series of men infatuated with Eva. His feelings for the attractive daughter of Chris Evans are evidenced in a 1906 letter he wrote to California governor George C. Pardee applying for a pardon. "I was in love with Miss Eva Evans," Morrell claimed, "and all my after course and actions can easily be read between the lines."[28] Although she was still a teenager shy of legal age, numerous men had already been romantically linked to Eva. There was, of course, her supposed fiancé, John Sontag, who was more than seventeen years her senior. Speaking of older men, there was her friendship with the notorious womanizer, Petey Bigelow (perhaps their shared trip to San Francisco wasn't completely innocent). Although little is known about Jim Evans, he and Eva were married (how legitimate or romantic their marriage was is open to speculation). And if speculating about Eva's romantic liaisons, William Fredericks presents himself as one more possible candidate, especially when considering the fond way she remembered him in her memoir (beyond writing that he was "really nice and I liked him very much," Eva later lamented his life of crime and although she had tried to help him, she suffered the sad news of his execution at San Quentin).

And now there was Ed Morrell. While it is titillating to speculate these men may have enjoyed Eva's company and perhaps even her bed, it is equally evident that they meant little to Eva. They were nothing more than temporary diversions, for her heart had always belonged to her father. And Eva and Ed Morrell were now united to serve his interest.

It is hard to know exactly how and when Morrell fell in with the Evans family. If Morrell's later writings are to be believed, he was a double agent working as an undercover detective for Will Smith. In his book, *The Twenty-Fifth Man*, Morrell claimed he met with "Big Bill Smith," who brashly demanded to know, "What is your business with me?" Morrell told the Southern Pacific detective that he was "familiar with his work and had come to offer a plan which would bring about the capture of the outlaws, provided however that [Smith] would do the square thing with [Morrell]." Morrell then informed Smith that he had a friend serving twenty years in San Quentin who was a former member of Chris Evans' gang of outlaws. "If you help me get this man out," Morrell told the brash railroad detective, "I can join the band through him. After that, you know, the rest is a mere matter of detail."[29] The genesis of these overblown claims of double agent detective work was probably his amatuer sleuthing work for the Evans family. Even later news reports noted that Morrell had been "a detective...in the bandit's employ for months." Morrell's claims that he befriended Evans only to infiltrate his gang and effect his capture were clearly a transparent alibi. [30]

Evidence of Morrell's association with Evans went back several months. In September, Morrell had been charged with threatening a local blacksmith. Unable to pay the one thousand dollar fine, he landed in the Fresno jail and became a cellmate to the infamous Chris Evans. The *San Francisco Examiner* noted another interesting arrest (especially when considering who made it) when it alluded to an incident where Morrell "was arrested in August by Officer Byrd for threatening to kill Charles Cummings, a man who had just been released from San Quentin." But Cummings, it was noted, "refused to prosecute Morrell and he was discharged from custody."[31] It isn't such a long stretch of the imagination to assume Morrell wanted to find himself back in jail, especially considering he made two attempts to get himself arrested. Even the *San Francisco Chronicle* made that speculation when it wrote that "it is now thought that he managed to get in jail for the purpose of releasing Evans."[32]

Morrell was released in time to attend the Evans trial. It was during this period that he obtained work at the Union Restaurant in Fresno (where he was known as Frank Morey) and provided the Evans family with information on prospective jurors. Morrell had earlier worked as a waiter in a Visalia hotel, where it was said he was very particular about his appearance. As the *Fresno Republican* later reported, "If any ladies chanced to take seats in the dining room, [Morrell] left everything else and waited on them. He even went so far as to powder his face, color his eyebrows, wax his mustache and paint his lips red. This finally disgusted his employer and he was discharged." The newspapers also reported that Morrell, when in Visalia, "was a frequent visitor at the Evans house."[33]

By Ed Morrell's own admission, he was enamored with Eva and greatly admired Chris. Whether he was recruited by Chris or Eva is unknown, but by late December he had helped set in motion a plan that, as Eva told Morrell, would be dangerous. "You might get sent up for years,"[34] she warned him.

CHAPTER FOURTEEN

On Tour Again

E VA EVANS AND ED MORRELL did not act alone in planning to break Chris Evans out of the Fresno jail. The strange story of Edward E. Deck is further evidence that they had help and that Chris Evans had many confederates. On the morning of December 28, 1893, Deck informed the conductor of the Southern Pacific's Porterville branch line that there would be a holdup near Lindsay later that day. He explained he knew because he was supposed to be one of the robbers, but "claimed that he wanted to save himself by giving the plot away."[1] His story caused every available Fresno deputy sheriff to be sent south right away to foil the impending crime. A diversion, it would seem, had been implemented.

Another alleged accomplice was Jim Hutchinson, who had married his own stepsister Grace Lee, the daughter of Morrell's friend from San Quentin. Morrell had stayed with the Hutchinsons for a time when he first came to Fresno. On the afternoon of December 28, Hutchinson rented a team of horses and a buggy from a Fresno livery stable and left them near the jail.[2] In the vernacular of later times, a getaway vehicle was now in place.

There was one person, very close to Chris Evans, who it can be argued knew nothing of the plan, which had now been set in motion. This was his easily upset wife, Molly. On the evening of December 28, Molly decided to go see Chris at the jail. "I was afraid to tell her not to go," Eva later wrote, implying her mother's ignorance of the plan. Eva tried to talk her mother out of visiting Chris that evening, but couldn't. "So I just prayed that she would not get in the way."[3]

MOLLY ARRIVED AT THE JAIL at dusk on what was a cold and foggy evening. She was shown to the upper corridor where her husband was guarded by Ben Scott. He was the brother of Sheriff Jay Scott and was substituting for the regular deputy in charge of the jail. While Molly was visiting with Chris in the corridor, a waiter arrived with the prisoner's evening meal. In the words of one historian, Molly, unaware of impending events, was horrified when she saw the contents of the platter. "Besides the dinner, she saw a revolver, which in a sense was to serve as dessert."[4] It is unknown if she recognized the waiter—her daughter's co-conspirator, Ed Morrell.

The inexperienced guard had locked the waiter Morrell in with Molly and the prisoner, after which he left them alone. When Scott returned to let the waiter out he was shocked to see a six-shooter pointed at him. Morrell ordered him to throw up his hands. "I supposed he was joking," Scott later recounted, "and did not obey. Just then Chris Evans stepped up and said 'That's right, Ben, put your hands up.'"[5]

Ben Scott was then forced to accompany Chris and Ed Morrell out into the street. Molly remained behind and had, reportedly, fainted. The heavy tule fog that evening favored their escape, but as they walked along Mariposa Street they encountered three men, one who happened to be the Fresno city marshal and another the former mayor. There followed a botched attempt to detain the escaping outlaw and his waiter/accomplice wherein the city marshal was wounded in the shoulder. The report of Chris' gun spooked their horse team stashed nearby and Evans and Morrell were forced to flee on foot.

Soon they came upon a delivery boy for the *Fresno Republican* newspaper. At gunpoint, young Bennie Cochran was ordered out of his horse-drawn cart. As the fugitives drove his news cart away into the inky night, Cochran yelled for help. He was near his house, and so his father and brother soon appeared and gave chase, but when Evans fired shots they quickly ceased their pursuit. Bennie had lost his horse and cart, which ironically he would really need the next day to deliver all the newspapers that Chris Evans would, once again, help him sell.

After the excitement in the streets of Fresno died down, Ben Scott returned to the jail and promptly arrested Molly Evans as an accessory to the escape. It is unclear whether she had recovered from her fainting spell.

THE *SAN FRANCISCO CHRONICLE* (which along with its competitor, the *Examiner,* were of the more sympathetic newspapers to the Evans family plight) reported that Molly Evans had "talked willingly" and denied all participation in the escape. The reporter empathetically described her situation. "She occupies rather a lonesome place in the jail, sitting alone and solitary in a little iron cage with no light except what can find its way in through the iron grating of the door." The *San Francisco Examiner* likewise described Molly as "a very sick woman yet. She lies on an iron cot in a steel-barred cell and complains bitterly of the treatment she received at the hands of Undersheriff Berry."[6]

The *Chronicle* further pointed out that it was said by friends of Chris Evans that he never took his wife into his confidence in any of his "undertakings of a questionable nature" because she was too nervous. This, the reporter surmised, strengthened the assertion that Molly Evans knew nothing of the escape plan. But, as the article also pointed out, Chris Evans "confided many things to Eva which he never told her mother." Although never stated outright, the *Chronicle* seemed to be pointing the finger of guilt at Eva and hinted that perhaps she should have been arrested instead.

With her prone-to-fainting mother languishing in jail and her father once again a hunted man, one has to wonder what was going through Eva's mind. Decades later, when penning her memoir, Eva never expressed any regret in helping her father escape. It would seem that in her mind, even upon reflection forty years later, she was merely doing what her father had asked. She was following orders. She was being a "good soldier." And even though her mother suffered the indignity of being arrested and held in jail, that was just an unfortunate consequence—collateral damage in her father's war.

Fortunately, after having spent several days in the Fresno jail, Molly Evans was arraigned in court and "was discharged from custody, there being no evidence to hold her." She returned to Visalia on the next train that evening.[7]

Molly was not the only suspected accomplice. As reported in the *Fresno Morning Republican,* there were a total of "six persons so far as known under arrest suspected of complicity in the Evans escape." In addition to Molly, the paper listed "Edward Deck, who drew the deputy sheriffs to Porterville, and the four Hutchinsons." The four members of the Hutchinson family arrested were "Jim, the oldest and the ringleader, Will and Henry Hutchinson, mere boys, and Rose Lee, a girl aged fourteen and the sister of Jim Hutchinson's wife."[8] The paper claimed the family had a "very bad reputation, nearly every member having been in jail," and that they "showed a desire to shield the desperadoes, and Rose seemed particularly anxious about Morrell." That Rose Lee, who was three years younger than Chris Evans' oldest daughter, ended up in jail had to be a frightening aspect for Eva. But strangely enough, in the words of historian Wallace Smith, who described Eva as the "brains and spark-plug in the clever and successful jailbreak," she was never "suspected, interrogated or arrested."[9]

None of the accused accomplices spent much time behind bars. Despite rigorous questioning, Ed Deck and the Hutchinsons all remained "very close-mouthed." A week or so later, charges were dismissed against Rose Lee and the two younger Hutchinson boys on the grounds that the evidence did not warrant a conviction. Charges were later dropped against Deck, and by the end of January, the case was also dropped against Jim Hutchinson.[10]

One known accomplice who remained at large was Ed Morrell. He was now with Chris Evans deep in the mountains in the dead of a harsh Sierra winter.

WITH A JAILBREAK AND JAIL TIME behind her, Molly Evans once again moved her family to San Francisco so she and Eva could resume their roles in the melodrama of their life. Newspapers reported that Molly and Eva would take the same parts they had in the old version, but in this revised revival, the younger Evans children would be "bunched on the stage whenever the occasion calls for a display of tow-headed children."[11]

Evans and Sontag: Up to Date was the title R. C. White now gave his blood and thunder drama, which included a new seventh act. As described by Eva, the addition "opens on the inside of the jail, with an iron-gated corridor in the back and papa and all the other prisoners behind it. Then Benny Scott, the Sheriff, comes in and walks up to the grating from the front. 'Well, Chris,' he says, 'your wife will be here soon. I guess you can come out here and eat your dinner at the table.' And he opens the gate and out comes papa."[12] Of course, everyone knew what happened next. White was wisely capitalizing on the recent interest after Chris Evans' escape had dominated the front page of every newspaper in the state, wringing every penny he could out of the play and taking advantage of every publicity stunt possible. In addition to now having all the Evans children on stage, he even went so far as to display the actual cabin from the famous shootout at Stone Corral in the lobby of the National Theatre during the San Francisco run.[13]

The ever-supportive *Examiner* offered the following review of the revival's opening night:

> "Evans and Sontag" filled the National Theatre last night, in spite of the weather and the late hour at which the engagement was announced.
>
> The play has been recast and altered in some portions, and another act has been added.
>
> Mrs. Evans was looking better than when she was here before, although "not feeling as well," as she said, and "no wonder."
>
> Miss Eva was blooming in every sense of the word, and carried off her difficult role with more abandon than formerly. Besides this there was a picked assortment of the Evans children, and as many as could be handled were to the fore. There were seven of them altogether—Eva, the oldest, being the star.[14]

Shortly after the play reopened in late January, newspapers were reporting more protests from Methodist ministers. "Evans Not a Proper Hero," bellowed one headline in the *San Francisco Examiner*. The article detailed how a delegation of clergymen, with the Reverend Dr. Hirst acting as spokesman, called upon the chief of police to see if he could assist them in banning the production. Dr. Hirst pointed out that the play was not fit for presentation to the youth of San Francisco, claiming it gave "youthful minds an evil tendency" and made "heroes of border ruffians, murderers and highwaymen." The police chief replied that he would consult the district attorney to see if there was any law "by which the drama could be suppressed." The chief then advised the ministers, in the meantime, "to attack the objectionable drama from their pulpits, and endeavor to influence their congregations to withhold their approval at least to the extent of remaining away."

When asked to comment on the clergy's attempts to shut down the melodrama, Eva took umbrage. "They talk of the play being immoral—why, they are crazy!" She didn't accept the theory that she was causing "innocent little boys to go about bristling with weapons." The play taught lots of lofty sentiment, Eva argued. "And when they talk about stopping the play because they say we are 'violating the law' they simply show their own ignorance."[15]

On that last point she was right. The following day the *Examiner* reported, under the headline "The Laws Are Inadequate," that the district attorney could find nothing on the statute books to prevent the Evans and Sontag drama from being publicly performed and that not even the youngest Evans children could be "kept out of the play."[16]

R. C. White offered his retort via a scathing curtain speech. The seasoned actor and theatrical producer opened by quoting Shakespeare. "All the world's a stage and all the men and women are merely players." The doctor, the lawyer, even the preacher were all, White pointed out, actors, but it was the thespian that had the great advantage. They were the "brief chroniclers of time, portraying human life and human passions as they are, not as the narrow minded gentlemen of the pulpit would have them." White stated that in his play they had merely chronicled facts. "We do not glorify Chris Evans or John Sontag or make heroes of them."

White pointed out that the Methodist preachers had never actually seen the melodrama, but had nonetheless deemed it demoralizing. He continued to hammer at the clergy who had condemned his production. "They are distorted images of the Great Creator whom they pretend to worship. They, the preachers, say this play will cause [young boys] to turn train robbers and murderers. What a ridiculous assumption."

White's speech was designed to arouse the audience, and it likely elicited whoops of support and cheers for the persecuted heroes of the play before the curtain even rose. White closed by flinging one final insult at the preachers. "With them, intellectual expansion is impossible, for their brains are confined to the covers of a single book. They are preaching against Evans and Sontag. Well, let them preach. I can preach as well as they and to larger congregations."[17]

The anger directed at the clergy was perhaps itself something of an act, for White was savvy enough to realize that the Reverend Dr. Hirst's efforts really only meant free publicity in the form of additional press coverage.

Eva's personal life also made its way into the newspapers during this period. When reporting that the Evans family had moved to San Francisco to resume the play, the *Examiner* noted that there were "internecine troubles" behind the scenes because "James Evans, the contract husband of Eva Evans, has not been acting right." He had shown no visible means of support, and Molly Evans told the reporter for the *Examiner* that they were drawing the line at Eva doing all the wage-earning. "Jim Evans thought he had a snap and was going to let Eva wear the boy's clothes and draw the pay, but he never got a bean out of Eva," said Mrs. Evans. "You can say that I am going to have that marriage of hers annulled and that it was the same as a civil marriage."[18]

A Visalia newspaper reported that "Miss Eva's reason for becoming single again is that she made a serious mistake in becoming the contract bride of Jim Evans." The paper noted that he had been a barkeeper in a Fresno saloon, but that soon after the marriage gave up his job, "deciding that Eva could make enough on the stage for both of them." While the paper concluded that Eva did support him for awhile, it was by the advice of friends that "she decided to separate from him." The article stated that the marriage had been annulled because Eva was a minor when she contracted it and "her mother fiercely opposed it."[19]

"OUR COURSE LED US on a section of road between the Sanger and old Summerville roads," Ed Morrell later wrote, describing their flight from Fresno after the jailbreak. "We could hear the clatter of horses and shouts of pursuing men on either side as we sped along in hope of gaining the bridge first. Once across that turbulent stream, the Tulare Mountains and liberty would be ours."[20] To the consternation of local lawmen, Evans and Morrell indeed made it into the mountains and Chris became a hunted fugitive once again. As December gave way to January, and February replaced the coldest month with little relief from the freezing conditions, the bitter struggle Chris faced in the mountains could hardly be described as liberty.

Eva could only imagine the hardships her father faced as she regularly saw headlines in the San Francisco dailies recounting the renewed manhunt. Headlines like "Outwitted by Chris Evans: The Bandit and Morrell Elude Their Pursuers" and "Evans is Not Caught Yet: The Pursuers Have Not Had as Much as a Glimpse of Him" offered hope. But other headlines were more ominous. "Footprints in the Snow: Sheriff Scott's Posses Moving on What They Think Will Be the Last Raid" was frightening for Eva, but proved to be all bluff. When Eva and her mother read in early February that "Evans Takes to the Plains: Seen a Few Miles from Visalia in Broad Daylight" they worried he was taking too many chances. A day later, headlines told of "A Fight With Chris Evans: The Outlaw and His Confederate, Morrell, Put Two Deputy Sheriffs to Flight Near Slick Rock."[21]

As Eva later recalled, history was repeating itself. "Only this time the man hunt was even more terrible for us, living in San Francisco, appearing nightly in the play, than it had been before. This time Dad was weakened from his long illness, he was handicapped by his partial blindness and that lost arm."[22]

Chris and Ed Morrell, despite the older fugitive's physical limitations, were covering a great deal of territory. They had spent time as far north as the Kings River and the Dinkey Creek area of Fresno County. But after trudging through the snow in strange surroundings, Evans longed to get back to more familiar territory and seek shelter. It was a cold, wet winter and hiding out in the mountains was taking its toll on his battered body. According to Morrell's embellished memory, Chris groaned with fatigue. "Man, do you hear? I am dead beat out. My blood is like ice water in my veins. I will freeze to death if I don't get under cover soon." Chris then complained that Morrell, who had "the endurance of a mountain deer," was "without the bowels of compassion."

In Morrell's self-aggrandizing version, he finally relented. "Since the jail break I had made a practice of humoring the Chief," Morrell wrote. "He had gone through enough to kill any other ten men. So, with a heavy load tugging at my heart, and premonitions of danger dogging my footsteps I plunged ahead, again taking the lead. We were soon within the confines of Camp Manzanita."[23] Morrell's premonitions, however, were not without merit.

Camp Manzanita was well hidden by dense manzanita and chaparral on all sides. Later news reports described the cabin, eight by ten feet in size, built against a large exposed granite slab. "The adjacent cleft of rocks furnished ample kitchen accommodations and a fine spring of water was at the door. In fact, it was an ideal hiding place."[24] Deliberately, no trail was ever made to it, and few besides Chris Evans even knew of its existence. The Downing family, however, did know. They were great friends of Evans and often supplied the outlaws. What Bill Downing did not know was that his children, after the capture of Evans and Sontag the previous summer, had told Walter Kirkland, a relative by marriage, of the secret hideout. Eva excused the children's indiscretion because, as she later explained, "they little thought it would ever be needed again." And so when Chris and Ed Morrell returned to Camp Manzanita, the Downing children were afraid to tell anyone what they had done and just hoped that Walter Kirkland would not reveal the secret to anyone else.[25] Whether the information came from this slip of the tongue or not, Camp Manzanita was soon discovered by lawmen.

"Evans Ran for his Life" headlines proclaimed on February 9, 1894. Bold print told how "the notorious outlaw and his companion" were "driven from their lair in the Sierra foothills." The bandits were forced to flee "Half-clad and with a slender supply of Ammunition." Finally, readers were intrigued to see in capital letters the proclamation that "EVANS LOSES HIS FALSE ARM."[26]

Morrell later offered this dramatic rendition of the surprise encounter:

> A rifle cracked sharply! I dropped the paper and sprang to my feet, Colt 45 in hand.
>
> I had been reading to the Chief, and did not notice him cross the floor and open the door, stepping just outside. There he had raised his good hand above his one remaining eye as if to penetrate the fog and look over the Dry Creek Valley far below.
>
> With the report of the rifle my partner wheeled and fell into the cabin, striking the door-jam with his head. He dropped upon the floor face down, to all appearances life-less.
>
> "Well, old man, you've got your final shot at last," I murmured, believing him dead, but not daring to lean over just then to pick him up.[27]

Evans survived the grazing shot to his head, which was evidently only dramatic embellishment on Morrell's part. News reports offered a rather different account of the surprise routing.

> When the posse came upon the cabin Evans was reading a paper, pausing to laugh with Morrell over something that seems funny, which was afterwards found to be an account of their doings. Leaving [posse men] Henry and Miles on guard, Peck and [deputy sheriff] Timmins crawled down the canyon about 100 yards in order to cross to the other side and get a cross fire on the cabin, and in doing so they accidentally made a noise which either caught Evans's ear, or else the actions of a pet cat which they had there gave them the alarm.
>
> Evans came out of the door and immediately darted back into the cabin, emerging a moment later with his rifle in his hand. It was then that Henry fired. As Evans and Morrell darted into a crevice at the side of the cabin Henry and Miles fired upon them. The smoke obscured the cabin for an instant, and when it cleared away the bandits had disappeared.[28]

The posse then searched the cabin and found it amply supplied with ammunition and food. After a portion of its contents were removed, the crude structure was set afire and completely destroyed. Among the items Sheriff Scott brought back to Reedley was Chris Evans' prosthetic arm. As Eva later claimed, authorities refused to return the artificial arm, which Molly had purchased for Chris while he was in the Fresno jail awaiting trial. They eventually put it on display in the jail museum in Fresno.[29] Rumors even circulated that the fake arm would be on display at the current Midwinter Fair in San Francisco.[30] As the *Fresno Republican* summarized, Evans and Morrell were again at large and were being "hard pressed by resolute men who are determined to make an end of the matter."

> It is known that they are in no condition to endure the storm now raging and are rapidly sapping their strength and endurance. It is expected that there will be sharp and bloody work when they are overtaken, as it is known that Evans has made up his mind thoroughly to die rather than to be captured.[31]

WITH HER FATHER AGAIN ON THE RUN, Eva found herself once more traveling with the melodrama. After playing San Francisco for a few weeks, *Evans and Sontag: Up to Date* went out on tour again. One of their first engagements was across the bay at the Oakland Theatre.

With the play now on the road again, Molly sent the younger children back to Visalia to live with her mother, Grannie Byrd. To ease the burden of caring for the four rambunctious boys, the family relied once again on a couple who had helped care for the children the previous fall. Mrs. Brighton, along with her husband, Jonas, had been friends of the Evans family since they arrived in Visalia the previous summer. In fact, they had recently rented the old Evans house from Sol Sweet and were now living next door to Grannie Byrd.

It was not entirely by accident that Jonas V. Brighton and his family came to live in the Evanses' old house, but at the time very few knew his background or what had brought him to town. As would only later come to light, Brighton was an undercover detective hired by Marshal Gard to develop evidence against Evans during the manhunt and later trial.

Brighton, who was born in 1847 in Indiana, was a combat veteran of the Union army and had been a prisoner of war in 1864, when he was freed in an exchange for Confederate prisoners. After two decades as a farmer in Kansas, Brighton began his detective career when he was hired by the Arizona Cattlemen's Association to investigate and pursue cattle rustlers. He infiltrated a gang of rustlers and eventually killed the notorious Ike Clanton, a member of the family that had so famously battled Wyatt Earp and his brothers in Tombstone, Arizona.

As one historian explained, Brighton relied on his less-than-noteworthy appearance and unobtrusive nature. "His method was to frequent saloons and get well-acquainted with the hangers-on and the tough element. He complained about how unfair life treated him, which endeared him to the malcontents. Soon he had their confidence." It was a method that worked in Visalia.[32]

As Brighton himself once recounted:

> I am a Deputy United States Marshal. I came to Visalia with my wife early in May, 1893. My purpose was to aid in "rounding up" Chris Evans and John Sontag. Only two or three persons with whom I was associated knew my plans at first....
>
> I continued to play the part of the rusty old "hayseed," and did all kinds of work; hoed weeds for people, worked on the streets, and accepted any kind of job that was offered. Mrs. Evans occasionally hired me to do a little work about the place...
>
> I gradually became well established in the good graces of Mrs. Evans and believed that the time had come when I could reach Chris through her...
>
> During the incarceration of Chris, when Mrs. Evans was away from home a good deal of the time, and while she and Eva were absent with the "Evans-Sontag" troupe, my wife and myself were employed to take care of the younger children....
>
> During all this time I was trusted implicitly by all members of the family and even up to and after his capture last Monday Chris believed I was his friend. He thinks so yet.[33]

It was Eva herself who most colorfully explained Brighton's role in the capture of her father. According to her memoir, after the close call at Camp Manzanita, her father was near exhaustion but was able to make it to Bill Downing's mountain ranch. While there, Bill went into town for supplies and Chris asked him to go to their old home, where the Brightons now lived and were caring for the Evans children, and see if they were all right. "Mr. Downing returned with a message that baby Carl was dangerously ill, and that if Chris wanted to see the little fellow alive to come at once," Eva later wrote. She explicitly noted that "Downing had no part in this. He believed Brighton when he told him that Carl was in danger of death, that he was so ill that Bill could not even see him."[34]

Although Eva claimed it was news of a sick child that brought Chris to his former home on February 17, 1894, initial news reports infer it may have been the lure of money. The *Examiner* reported that "it has been known for several days that Mrs. Evans, who is on the road with the drama *Evans and Sontag*, had saved about $300 from her earnings, which she intended to send to her husband. It was also known that Evans and Morrell intended to come [to Visalia] and get the money and then leave the country." Evans himself indicated in a later interview that it was sheer exhaustion that motivated his ill-advised foray into town. He had been "hunted so hard in the hills" that he had to get out.[35]

But Eva maintained that because of his devotion to his children, "now without the protection of Mother and me, my father walked into a second trap, for he decided to start at once to his dying child." For whatever reason, Chris and Ed returned "to the house which had been the scene of the first troubles" and, as Ed Morrell later recalled, "a welcoming light gleamed out through one of the back windows."[36] Weak from hunger, the men staggered and stumbled through the door and Mrs. Brighton quickly offered them food.

According to Eva, Chris was told his sick child had suddenly recovered. It was then, Eva asserted, that he knew Brighton for a traitor. "It would do no good to kill him," she added, "as daylight disclosed the house surrounded."[37]

THE FINAL ACT IN THIS LONG-RUNNING SAGA offered one supporting character his finest moment while showing Chris Evans at one of his worst. Eva would read in the *San Francisco Examiner* how Sheriff Kay had learned that Evans and Morrell were in town, having gained his information from a "trustworthy agency." The desperadoes had come to Visalia, the paper stated, "for the purpose of getting the money which Mrs. Evans intended to send them, but which had not arrived."

Sheriff Kay immediately wired Marshal Gard and posted a small posse to guard the roads until morning. In the meantime, Marshal Gard arrived and held a consultation with Sheriff Kay. It was decided not to do anything until morning. The *Examiner* further recounted:

J. V. Brighton came down town about eight o'clock and was promptly placed under arrest by Sheriff Kay and locked up in jail on a charge of being a confederate of Evans and Morrell.

The news that Evans was surrounded drew a large crowd of people to the house. The officers had established a cordon around the Evans house, cutting off all avenues of escape. Mr. Brighton sent word to his wife that he had been placed in jail, and asked her to leave the house. Mr. and Mrs. Brighton have been taking care of the younger members of Evans' family since last fall. Evans refused to let Mrs. Brighton leave with the children.[38]

A follow-up in that very issue of the *Examiner* elaborated on the cornered fugitive's attitude toward Mrs. Brighton. Regardless of Kay's ruse of arresting Brighton to deflect suspicion, Evans now knew his true colors. As Morrell later recalled, when they woke up to find the house surrounded, it was obvious. Mrs. Brighton's husband had evidently "slipped out some time during the night to give the alarm. They were traitors and had sprung the trap!"[39]

The *Examiner*, citing as its source "others in the house," told how when Mrs. Brighton "received the note stating that her husband was in jail, Evans picked Mrs. Brighton up and threw her into a bedroom and kicked her in the ribs. He was going to kick her again, when Morrell interfered. Mrs. Brighton fainted many times during the day and suffered much from her injuries."[40]

Evans later "denied emphatically that he had abused Mrs. Brighton, saying that he had never spoken to her except kindly, and that he did not blame her husband for their capture."[41] Eva never mentioned in her memoir what she had to feel was a vile accusation against her father. Why would she want to remind readers—or herself for that matter—of what she had to see as one of her father's lowest acts: throwing down and kicking a woman? Perhaps Eva, aware of the temper her father possessed, knew in her heart it was true.

Who those "others in the house" were was answered with another example, reported in the newspapers, of Chris Evans' volatile temper during this tense time. Grannie Byrd had returned from a trip to Bakersfield and when she went to the old Evans home to see the children in the care of the Brightons, she was surprised to find Evans and Morrell there. She told the *Examiner* that about an hour later her son, George, came in and Evans drew his Winchester, called him an unprintable name, and threatened to kill him. Grannie Byrd stepped toward her enraged son-in-law and said, "Chris, child, what do you mean?"

He said he meant to kill George Byrd and that he was a traitor. "He then abused me in the most shameful manner and all the Byrd family, and said he would not have his children raised by any of us. He said he intended to kill Perry and George Byrd. He said he had no fault to find with his wife. After talking with him for a time he became calmer. I came to my own house later with George and went to bed, but not to sleep. No one knows how sorely I have been tried during the last twenty months on account of Chris. I hope this will be the last of it."[42]

And so it was that Eva, 200 miles away in Oakland, could read about personal family tensions. It pained her to see them aired in public. Again, Chris denied any harsh words toward his mother-in-law. But because Eva had testified in court that there was friction between the Evans and Byrd families and suspicions of betrayal by her uncles, the threats and comments attributed to Chris Evans rang true.

It was Sheriff Kay, with tact and intelligence that even Eva would later praise, who effected Chris Evans' peaceful surrender. Again, like so much of this ongoing drama, it involved the children of Chris Evans.

With his posses and a gathering mob surrounding the house, Sheriff Kay wrote Chris Evans a note imploring him to "surrender and we will protect you. If not we will take you anyway." A young man volunteered to take the note to the bandits for the fee of one dollar. Chris read the note and he and Morrell debated surrender. Chris then dispatched his nine-year-old son, Joe, to the sheriff with his written reply. (The original note-bearer was apparently too frightened to continue his messenger duties.) After the exchange of two more notes, with little Joe Evans serving as courier, Evans agreed to surrender if Kay would disperse the crowd and bring only Deputy Hall with him to the porch to talk. "You are the sheriff of this county, and I am willing to make terms with you, but with no one else," his note explained.

"Just as Kay and Hall reached the dilapidated gate," the *Examiner* reported, "Evans and Morrell came out on the porch and held up their hands as a signal of surrender. The two officers walked up to the porch and Evans said: 'Our word is good. If you protect us, we will surrender.'"[43] Kay made the final arrest of Chris Evans and brought him safely through the crowd to jail.

Several decades later, Eva wrote a letter to Kay expressing her gratitude for his masterly handling of the overly-excited mob, his consideration for her father, and the kindness he'd shown her mother on more than one occasion. Near death and debilitated from a stroke, the aged Eugene Kay was moved by Eva's "voluntary gratitude" and sincerely sent his own thanks for extending the appreciation.[44]

So many years later, there survived this respect between the sheriff and the train robber's daughter.

CHAPTER FIFTEEN

Hard Times

A FTER BEING TAKEN TO THE VISALIA JAIL, with his sentencing pending, Chris was moved to the Fresno jail. Concerned with the threat of lynching, officers didn't wait for the next train but transported him at midnight by horse and buggy. After receiving his official sentence of life in prison the next day, he was transported via train to Sacramento, where he was then taken to Folsom State Prison. Molly joined her husband on the train ride up to Folsom, but Eva stayed behind in Visalia. News reports commented on how Chris Evans "bowed and smiled at the thousands of people congregated at the depots to see him as he passed through the San Joaquin Valley."[1]

On February 21, 1894, Chris Evans arrived at Folsom Prison. Warden Aull of Folsom was quoted in the newspaper that he would not let Evans be seen or interviewed as he wanted to put an end to the notoriety the bandit had received. Aull pledged that the "sentimentality over the outlaw will be ended for all time to come." Evans would be treated no better than the meanest criminal within the walls of the penitentiary and would be obliged to observe the rules and regulations of the prison.

Established in 1880, Folsom Prison was situated at the site of a former mining camp near the American River. The prison was largely self-supporting due to the sale of convict-quarried granite (which was also used in the construction of prison facilities), shoe and tailor shops, and a prison farm. Power supplied by a nearby dam operated electric lights throughout the facility. (Folsom was the first prison in the world to have electric power via California's earliest hydroelectric power plant.)[2] Despite its modern touches, Folsom harbored a reputation as being a notoriously harsh, cruel and even barbaric facility.

It wasn't until several days after Chris arrived at Folsom that Eva was able to visit him. She was apprehensive as she rode the train to Folsom, some twenty miles east of Sacramento. She tried to prepare herself for the moment she would see him. She assumed his head and face would be clean-shaven and that he'd be wearing the prison stripes. These thoughts made her recall a time when, as a little girl, she waited for her father outside a barber shop. When he came out and picked her up, she didn't recognize him. She struggled and tried to escape his arms. Chris, freshly shorn of beard, laughed. It wasn't until he called out her name that little Eva realized she was in her father's arms. It was the only time she'd ever seen him without whiskers. She made him promise to grow them back and never shave again.[3]

Eva arrived at Folsom Prison, its hand-hewn gray granite walls looking so impenetrable, the vaulted gates and peaked Gothic guard towers so foreboding. The still-teenaged young woman was nervous, but she was soon directed to the warden's office, and upon stating that she was the daughter of Chris Evans, was shown to another office and told by a prison official that the prisoner would be brought to her.

> I wait; minutes pass. A prisoner with an armed guard enters and they go to a desk where a clerk is at work. The prisoner has not looked in my direction—is facing away from me. I notice his clothing; wide, dirty looking black and gray stripes running around the body; coarse material, loose, ill-fitting. He turns to come toward me, and I see the missing arm and the blinded eye. O, God! This is my father—this man with a face the color of granite—the large mouth—the sensitive lips—the lower one trembling a little.
>
> "Eva! Little daughter, how are you?"
>
> My arms go around his neck—and then—that smell, like a surgical ward in a hospital; he who had always smelled so good—how can he endure it?
>
> "What is it, Dad? What do they put on you?"
>
> "O, it's just a necessary sanitary measure. All the convict clothing is washed with a strong solution of iodoform in the water. Don't think about it. It will soon disappear."
>
> My throat aches, and I want to cry, but if I do I know what he will say— "You are showing the white feather. Keep a stiff upper lip."[4]

For weeks after visiting her father, Eva would awaken in the middle of the night with that institutional odor in her nose. The unpleasant memory-smell awakening thoughts of her father—troubling thoughts— it was as if that stench were bearing down on him, preventing him from seeing or feeling sunlight, from breathing in fresh air, from sending out thoughts to his family so far beyond the gray granite walls of his cell. Even forty years later, Eva would be unable to erase the terrible odor from her mind, and she would forever associate it with seeing her father in prison.

WHILE EVA STRUGGLED TO MAINTAIN her career as an actress and faced the barbs of negative publicity that came with her celebrity status, other men in Eva's life faced the prospect of time in prison.

Ed Morrell's conviction for highway robbery (he was charged with armed robbery—taking Fresno City Marshal Morgan's gun—as well as aiding Evans in his escape, but stood trial on the robbery charge) was the price he paid for his devotion to Eva and her father.[5] At his trial, the jury delivered their guilty verdict after only ten minutes of deliberation. The *Fresno Daily Expositor* reported how Morrell, "the whilom friend and companion of Chris Evans, was dazed…by the remarkable rapidity with which his case was disposed of."[6]

On April 16, 1894, Morrell appeared in Fresno County Superior Court for sentencing. After a stern lecture from Judge M. K. Harris, he was handed his sentence. "Life!" angrily thundered the judge. As Morrell later wrote, the word rang in his ears. "My doom was sealed. It had come at the end of a long harangue by the magistrate who, at this solemn moment, took occasion to drone out a moral diatribe on my evil criminal career." He was sent in shackles on the next morning train to Folsom, where he would be "confined at hard labor in the rock quarries of Folsom State Prison for the balance of [his] natural life!"[7]

That same spring, another of Eva's former co-conspirators faced an even stiffer sentence. On March 23, 1894, William Fredericks, whom Eva once helped to secure weapons for George Sontag's failed prison break, badly botched a bank robbery in San Francisco.

Eva, admitting the "rather strange coincidence" of it, claimed she heard a revolver shot on her way to the theatre one morning. "I knew it meant some kind of trouble, and I wondered what," she later recalled.[8]

That evening, the papers described the trouble in boldface type. It was "Fredericks' Crowning Crime" according to one headline, while

another banner described it as a "Desperate Deed by Outlaw Freder
icks" under an even bolder declaration that he was "CHRIS EVANS'
PAL."[9] The papers related how at nine-thirty that morning, a man entered the branch office of the San Francisco Savings Union at Market
and Polk streets. He walked over to cashier William Herrick and presented a note, demanding money. The note stated that if the demand
was refused, the bearer would blow the building to "everlasting nothingness." At the bottom of the note, in red ink, was a rudely sketched
skull and crossbones.

Herrick handed the paper back, shaking his head, whereupon the
desperado drew a pistol and fired, missing his mark. Herrick drew a
pistol he had hidden nearby and returned the shot, also missing. Then
the assailant shot a second time, the bullet striking Herrick in the heart,
causing instant death.

The assassin ran, pursued by a crowd, and was captured a short
distance from the scene and placed under arrest. It was not long before authorities recognized in their prisoner a "desperate criminal for
whom the authorities throughout the state had been searching for some
time."[10]

Eva was no doubt saddened when she learned the identity of this
self-described "despondent man" (which was how he signed his note to
the bank teller). Saddened, but perhaps none too surprised, she recalled
getting to know Fredericks.

> In the days that we waited to get the guns [for George Sontag's
> escape attempt], this strange lad told me all about himself. He was
> not over twenty-five, and looked much younger. His people, in
> Germany, belonged to the lesser nobility. His father was a baron.
> He had run away and come to America for adventure. He was not
> exactly mad—just some of the parts had been lost while he was
> being assembled. He was really nice; I like him very much.
>
> He had robbed a Yosemite stage, had been caught, and sent to
> Folsom Penitentiary under the name of William Fredericks. Ac
> cording to Christian standards, he had no regard for human life. I
> am quite sure he would have killed anyone I asked him to in the
> same spirit that he would bring a bouquet of flowers.[11]

One Fresno newspaper declared that "the notorious Fredericks...at
one time was a confederate of Bandit Chris Evans. He killed Sheriff
Pascoe of Nevada County. He subsequently killed a Southern Pacific

brakeman and is the man who supplied arms to George Sontag and his companions at the time they made their futile attempt to escape from prison."[12]

At least Eva could take solace that the papers didn't link her with Fredericks, at least not until she chose to visit him in jail a week later.

On April 3, 1894, the *San Francisco Examiner* reported that "Eva Evans, the yellow-haired daughter of Chris Evans, yesterday paid a visit to Fredericks, the man who killed Bank Cashier Herrick, in his cell at the Larkin Street prison."

Eva later recalled that when she asked Fredericks why he did it, he claimed he hadn't shot the bank cashier, but "would have if he didn't give me some money." He was broke and hungry, he told Eva. When she asked him why he had come back to California when he promised that he would not return to the West Coast, he replied, "I meant to find you. I knew you'd help me till I'd get work. But I couldn't find you. I asked at a lot of theatres, but no one knew. I'd been here two weeks, and I haven't had much to eat."

Had she but known, Eva later lamented, she might have saved his life. But the end for Fredericks, she sadly realized, would probably have turned out the same.[13]

According to the *San Francisco Examiner* account, after her visit someone asked who the young woman was and upon learning it was Eva Evans, Fredericks' cell was immediately searched. Evidence disturbing to authorities was discovered—a small hole bored into the wall of the cell. The *Examiner* explained that "the police, knowing that according to Fredericks' statement some of the weapons...which were used by George Sontag and other convicts in an unsuccessful endeavor to escape had been furnished by Miss Evans, at once associated her visit with some plan for the liberation of Fredericks" and "issued orders that no more permits to see Fredericks should be given to any one, particularly Miss Evans."[14]

To be accused in the papers of being an accomplice in the attempted Folsom Prison escape and a potential accomplice in a plan to help Fredericks was certainly a low point for Eva's public image. But by now she had long been a recipient of less-than-flattering press.

One publicity stunt, undoubtedly designed to boost interest in the play, backfired and left Eva open to jeering criticism. The Associated Press sent out the following account of a public spectacle in San Francisco that headlines called "Eva Evans' Latest Exploit for Coin":

Eva Evans, the daughter of Visalia bandit, Chris Evans, competed against Mme. Marantette, a professional horsewoman, in a five-mile race on horseback at Central Park this afternoon. Fifteen hundred people witnessed the contest. Mme. Marantette wore a lady's habit and rode a lady's side-saddle, while the Visalia girl wore tights and rode astride a Mexican saddle. The riders changed horses every mile.

Though the Visalia girl seemed to be the favorite with the crowd, she was out ridden from the first, and at the end of the race was a lap and a half behind the other woman. The Evans girl was lifted from the horse in a semi-unconscious condition from exhaustion, and carried to a dressing room. This is the girl who appears on stage as the heroine in the bloodcurdling drama, "Evans and Sontag, Up to Date."[15]

Even back in her hometown, readers were offered a castigating description of Eva's equestrian skills. The *Visalia Weekly Delta* (in a reprinted account from the *San Francisco Examiner)* declared that as a rider, Eva was not a success. "She bounced all over the saddle, while her gum chewing kept time to the music of the band."[16]

As long as she was in California, Eva would be subjected to negative press. Even a visit to her father in prison prompted a comment from the warden printed in the Visalia paper. Warden Aull was quoted as saying he had only allowed Chris to see Eva and Molly with a guard posted between them. "I would not trust those women for a fraction of a moment," Aull noted, adding that he didn't think "they possess any conscientious scruples that would prevent them from stooping to aid Chris in regaining his liberty."[17]

It had to be trying for the seventeen-year-old girl to see herself so frequently portrayed in the newspapers in such a negative light. Eva was learning the hard lesson that there was a price to pay for fame, and infamy came with even a higher cost.

With news that the Evans and Sontag Combination would soon be taking the melodrama on tour to Oregon, Eva undoubtedly looked forward to a chance to escape the constant reminders in print that people thought of her as nothing more than a train robber's daughter. Sadly, it was just that public perception on which the play depended, and Eva would not succeed on stage without embracing the baseness of the role she filled in real life.

OREGON REPRESENTED A MUCH-NEEDED CHANGE of scenery, and it soon became evident that just one state to the north, Eva and her father's exploits were not quite as notorious as in California. This may have been a relief to a press-weary Eva, but it wasn't necessarily good for box-office business. While Eva later remembered that ticket sales fell off as soon as the tour reached Oregon, the production actually attracted "fair business" from April 29 through May 5 in Portland. That, at least, was what someone connected with the production scribbled on the sheet music for the play's underscoring. That same source noted that they "turned 'em away, for two nights in Astoria," where the local newspaper called the play "a most exciting one and excellently constructed, with a fine comedy vein running throughout." The review even went so far as to claim that "a more truthful story never was portrayed upon the stage, or a more salutary lesson on the ethics of right and wrong ever woven into a drama."[18]

Astoria was the high point of the Oregon tour; things went downhill from there as they headed to eastern Oregon and the town of Heppner, situated at the head of a long, narrow valley about forty miles south of the Columbia River.

On May 29, 1894, the *Heppner Gazette* reported that the previous Saturday and Monday evenings, the "White Dramatic Co. produced the drama, 'Evans and Sontag,' to small audiences." While it was admitted that the production was filled with "good acting, and the comedy parts are fine," the paper also pointed out that "much objection has been made to the play on moral grounds."

Immediately below the brief review of the play ran a somewhat more ominous notice. Under the heading of "High Water," the *Gazette* informed readers that the Columbia River was "now higher than ever before known in the memory of civilized man." The paper went on to report that the flood had inundated the Union Pacific tracks. "Trains are blocked and all traffic is stopped, and as the flood is not yet at its highest, the blockade may last several days." This was not only the worst flood in recorded memory to that date, but more than 110 years later, it remains the Columbia River's greatest flood in history.[19]

The rain Eva and the company experienced could not have been pleasant, but the more than two months they spent marooned in Heppner became even more disagreeable for a number of reasons.

Unable to continue their tour, White and his company were faced with no means of income. Money was so tight, Eva later remembered, that they couldn't afford a hotel, "so Mr. White rented a furnished house" and he, his two daughters, two of the men in the company, Molly and Eva moved in to wait for the trains to begin running again. White then did the only thing he knew to try to survive. On June 5, the *Heppner Gazette* reported that the "White Dramatic Company" would perform the celebrated melodrama *The Gambler's Wife, or Never Too Late to Repent*. Two weeks later, the paper ran notice of *The Curse of Rum* at the opera house, commenting that "while the play was much appreciated, it would have been more successful had some of the actors been more familiar with their lines." White and company took to the boards, cobbling together productions as best they could. But illness was also taking its toll on the company. The local newspaper reported the lead actor in one performance, Mr. Ellis, had to be replaced at the last minute "owing to sickness."[20]

It is unclear if Eva was able to perform in either of these two plays, as she too had taken ill owing to the back injury she had received in Oakland. "Mr. White would not give us a penny," Eva bitterly recalled. She complained he hadn't given them any money for quite some time. He told Eva and her mother there were no profits.

Molly finally contacted the local doctor, who was well-known in Heppner as a kind and caring man. When Dr. McSwords learned of their situation, he came at once to see Eva and took care of her. Eva claimed the kind-hearted doctor even bought her food, "knowing that we were living on the most meager fare." Eva would forever be grateful to Dr. McSwords.

By mid July, Eva was apparently well enough to perform. She was listed as one of the players in an advertised production of Bret Harte's western drama *M'Liss, or the Waif of the Sierras*, although she was a mere supporting player; White's daughter, Laura White Wolf, received top billing as the waif.[21]

By the end of July, repairs had been completed on the railroad between Heppner and Portland, and over the next few days members of White's Dramatic Company left Heppner. The tour would not resume. The Evans and Sontag Combination had dissolved. Some company members left Heppner immediately upon reopening of the route—Arthur Ellis (the actor who had earlier fallen ill) left for Portland on one of the first trains out; Joe Roberts (another actor) departed for Spokane a couple of days later. The local paper reported that "Mrs. Chris and Miss Eva Evans departed for their home at Visalia, California," more than a week later; and finally, later in August, White's two daughters, Laura and Nora, and his son-in-law, Dan Wolf, departed for "their home in 'Frisco."[22] The ordeal in Heppner was over. Or so Eva thought.

On the trip back to Portland, at Heppner Junction near the Columbia River, Eva claimed she almost lost her life. She wrote of the incident some forty years later. She explained how during the summer at Heppner, a member of the company named Jack Ellis had brought a young professional foot racer, who was in town visiting his parents, to the house. His name was Whetstone and Eva described him as a quiet chap; she paid him little attention and she had "in no way any warning of the thing that was to happen."

He was on the train out that night, and while we were waiting for the Portland train he asked if I wanted to walk down the tracks and see the Columbia in the moonlight. There is a bend in the river at this point, and it is beautiful. There is such power under its smooth ripples.

Suddenly as we walked along, without saying a word, he threw his arms around me and forced me to the ground, with my back across the iron rail of the track, and tried to assault me. Now, I'd never taken much stock in these stories of women being overcome against their will. I thought I could protect myself against any man. He wasn't the first man that had "gotten rough." I clawed and bit and kicked, but the pain in my back took my strength.

Suddenly I felt a vibration; the train was coming! That renewed my strength. Then it whistled, and I said, "Let me go; we'll both be killed!" But he did not release me until the engine was almost upon us. I rolled to one side, and the steam and cinders stung my face.

I was battered and bruised, my clothing almost torn from my body; the pain in my back was so intense I could hardly speak, but the iron monster had saved me from the humiliation of that human brute becoming the victor. The train came to a halt and the engine crew ran back to me. The engineer said he was slowing down for the "junction" when the headlight struck me. They carried me to the station house and organized a crew.

Someone said, "If we get him, let's lynch him!"

Another man said, "No, we'll hold him and let the girl shoot him!"

They did not find him, nor did I ever hear of him again.[23]

EVA DIDN'T GO BACK TO VISALIA with her mother, but returned to San Francisco. The failure of the Oregon tour was explained away by Eva in an interview with the *Examiner* wherein she basically blamed tour management and the Oregon audiences. "First of all," she complained, "we were mismanaged—or not managed at all, as I told you—and then I sometimes think that perhaps the story of Evans and Sontag was misunderstood. But did you know the Oregonians were so ignorant?!" She was also quoted as using phrases like "not cultured up to appreciating" and "kind of jay" when describing the "mossbacks" in Oregon. She then related her plans to continue acting. "I love the stage, you know, even after the Oregon tour. I am coaching for a new part already." The play was *Muldoon's Picnic*, and Eva explained it would include "a Chinaman's part and a darky part that has been cast to a real colored man." She claimed she had been cast in the juvenile lead and noted that the cast included her friend, Mr. Ellis.[24]

Not surprising, the Oregon newspapers reacted to the insult. The *Heppner Gazette* retorted that the reason the play failed was because "the people of Oregon were not in sympathy with the bandits, nor the dramatic element of the family. They could not endorse a drama that pictured those train robbers as innocent when no one doubted their guilt." The *Gazette* couldn't resist taking its own swipes at the young woman who had claimed that "the ignorant mossbacks up in that jay state" weren't "cultured up to appreciating" her talents.

The paper pointed out that Eva was set to play the juvenile lead in *Muldoon's Picnic* with a cast consisting of "herself, a pig-tail chinaman and a tar-heel Negro. All stars. A wonderful aggregation, isn't it," the paper editorialized, dripping sarcasm. "We now trust that Eva Evans has got back to a country where such gross and inexcusable ignorance does not prevail, and that her audiences may be highly enough cultured to fully appreciate her talent."[25]

Muldoon's Picnic, if she ever actually performed in it, was apparently not the success she'd hoped. Nor was a subsequent production in which she performed. One Fresno newspaper reported that Eva had joined Harry Knox's play, *The Great Railroad Strike*, which did not seem "a very great financial strike." Eva left the play and "complained that she was short of funds." By late September, newspapers were reporting that Eva Evans had "finally and completely failed as an actress." She told a reporter she planned to go back to Visalia to live with her mother and the other children.[26]

Before returning to Visalia, Eva went to visit her father at Folsom Prison. He was shocked by her appearance. She told him she'd been ill, but she did not tell him how she and Molly had suffered from "the lack of nourishing food, or of the difficult time the family was having."

Eva admitted she had to lie to her father during those hard times. She had thrown overboard the most important part of their family code—thou shalt not lie. "It [lying] was the one thing we could do [to hide our suffering]," she rationalized, "but I am sure we never fooled Dad any more than he did us."[27]

"THREE TIMES MARRIED," blared the heading of an article in the *Tulare County Times* in May 1895. (It was actually a reprint of an article from the *San Francisco Chronicle*, which the *Fresno Daily Evening Expositor* also reprinted.) The article was prompted by a report that Eva Evans had brought suit to recover interest in a mine in the Fresno mountains that was owned by John Sontag on the grounds that she was actually the widow of the deceased outlaw. It is unknown if such a suit ever existed, but it is doubtful, as no evidence or mention of it occurs anywhere else, and there was never any evidence that Eva married John Sontag. But the article didn't stop with just that rumor. It went on to claim that "Miss Evans married an actor, John Ellis, who played in the thrilling drama, *Evans and Sontag*." Not only was he in the play, but ironically he played the part of John Sontag.

While the all-but-forgotten fact that Eva was still legally married to James Evans precludes a legal marriage to Ellis, this does not mean there wasn't substance to the rumor. There was an Arthur Ellis in the touring company of the play—who may have used the first name John as well—and Eva wrote of a "Jack Ellis" who apparently stayed at the house that she and members of the White family shared during their forced two-month stay in Heppner. Later news reports also stated that Eva performed in a play that included "her friend, Mr. Ellis," in the cast.

This, coupled with the fact that the *Chronicle* even listed an address for the couple in Oakland, leads one to believe this wasn't just mere fabrication.[28] Also important to consider was Eva's eventful history of relationships with men. Though she had just turned eighteen, Eva had been romantically linked to a number of men. The rumors of romance that swirled around the attractive young actress were very much the nineteenth-century equivalent of the sordid tabloid sex scandals so prevalent today.

So if Eva was running around with John Ellis, where was her husband, Jim Evans? While the *Chronicle* report stated that Eva was "divorced from him, and then contracted the next alliance with Ellis," they were, in fact, still legally married. This is known because in the spring of 1896, she legally divorced Jim Evans. But in 1895, he was already out of the picture. According to court papers, he abandoned her only months after their 1893 marriage—in March 1894—and "ever since has and still continues so to willfully and without cause desert and abandon said plaintiff [Eva Evans]." When the divorce decree became final and made public, one Fresno newspaper posed this question: "Now that it is all over, do you suppose that she would be willing to tell what under the sun she married him for? That is what always beat everybody, you know."[29]

It is unknown what became of John/Arthur/Jack Ellis, but as there never was a legal marriage, there never was a divorce. The one brief mention of him in her memoir—he was the man who introduced the would-be rapist to her—sheds absolutely no light on his destiny.

About that same time, the fate of another man from her past was sealed. In her memoir, Eva quoted in full a lengthy article, written by Charles Michelson (a reporter who had filed numerous stories about Evans and Sontag) for the *San Francisco Examiner*. The moving account opened with "Fredericks, the murderer who was executed at San Quentin yesterday, was the gamest man I ever saw hanged." Michelson was by no means an apologist for Fredericks. He portrayed him as cold and calculating. And the strength of Michelson's account of the execution lay in his straightforward and unsentimental description. Still, in the end, Michelson couldn't help but wonder what might have been, and his comments echoed Eva's feelings.

> In one of my talks with the condemned man [wrote Michelson], he told me that when he had left the little school in Germany his ambition was to be a soldier, and the career that he had marked out for himself was that of a commander of men.
>
> Possibly if the boy Fredericks had been given a cadetship instead of being forced by his necessities to go to sea and generally make his way among the hard walks of life, there might have been a Captain Fredericks or a Colonel Fredericks, whose dashing courage would have made him world famous. At all events, that

is the thought that came to me when they cut his muffled body down.[30]

The next year, Ed Morrell, who would one day confess to having been smitten by young Eva, was transferred to the state prison at San Quentin. Before long, he was banished to solitary confinement and struggled to hold on to his last vestiges of sanity.[31]

CHARITABLE KINDNESS HELPED SUSTAIN the Evans family during the years that followed. Claims by the family that they were penniless, though perhaps exaggerated, are supported by mentions in the local newspaper that Molly took in laundry and worked in local packing houses and that Eva picked fruit in local orchards.[32] The family had little money and became, by necessity, somewhat fractured; the charitable kindness came to them in the person of Father Farrelly, the Catholic priest who had befriended them during their troubles and who had even stood as godfather to Chris during his jail-cell baptism into the Catholic faith.[33] Eva, herself, had started to attend Catholic services in Visalia, and she often noted to herself a resemblance between Father Farrelly and her father.

The kind priest had undoubtedly become a father figure to Eva in more than just a spiritual way; Father Farrelly made arrangements to help care for the rest of the children. He was able to send the boys—Louis, Joe and Johnnie—to a boarding school in Watsonville tuition free. Eva's two younger sisters were of high school age and were also sent away for their education and well-being. As Eva later explained, "the Sisters of Charity, Order of Saint Vincent de Paul had a convent and school for orphans and half-orphans in Los Angeles. If there was anyone to pay for you, you were expected to pay something; so Father Farrelly put Ynez and Winifred in this school and paid for Ynez for four years and Winifred for three."[34]

This left only Molly, Eva and Baby Carl (as they continued to call him, even though by 1895 he was four years old) to continue their daily struggle in Visalia, a struggle complicated by health issues that only worsened as the difficult years plodded by.

Carl had, as a toddler, fallen off the back porch at Grannie Byrd's house. Although Molly initially thought he hadn't been seriously hurt, she later noticed a raised up vertebra, painful to the touch, which kept getting worse and worse. Doctors told her there was nothing they could do, and Carl became increasingly crippled. "Only the hump seemed to grow on the little body, the arms and legs grew thin," Eva remembered.

Eva, too, was suffering physically during this period. This was due, she claimed, to the old back injury she had sustained during an Oakland performance of the melodrama. In a scenario that rings almost cliché to the modern reader, Eva had been prescribed morphine for the pain. It is pure conjecture to hint that she had become addicted, but (by her own admission) she had become so depressed that suicide became a viable option in her mind.

Offering the excuse that she "suffered a great deal," Eva wrote in her memoir how Dr. Page had given her morphine tablets for her to take "when the pain was too much." Though she didn't use the word suicide, Eva described how she had decided to save the pills until she had a sufficient supply available "to open the door......" To open the door, followed by an extended ellipsis; this was how Eva admitted, without using the actual words, that she had tried to take her own life. Her memoir is, understandably, the only source for this painful personal admission. It was an admission she did not dwell on. She simply wrote that "Mother found me in a coma, shook me into consciousness, and I told her what I had done. She gave me mustard and warm water and sent for Dr. Page." It was three months before she was out of bed, and Eva admitted she had only made things worse.

We just went on like this through the weary months, worried about the little boys in Watsonville... By the spring of '97, a year and half after they went away, Mother had saved enough money to go to Watsonville to see them. Joe and Louis begged her to take Johnnie home, saying that they would stay, realizing how poor we were, but she brought them all home, and we somehow managed to get along.

I was determined now to live and do something for the children. My body grew stronger, but the heartache increased. I had not visited my father since my return from San Francisco, nor had I seen Ynez or Winifred.

In the fall, some old houses were being moved away from the Douglas Block. Father Farrelly bought one of these for twenty dollars and had it moved onto the triangular block, containing about five lots, which we still owned in front of our old place. We fixed it up, and were again in a home of our own... We put out fruit trees, and Joe, who was now thirteen, planted a garden. Winifred came home. Louis, who was eleven, but looked sixteen, got a man's job driving a team at two-twenty-five a day.[35]

The hard times were far from over, but as Eva concluded this chapter in her memoir, they "were almost happy."

ACT FOUR

MOVING ON

Chapter Sixteen

Oregon Portraits

———◦◦———

A COMPLETE CHANGE OF CLIMATE was the recommendation made by Dr. Page for the insomnia and depression that Eva continued to battle. Perhaps the good doctor had rethought the wisdom of giving her morphine tablets. As Eva later recalled, "a friend" made it possible, in 1898, for her to go to Oregon. Eva declared that while there might be lovelier cities in the world than Portland, she had not yet seen one.

A clue as to who the friend was that made her relocation to Portland possible is found in the Tulare County marriage records. In April 1898, Eva Evans married a man named Albert F. Cribbs. As Eva never mentioned this husband in her memoir (at least not by name nor as her husband), little is known about him. From marriage and death records, one can discover that Cribbs was born in Pittsburgh, Pennsylvania, in 1860,[1] making him thirty-eight years old when he married Eva, who was only twenty-one years old. Cribbs was close in age to John Sontag (born only a year later), and although it is impossible to know the age difference of her first husband, James Evans, or her other rumored husband, John Ellis, it is highly likely that these men were also older than Eva. As independent and strong-willed as she always portrayed herself to be, Eva had, since she was barely in her teens, been continually involved (as fiancés, husbands or lovers) with men, often (if not always) very much older than her.

What Molly (or Chris, for that matter) felt about this marriage to a middle-aged man is unknown, but Eva could point out to her parents the difference in their own respective ages and had probably done so with her previous suitors. Besides, she might also argue, she was now an adult and could do as she wished. The argument could be made that

Eva had been doing exactly as she wished when it came to men and marriage for a long time now.

In her memoir, Eva didn't give Cribbs any credit for helping her relocate to Oregon or for helping her regain her health—she claimed it was "that emerald land [that] laid a healing hand upon my heart" and "in less than a month, I could sleep around the clock"—but he must have had some positive influence on the change. Nonetheless, at some point the marriage became, in Eva's mind, a mistake and so she later simply pretended it never existed.

So whether credit is due to Dr. Page for suggesting the change, or Albert Cribbs for making it possible, or the cool, wet breezes and verdant scenery of Oregon, Eva was able to recover from her awful insomnia, and as soon as she was strong enough, "secured work in a photograph gallery and began planning to get the family away from Visalia."

Eva was sensitive to the shameful stigma her family faced in Visalia, where they were well-known as the family of an outlaw. Having spent time in big cities like San Francisco and Portland, Eva now saw Visalia as a small town where everyone knew, and stuck their noses in, everyone else's business. She deeply wanted her younger brothers and sisters to have greater opportunity for success and relief from whispered abuse that would only be available far away from the site of so many earlier troubles, but, as she later admitted, she worried that wish was perhaps "just a dream."[2]

JOAQUIN MILLER CONTINUED TO HELP the family achieve that dream, and sometime during the waning years of the 1890s—after Ynez had graduated from the convent school in Los Angeles and returned to Visalia to rejoin her mother, sister Winifred, and the boys—the celebrated poet again offered a helping hand.

Miller invited Eva's sisters to stay at a cottage on his Oakland estate called "The Hights." If the florid descriptions of the poet's estate in various magazines of the day are to be believed, Ynez and Winifred had come to live in an idyllic setting.

One magazine described a visit to the hills above Oakland, where "round and round the mountain winds the road until it reaches the poet's home, and goes no farther."

> After crossing the little wooden bridge that spans a tiny rushing brook, the first house approached is occupied by Joaquin Miller's

foreman; then through a little avenue of roses planted each side of the highway we reach the gates of a place half wild, wholly beautiful. Two narrow rustic bridges bring us to the entrance of the small white house which is the poet's habitat.

A little farther up the hillside is the house of Joaquin Miller's mother, a sweet old lady with a gentle, kindly manner. All the mountain and the canyon behind it belongs to the poet, and his time is spent in making it a veritable paradise of birds and flowers and little crystal streams.[3]

There were a number of detached cottages on Miller's hillside estate. Eva remembered that her sisters had use of one called the Rose Cottage. "Fancy a mile of roses of every sort," a visitor once wrote. "The heavy perfume and glorious mass of color almost intoxicate the senses." And every writer who visited Miller's domain commented on the panoramic view from "far up on the hilltops, looking down on peaceful Oakland slumbering quietly below, over the shining waters to stately San Francisco, and out through the famous Golden Gate to the ocean beyond."[4]

Surely Eva envied the famous poet, and now her younger sisters, their ability to escape the drudgery of everyday life in this Edenic setting. As one journalist of the day was prompted in purple prose to profess: "Looking out upon the broad expanse of hill and vale and sea, it is small wonder Joaquin Miller is content to live apart from men and all the busy strife in marts of trade, to read each day in Nature's book some new unraveling of Nature's plan, whose threads are woven in supremest harmony in all the lights and shades that mark the handiwork of God."[5]

With Eva now in Oregon, and Winifred and Ynez in Oakland with Joaquin Miller, Molly was left on her own to care for the four boys. At some point, she found she could no longer give her youngest, crippled little Carl, the care he needed and he was sent to the Little Jim Hospital in San Francisco. Although Eva doesn't mention that Joaquin Miller had anything to do with this, it is possible he also had a hand in these arrangements.

The Little Jim Hospital was actually a wing of the Children's Hospital of San Francisco, and its establishment was due to the *San Francisco Examiner* and a writer that Eva once met on her visit to that newspaper's offices with Petey Bigelow. As the story goes, a mother once took her crippled child to the hospital's noted orthopedic department, only to find there was no room for her little boy. The plight of the crippled boy caught the attention of Winifred Sweet, known to readers as Annie Laurie, the original sob sister. The story prompted sympathetic readers to raise $30,000 to erect a new building, which was named for the crippled child in Annie Laurie's story: Little Jim.[6]

Eva recalled that with her sisters now living at The Hights, they could visit Carl at the Little Jim Hospital. On one such visit, little Carl begged Winifred to take him away from the hospital. She was told it was impossible without written permission from their mother. But she could not resist her little brother's pleading and so snuck him out. "She picked him up in his nightgown, tucked him under her cape, walked to the street car on Market, crossed the bay on the ferry boat, took a train to Alameda, a street car to Dimond, and walked a mile and a half up a mountain, with this six-year-old boy in her arms." Eva always admired Winifred's devotion to family.

Carl became a fixture around The Hights, carried around in his big sister's arms. One day, he said "Winnie, put me down; I can walk."

She did, and he was able to walk a few steps. He walked a little more each day, and before long he was able to clamber around the hillside paths. Joaquin Miller always liked flowers for the table, and one day he said, "Carlton, you have a new name; you are Lord Flowers. From this day on, your duty will be to gather flowers for every meal and place them beside the plates."[7]

In his 1927 book, *Joaquin Miller and His Other Self*, Harr Wagner recalled that the poet's association with the Evans family was "the only time that he slipped back to the days of Joaquin Murrieta and his association with men of the bandit and renegade type." Wagner was a close friend and publisher of Joaquin Miller (and lived for a time at The Hights) and wrote that he doubted Miller enjoyed his association with Mrs. Evans and her daughters. Wagner seemed to base this on the fact that Miller "never wrote or talked much about the Evans family as his guests," nor did he ever mention, Wagner claimed, "that the Evans family took care of his two sons for several years." According to Wagner, Miller paid Mrs. Evans fifty dollars a month for their board and care.[8]

This could be seen as evidence that Molly Evans later did what she could to repay Miller's hospitality, but, of course, she would have greatly benefited from the added income, and so this, too, can be seen as one more favor provided by Joaquin Miller. By his comments, Wagner inferred that he felt the Evans family—the family of a convicted criminal—was taking advantage of his friend, the magnanimous and highly cultured poet.

THE REDWOOD RANCH ULTIMATELY MADE ESCAPE from Visalia possible for Molly and the boys. Just after the turn of the century, in January 1900, Molly and Chris deeded the property, which had been their cherished summer home, to Molly's mother in consideration of the sum of ten dollars. Molly traveled to Folsom to have Chris sign the document in front of a notary, and this was only the first step involved in ultimately transferring the property to the United States government as part of the forest preserve.

Molly's mother, Isabella Byrd, in turn deeded the property to a Tulare County man named S. B. Patrick, again in consideration of ten dollars, but this wasn't until June of that year. Patrick turned right around and deeded the property to John Lillis in Santa Barbara, who the very next day deeded it to the United States of America, who would "select the same number of acres of other vacant public lands" and conveyed that to Lillis.[9] This land was then sold for four hundred dollars, and thus the transfer was complete (although Eva later recalled, in far simpler terms, that the government had offered Molly five hundred dollars for the property). This somewhat complicated procedure took some time. Molly was still living in Visalia as late as May 1901, but according to Eva, it was proceeds from the sale of the Redwood Ranch to the government that finally made it possible for her mother and brothers to move to Portland, Oregon, sometime around the turn of the new century.

> So in this way [Eva later wrote] the Evans family really began a new life. We were farther from our father, but we had so little money that it was difficult for us to visit him anyway, and there was a chance here in this larger city for the boys to make a better living. They were still only children, but Louis at fourteen seemed almost grown, and he had been doing a man's work since he was eleven. He went to work in a saw mill, loading lumber on wagons. There was nothing for them but hard labor, but in Oregon, at least, they would escape hearing, "Your father was a train robber."

Eva also noted that the sale of the Redwood Ranch put the property into the boundaries and possession of a government forest reserve that eventually became Sequoia National Forest. Although not as protected as nearby Sequoia National Park, this nonetheless meant that her father's cherished forest of pine, fir, and beloved giant sequoias would be far less likely to fall to the lumbermen's saws. "I knew this would please my father, who so loved those trees," Eva wrote.[10]

At some point, Ynez and Winifred left The Hights and joined Molly and the boys in Portland and before long, Eva's youngest sister had married. Winifred was twenty years old when she married Walter Burrell, but it is unknown if, like her sister Eva, she married a much older man. And, like Eva's marriage to Albert Cribbs, the details of the union are unrecorded.

Regarding Eva's marriage, one can only make assumptions. But based on her memoir's utter silence on the years with Cribbs, one easy assumption is that these years were not happy ones. Little is known of what Eva did or thought during this period in her life. In 1903, she did have a reminder of her past troubles. There was a great flash flood in Heppner, Oregon, and among the 250 people killed was Dr. McSword. It is unclear how soon after the tragic flood Eva heard the news that the doctor who had shown her so much kindness had perished, but as she mentioned it in her memoir, she probably read about it in the newspapers.[11]

If one assumes that Eva's marriage wasn't a happy one; neither, apparently, was Winifred's. Although she and Walter had a baby, their marriage didn't last more than a few years. By 1904, Winifred had moved to Sacramento. It is unclear if this was with or without her husband, but in less than three years she remarried.

Ynez also married at some point during this period, as she now carried the last name of Mason.[12] Like both her sisters, this early marriage would not turn out to be a successful one. One thing the Evans girls had found in Oregon were husbands, but unlike their mother's, these husbands would not last. Would Eva look at her mother and wonder how she had gotten it right the first time? Was Chris Evans, for Eva and her sisters, the model of a good spouse, regardless of the fact that he was now serving a life sentence in Folsom Prison? Perhaps they all saw him as the perfect husband, and no man could live up to him. Or was he an absent father that his daughters sought to replace with hasty marriages? Whatever the answer, they all—Molly included—held out hope that someday, regardless of that life sentence to Folsom, Chris Evans—beloved husband and father—would return to them.

Parole was the hope to which Eva, her mother, and sisters clung. In late 1904, Winifred, now in Sacramento, threw herself into seeing that hope realized. Chris Evans had applied for parole in 1901, but was denied. Now Winifred organized a more concerted effort that brought out some surprising, and not so surprising, support.

It was of little surprise that Joaquin Miller would offer to write a letter to the governor of California on behalf of Chris Evans. Following a visit to Molly and the family in Oregon in 1905 (perhaps this was when he left his sons with Molly), Miller penned a lengthy letter describing the persecution of Chris Evans, the hardships faced by the family, and the incompetence of their lawyers. He told how he had advised them to drop their lawyer and appeal directly to the governor. He described the children as all hardworking, who gave any money they earned to their mother to help get their father out of prison.

"I never in all my life saw such devotion," Miller wrote. "These girls and boys, as well as the mother, came [to Oregon] to work in the saw mills after they had spent their last dollar in California. They never changed nor denied their name nor the sad story of the family. I know nothing so beautiful as the way in which Mrs. Evans has brought up and educated these six [*sic*] children through all this trouble."

Miller closed by asking the governor if he would meet with Mrs. Evans and one or two of the children. "I promise you there will be no pleading, no waste of time, no tears," Miller assured, but pointed out that he wanted the governor "to see they are honorable, earnest, refined and educated far, far above their misfortune." The boys, he concluded, were still in their teens and "deserve better than the death of the father in prison."[13] The letter had little effect, but does serve as a contradiction to Harr Wagner's theory that Joaquin Miller did not think very highly of the Evans family.

In 1906, Winifred stepped up her efforts, traveling to Fresno County to obtain letters of support for a petition to the governor to commute her father's life sentence. She received support from some surprising sources, including jury members, prosecuting attorneys, and even former law officers.

Jury foreman J. N. Reese wrote that he did not believe Chris Evans, owing to his "age and physical condition," would ever attempt another crime and that he had no hesitation in recommending that his life sentence be commuted to twenty years.

Alva Snow, a deputy district attorney who had participated in the prosecution, commented that one thing that impressed him at the trial "was the high esteem which Chris Evans was held by his neighbors" and that his "reputation was as good in every respect as the best citizens of the community." Snow went so far as to claim Evans "seemed to have been led astray by two men named Contant, alias Sontag." And while he claimed there was no question "but what he committed the offense for which he was convicted," Snow felt "he'd been sufficiently punished" and asked that the petition for commutation be granted.

Former Fresno sheriff Jay Scott, who in 1903 had called Chris Evans "one of the hardest criminals ever sent to prison" and recommended to the parole board that he "should stay where he is," wrote only three years later, in a letter to Governor Pardee, that Evans was "old, maimed and disabled, and prior to the year of 1892 he was a hard working, highly respected citizen of Visalia." He pointed out that he'd been a model prisoner, and that his family were "worthy and respectable people." That said, Scott recommended clemency and commutation of his sentence.[14]

In December, Winifred presented her plea in person to Governor Pardee and was denied. The family was discouraged but determined not to give up.

Eva was ever grateful for her younger sister's hard work. One later newspaper report, however, had confused which of the Evans daughters was leading the charge. It reported that "Mrs. Eva Burrell of Oak Park, a suburb of Sacramento, is the author of this latest movement to allow Evans to spend his few remaining years in freedom."[15] With all their recent marriages, this mistaken melding of Eva Cribbs and Winifred Burrell by the press was forgivable, but Eva herself readily confirmed that it was Winifred who performed "untiring efforts" in obtaining their father's release from prison.[16]

PHOTOGRAPHY BROUGHT EVA BACK to California and reunited her with Winifred in 1907, when she had the opportunity to work for Grace Hubley at her photography studio in Sacramento. This return to California also marked a return to the pages of her own memoir, for she had seemed to disappear from the narrative ever since her never-mentioned marriage to Albert Cribbs.

Grace Hubley earned her place in the early history of women photographers in San Francisco during the first years of the twentieth century. Having won an amateur photo contest sponsored by the *San Francisco Chronicle* in 1900, she began to have photos exhibited and published and became a member of the California Camera Club. In 1904, she mounted an exhibit of her work in the offices of the California Camera Club. Hubley later attended the Aristo School of Photography and told Eva she had studied with the noted photographer Arnold Genthe.[17]

Hubley, like her mentor Arnold Genthe and a number of prominent photographers in San Francisco, saved little or nothing of their work from the flames following the great earthquake in April 1906. Undaunted, Hubley continued to study and work in San Francisco until she relocated to Sacramento in 1907.

It is unknown how Eva came to be "offered a position in the Grace Hubley Studio" in Sacramento. She had gained some experience working in a photo studio in Portland. With this new opportunity in California, she was thrilled because she would be able to "learn the highest type of photographic art," but above all else, she could join her sister Winifred and be near her father.

Eva wasn't able to see her father as much as she'd like; her work schedule and his limit to one visitor per month precluded frequent visits. But knowing she was only two hours away comforted Eva. She didn't work for Grace Hubley very long; only a few months. But during that time, which may very well have been a time she was recovering from another failed marriage, she gained, in her own words, "courage and knowledge." It was that courage and knowledge that spurred Eva to act on a plan she and Ynez had been mulling over for some time. They decided to open their own photographic studio in Marshfield, Oregon.[18]

Both their marriages had apparently failed, and it is unknown if Eva and Ynez were left with anything more than the surnames of their respective husbands: Cribbs and Mason. But they had saved every penny they could get their hands on, and in December 1907, Mrs. Cribbs and Mrs. Mason journeyed to San Francisco to buy supplies. They found the downtown district, twenty months after the earthquake and fire, still a mass of ruins. But they were also impressed with the thriving business district that had sprung up on Fillmore Street as the city rebuilt. Attending a New Year's celebration, Eva was taken with the strength of spirit in San Francisco that had flared out from the rubble and ashes. Did it dawn on her that she and Ynez were themselves setting out to rebuild a new life out of the rubble and ashes of failed marriages and a troubled past?

By early 1908, ads began appearing in the *Daily Coos Bay Times* of Marshfield, Oregon, listing the photography studio of Cribbs & Mason in the Coos Bay Monthly building on Front Street. Eva and Ynez, presumably alone and without their husbands, had hung out their shingle.

EVA AND YNEZ WERE NOT THE ONLY ONES to get a fresh start that year. In 1908, both George Contant (alias Sontag) and Ed Morrell were released from prison.

George's sentence was commuted and he walked out of Folsom Prison on March 21, 1908. This undoubtedly angered Eva, but considering that she always believed he had made a deal with the railroad in return for his testimony against her father, it hardly surprised her. She knew if the railroad wanted, it could get George paroled. Eva didn't doubt that he had suffered during the sixteen years he served in Folsom, and more than once during those years tragedy had touched George's family outside the walls of his prison. In 1897, his nine-year-old son was killed on an errand to the store—run over by a switch engine in the rail yard near his home. Less than two years later, his wife, Theresa, fell ill and died. "Was ever a man being more thoroughly punished than I?" an utterly depressed George asked himself.[19]

The years in prison had taken their toll on George, now in his forties. One newspaper described him upon his release as "crippled with rheumatism, bullet-scarred and broken in health…he is only a shadow of his former vigorous, robust self. Sixteen years ago he was not afraid to meet any man in deadly combat, or even to lead a prison revolt, but as he turns his back on Folsom Prison, he is almost as helpless as a child."[20]

The suffering Ed Morrell endured in prison became legendary, although his penchant for exaggeration shaded that legend. Having been transferred to San Quentin in 1896, Morrell labored in the jute mill, which he likened to Dante's Inferno. In 1899, he became involved in an escape plot that (according to him) turned out to be a set up. Betrayed by his co-conspirator, Morrell ended up in solitary confinement, and because he couldn't give answers to questions prison officials asked, he was considered an incorrigible and languished in solitary. Prison records indicate Morrell was kept in solitary confinement for four years and seven months.

Morrell claimed to have saved his sanity by utilizing his mind to transport himself away from the torment of this deeper circle of hell to which he'd been sent. He would communicate with another "solitary" by tapping on the wall of his nine-by-four-and-a-half-foot cell. The hell he experienced in solitary may be the one thing he didn't need to exaggerate.

After his release from solitary, Morrell became a model prisoner and began spending every spare moment working toward securing his freedom, even garnering letters of support from the Fresno judge who originally sentenced him and the former marshal, John Morgan, who had been shot by Evans during the Fresno jailbreak.[21]

It is unknown what Eva thought about Ed Morrell's release from San Quentin in March 1908, but it had to fill her with hope that even Morrell was able to obtain parole. At the same time, there was a growing frustration that everyone *but* Chris Evans was getting paroled. A grudge-bearing and politically powerful railroad could be a factor, Eva realized, and as hard as her sister worked in Sacramento, their father's release still seemed an unattainable dream.

In May 1908, a celebrity visited Marshfield, Oregon, and it made headlines in the local newspapers. "Joaquin Miller, the 'Poet of the Sierras,' is feasting his beauty loving soul on the water girt ways and forest clad hills that surround Coos Bay," the paper reported.

> A pretty incident of the trip, "one of the prettiest in my life," the poet said with gentle graciousness, was his arrival and greeting at North Bend, whither his Marshfield friends, Mrs. Mason and Mrs. Cribbs, whose guest he is, went to meet him. The steamer was delayed at quarantine and the ladies wandered up to the hillside at Simpson park where the Rhododendrons grow in great profusion, and they plucked arms full of the blossom laden boughs. As the steamer approached the dock the poet's eye quickly found the flowers. He remarked to a companion that there was a beautiful welcome awaiting someone, but did not think it for him. When he landed, he said "the flowers beckoned" to him and then he received a royal welcome.
>
> The poet is stopping in Marshfield at the home of Mrs. Mason and Mrs. Cribbs in the rear of their studio on Front Street.[22]

Certainly Eva and Ynez knew how much Joaquin Miller liked flowers. He was also very fond of having his picture taken, so while Miller visited his photographer friends, several images of the poet were made.

One photo was taken during a picnic outing to Hilborn's Landing. This excursion, too, made the local papers, which reported that in addition to Joaquin Miller and Mesdames Cribbs and Mason, "other members of the party were Messrs. McCullough and Mr. Jensen."[23] It can only be assumed that Mr. Mason and Mr. Cribbs were, literally and figuratively, no longer in the picture.

The Messrs. McCullough the society item referred to were two brothers—Bret and Perry McCullough—who had recently moved to Marshfield and operated the Crystal Theatre, said to be the first moving picture theatre in the growing harbor city. Norris Jensen was a well-known Marshfield businessman who owned and operated a tailor shop.

Eva had only recently met Perry McCullough. She would always recall that it was in May that he showed up in the reception room of their photo studio. She was sure it was May because the studio was decked out with pink and white rhododendrons, which "one could just go out in the woods and gather by the armful."[24] (Perhaps these were the same rhododendrons she and Ynez had gathered for Joaquin's arrival.)

Perry, who had the coloring and fair hair of Eva's younger brothers, was born in Nebraska in 1886, making him a full ten years younger than Eva, who was thirty-two years old at the time.

He had worked at a bank in Omaha when he read about Coos Bay in *Sunset* magazine. With the "best harbor on the coast between the Puget Sound and San Francisco," the coming of the railroad, vast and virgin lumber and other natural resources, the region was being touted as "The Next Metropolis on the Pacific Coast,"[25] and the McCullough brothers smelled opportunity. So Bret and Perry, much like the Evans sisters, had come to the Oregon coast with dreams of finding business success. Though Perry, because of his age and looks, may have reminded Eva of a younger brother, her feelings for him quickly developed into something far more than sisterly. Ynez, meanwhile, began to develop feelings for the more mature and established Norris Jensen.

Before 1908 drew to a close, Ynez and Eva once again made the local society pages. It was reported that a "Popular Couple Wed: Norris Jensen, prominent business man, and Mrs. Ynez Mason married Monday afternoon."[26] The paper didn't mention that it was fifteen years to the day since Ynez's father, Chris Evans, had escaped from the Fresno jail. Indeed, there was no mention and likely no knowledge that the father of the bride was one of America's most famous outlaws. One valuable thing all the Evans girls got from their respective husbands was anonymity through different last names: names that were mentioned when the newspaper noted that both Ynez's sisters attended—Mrs. A. A. Gutierrez (Winifred, who had herself recently remarried) from

Sacramento and *Mr. and* Mrs. A. F. Cribbs of Marshfield. Perhaps the reporter mistook the handsome young man on Eva's arm for her legal husband, Albert Cribbs. It was in all likelihood, however, Perry McCullough. She married him in Vancouver, British Columbia, sometime the following year.

What brought the couple to Canada was, ostensibly, work for a lumber company. Neither the Evans sisters nor the McCullough brothers seemed to find lasting success in their Marshfield business ventures. By early 1909, ads for Cribbs and Mason Photographers disappeared from the newspaper, and Bret McCullough had taken a job at a movie theatre across the bay in Coquille, indicating failure of the theatre he and Perry ran in Marshfield. But Eva and Perry had found something they hoped would have real staying power: each other.

It is not clear exactly when Eva was divorced from Albert Cribbs, and perhaps she never legally was. Could that be one reason Eva and Perry went to Canada to get married? Eva had already shown that she played fast and loose with the marriage laws. Accusing her of polygamy, compared to some of her other crimes, doesn't seem like such a harsh indictment. And for Eva, the mere bending of a law surely seemed like a small thing compared to the lifetime of happiness she now looked forward to with Perry.

CHAPTER SEVENTEEN

Utopian Dreams

*How long I slept I know not, for when I awoke my boat was
close to shore, and to my astonishment I was in strange waters.*

—CHRIS EVANS, *EURASIA*

MARITAL BLISS WAS DAMPENED when Perry came down with
pneumonia while he and Eva were living in Spokane, Washington. Perry developed tuberculosis, and doctors recommended a drier, warmer climate. Rather than return to Eva's home state
of California, the couple moved to Arizona,[1] but it is not known what
work, if any, Perry was able to get in that desert state.

Winifred, meanwhile, had remarried. Adalberto "Albert" Gutierrez
was about the same age as Winifred and, as his name would indicate,
of Hispanic descent. He was a dark contrast to the blonde-haired, blue-
eyed Winifred, and the two made a striking couple. The only other thing
known about Albert Gutierrez is that he evidently owned a farm, for
early in 1910 he promised the prison parole board that he would furnish
Chris Evans, if he were to be released, employment as a farmhand on
his place east of Sacramento.[2] Winifred was eliciting the help of everyone she could in her long-continuing effort to win her father's release.

Hope of that release glimmered anew as the California gubernato-
rial race got under way in 1910. Hiram W. Johnson, a successful lawyer
from Sacramento, won the Republican nomination and was supported
by a group of reformers within the party known as "Progressives." Like
many others, Johnson believed that the greatest source of corruption
in California was that dreaded "octopus": the railroad. He pledged to

"return the government of California to the people and take it away from the political bureau of the Southern Pacific Company." As historian William Deverell observed, Johnson's myopic concentration on the Southern Pacific was hardly accidental. The Progressives' adherence to a single-issue campaign stood in stark contrast to the much wider reform agenda embraced by other groups to the left of the insurgent Republicans.[3] And it was a strategy that resonated with voters.

Sometime during 1910, with funds running low, Perry and Eva moved to Los Angeles. It isn't known if Eva returned to California in time for the fall election, but in spirit she undoubtedly supported Hiram Johnson. (Even if she did live in California, her support of Johnson would have to be in spirit only, as women were a year away from having the right to vote in California and nearly a decade from the constitutional right nationwide.) Anyone who pledged to fight the railroad like Hiram Johnson was a friend of Chris Evans and thus worthy of her support. And such a governor might just be receptive to considering his case and granting him clemency or parole, if not an outright pardon.

In January 1911, Hiram Johnson was inaugurated as the twenty-third governor of California. The emancipation of California from railroad rule could begin, but for Eva McCullough, it was the emancipation of only one man that mattered.

LESS THAN A MONTH AFTER HIRAM JOHNSON took office, attorney R. T. McKisick of Sacramento presented the new governor an application for a commutation of sentence along with numerous supporting documents that had originally been presented to his predecessors. Among the papers were the numerous letters of support Winifred had obtained, reports on Evans' exemplary behavior in prison, and even a certificate from the Fresno County clerk confirming there were no pending indictments against Evans.[4] It was all material that had already been gathered—all the hard work had been done—but now it could be submitted to a more receptive set of eyes.

When the Board of Prison directors met a little more than two months later, they found "good and sufficient reasons why the parole should be granted" and on April 15, 1911, Chris Evans received notification of their decision.[5] He had been in prison for more than seventeen years. That same day he sent a letter, handwritten on Folsom Prison stationery, to Eva. She kept it the rest of her life.

My Darling Eva,

I am paroled to take effect the 1st of May and I am going to make
my home at Portland, Oregon with Mama and the boys. You and
I will have a good time yet and you will be my companion in
another exploring tour. Cheer up, my darling, we will be having a
happy time in the sweet bye and bye.

Your loving Dad,
Chris Evans [6]

Although one newspaper reporter opined, upon announcement that
sixty-four-year-old Chris Evans was to be paroled, that "the broken old
bandit did not realize that the real sentence meted out to him is that he
has been forgotten,"[7] his release from prison made headlines in papers
throughout the state.

Jack Jungmeyer, of the *Sacramento Star,* was one of the many reporters gathered outside the gates of Folsom Prison on a glorious May
Day morning. "We watched him come to the great iron gate and pause
while the keeper unlocked it—a stooping figure with hair grayed to the
color of prison walls and a sad smile upon his lean cheeks."[8]

Eva, however, was unable to be there. Perry's illness had relapsed
and so Eva dared not leave their home in Los Angeles. She could only
read about the day she had so long dreamed would come. She pasted
more than a dozen newspaper clippings, along with the letter from her
father, in a scrapbook. These news reports described her father's exit
through the open gates of Folsom; his reunion with a waiting Winifred;
many recounted his earlier exploits with varying accuracy; most included comments from the recently freed man such as: "My battles are
over" or "I'm not a reformed crook. I had nothing to reform." Winifred
was mentioned in most every article, with credit given to Evans' youngest daughter who "year after year pleaded for mercy for her father,"
although many newspapers mistakenly still referred to her as Winifred
Burrell (she was now Winifred Gutierrez).[9]

One facet of Chris Evans' release from prison that was detailed in
newspapers was especially indicative of the interest he still aroused and
reminds us that an intrusive media is as old as the medium itself.

The *Sacramento Star*'s Jack Jungmeyer wrote a side-bar to his
front page account of Evans' release. Under an "Exclusive photograph
of Chris Evans," the following headline announced "STAR HAS A
THRILLING AUTO CHASE OVER THE HILLS, BUT CAPTURES
EVANS AND PICTURE."

No posse of Southern Pacific and Wells-Fargo blood-money men [Jungmeyer wrote] ever had a more exciting chase in an endeavor to capture Chris Evans, one time chieftain of the famous Sontag-Evans gang of train robbers, than that the former bandit gave me this morning when I undertook to capture the paroled man to get his photograph.

I succeeded only after an automobile chase of 30 miles during which the machine in which Evans and his daughter, Winifred, and a party of friends were being carried to Sacramento and the machine in which I rode, held to a mile-a-minute pace over the greater part of the road.

Luck was against the Evans party or I might never have secured his picture.

In laughing over the experience afterward he said, "You never would have overtaken me had it not been for that freight train. I thought I was done with the Southern Pacific, but I see they are still my hoodoo. They blocked me again just at the critical time."

"But I enjoyed the man-hunt immensely" he added, with a smile that came from the bottom of his heart. "It was not quite so tragic as some I have taken part in, but I was in it heart and soul while it lasted. We gave you a good run, anyway."[10]

Eva would be comforted to read that her father still maintained his sense of humor, and she would probably chuckle to think his first ride in an automobile had been so eventful.

Another thing the papers all reported was Chris Evans' plan to go to Portland to join his wife and boys—indeed, a condition of his parole was that he "reside outside the State of California, to wit, in the state of Oregon."[11] Of course, this meant he would be heading farther away from Eva, and with her current situation in Los Angeles (a sick husband and little money), she didn't know when she'd ever get to see her father.

On his way to Oregon, Chris Evans made a stop in Oakland to visit an old friend. This, too, made it into the newspapers and subsequently into Eva's scrapbook.

A photo taken during that visit was published in the *San Francisco Star*. Joaquin Miller, who arose from his sick bed to be photographed with his friend, Chris Evans, always did like to have his picture taken. In the photo, Miller is seated with a large woolly blanket draped over his lap, his hands folded atop a sheaf of papers. He wears an oddly blank stare, looking straight into the camera; even in the faded and fold-ed clipping pasted into Eva's scrapbook there is discernable a haunting hollowness that draws attention to his eyes.

Chris is seated next to the poet, wearing a dark suit, with one leg crossed up over the other. He is shorn of beard and his head is still prison-shaven. Although Chris, too, is facing the camera, both his eyes are lost in shadow. Half of his face falls away in darkness due to the directional light. The deep-set socket on the illuminated side of his face disappears in a black hole of shadow, where his bad eye sees only ever darkness.

The photo, which ran dead-center on the *Star's* front page on May 20, 1911, is captioned "Concerning Two 'Outlaws.'" The entire com-position, with its dark background and dramatically lit subjects, has the feel of a Rembrandt painting—Joaquin Miller as a subject is even reminiscent of the Dutch painter himself. Chris Evans, on the other hand, looks content to disappear into the shadows. "All I now want is to get off to a quiet spot with my family, there to regain my health and live in peace and quiet," Chris told a newspaper upon his release. "I'm done fighting."[12]

EVA'S EXISTENCE IN LOS ANGELES was a difficult one. She and Perry moved to Southern California and rented a tiny three-room house for ten dollars a month. With just a few dollars left to their name, Eva found work in a cafeteria. She would often work twelve-hour days, while Perry had to stay home in bed. "I'd give him his breakfast and put his lunch on the table beside him, and go to work," Eva later recalled. "His heart was bad; the doctor thought that it would kill him before the TB was much further advanced, but he didn't know this." Eva would be relieved when she came home late at night to a light burning in their little house, for this meant Perry hadn't died during the day.[13]

After a full year bedridden, Perry was finally able to get out of bed for a while in the morning and soon could help with housework and even work an hour in the garden. Eva found employment in a photog-raphy studio, with better pay and easier hours. With her father settled in Oregon and Perry now able to take care of himself, Eva was finally able to travel to Portland to visit her father. The visit was short, as she could only get two weeks off from her studio job and it would take five days travel by boat, which was all she could afford.

"No one knows what it meant to me to see my father out of a prison," she wrote. "No hideous prison stripes—no smell of iodoform. We sat for hours in the back garden, and talked and talked. He didn't want to stay in the house; he just couldn't get enough of the sun and the sky."

Eva was able to extend the visit a little when her brothers gave her enough money to take the train home, thus cutting her travel time by a couple of days. Eva fondly remembered spending time with her brother, Louis, on a sun-drenched afternoon before she left. They talked, and Louis intimated to his sister that he wasn't entirely happy in his new marriage (a subject his sister Eva could no doubt appreciate). He had nothing but praise and admiration for his new wife, however, and when Eva asked why it was he wasn't happy, all he could think to say was: "Billee, it's just because Florence is not like you."

Louis had years before given Eva the nickname that more and more of her friends and family continued to call her. As family legend had it, little Louis had starting calling his oldest sister Pete. One day, Grannie Byrd asked him why he called his sister Pete. "That's a Chinaman's name," she admonished him.

"Is it?" Louis replied. "Then I'll call her Bill."

When asked why he should give her a boy's name instead of the perfectly lovely name she already had, Louis responded, "She's too good a fellow to have a girl's name."[14] Eva returned to Los Angeles the next day not realizing that she would never see her brother Louis again.

Back at work, Eva eventually saved enough money to buy a lot on the east side of town, where it was drier and warmer and Perry might continue to improve. They put a tent with a floor and low siding on the lot and lived in it for years before they were able to convert it into a real house. Times were tough, but they were able to get by. Many were not so lucky. More and more, Eva had begun to think about the hardships faced by so many. She became "intensely concerned with the injustices under which working people labored." Perry, with time on his hands, read and thought deeply about these social questions as well. They spent many evenings discussing these problems and shared their frustration that little was being done.

One day, Eva read an article about Emma Goldman, and Perry encouraged her to attend one of the famous anarchist's lectures. "She, at least, is doing something!" Perry told Eva. "She's not sitting supinely like most of us, letting everything go wrong. Perhaps we can help in our way, small though it be. Go, by all means, and tell me all about it."[15]

EMMA GOLDMAN, EASILY THE MOST NOTORIOUS woman of her day, was many things. She was a practicing anarchist, a labor agitator, a pacifist during World War I and, yet, an advocate of political violence, a feminist and a proponent of free love and birth control, a communist and a street-fighter for justice. She had come to America from Russia in 1886 as a teenager. As the back-cover blurb of her still-in-print autobiography recounts, "After an encounter in the sweat shop and an unfortunate marriage, she plunged into the bewildering intellectual and activist chaos that attended American social evolution around the turn of the century. She knew practically everyone of importance in radical circles. She dominated many areas of the radical movement, lecturing, writing, haranguing, and publishing to awaken the world to her ideas."[16]

During the years Eva and Perry lived in Los Angeles—basically the second decade of the twentieth century—Emma Goldman kept up a constant lecture tour, usually speaking on the West Coast during May or June. It was after one of these lectures—the topic of which may have been: "Anarchism, the Moving Spirit in the Labor Struggle"; "Woman's Inhumanity to Man"; "The Failure of Charity"; or even "Sex, the Element of Creative Work"[17]—that Eva McCullough waited around for the opportunity to introduce herself to the most notorious woman of her day. Eva mentioned that her father, too, was notorious, and Emma well remembered hearing of Chris Evans. She invited Eva to come back to her apartment for supper and to meet some of her comrades-in-arms.[18]

"Emma was a good cook," Eva recalled, noting that the matriarch of the anarchist movement regularly hosted dinners for her working crew—the ones who sold books and took tickets and such—in her apartment. Surrounded by her admirers, Emma was at her best at these gatherings, and Eva felt privileged to be a part. Like most who met her, Eva was taken with the magnetism of Emma Goldman. Men had often described how sexually attractive she was, even though she was not what anyone would consider conventionally beautiful. Eva offered this physical description. "Her body was too short and stout for beauty, but her hair was a lovely light golden brown and wavy...and her eyes were the most beautiful shade of deep blue, almost violet."[19] Eva considered Emma Goldman the most intelligent woman she ever met.

Before long, Eva and Perry became regulars at these gatherings and got to know Emma and her circle of friends, associates and admirers. They met Ben Reitman, Emma's longtime manager and sometime lover, whom Eva described as "one of the least understood men" she had ever known. In 1912, following IWW (Industrial Workers of the World) riots in San Diego and Emma's comments at the Los Angeles funeral for IWW agitator Joseph Mikolasek, who'd been killed by San Diego police, a vigilante mob waited for her and Reitman to arrive in San Diego. Emma was able to flee town and return to Los Angeles, but Reitman was kidnapped by the mob. Taken to the outskirts of town, he was stripped, tarred and feathered. According to Eva's account, when someone suggested they brand "IWW" on his bare ass with a hot cigar, Reitman protested: "I'm not an IWW!"

"What are you then?" one of the mob retorted.

"I'm just a sympathizer," Reitman pointed out, to which his angered captors replied, "All right, you'll get that then: 'IWW Sympathizer.'"

"Okay," said Reitman, "Just let it go at 'IWW.'"[20]

Eva was obviously repeating a version of history that Ben Reitman had probably told numerous times, and one can well imagine the roar of laughter (and the shudder of fear) it inspired in a room full of IWW sympathizers.

Eva and Perry met and socialized with many like-minded people during Emma's annual stays in Los Angeles, but they didn't tend to meet at other times of the year. At Emma's suggestion, they tried to organize a Radical Dinner Club to meet once a month when Emma was not in town. But the idea only served to highlight the genius Emma had to bring people together. Their meetings were unsuccessful, degenerating into nothing more than raucous shouting matches.

But every year they continued to attend all of Emma's local lectures. In 1914, they had Winifred's little boy—who was only eleven or twelve years old—with them. Eva described her young nephew, Billy Burrell, as "good to look at and intelligent far beyond his years." She thought it would be good for him to meet Emma Goldman. He wanted to help sell books on the floor at one lecture. "So one night at her lecture on birth control," Eva later recalled, "this handsome lad was going up and down the aisles, holding a pamphlet above his head, crying *What Every Girl Should Know* by Margaret Sanger, twenty-five cents!"[21] This would have been considered utterly shocking, for those were times when people such as Margaret Sanger were regularly arrested for even distributing birth control information.

In 1915, Emma wrote to Billee (as she called Eva, utilizing the family nickname) and Perry that her friend, Alexander Berkman, was coming to the West Coast, and she asked them to look out for him and see that he meet the "gang." Berkman, like Goldman, was a Russian-born anarchist, and the two had even had a brief romance when both were becoming involved in radical political activism. In 1892, at the age of twenty-two, Berkman attempted to assassinate Henry Clay Frick, a wealthy industrialist involved in a bitter dispute with steelworkers in Homestead, Pennsylvania. It was, in Emma Goldman's words, "the first Anarchist act of economic terror in the United States, and Alexander Berkman had to pay dearly for his revolutionary protest."[22] Convicted of attempted murder, Berkman served fourteen years in prison, many of them in solitary confinement. He was released in 1906.

Nearly a decade later, when he and his secretary/lover, Mary Fitzgerald, arrived in Los Angeles, they stayed with the McCulloughs. Berkman was said to be at work on a book. When Perry, doing much better physically, had the opportunity to go to San Francisco and work at the fairgrounds, he and Eva jumped at the chance. They let Sasha and Fitzie (as Berkman and Mary were known) stay at their house, while Berkman continued to work on his writing.

One book of Berkman's, published just a couple of years earlier, that Eva could especially appreciate was his *Prison Memories of an Anarchist*, which he dedicated to "all those who, in and out of prison, fight against their bondage." In the copy he gave to Eva, Berkman added the following inscription:

> To the Tribe of Evans—May Their Shadow Never Grow Less— Whose social outlawry reflects their intense hatred of injustice and tyranny, their love of liberty, and the rare and unique personalities that are still extant, here and there, in spite of our rotten, leveling civilization.
>
> —Sasha[23]

ALEXANDER BERKMAN WAS NOT THE ONLY PERSON Eva knew to publish a prison memoir. Since the spring of 1909, George (Sontag) Contant had been promoting *A Pardoned Lifer*, which was his life story as told to author Opie L. Warner. "In introducing the book," the *Visalia Delta* noted, "Mr. Sontag says his one desire is to render an object lesson. The paths of crime lead unerringly to punishment, and he believes a call setting forth of the causes which led him into crime, and the ultimate results, will act as a lesson and a deterrent on others."[24] George traveled all over the country on the lecture circuit, including a stop in his hometown of Mankato, Minnesota, in the fall of 1910. The local newspaper wrote that his presentation, entitled "A Life of Crime," was "as good a sermon to young men as was ever preached in this city."[25]

One primary element of George's book and lectures was his description of the train robberies committed by him, his brother John, and Chris Evans. He was, in essence, repeating the confession and testimony that Eva saw as either a coward's betrayal or—depending on who is to be believed—a traitor's lies. She undoubtedly resented George's attempts to capitalize financially on their troubles. There was much in George's book that contradicted Eva's side of the story—she still echoed her father's assertion that Chris Evans never robbed any trains—and that she found personally offensive. But it was all the more loathsome to her when George maintained he was only motivated by his desire to help mankind with his lesson that "crime does not pay." George was doing his best to prove that cliché false, and Eva knew from personal experience on the stage that exploiting crimes already committed paid pretty darn well.

Ed Morrell also knew this, although he overestimated the money to be made from his life story. In a letter to Jack London, Morrell predicted he could earn as much as one thousand dollars each for a series of lectures. Morrell claimed that motion picture and vaudeville agents had approached him, begging him to "turn from my chosen work and reap a harvest of golden coins" exploiting his eventful life. Morrell's "chosen work" was prison reform, and it was through these efforts that he met Jack London.

London became fascinated with Morrell's experiences in prison, with his suffering in solitary, with his astral projections and knuckle-rapping communications, and proposed a biographical treatment of his story. What London eventually came up with was *The Star Rover,* published in 1915. Morrell, relegated to a minor supporting character in the book, was disappointed; it was probably about this time that he formulated the plan of writing his own autobiography. In 1917, a year after London's untimely death, Morrell married the author's former assistant, Mildred McEwen. The two began working on a book, and in 1924, *The Twenty-Fifth Man* by Ed Morrell (although Mildred McEwen is assumed to be the real uncredited author) was published. In the words of noted California outlaw historian Bill Secrest, the book "raised eyebrows for years because of Morrell's exaggerations and self-serving attempts to make himself more important than he was."[26] It is unknown just how high Eva raised her eyebrow at her former accomplice's literary effort, but surely Morrell's book wouldn't cause her to spit in disgust as did George Sontag's.

CHRIS EVANS, TOO, WROTE A BOOK while he was in prison, and three years after his release, James Barry, editor of the *San Francisco Star*, published it. Eva's father, however, didn't set out to exploit his life story, nor preach against a life of crime, nor even present his defense or deny his crimes. In his modest little book, entitled *Eurasia*, Chris Evans sought to provide the blueprint for nothing less than social utopia.

Borrowing (if not outright lifting) the form and concept of Edward Bellamy's *Looking Backward,* Evans' own utopian vision relied heavily on that 1888 classic work that influenced the formation of the Nationalist political movement (so named for their belief in nationalizing industy and eliminating private capitalization) and several utopian living experiments during the 1890s.

One such utopian experiment influenced by Bellamy's *Looking Backward* was an endeavor with which Chris Evans was directly familiar. As he had once noted in a newspaper interview following his final capture, Evans "used to know a lot of the anarchists" at the Kaweah Colony. The Kaweah Co-Operative Colony was an attempt at establishing a self-sustaining society based largely on Laurence Gronlund's 1884 published treatise, *The Co-Operative Commonwealth: An Exposition of Modern Socialism*. The group, composed largely of San Francisco labor reformers and radicals, sought to subsist on logging claims they had filed in 1885 in Tulare County's Sierra Nevada. With an office in Visalia, and four years work in the mountains near Chris Evans' Redwood Ranch, there is no reason to doubt his claim that he knew members of the colony. And his labeling them "anarchist" is especially apt, considering the radical and even anarchistic writings of the Kaweah Colony's founder and driving force, Burnette Haskell. Chris Evans and the Kaweah Colony also had a common nemesis, as it was ultimately (though not exclusively) due to the political behind-the-scenes maneuverings of the Southern Pacific Railroad that the Kaweah Colony lost its timber claims and saw their land turned into Sequoia National Park in the fall of 1890.[27]

When Bellamy's *Looking Backward* was published in 1888, Haskell and the Kaweah Colony adopted it as an almost sacred text, and when the subsequent Nationalist movement flourished, Haskell became a tireless organizer of Nationalist Clubs in California, seeing the movement as a means to promote and support his own Kaweah Colony. Although the Kaweah Colony's political and social structure was actually based on Gronlund's *Co-Operative Commonwealth*, Bellamy's utopian look at the future proved more accessible to the general reading public. While Gronlund had provided a blueprint of socialist cooperation, Bellamy came up with the full-color model. It wasn't long before Haskell was claiming that the Kaweah Colony was Bellamy's model realized.[28]

And so just as Bellamy influenced Haskell and Kaweah, so, too, did he influence Chris Evans. *Looking Backward* opens with an aristocratic insomniac waking up from a "mesmerized sleep" only to find himself in the Boston of A.D. 2000. Leaving behind a nineteenth-century world dominated by the waste, greed, cruelty and madness of the capitalistic system, the inadvertent time traveler finds an unrecognizable America of the future. The country operates under a system of state socialism; private property has been abolished and all share equally in the wealth of the country. Cooperation has replaced competition.

Chris Evans' book, which the preface promises will describe "an ideal republic where many of the problems that confront us are worked out," opens with the narrator falling asleep in his rowboat. "How long I slept I know not," he tells us, "for when I awoke my boat was close to shore, and to my astonishment I was in strange waters."[29] Upon going ashore, he meets a man who in accented English tells him he has landed in Eurasia. He is taken the next day to tour the country and meet its officials. What follows is a department by department description of this country that has happened upon a social system not entirely unlike the one Bellamy described. What Evans' deemed most important is probably best gleaned by the order of departments his narrator visits. For example, the second chapter includes a visit to the Minister of Justice and the very next chapter is about a visit to the state prison, where prisoners are given military-like rank, treated humanely yet sternly, and upon parole "if he does not have friends to take care of him, is given employment by the Government."

Eva appreciated many of the other reforms suggested by her father's book, reforms that Edward Bellamy, or Burnette Haskell, or Emma Goldman would also appreciate. Eurasia's court system was free to complaintant or defendant, but a complaint without just cause could result in imprisonment for a year at hard labor. Industry was nationalized, and the government drew revenue from sales of goods and controlled the only bank. All young men and women were drafted into military service but were well paid during their service in the great industrial army, which besides offering civil defense served as a labor force in the department of railways, mines, commerce and agriculture. A woman ran the Department of Labor, all wages were fixed by law, and the eight-hour work day was strictly enforced. Children were not allowed to work for wages under any circumstances. The government granted a pension to every working man and woman—half his yearly wages at age sixty and full pension at age seventy.

Thus, it was natural that Eva would hope her father could meet her friend Emma Goldman. In August 1915, Goldman's lecture tour made a one-week stop in Portland, Oregon. A handbill advertising the series of lectures at the Scandinavian Socialist Hall included such subjects as "The Philosophy of Anarchism," "Misconceptions of Free Love," and "War and the Sacred Right of Property."[30] Eva wrote Emma and asked if she would send tickets to her father so he could attend one of her lectures.

Chris later wrote his daughter that "Miss Goldman called on us, and gave us tickets to her lecture." Chris attended a lecture on "Jealousy—Its Cause and Possible Cure." Perhaps he would have been more enthused hearing her speak on The Philosophy of Anarchism or the Misconceptions of Free Love. He told Eva he thought her an eloquent speaker and he had "no doubt of her honesty of purpose," and felt compelled to add that "that Dr. Reitman is a character."

Reflecting on it, Eva admitted that she might have known her father, that "darned old conservative," would have such a reserved reaction. But still, Eva had "hoped that Emma Goldman would give him a thrill."[31]

CHRIS EVANS, AT THE RISK of violating his parole, had visited his beloved daughter Eva in Los Angeles the previous year (1914). Eva stated in her memoir that the prison board had granted her father permission to travel to Sacramento to see Governor Hiram Johnson to ask for a pardon. The request was denied. "His health was very poor, and he feared he would die without seeing me again. So he risked his freedom once more by traveling to Los Angeles to have one last visit with me."[32]

Eva described coming home one day to find her father sitting on his suitcase by her back door. He seemed so ill she took him to a doctor, thinking he could stay with her until she nursed him back to strength. But according to her memoir, he soon received a letter from the parole board. They had been alerted to his presence in Los Angeles and he was ordered to report to "the deputy parole office, 525 Exchange Building, Los Angeles, and make arrangement to return to your family in Portland, Oregon, as soon as possible." Eva pleaded to let him stay, but he was ordered to leave for Oregon at once. "A boat was sailing that afternoon from San Pedro for Portland. I said good-bye at the dock."[33] It was the last time she ever saw her father.

EVA EVANS, OR BILLEE McCULLOUGH as she was now comfortably known, turned forty in the spring of 1916, a milestone in any life. She was childless. And with a husband who endured recurring bouts of TB, there was little likelihood of her ever having children. How that weighed on her is unknown—she had come from a large, tight-knit family who were now all separated from her by hundreds of miles. On the other hand, having been the oldest of seven surviving children and almost a mother-figure to her youngest brothers, perhaps she had had her fill of raising children. Eva had always had a self-centered streak—it's what made her a natural as an actress, a vocation where egoism is a necessity—and motherhood can be hard to bear for the self-centered type.

At a certain age, it is common to contemplate one's life. Was a mature Eva forward looking or nostalgic? As she was at a traditional halfway mark, one would assume she was both. Did she have regrets? Did she suffer from guilt? And what were her hopes for the future? If turning forty didn't make her reflect upon her life, another milestone less than a year later certainly would.

On February 9, 1917, Eva was awakened by a ringing telephone in the middle of the night. She stumbled through the dark house to reach the phone.

My father was dead. Free at last from grief and pain. The palsied hand still: looking alike now—both the seeing and the unseeing eye.

Returning to bed, I cried the night through; not for what had happened, but for what had not. Now I realized fully that I had always clung to the hope that he and I would walk again the paths to the beauty spots at the Redwood Ranch.

If I could go to the ranch again, would you come to me with the dawn wind—that miracle, over so soon, that you taught me to feel? First, there is an electric feeling in the air, and then a little breeze, even on the stillest morning. It comes just ahead of the light. You said even miners in the depths of the earth feel this vibration, and know that day is coming. In the pine trees, you hear the wind better. Would I hear your voice there?

Camping out, and sleeping in the hay for the horses, you first told me about the dawn wind. You would come to me while it was not yet light, and tell me to wake and listen....and then you would take off my gown, and hold up my clothing to be slipped over my head, and say what I thought for years was "Up, Guards, and Adam!" (Up, Guards, and at 'em!) Then breakfast in the growing light, and away on the road to the music of the tug chains. In memory I hear your voice reciting lines from "Locksley Hall"

> *For I dipped into the future, far as human eye could see;*
> *Saw the vision of the world and all the wonders that would be;*
> *Saw the Heaven filled with commerce, argosies of magic sails;*
> *Pilots of the purple twilight, dropping down with costly bales;*
> *Heard the heavens fill with shouting, and there rained a ghastly dew*
> *From the nation's airy navies, grappling in the central blue,*
> *Far along the world-wide whisper of the south wind rushing warm,*
> *With the standards of the peoples plunging thru the thunder storm,*
> *Till the war drums throbbed no longer, and the battle flags were unfurled,*
> *In the Parliament of Man, the Federation of the World...*

How your voice rang on that last line! You believed in Tennyson's vision. You told me, too, that some day the most rapid transit would be enclosing a person in a rocket, and shooting them to their destination.[34]

Eva couldn't help looking backward, but forced to deal with the present, she could only hope that her father had finally awakened from the sleep of life on this earth to discover he landed in Eurasia, his utopia. And to contemplate the future, could she ever believe—like her prophetic father did—that men would fly through space in a rocket ship, journeying to and walking on the moon in her lifetime?

Chapter Eighteen

Writing a Legacy

S A TEENAGER, EVA EXPERIENCED the "Champagne Days" of the 1890s in San Francisco, but as a middle-aged woman she found herself living in another California city just coming into its heyday. Los Angeles was experiencing an unprecedented period of growth and prosperity. Over one million Americans migrated to Los Angeles County in the 1920s. The population in Los Angeles more than doubled, making it the fifth largest city in the United States by the decade's end. Many of the other cities in the county—Long Beach, Pasadena, Glendale, Santa Monica—likewise doubled, tripled, or even quadrupled their populations. In the words of historian Carey McWilliams, during "the bonanza years from 1920 to 1930, Los Angeles had all the giddiness, the parvenu showiness, and the crazy prosperity of a gold-rush town."[1]

Without health, that prosperity was out of reach. During this period, Perry suffered another bout with tuberculosis and was bedridden for an extended period of time—four years by Eva's account. In 1925, Eva's brother, Louis, made plans to come down from Oregon to help out his sister in Los Angeles. She had been struggling so long taking care of her invalid husband while trying to make ends meet.

In early February, with Eva daily expecting her brother's arrival, a telegram came. "Louis seriously injured in automobile accident. (Signed) Mother." Eva later learned of the details. Louis had borrowed a car from a friend to take his mother out for a Chinese dinner. On the way home, they took a drive in the country, the use of an automobile being somewhat of a novelty. Louis lost control and the car skidded across the road, striking the bank and overturning. The top was torn off the vehicle as it scraped back across the slick road and turned over again. Molly was thrown out onto the soft embankment and only slightly injured. Louis was tossed onto the highway, striking his head.

Three days later, on February 10, 1925, Eva received another telegram, this time from her sister, Ynez. "Louis died today at ten a.m."[2] Eva would always remember him as the fair-headed little boy who insisted she was too good a fellow to have a girl's name.

LITTLE IS KNOWN OF EVA'S LIFE in Los Angeles during the 1920s, but as the decade drew to a close she was interviewed by a writer working on a book about her father. Carl Glasscock, who was born in Ventura, California, in 1884, had studied at the University of California in Berkeley before launching a career in journalism.[3] In 1929, while living in Los Angeles, his book *Bandits and the Southern Pacific* was published by the Frederick A. Stokes Company of New York. In the foreword of the book, which "is primarily the story of John Sontag and Chris Evans, the two San Joaquin Valley men accused of having held up the Southern Pacific," the author acknowledges his indebtedness to old newspaper files in the Fresno and Los Angeles public libraries, cites various regional history books, and finally expresses his gratitude to "those who have helped to round out the record by permitting quotations from their recollection of the events they had a part." Most significant, judging by the number of times she is quoted, was Eva Evans. She must have spent many hours with Glasscock telling her story, and perhaps she even supplied him with written accounts. The book quotes Eva at length on numerous occasions and includes many events that only she could have known, such as her part in helping Fredericks supply guns for George Sontag's ill-fated escape attempt from prison.

It is also clear that Glasscock did a very careful and thorough scouring of the newspaper files, and his telling of the saga of Evans and Sontag was by far the most complete and detailed account to date. This is not to say it wasn't without glaring errors. For instance, Glasscock claimed Evans had joined the Settlers' Land League and lost his farm holdings in the Mussel Slough affair. "Chris Evans was one with the hundreds of other victims. His home was taken from him and the labor of years went to swell the profits of the corporation," Glasscock wrongly asserted.[4]

A review of the book, found pasted in a scrapbook Eva compiled, noted that "as narrated here by Mr. Glasscock, the reader is left to draw his own conclusions as to whether or not either Sontag or Evans was guilty of train robbery. He maintains an impartial attitude, setting forth the facts as seen by both sides. As to where his sympathies are it is not difficult to guess." Perhaps Glasscock couldn't help but be influenced by his star source: the daughter of Chris Evans who "idolized her father and who insisted then and insists today that he was the victim of the railroad's tyranny."[5]

It is hard to imagine Eva being completely satisfied with Glasscock's book, but she certainly would have viewed it as a much more accurate effort than Morrell's self-aggrandizing *Twenty-Fifth Man*, which appeared five years earlier. But even as Glasscock himself noted at the end of *Bandits and the Southern Pacific*, the many legendary tales surrounding Evans and Sontag had embellished and distorted the memory of the outlaws. As an example, Glasscock cited the numerous obituaries, reciting the details of his life, in newspapers throughout the West when Chris Evans died in 1917. "There were no two stories alike," Glasscock pointed out. "According to some, Evans was a Robin Hood; according to others, an unmitigated villain. Some had Evans and Morrell escaping from Folsom Prison years after their incarceration. Some made Evans the hero of the Mussel Slough tragedy." And so on, but Glasscock maintained that even though the characters and their adventures had become legendary, "it is fact, history if you will, not legend, which makes up this narrative."[6] With so many years having passed, one has to wonder if even Eva herself was having trouble separating the fact from the legend.

That same year, Eva and Perry moved out of Los Angeles. They settled in the tiny seaside community of Laguna Beach, sixty miles to the south. Settled in the 1870s and further developed as a tourist destination around the turn of the century, by the 1920s Laguna Beach had become known as a haven for artists and writers. Nestled amongst steep cliffs, water-etched coves and beaches, rolling hills and deep canyons, the seaside village held irresistible charm for Eva and Perry. Although it is unknown how they found the opportunity to move to there, before long, Perry established a real estate and insurance business with his office on South Coast Boulevard, as the Pacific Coast Highway was known through Laguna Beach.[7]

IN THE AUTUMN OF 1929, EVA RECEIVED A LETTER from an old friend. "Dear Billy [*sic*] McCullough," the letter began. "I know you will be surprised to hear from me. It isn't that I have forgotten you which made writing seem unnecessary. It is that so many things have happened in my life since I saw you last in 1915 that it appeared ridiculous to start in a correspondence after so many years."[8] Much had indeed happened to the writer of the letter, for it was from Emma Goldman, writing from St. Tropez, France. Most significantly, the notorious anarchist had been imprisoned and then deported back to her native Russia for her relentless anti-war and free speech agitation. Now at work on her autobiography, Emma had contacted Eva seeking information.

After apologizing that her letter had to be brief because she was on a deadline to finish her manuscript, Emma wrote that "I would like to have a little data about Ed Morrell's part in the attempt to rescue your father." Emma explained that she had written about meeting Morrell in San Francisco, and that he had made quite an impression on her. (Undoubtedly, she found his prison experiences of interest.) "And the fact," Emma's letter to Eva continued, "that you should have happened to be the girl who inspired him as a young boy to an adventurous act made him even more interesting. I would like to be quite sure that I did not mix my data and would appreciate it as a great favor if you would let me know the particulars of the episode which landed your father as well as Morrell in prison." Emma then closed, expressing her warm desire to hear about her and Perry and his brother, Bret, and all "the other friends we used to know in our carefree days."

Eva and Perry were thrilled to hear from Emma. Perry wrote back on their behalf (as he "runs the typewriter and can do it easier") and enclosed "a short resume of the old trouble and Ed's connection with it," along with their fondest wishes that "your health is good, that you are situated in congenial surroundings, and that the book will be as big a financial success as I know it will be from an interesting and historical personal document."

Upon receiving the reply, Emma wrote back to thank Perry for the information about Billee's father and Ed Morrell. She told him she had not forgotten the cause that led to the feud between the farmers and the Southern Pacific Railroad. "Yes, indeed," she told Perry, "I have read Norris's work, *The Octopus,* which so vividly describes that struggle."

On a more personal note, Emma admitted the real reason she had been so long out of touch.

I, too, have wondered about you and Billie [*sic*] and your brother, I often longed to hear from you. So few of my American friends have kept in touch with me since my forcible eviction from my erstwhile country. The reason I myself have not written you before is that I did not wish to impose myself on you. You see, old man, a number of my so-called friends have never forgiven me my stand on Russia. Frankly, I was afraid that you may be among these, that you may have gone back on your friendship. You will not feel hurt for my saying so, I hope; but, when one has had so many blows in one's life, one grows somewhat skeptical.

Give Billie my love, and also your brother. Yours affectionately.[9]

In 1931, Emma Goldman's autobiography, *Living My Life*, was published by Alfred Knopf. It ranks among the finest autobiographies ever written in the English language and is still in print today. The two volumes are chock-full of the many radicals and anarchists and reformers and writers and agitators and political figures and even criminals Emma Goldman knew or with whom she crossed paths. It was so full that there wasn't room for Ed Morrell or Chris Evans. Neither was mentioned in her book.

It is unknown if this disappointed Eva, or if she even read Emma's autobiography for that matter. But the idea of Emma writing her life story tucked away in "a picturesque fisher nest in the south of France,"[10] the nostalgic reconnection with an old friend after so many years, the effort to get the story of Ed Morrell and Chris Evans right—all this had to have set Eva to thinking. Couple this with frustration at the various errors about her father that had recently found their way into print. Then consider the encouragement from an increasing number of Laguna friends who were writers, including her husband who dabbled at poetry. Eva had asked a number of friends with literary aspirations to consider her father's story, but as she once related, they all said "Billee, you write it yourself. You are the one to do it."[11] And so the idea lodged in Eva's mind.

Eva did not completely trust her memory, but "went to the State Library at Sacramento and checked my story carefully with the daily papers of this period" when she set out to tell the story of her father. She also elicited the help of her family. Her sister, Ynez, wrote in a letter that she had "been trying to get some dates from mother, but her memory is very bad." Ynez was able, however, to list for Eva a number

of milestones in the Evans family history, from their father's coming
out to California, to his marriage to fifteen-year-old Molly at the Rattlesnake Ranch, to his going to the Cerro Gordo mines where he got a job
on the *Bessie Brady*, to his acquiring the Redwood Ranch, to building
their first house in Visalia ("a one room shack facing the county road").
Ynez cited the birth of Chris and Molly's first child, a son who died after only a couple of hours at the Redwood Ranch; the births of Eva and
Elmer at the Rattlesnake Ranch; and the death of Elmer shortly before
Ynez was born. "They then built the house we were raised in and all the
other children except Carl were born there."[12]

Perhaps most inspiring to Eva's muse as she prepared to write her
memoir was a trip back home. In September 1933, Eva found herself
"at last, on my way to the Redwood Ranch." To write the story of her
father, she went to that place imbued with his spirit. She felt regret
that:

> In the twenty-four years that my father lived after he was sent to
> prison, I spent less than twenty-four days with him.
>   No need to give the reasons for the meagerness of our days
> together. Circumstances can imprison as well as stone walls and
> iron bars.[13]

Now she was making a nostalgic journey back home. It was the first
time she had been in the Central Valley in perhaps thirty years. As she
and Perry traveled north toward Visalia, she couldn't help but think of
her family history. Seeing the orange groves, she remembered how her
father had predicted citrus would one day thrive in the thermal belt lying at the foot of the Sierra between Porterville and Lemon Cove. As
they pulled into Farmersville, Eva inquired about a great oak where
her great-grandfather had set up his forge, but learned it had been cut
down to make a new road. She visited the Deep Creek Cemetery, near
Farmersville, which she remembered as a "tangled, weed-grown spot,
without tree or flower," where the faded wooden headboards of her
great-grandparents had once stood. She walked through a tangled mass
of salt grass, unable to find them. "All I find is a barren spot, but I feel
sure that it is here they were buried," she lamented.

In Visalia, she was unable to find her old house. The entire neighborhood was changed. They stayed in an auto camp in the northeast
part of town, which they later learned was right where their house once
stood. When Perry asked if it was around there that the Evans and Son-

tag trouble started, the proprietor of the auto camp proclaimed: "You're right on the fightin' ground, my boy, right on the fightin' ground."

Later that day, Eva and Perry set out for the Redwood Ranch, stopping to see Stone Corral. "We had difficulty locating it because the road no longer goes that way. But hills do not change." Then a few more miles and they came to Eva's birthplace, the Rattlesnake Ranch, and were given permission by the current residents to go inside. Eva saw pale sunlight through dust and cobwebs in the bedroom where she was born.

As nostalgic as all these visits were, they paled in comparison to emotions brought up when, after winding its way into the forest nearly fifty miles from Visalia, the road turned sharply to the right and Eva saw a sign that read: "SEQUOIA RANGER STATION." In a moving ending to her memoir, Eva described her visit to the Redwood Ranch, now a ranger station.

I look ahead, and there it is; the place of my dreams; the little old cabin under the cedar trees. How small it looks, I used to think it quite a house! The rock chimney of the fireplace is gone, and the steps, made of round blocks of trees, have been replaced by sawed boards; otherwise it is just the same. To the left is a new house, and down the steps comes a stalwart man, looking just like a ranger ought to look—in fact, a perfect picture of the Northwest Mounted. We walk to meet him.

"What can I do for you?" he asks.

"We would like permission to camp here. I used to live here when I was a little girl. I'm Chris Evans' daughter; perhaps you have heard of my father."

"Yes, I know all about your father, and I'm glad to meet you. I'm Jess Waller, the ranger in charge here. Would you like to have your old house? We use it for a store room now, but there is a cook stove and bunk in it. I can clean it out enough to make you comfortable."

We lend a hand with the arranging of the room, and Jess Waller says, "In the morning, if you can remember the spot, will you show me where the babies of Chris and Tom Evans are buried?"

I show my astonishment, and he explains, "One of the mountain people told me about it, long ago, and since then several have asked to be shown the graves. But I've never found anyone who had the least idea where they were. If you can locate them, I'll make a marker for them."

Night in the cabin, with only the flicker of firelight from the front of the stove. We talk, far into the night, of things that happened here so long ago.

Can wood absorb something from the dynamic mind of the man who assembled the boards, and from whom thoughts emanated for so many years within its four walls? Or do I just imagine I can feel my father, as I see him in fancy, walking the floor by candle light, with a baby in his arms, crooning Tennyson to a half-asleep child?

It is still dark when I awaken suddenly. I raise up on one elbow and listen intently.....Then I hear it. At first, only from my inner mind; then a soo-o-o and a swish in the trees.

The Dawn Wind! Now, if ever, I'll find him! Listening with all my soul! The wind dies!... A sense of infinite rest. Like a benediction after prayer. "Go in peace, my child."

I dress and go out into the fragrance of that cool September morning. The birds are beginning to sing, just a faint twittering in the trees....Presently, shafts of light come across the meadow over the top of Redwood Mountain. One strikes the red bark of the tree by the road. His tree! His body is not in it—that is unimportant. Long ago he made it his, when he asked me to promise that when he died he should be buried in its heart.

Now the sun is through in full glory. "A mountain meadow bathed in sunlight, circled round with pine." How I wish my arms could go around it, like the pine trees.

I rejoice that this place belongs to the Government. Safe for animals, protected from the vandalism of man. Other children can see what we did.

I turn at the sound of footsteps, and Jess Waller joins me, saying:

"Shall we look for those graves now? My day begins pretty early. I have to plan the forestry work for the boys at the Triple C. You should see that camp before you leave the mountains. It's only about a mile from here, down on the site of the old Wagy Mill. You can go down with me if you like."

I thank him, and we walk up the winding path to the "Half Moon" spring, under a giant cedar nearby. I point out the spot where the babies are buried. It is covered with small cedars. I tell

Mr. Waller I should like to have a tiny one to take away, and, if it lives, later I will plant it on my father's grave, on that Oregon hillside—another green land looking much like this. He says he will have one of the boys dig several for me, and any other small trees or shrubs I should like. Again I thank him. He returns to the house, and I go to seek the place where the tiger lilies grew.

Before I reach the spot, I hear the little brook singing its way down from Redwood Mountain—"for men may come, and men may go, but I go on forever..."

There it is; the deep pool and mossy bank—the ferns—but not a single tiger lily. I lie down on the bank and bury my face in the cool, sweet moss. Once my father smelled like this, and not like iodoform. Why can I not make this erase forever that terrible odor! I must—I must—leave him here. This is the garden of my heart. I must bury him in it.[14]

Historians have questioned the veracity of Eva's memoir, and admittedly there are sections where it is obviously a carefully constructed defense for her father. But Eva was diligent in checking her facts. The aspects of the story she didn't purposely shape to conform to an alibi and defense for her father are consistently accurate. Any lies she put forth (and there certainly are some) were motivated by her desire to maintain her father's innocence and so, while not necessarily forgivable, are certainly understandable. But the narrative was well written and, as the above passage indicates, a moving example of a daughter's love for her father. Eva's memoir, which she entitled "An Outlaw and His Family," provides unparalleled insight into the personal life of California's most notorious outlaw. It also gave Eva a chance to do something she may not have even realized she wanted—and needed—to do: to tell her own story.

IN LETTERS TO PROSPECTIVE PUBLISHERS, Eva explained her motivation for writing "An Outlaw and His Family." "I am the daughter of Chris Evans, a California outlaw of the nineties," she informed the editors of Colliers. "And I have been patient through all the years, with the several books and magazine articles which contained untruthful and erroneous articles about my father." She went on to note that the late Annie Laurie had claimed in print that Evans and Sontag had killed ten or twelve men. "Now she knew better than this because she was an *Ex-*

aminer reporter during the years of this tragedy, but she had forgotten and the truth in regard to it was not important to her," Eva pointed out, failing to mention that the truth was closer to six men killed.

Eva also complained of an unnamed "recognized authority on California history" who made a statement that Evans and Sontag were never in the Sierra Nevada mountains. "Now if a historian would ignore this important fact, one easy to prove or disapprove [*sic*], in time there will remain not one iota of truth about this remarkable man, so I decided to write the truth as I knew it."[15]

Both Eva and her husband wrote to numerous publishers in 1937 and 1938, including Random House, Atlantic Monthly, Houghton Mifflin, Greystone Publications, and Alfred A. Knopf, but they were unable to interest any enough to publish the book. Some of the rejection letters carried encouragement—one editor claimed the staff read the story with much interest and that it was "above the average and held our readers to the end," but ultimately they felt it was "too personal in its reminiscences" and was "not suitable to the needs of the market"—while others offered little more than form letters—"We are sorry to inform you that the work projected by you is not quite adaptable to the special needs of the Random House list."[16]

They were able to interest a New York literary agent. In a letter to Ruth Boyd, Perry listed several of the publishing houses they had already contacted and added that they had received several favorable responses. "The general attitude was that they questioned whether the book would sell enough copies to pay for publication," he told her, adding that he and Eva were confident it could be a commercial success and "will have an audience." Although the agent said she thought the story would make exciting reading and that she believed "there are also magazine and motion picture possibilities," nothing ever came of the agent's interest.[17]

ALTHOUGH FRUSTRATED AT THE INABILITY to find a publisher for her memoir, Eva did not sour on writing. In fact, she became enamored with the idea of being a writer and had started trying her hand at short stories. She subscribed to *Writer's Digest* and began entering short story contests sponsored by the publication. In 1938, she signed up for a correspondence course they offered in short story writing. The instructor evidently requested some personal information from Eva, and her reply amounts to what can be described as a biographer's bonanza.

I have two important reasons for wanting to write, first, I have always led a very active life. When I was young I was "on the stage," but an injury forced me to give that up. When I finally recovered, the procession had moved on. For the last twenty-five years I have been landscape gardening and remodeling old houses. I like to work in the soil with my hands.

Now I am sixty-two years old and I am slowing down but my mind must have something to do. I am the daughter of a California outlaw of the early '90s. Two years ago, growing weary of the lies that still continued to be published about my father, Chris Evans, I wrote his story, "An Outlaw and His Family," without any training whatsoever for writing. I have only a grammar school education. As yet I have not found a publisher though appreciation and kind words have been plentiful. It may be necessary to rewrite my book. This is reason number two.

Now to answer your other questions.

I do not like people very well but I am interested in them and like to know what makes them behave as they do, especially criminals. My few friends are mostly writers. I live in a high white house at the head of a canyon: when I look down there is my lovely garden, and when I look out—6,000 miles of ocean. I live alone all day and like it better than anything else that could happen to me.

My people came to California from the south in 1852 in a covered wagon. For three generations we have never crossed the "Rockies," but I do know my Pacific Coast.

I am just as provincial as any New Yorker I've ever met; I think Laguna Beach is the only place to live. When young, I read the older classics. Now I find it more difficult to find books to read but I can still read avidly the few things I like. I thought Dr. Cronin's "The Stars Look Down" a great book, but I could not finish "The Citadel." Mostly I like my fiction disguised as history and biography.

The things I like to talk about—international politics and animals, especially cats. I like "garden" magazines and my favorite newspaper is the Manchester Guardian. I have not had any "pictures taken" for many years, just deepen the lines and add some crow's feet to this one; it's just the best I have to offer.

I enclose a copy of one of two stories, "No Death is Untimely," a short story that I have submitted in your short story contest. It is based upon the death of my brother and his wife, the idea unconsciously suggested by my sister who has a metaphysical mind (I have not) when she said "Margaret came and got him."

A year ago I subscribed for the Writer's Digest. Occasionally I buy the other writer's journals and so forth but they do not compare with your magazine. I keep a notebook on stimulating ideas contained therein. Thanks for the book, "The Art of Inventing Characters." I appreciate the thought, but it's just "Greek to me."

Sincerely, Mrs. Evelyn McCullough. —Pen Name: "Eva Evans"[18]

There is a dark and fatalistic streak in Eva's short stories and the quality of the writing does not compare to her memoir. This might be a hint that she had help writing "An Outlaw and His Family" from Perry.

One story, entitled "The Polar Bear Rug," was a confusing story about a young family who lose their house and all possessions in a flood but escape with their lives. "The Basement Door" told the story of a sensitive immigrant who falls in love with a young woman in a New York boardinghouse and is killed when he rescues her from an attacker on the basement stairway. Another story was based, as she told *Writer's Digest*, not only on the deaths in close succession of her brother, Louis, and his wife, but on a newspaper article about a lawyer who was killed in an accident (coincidentally on the same road as Louis) only two days after the death of his wife. The story ended up being thin and underdeveloped, only a few pages long, about a newly-widowed man who dies before he can even mourn his wife's death. It never addressed the similarities with her brother's death (even the date was nearly the same) but those who knew Eva well realized, of course, she was writing about Louis when she described the crash on Hillsboro Road. "A splintering, grinding crash and he was lying clear of the car by the side of the road. Soft flakes of snow touched his lips and he murmured, 'Margaret.' Then the soft sweet dark claimed him. He remembered no more."[19]

EVA'S MOST INTERESTING SHORT STORY, and by far her most ambitious at over a hundred pages, was a fictionalized account of an infamous California outlaw and his flight from justice. Now this wasn't the outlaw saga she knew so intimately (and had told of in her earlier memoir).

No, this was the story of an outlaw with whom she had only a passing familiarity.

Perhaps Eva had more familiarity with the subject of her historical novella, *Grat Dalton's Ride*, than she admitted. Her story told of the Dalton brother's flight from California after his arrest for the Alila train robbery. She began her account with Grat receiving a visitor in the Visalia jail:

> "A visitor for you Dalton, this man wants to talk to you," Williams the jailer announced as a man about Grat's own height stepped into the cell and the door swung to behind him. It was a sultry cloudy day and the dim light in the cell did not permit all at once a clear picture of the man. He noticed the man's small feet and hands, so like his own. Then the man spoke, a simple salutation.
>
> "Dalton, how are you?" The voice, low, vibrant, electric, thrilled Grat Dalton as he looked into eyes that matched the voice, penetrating, dark gray eyes with a will to power in them. They sat side by side on the cot and no word was spoken until the sound of the jailer's footsteps died away.
>
> "I've only fifteen minutes," the man said briskly. "I'll talk fast and you are to listen. Want to get out of here?"
>
> "You're damn right I do."
>
> "All right, do exactly as I tell you. Don't ask questions, just take orders. It's tonight or never so far as I am concerned."[20]

Grat's mysterious visitor then outlined a plan that was to be implemented that night. During the escape, Grat heard one of the other prisoners address their secret accomplice, calling him Chris. "I wish he'd use his last name," Grat thought.

The author's implication was clear. Eva and her father had always denied rumors (and Sheriff Kay's assertion) that Chris Evans helped break Grat Dalton out of the Visalia jail. Had Eva, with a wink and a nod, finally admitted it? And if so, what else might she admit to in her old age?

CHAPTER NINETEEN

Laguna Beach Passings

E VELYN (THE NAME EVA NOW USED) AND PERRY settled down to live out their golden years in Laguna Beach. Perry stayed healthy long enough to maintain his real estate and insurance business. Ynez, who was widowed, moved to Laguna Beach and became his office manager. She lived just a couple of blocks from the office in a two-story house on Catalina Street. Molly, who was now nearing eighty, also moved to Laguna Beach to be with her daughters, Eva and Ynez. She moved into the Catalina Street house and brought her youngest son, Carl, to live there as well. The roomy house, set well back from the street, had plenty of space for a rambling garden, which undoubtedly appealed to the little lord of flowers. Carl eventually found work as a shipping clerk at a nearby pottery store.[1]

By 1938, Perry was able to purchase a house closer to downtown Laguna. It was situated at the top of a steep hill on Third Street with a magnificent view of the ocean. It was here, a few miles away from Perry's office and the rest of her family down on Catalina Street, that Eva would look out at 6,000 miles of ocean and spend her days alone, liking it better than anything else that could happen.

It is impossible to say if Eva resented having so many of her family members now living nearby. Family had always been important to Eva, but she was also the most independent and headstrong of the Evans brood, and the one family member who understood this best was gone. Eva, even as an older woman, remained her father's daughter, and now that she began to think of herself as a writer, she could rationalize her self-absorbed streak as an artistic asset.

Eva still clung to a stubborn hope of seeing her memoir published. In 1940, she traveled to Reedley, a small San Joaquin Valley town on the Kings River not far from where Evans and Sontag had roamed fifty years earlier, to visit a writer and historian she hoped would finally tell her father's story accurately. Eva lent Wallace Smith her manuscript and told him to "use any of my material you choose, because if my story is ever published, your having it would aid instead of detract...If you write a story about Chris Evans from my point of view I would benefit by it if my book is ever published, and that, to me, would be ample compensation."[2]

EVA'S HUSBAND, PERRY, ASPIRED to be a poet. He was quick to point out that his middle name was Emerson, after distant relative Ralph Waldo Emerson. As one friend put it, "maybe the yen to scribble and the overwhelming desire to wax philosophical is in the blood."[3] For a couple of years, Perry wrote a column in the local Laguna Beach newspaper entitled "Through the Years." The column was mostly remembrances of the unique places and people Perry had known or visited over the years. It was filled with local history and anecdotes, but rarely did he ever mention his wife. It was almost as if her remarkable history was off-limits.

That books and literature were important to Perry is evidenced by his work on the Laguna Beach Library board. He was instrumental in getting a bond issue passed to build a new library in Laguna Beach in the late 1930s.[4] His work on the library board, the grind of writing a weekly newspaper column, and a full-time real estate and insurance business indicate a much hardier man than Perry had ever been. In his mid-fifties now, this was perhaps the most productive time of a life long saddled with health struggles.

By the spring of 1941, it all caught up with him. He became too ill to write his newspaper column and a friend replaced him until he could recover. The guest columnist explained how Perry was sick in bed with a doctor and nurse attending him. "The nurse is in love,"[5] he chided, obviously referring to Eva, who once again had become caretaker to her bedridden husband. It was a recurrent theme in their thirty-year marriage.

Perry never did return to writing his weekly column. On July 7, 1942, fifty-six-year-old Perry McCullough succumbed to illness, dying at his home. The cause of death was attributed to a heart attack; the front-page obituary noted that Perry had been critically ill for several months and the illness had evidently weakened his heart.[6] He left behind his widow, Evelyn, the paper noted, making no mention of how terribly her heart was affected.

IN 1944, EVA'S EIGHTY-FIVE-YEAR-OLD MOTHER, Molly Byrd Evans, died. With her mother's passing, Eva, now sixty-eight years old, became the senior member of the family. She herself never had any children, but she was now the family matriarch. Although Molly had lived at the Catalina Street house with Ynez and Carl, it can be assumed that Eva did a good deal of caring for her aged mother (both Ynez and Carl had jobs). Thus Eva, who had nursed her sickly husband for so long, who looked after her elderly mother to some degree, and who cared for her younger crippled brother, had settled into the role of family caretaker in her older years. That self-absorbed streak would have to have been held in check.

In another sense, Eva served as caretaker of her family (and her father's) reputation.

Her memoir, "An Outlaw and his Family," was a tool meant to protect that reputation, and it had been a decade since she lent that tool to the writer, Wallace Smith. In 1951, his book, *Prodigal Sons: The Adventures of Christopher Evans and John Sontag,* was published. He freely and liberally (and not always with proper credit given) quoted Eva's memoir. How Eva felt about this book is evidenced in the rumor that she tried to sue Smith for plagiarism.[7] Smith evidently had some sense that such a reaction might arise—he made a point in the book's acknowledgments to quote a letter Eva wrote encouraging him to use her memoir as much as he should choose. And he chose to use it a lot. Reading Smith's book, one will note large sections that are incredibly similar to Eva's unpublished manuscript. And although he uses her exact words liberally, he seldom presented them as direct quotes. He was, however, careful to cite her memoir frequently in the book's endnotes; so while an argument could be made for plagiarism, nothing ever became of the supposed lawsuit because it could as easily be argued against.

IN 1954, CARL EVANS DIED. His death certificate noted that bronchial pneumonia was the cause of death and that he had suffered from cancer of the mouth. Six months prior to his death, he had his lower jaw and more than half of his tongue removed.[8] His last years couldn't have been easy, but Carl had always faced physical challenges. It was perhaps surprising that Carl lived to be almost sixty-three years old. Although he certainly wasn't a baby when he died, he would always be Baby Carl to Eva, who was nearly seventy-eight years old at the time of his death. Carl undoubtedly thought of Eva as something of a mother figure. She had often looked after him when he was a baby and their mother was so deeply affected by the stress of their "family troubles." Picturing fifteen-year-old Eva holding a tiny Baby Carl in her arms and remembering the supposed romance between her and John Sontag, is it such a stretch to wonder if perhaps he was really Eva and John's child? While there is absolutely no hard evidence for this speculation, a rereading of the family history from the period of Carl's birth (May 1891) shows it might be plausible.

Even discounting this fanciful theory, Carl's death had to have affected the now-elderly Eva much like the death of a child. She was now at such an advanced age that she was surviving a younger generation. It was a lonely feeling.

WITH PERRY DECEASED, EVA NOW lived alone in their Third Street house. And with Molly and Carl now gone, Ynez had the entire two-story house on Catalina Street to herself. Rather than the two elderly sisters moving in together, Ynez rented out one floor of her house to a boarder. According to city directories, Andrew Kinkela, a retired gardener, began living at 1142 Catalina Street in the early 1960s, sharing an address with the eighty-year-old widow, Ynez Jensen. Perhaps he had been her gardener, as there was a lush almost-jungle fronting the house so deeply set back from the street. One can imagine that Ynez liked having someone around to help her out, and Andy Kinkela was a kind, thoughtful man who—although in his retirement years—was still active and quite handy. He represented the perfect tenant, and he became a valued friend. It is natural that through Ynez, Andy became acquainted her sister, Eva.

Andy began to spend more and more time with Eva (or Evelyn, as he knew her). Perhaps he helped with her garden as well. Eva had a great love for trees and plants, sometimes even preferring them to the company of people. And although she cherished her solitude, Andy shared her love of plants and was a welcomed relief from loneliness.

Once he got past her sometimes stern exterior, Andy saw Eva as a lady of considerable charm. She was a diminutive woman, shy of five feet in height. Age had rounded her face and squared her figure. Her smile was subtle; a Mona Lisa-like expression with the barely up-turned corners of her mouth ending in little vertical indentations, not quite dimples, but endearing nonetheless. Andy could imagine she had been quite an attractive young woman and that the sadness in her eyes mourned, among other things, the loss of youthful beauty.

Ynez started to feel jealous of her older sister.[9] The octogenarian sisters were almost like teenage girls, competing for the attention of a nearly seventy-year-old man who (at least they could imagine in years' past) had once been tall, dark and handsome.

While Eva sometimes claimed she didn't like people very much, Andy soon discovered that she enjoyed telling stories about the many interesting people she'd been fortunate to know. Eva had been friends with many famous writers and poets and actors and even an anarchist or two, and Andy was always an appreciative audience. But more than anything, Andy cared for, and took care of, Eva. As her age advanced, she needed Andy's care more and more, and their relationship grew closer and closer.

ANDY'S DAUGHTER, LILLIAN, WAS SHOCKED to receive an invitation to her father's wedding. There had been a time when she would have been shocked to even hear from her estranged father, but the two had mended their relationship and even become close after her own wedding, ten years prior, opened the door to reconciliation.[10] And now the news of his impending marriage was a little hard for Lillian to believe. It wasn't just that her father, a man of considerable age, would marry again. It was that, in the autumn of 1964, he planned to marry an eighty-eight-year-old woman in Laguna Beach named Evelyn McCullough.

After attending their wedding, Lillian often visited with her father and Eva at their home in Laguna Beach. Sitting with the aged Eva in her little white house perched high on a hill that overlooked the ocean—sharing the indulgence of champagne cake that Lillian always made sure to bring—they traded life stories. Eva, who still fancied herself a writer, eagerly questioned her new stepdaughter about her remarkable life, for Lillian had, in her forty-five or so years, experienced a great deal of history.

Lillian Kinkela Keil was born in 1918. She was raised in a convent in Eureka, California, after her father abandoned the family when Lillian was just a little girl. Growing up, she watched the nuns take care of the sick and was drawn to nursing. Upon completing high school, she became a student nurse in San Francisco and launched her professional nursing career.

It wasn't long until her career path took a decidedly different course. In 1938, Lillian's mother suggested she might like being a "stewardess." In the early days of commercial aviation, stewardesses were required to be trained nurses, and her mother heard an airline was looking for some. Lillian had never heard of a stewardess. After all, United Airlines had only recently invented the profession. Furthermore, Lillian didn't know anything about aviation. She had never even seen an airplane. Curious, Lillian ventured across the San Francisco Bay to the airline's base of operations in Oakland. There she saw the glistening airplanes and immediately was hooked on the idea of flight. Within days, Lillian was tending to passengers with the same care she had given her patients.[11]

After America entered the war in 1941, Lillian joined the Army Air Corps. Not only did it provide further opportunity to combine her two great loves: nursing and flying, it offered the patriotic and adventurous young woman a chance to join the war effort. She became a flight nurse, flying convoys across the Atlantic. She was later stationed at a B-17 air station in England and then, following D-Day, served on troop carrier planes for Patton's Third Army across France, Belgium and the Rhineland.

By war's end, Lillian had flown 250 missions and had crossed the Atlantic twenty-five times. After the war, she returned to her job at United Airlines, where she was promoted to Assistant Chief Stewardess, but she returned to active military duty in 1950 during the Korean Conflict. After sixteen grim months in Korea, accruing 1,400 flight hours and flying 175 evacuation missions, she stayed on with the Air Force with assignments at Castle Air Force Base in Merced, California, and then Hamilton Air Force Base near Ignacio, California.

After twelve years of service, Lillian was among the most decorated women ever to wear a United States military uniform. Her life was the stuff of movies, and, indeed, in 1953, she was "loaned" to Republic Pictures Studio as technical adviser for their production of *Flight Nurse*. The movie, which starred Joan Leslie, was based on Lillian's experiences while serving with the 801st Medical Air Evacuation Transport Squadron.[12]

While doing public relations for the Air Force in 1954, Lillian met Walter Keil, who had been a Navy intelligence officer stationed in Guadalcanal during World War II. It was a whirlwind romance and the two war veterans set a wedding date within a matter of weeks.[13]

Over the years, Andy Kinkela often read about Lillian in the newspapers. He kept track of his famous daughter, and although he was undoubtedly racked with guilt, he also beamed with pride. When he heard that she was about to marry, he knew it was time to take that difficult first step toward re-establishing contact. It was a step that happily led to him walking his daughter down the aisle at her wedding.

HOW FORTUNATE FOR EVA that Andy and Lillian reconciled. How exciting for Eva, who never had any children of her own, to now have a stepdaughter. And a war hero, no less!

Eva loved to hear Lillian tell her stories of flying dangerous missions in Europe during World War II and of providing comfort for injured soldiers during perilous air evacuations behind enemy lines. When Lillian told of the movie based on her experiences, Eva gave a wry chuckle. "But they got someone else to play your part?" Eva teased.

"Well, sure," Lillian admitted. "It was a movie. They needed a big star to play me."

"When they did my story, *I* was the star," Eva proudly proclaimed. Lillian smiled at the jest, but soon realized her elderly stepmother was dead serious. Of course, the statement begged further questioning, and Eva patiently waited for Lillian to take the bait.

"Are you telling me they made a movie about your life?" Lillian asked.

"Dear, this happened a very long time ago. There was no such thing as movies back then. No, I portrayed myself on the stage."[14]

Eva then proceeded to tell Lillian her own life's story. It left the highly-decorated war veteran utterly dumbfounded. It simply couldn't have been all true. Although Eva seemed remarkably sharp for her age—she didn't exhibit any signs of senility or forgetfulness—the tales she told must have been borrowed from books or movies or even figments of an overactive imagination. Maybe Eva's true calling in life was that of a Western romance novelist, for she certainly spun a doozie of a yarn for Lillian.

It couldn't have all been true; but, of course, it was. All Lillian had to do was go to the library and do a little research, which she did, to realize that Eva's father and her fiancé were indeed two of the most famous outlaws in the Old West. They really had achieved the status of folk-heroes in California, not unlike what Jesse James had done in Missouri. It was true that John Sontag was tragically gunned down at the famous shootout at Stone Corral. The teenage daughter of Chris Evans had indeed been engaged to Sontag, and she really did star as herself in a sensational and lurid melodrama.

Lillian was good friends with the legendary film director John Ford, who made some of Hollywood's greatest Westerns and helped promote the cultural myth of the American West. Lillian brought the saga of Evans and Sontag to Ford's attention, thinking it would make a great movie. But he scoffed at the idea, claiming it was too cliché a story, too much like "every other damn western ever made."[15]

The neighbors in Eva's Laguna Beach neighborhood would never know, nor ever imagine, the story behind this little old woman. As famous as Evans and Sontag had been in their day, history had relegated them to near obscurity. Perhaps this was all just as well. Eva had had her day in the spotlight. She was no longer Miss Eva Evans, the beloved daughter of Chris Evans, the beautiful fiancée of John Sontag, the subject of newspaper headlines and the star of a blood-and-thunder melodrama. That was all a lifetime ago in an era gone by. Now she was a frail, elderly woman named Evelyn Kinkela. She was Ynez's sister and Andy's wife and Lillian's stepmother and friend.

Eva no longer felt the burning desire to tell the world she was the daughter of a man branded "outlaw." Years before she had tried. She had so wanted to set the story straight—to proclaim to the world that she was so gloriously proud of her father. In her remarkable memoir she had told—better than anyone else could—the story of Chris Evans, her father and the enduring love of her life. But sadly, it was never published. Maybe it was just as well that her painful past would not be dragged up again.

YNEZ, THE SISTER WHO HAD SHARED so much of her life with Eva—an eventful childhood, hard times and failed marriages, heading out on their own and running a photography studio in Oregon, and decades together in Laguna Beach—died less than two years after Eva married Andy. Although she still had one brother, Joe, alive up in Oregon, she had outlived everyone else. And it began to feel as if she had even outlived her father's infamy.

Feeling that the story of her father (as she chose to tell it) needed safekeeping, Eva donated her never-published memoir to the Huntington Library in San Marino, California. Established in 1919 by Henry and Arabella Huntington, the library is today considered one of the largest and most complete research libraries in the country and is an especially valuable resource for historians of California and the American West. The beautiful library, with its adjoining art collection and botanical gardens, serves as a major attraction in Southern California.

Henry E. Huntington, who had held several executive positions with the Southern Pacific working alongside his uncle, Collis P. Huntington (one of the original Big Four railroad barons), inherited much of the Southern Pacific fortune when Collis died in 1900. He also married his uncle's widow, Arabella, and it was at her behest that they use a portion of that fortune to establish the library and art collection. Surely Evelyn Kinkela—the former Eva Evans, daughter of California's most notorious train robber—was aware of the irony of donating her written account of Evans and Sontag to a venerable institution made possible by Southern Pacific Railroad wealth.

If she hoped, by housing her memoir in the library the railroad built, to keep alive a contention that her father was innocent, it was a contention that survived only in print. She and Lillian shared many a story and secret over their champagne cake visits. And when the subject of train robbery came up—when Eva discussed what she and her father had for so long denied—she freely admitted that her father, Chris Evans, had indeed robbed trains. "That's how we got our money," she matter-of-factly told Lillian.[16]

ANDY CARED FOR the increasingly infirm Eva, but eventually she needed to be moved to a nursing home. Andy had done all he could, and one has to wonder if his caring had become a compulsion. He had abandoned his first wife and children, and perhaps his devotion to a woman who needed him (and Eva was not the last elderly woman he would marry and care for) was, however subconsciously, a self-imposed penance of sorts.[17]

Lillian visited Eva at the nursing home just blocks from the Third Street house where she had lived for three decades. Being a former nurse herself, Lillian sometimes raised hell with the staff when she noticed that Eva was developing bedsores or was otherwise lacking in proper care. Eva, now in her nineties, suffered from many of the ailments typical of such advanced age: congestive heart disease, hypertension and diabetes.[18]

PONDERING THE NOW FRAIL AND ELDERLY EVA, one can't help but picture her lying in bed in a depressing and drab room. The odors of a convalescent hospital inescapable: the reek of urine-soaked linen mixed with disinfectant on cold stainless steel and less-than-appetizing cooking smells. How Eva longed to be outside in the fresh air. Like her father, she had always preferred the outdoors. Although it was winter outside, the weather in Laguna Beach was warmer than the mountains where Eva more and more imagined herself. She had always loved the mountains. She longed to be there.

I look ahead, and there it is; the place of my dreams; the little old cabin under the cedar trees. How small it looks, I used to think it quite a house! Can wood absorb something from the dynamic mind of the man who assembled the boards, and from whom thoughts emanated for so many years within its four walls? Or do I just imagine I can feel my father, as I see him in fancy, walking the floor by candle light, with a baby in his arms, crooning Tennyson to a half-asleep child.

It was the hour before dawn and Eva hovered between sleep and waking, between consciousness and something else. She was cold, chilled to the bone. Surely Andy or one of the attendants hadn't left her window open. The nursing home was utterly silent, but Eva heard the wisp of something. Did the curtain on her window rustle? Or was it a voice? And who was calling her?

It is still dark and I awaken suddenly. I raise up on one elbow and listen intently...then I hear it. At first, only from my inner mind; then a soo-o-o and a swish in the trees.

The Dawn Wind! Now, if ever, I'll find him. Listening with all my soul! The wind dies!...A sense of infinite rest. Like a benediction after prayer. "Go in peace, my child."

I dress and go out. The birds are beginning to sing, just a faint twittering in the trees....Presently, shafts of light come across the meadow over the top of Redwood Mountain. One strikes the red bark of the tree by the road. His tree! His body is not in it—that is unimportant. Long ago he made it his, when he asked me to promise that when he died he should be buried in its heart.

Now the sun is through in full glory.

Eva no longer shivered. Her breathing became shallow, but less labored. It was now morning and Andy sat with her, holding her hand.

Way down in the meadow where the lily first blows,
Where the wind from the mountains ne'er ruffles the rose;
Lives fond Evelina, the sweet little dove,
The pride of the valley, the girl that I love.
Dear Evelina, sweet Evelina,
My love for thee shall never, never die

Looking down at his unconscious wife, he could see she was far away.

I go to seek the place where the tiger lilies grew. Before I reach the spot, I hear the little brook singing its way down from Redwood Mountain—"For men may come, and men may go, but I go on forever..."

Eva died on January 10, 1970. In the end, she joined her father in the garden of her heart. It was all she ever wanted.

NOTES

A CURTAIN SPEECH

1. Handwritten draft of R. C. White's curtain speech that prefaced productions of his play, *Evans and Sontag: The Visalia Bandits*. This speech was in response to efforts by a group of Methodist ministers to halt performances by the Evans and Sontag Combination, as the touring company was known (Bob Lilley Collection, Tulare County Museum).

2. *Laguna News-Post*, January 17, 1970.

3. William B. Secrest, *California Desperadoes: Stories of Early California Outlaws in Their Own Words* (Clovis, Calif.: Word Dancer Press, 2000), p. 191.

4. Author's conversation with Harold Leland "Lee" Edwards, author of various magazine articles and *Train Robbers and Tragedies: The Complete Story of Christopher Evans, California Outlaw* (Visalia, Calif.: Tulare County Historical Society, 2003), who first told me where to obtain a copy of Eva's memoir during a Tulare County Historical Society picnic in September 1999.

5. Eva Evans McCullough correspondence to Louis Rice, Sept. 8, 1937 (Kinkela/Keil Collection, Tulare County Museum).

6. *Fresno Bee*, January 18, 2002.

7. In the fall of 2002, the author had the opportunity to help bring the play to life at the historic Fox Theatre in Visalia, Calif., utilizing the talents of the College of the Sequoias drama department and members of the community. A permanent museum exhibit, funded in part by the California Council for the Humanities, was also installed that year at the Tulare County Museum, entitled "From Headlines to Footlights: The Sensational Saga of Evans and Sontag." The Evans and Sontag Project (as the consortium of non-profit organizations involved came to be known) was the result of Bob Lilley bringing his material to the attention of Terry Ommen and Kathy McGowan at the Tulare County Museum.

8. *Los Angeles Times*, July 10, 2005.

9. Author phone interview with Lillian Keil, June 29, 2004.

10. Eva Evans McCullough, "An Outlaw and His Family," unpublished manuscript (Kinkela/Keil Collection, Tulare County Museum). This copy of Eva's memoir only recently came to light. The Huntington Library in San Marino,

Calif., has the only other known copy, which Eva donated to the institution in 1967. Note: Page citations are from the copy housed at Tulare County Museum. Pagination is the only apparent difference between this copy and the one housed at the Huntington Library. The text of the two typewritten manuscripts appears to be identical (although I only did a spot comparison), indicating Eva at one point completely re-typed her memoir word for word.

ACT ONE – A FAMILY

CHAPTER ONE/RATTLESNAKE RANCH WEDDING

1. "An Outlaw and His Family," p. 274; Tulare County marriage license (copy courtesy of Arleen Anderson).

2. "An Outlaw and His Family," p. 4.

3. Canadian Census; Harold L. Edwards, *Train Robbers and Tragedies: The Complete Story of Christopher Evans, California Outlaw* (Visalia, Calif.: Tulare County Historical Society, 2003), p. 10.

4. *San Francisco Examiner,* February 2, 1894. The *Examiner* published excerpts of Chris Evans' jailhouse autobiography under the sub-headline "The Book the Famous Bandit Wrote Just Before his Escape from Fresno Jail—Voluminous Extracts from the Story of his Life Told in his Own Words."

5. *Visalia Daily Times*, August 13, 1892; Wallace Smith, *Prodigal Sons: The Adventures of Christopher Evans and John Sontag* (Boston: The Christopher Publishing House), p. 17. (A re-issue of Smith's book was published by Craven Street Books of Fresno, Calif., in 2005 with the slightly revised title of *Prodigal Sons: The Violent History of Christopher Evans and John Sontag* and includes an afterword by William B. Secrest, Jr.)

6. *San Francisco Examiner*, February 4, 1894; "An Outlaw and His Family," p. 6.

7. *History of Tulare County* (San Francisco: W.W. Elliott & Co. Publishers, 1883).

8. *San Francisco Examiner*, February 4, 1894.

9. Edwards, *Train Robbers and Tragedies,* p. 19; Leland Edwards, "Chris Evans' Early Troubles," *Los Tulares*: *Quarterly Bulletin of the Tulare County Historical Society*, No. 204, June 1999; *San Francisco Examiner*, February 2, 1894.

10. "An Outlaw and His Family," p. 8; United States Census records.

11. Wallace Smith, *Garden of the Sun* (Los Angeles: Lymanhouse, 1939), p. 196.

12. Mark Arax and Rick Wartzman, *The King of California: J.G. Boswell and the Making of a Secret American Empire* (New York: Public Affairs, Perseus Book Group, 2003), p. 74.

13. "An Outlaw and His Family," pp. 8-9.

14. Monroe C. Griggs, *Wheelers, Pointers and Leaders*, Joseph Doctor and Annie Mitchell, eds. (Visalia, Calif.: Valley Press, 1985), p. 28; *History of Tulare County* (W.W. Elliott & Co., 1883), p. 159. Regarding the logging of giant sequoias: in 1883, Smith Comstock, a lumberman from the Santa Cruz area, began cutting old growth giant sequoias at Big Stump, near the famed General Grant Grove, and by the turn of the century the Sanger Lumber Company had completely decimated one of the largest groves of giant sequoias at nearby Converse Basin. See Hank Johnston, *They Felled the Redwoods: A Saga of Flumes and Rails in the High Sierra* (Fish Camp, Calif.: Stauffer Publishing, 1996).

15. Griggs, *Wheelers, Pointers and Leaders,* p. 21.

16. *San Francisco Examiner*, February 4, 1894.

17. "An Outlaw and His Family," p. 267; County of Tulare marriage license and certificate (copy via Arleen Anderson).

18. "An Outlaw and His Family," p. 9; *San Francisco Examiner*, February 4, 1894.

19. Ibid., pp. 10-11.

20. Edwards, *Train Robbers and Tragedies*, p. 20; Edwards, "Chris Evans' Early Troubles," *Los Tulares,* No. 204, June 1999; *San Francisco Examiner*, February 4, 1894.

21. "An Outlaw and His Family," p. 12.

CHAPTER TWO/EARLY CHILDHOOD

1. "An Outlaw and His Family," pp. 13-14, 18.

2. Ibid., p. 12.

3. W. A. Chalfant, *The Story of Inyo*, 1933, p. 280. See also William Secrest, *Perilous Trains; Dangerous Men* (Sanger, Calif.: Word Dancer Press, 2000).

4. Chalfant, *The Story of Inyo*, pp. 270-71.

5. "An Outlaw and His Family," p. 16.

6. Ibid., pp. 16-17.

7. Edwards, *Train Robbers and Tragedies*, p. 12; California State Archives; Sacramento, Folsom Prison Records, C. Evans #3055 Biographical Sketch.

8. "An Outlaw and His Family," p. 19.

9. *Visalia Weekly Delta*, May 14, 1880.

10. Ibid.

11. In summarizing the events at Mussel Slough, the following sources were considered: William Deverell, *Railroad Crossing: Californians and the Railroad, 1850-1910*, (Berkeley: University of California Press, 1994), pp. 56-57; Irving McKee, "Notable Memorials to Mussel Slough," *Pacific Historical Review*, No. 17, February 1948; Richard J. Orsi, "The Octopus Reconsidered: The Southern Pacific and Agricultural Modernization in California," *California Historical Quarterly*, No. 54, Fall 1975; and J. L. Brown, *The Mussel Slough Tragedy* (1958).

12. Frank Norris, *The Octopus*, *A Story of California* (Signet Books, 1964, originally published in 1901), p. 42.

13. Brooks D. Gist, *Empire Out of the Tules: A True Story of the San Joaquin Valley in California* (Tulare, Calif., 1976), p. 45; Annie R. Mitchell, *Visalia: Her First Fifty Years*, (Exeter, Calif., 1963), pp. 30-31.

14. "An Outlaw and His Family," pp. 22-23.

15. Edwards, *Train Robbers and Tragedies*, p. 13.

16. "An Outlaw and His Family," pp. 24-25.

17. Smith, *Prodigal Sons*, p. 18.

18. "An Outlaw and His Family," pp. 27-28.

19. Smith, *Prodigal Sons,* p. 31.

20. Annie Mitchell, *Sites to See* (Visalia, Calif., 1983), p. 25; "Tulare County Schools," compiled by Sigma Chapter, Delta Kappa Gamma, 1961 (copy furnished to author by Terry Ommen).

21. "An Outlaw and His Family," p. 29.

22. *Prodigal Sons,* pp. 41-42.

Chapter Three/Concerning John Sontag

1. Mark Aldridge, *Safety First: Technology, Labor, and Business in the Building of American Work Safety, 1870-1939* (Baltimore: Johns Hopkins University Press, 1997), pp. 9, 14-15.

2. John J. Koblas, *Robbers of the Rails: The Sontag Boys of Minnesota* (St. Cloud, Minn.: North Star Press, 2003), p. 36.

3. Smith, *Prodigal Sons*, p. 49.

4. Koblas, *Robbers of the Rails*, pp. 4-9.

5. Census Report; "An Outlaw and His Family," p. 47; Opie L. Warner, *A Pardoned Lifer: Life of George Sontag* (San Bernardino, Calif.: The Index Print Co., 1909), p. 38.

6. Blake Gumprecht, *The Los Angeles River: Its Life, Death, and Possible Rebirth* (Baltimore: Johns Hopkins University Press, 1999), pp. 32-33; Warner, *Pardoned Lifer*, p. 38.

7. Mitchell, *Visalia's First Fifty Years*; Kathleen E. Small, *History of Tulare* (Chicago: S. J. Clarke Company, 1926), pp. 160-65.

8. C. G. Glasscock, *Bandits and the Southern Pacific* (New York: Frederick A. Stokes Co., 1929), pp. 82-84.

9. *San Francisco Examiner*, July 13, 1893.

10. Warner, *A Pardoned Lifer*, p. 40.

11. John K. Winkler, *W. R. Hearst: An American Phenomenon* (New York: Simon & Schuster, 1928).

12. William Randolph Hearst, *A Portrait in His Own Words*, edited by Edmond D. Coblentz (New York: Simon & Schuster, 1952), p. 37.

13. David Nasaw, *The Chief: The Life of William Randolph Hearst* (Boston: Houghton Mifflin, 2000), p. 70.

14. "An Outlaw and His Family," p. 45. See also the afterword, by William Secrest, Jr., to the re-issue of *Prodigal Sons* (Fresno, Calif.: Craven Street Books, 2005). Secrest notes that it was the Grangers Bank of California that employed Chris Evans, not the Bank of California as Smith stated in *Prodigal Sons* and as Eva claimed in her memoir (which was obviously Smith's source for the error).

15. *Visalia Times-Delta,* June 25, 1959 (Special Centennial Issue), Article entitled "Bonanza Wheat Farms."

16. Jay O'Connell, *Co-Operative Dreams: A History of the Kaweah Colony* (Van Nuys, Calif.: Raven River Press, 1999), p. 6.

17. *Visalia Times-Delta,* "Bonanza Wheat Farms," June 25, 1959.

18. "An Outlaw and His Family," pp. 48-49.

19. Ibid., p. 50.

20. Ibid.

CHAPTER FOUR/COMING OF AGE

1. *Tulare Evening Register*, February 23, 1889.

2. Edwards, *Train Robbers and Tragedies*, p. 22; Secrest, *California Desperadoes*, pp. 194-96; *Tulare Evening Register*, February 23, 1889.

3. *Visalia Weekly Delta*, February 28, 1889.

4. Ibid.

5. T. J. Stiles, *Jesse James: Last Rebel of the Civil War* (New York: A. A. Knopf, 2002).

6. Koblas, *Robbers of the Rails*, pp. 13-14; Smith, *Prodigal Sons,* pp. 67-69.

7. *Visalia Weekly Delta,* January 23, 1890.

8. Richard Patterson, *The Train Robbery Era: An Encyclopedic History* (Boulder, Colo.: Pruett Publishing), p. 75.

9. *Fresno Weekly Republican*, January 24, 1890.

10. "An Outlaw and His Family," p. 53.

11. Ibid., pp. 53-54.

12. *Modesto Evening News*, January 3, 7, 1891.

13. "An Outlaw and His Family," p. 33.

14. Ibid., p. 28.

15. Ibid., pp. 54-55.

16. Robert O'Brien, *This is San Francisco* (New York: Whittlesey House, McGraw-Hill Book Co., Inc., 1948).

17. "An Outlaw and His Family," pp. 54-55.

18. Ibid., pp. 37-38, 56.

19. Ibid., p. 52.

20. *Modesto Daily Evening News*, January 7, 1891.

21. "An Outlaw and His Family," p. 58.

ACT TWO – THE TROUBLES

Chapter Five/Robberies and Suspects

1. *Modesto Daily Evening News,* January 7, 1891; "An Outlaw and His Family," p. 58.

2. Edwards, *Train Robbers and Tragedies*, p. 15.

3. *Modesto Daily Evening News*, March 3, 1891; Warner, *A Pardoned Lifer*, p. 46.

4. Edwards, *Train Robbers and Tragedies,* p. 25; *San Francisco Chronicle*, February 7, 1891; *Tulare Register*, February 7, 1891.

5. Frank F. Latta, *Dalton Gang Days* (Santa Cruz, Calif.: Bear State Books, 1976), p. 84.

6. Latta, *Dalton Gang Days*, p. 87.

7. Ibid., p. 9.

8. Wallace Smith, *Garden of the Sun* (Los Angeles: Lymanhouse, 1939), p. 308.

9. Latta, *Dalton Gang Days*, p. 8.

10. Edwards, *Train Robbers and Tragedies*, p. 27; Latta, *Dalton Gang Days*, pp. 98, 118-19.

11. Latta, *Dalton Gang Days*, p. 31.

12. *Tulare County Times,* July 9, 1891; *Visalia Delta*, July 9, 1891.

13. "An Outlaw and His Family," p. 61.

14. *Fresno Morning Republican*, December 2, 1893; Warner, *A Pardoned Lifer*, pp. 47-48.

15. Latta, *Dalton Gang Days*, pp. 147-8.

16. Ibid., p. 138.

17. Ibid., pp. 147-48.

18. Edwards, *Train Robbers and Tragedies*, p.15.

19. John Boessenecker, *Badge and Buckshot: Lawlessness in Old California* (University of Oklahoma Press, 1988), pp. 205-6.

20. Latta, *Dalton Gang Days*, pp. 137-38.

21. Smith, *Prodigal Sons*, pp. 89-90, 419.

22. Ibid., p. 90.

23. "Tulare County Schools," compiled by Sigma Chapter, Delta Kappa Gamma, 1961; "An Outlaw and His Family," p. 60.

24. "An Outlaw and His Family," p. 61.

25. Warner, *A Pardoned Lifer*, p. 50.

26. Koblas, *Robbers and the Rails*, pp. 26-29.

27. Warner, *A Pardoned Lifer*, p. 53.

28. Koblas, *Robbers and the Rails,* p. 77.

29. Edwards, *Train Robbers and Tragedies*, p. 14; Koblas, *Robbers and the Rails*, pp. 79-80.

30. "An Outlaw and His Family," p. 61; Edwards, *Train Robbers and Tragedies*, p. 36.

31. Warner, *Pardoned Lifer*, p. 56; Koblas, *Robbers and the Rails,* p. 86.
32. Edwards, *Train Robbers and Tragedies,* pp. 34-35.

Chapter Six/Collis Changes All

1. Koblas, *Robbers of the Rails*, p. 95; Warner, *Pardoned Lifer*, p.58.
2. Warner, *Pardoned Lifer*, p. 58.
3. Latta, *Dalton Gang Days*, p. 206.
4. *Fresno Daily Republican*, December 3, 1893.
5. *Fresno Daily Republican*, December 2, 3, 1893, recounting George Sontag's testimony at Chris Evans' trial.
6. "An Outlaw and His Family," p. 64.
7. Kerman Photo History, A Brief History of Kerman, Calif. (www.tosteph-armd.net/kerman photo/history).
8. *Los Angeles Times*, August 5, 1892.
9. *San Francisco Examiner*, August 5, 1892.
10. Koblas, *Robbers of the Rails*, p. 101.
11. "An Outlaw and His Family," p. 64.
12. Koblas, *Robbers of the Rails*, p. 102.
13. "An Outlaw and His Family," p. 64.
14. Ibid., p. 65.
15. Ibid.
16. Edwards, *Train Robbers and Tragedies*, p. 39.
17. Glasscock, *Bandits and the Southern Pacific*, p. 87.
18. Edwards, *Train Robbers and Tragedies*, p. 38.
19. *San Francisco Examiner,* August 6, 1892.
20. *San Francisco Chronicle*, August 6, 1892; *Los Angeles Times*, August 6, 1892.
21. "An Outlaw and His Family," p. 65.
22. Ibid., p. 66.
23. Ibid.
24. *San Francisco Examiner*, August 6, 1892.
25. Boessenecker, *Badge and Buckshot*, p. 186; Edwards, *Train Robbers and Tragedies*, p. 39; Latta, *Dalton Gang Days,* p. 98.
26. "An Outlaw and His Family," p. 66.
27. *San Francisco Examiner,* August 6, 1892.
28. Transcript of Testimony in the Trial of Chris Evans, Indicted for Murder of Vernon Coke Wilson, in the Superior Court of Fresno County, Calif., Dec. 6-11, 1893, Vol. II. (Bancroft Library, Berkeley, Calif.), p. 1086; "An Outlaw and His Family," p. 67.
29. *San Francisco Chronicle*, August 6, 1892; *San Francisco Examiner*, August 6, 1892.
30. "An Outlaw and His Family," pp. 67-68.
31. *San Francisco Examiner*, August 6, 1892.

32. "An Outlaw and His Family," p. 68.
33. Koblas, *Robbers of the Rails*, p. 109; Edwards, *Train Robbers and Tragedies*, p. 42.
34. *San Francisco Examiner*, August 7, 1892; Smith, *Prodigal Sons*, p. 137.
35. Edwards, *Train Robbers and Tragedies*, pp. 42-43.
36. "An Outlaw and His Family," pp. 70-72.
37. *San Francisco Examiner*, August 7, 1892.
38. "An Outlaw and His Family," p. 73.
39. *San Francisco Examiner*, August 1892.
40. "An Outlaw and His Family," p. 73.

CHAPTER SEVEN/A HEADLINE SENSATION

1. *San Francisco Examiner,* August 7, 1892.
2. "An Outlaw and His Family," p. 75.
3. *Visalia Daily Times,* August 8, 1892.
4. "An Outlaw and His Family," p. 75.
5. *Los Angeles Times*, August 8, 1892.
6. "An Outlaw and His Family," pp. 75-76.
7. *San Francisco Examiner*, August 9, 1892.
8. "An Outlaw and His Family," p. 78.
9. *Los Angeles Times*, August 9, 1892; *Fresno Expositor*, August 9, 1892; Glasscock, *Bandits and the Southern Pacific*, p. 108; Edwards, *Train Robbers and Tragedies*, p. 51.
10. *San Francisco Examiner,* August 9, 1892.
11. "An Outlaw and His Family," pp. 80-82.
12. Author interview with Lillian Kinkela Kiel, June 2004.
13. Edwards, *Train Robbers and Tragedies*, p. 49.
14. *San Francisco Examiner,* August 12, 1892.
15. *San Francisco Examiner,* August 14, 1892.
16. *San Francisco Examiner, San Francisco Chronicle*, August 31, 1892; *Visalia Weekly Delta*, September 1, 1892.
17. *Visalia Weekly Delta*, September 1, 1892.
18. *San Francisco Chronicle*, August 31, 1892.
19. *Visalia Delta*, September 1, 1892.
20. "An Outlaw and His Family," p. 82.
21. "An Outlaw and His Family," p. 1; *San Francisco Examiner*, August 14, 1892.
22. *San Francisco Examiner*, August 14, 1892.
23. *Visalia Times*, September 17, 1892; "An Outlaw and His Family," p. 99.
24. *San Francisco Examiner*, August 13, 1892.
25. *San Francisco Examiner*, August 14, 1892.
26. *Los Angeles Times*, September 11, 1892; *Visalia Daily Times*, September 17, 1892.
27. Edwards, *Train Robbers and Tragedies,* p. 53.

28. "An Outlaw and His Family," p. 85; Smith, *Prodigal Sons*, pp. 153-54.
29. *San Francisco Examiner,* September 6, 1892; *Visalia Weekly Delta*, September 8, 1892.
30. *San Francisco Chronicle*, September 6, 1892; *Tulare County Times*, September 9, 1892.
31. "An Outlaw and His Family," p. 83; *Tulare County Times*, September 9, 1892.
32. Glasscock, *Bandits and the Southern Pacific*, p.130; "An Outlaw and His Family," p. 89.
33. "An Outlaw and His Family," p. 89; Trial Transcript, p. 1115.
34. John Boessenecker (author of *Badge and Buckshot: Lawlessness in Old California*), his specific comments about Vic Wilson and Frank Burke via correspondence with the author, June 2007.
35. Glasscock, *Bandits and the Southern Pacific*, p. 130, Glasscock wrote his account before Eva wrote her memoir, but he did interview her sometime in the 1920s.
36. Smith, *Prodigal Sons*, p. 144.
37. *Visalia Weekly Delta,* September 8, 1892.

CHAPTER EIGHT/DEFIANCE

1. Edwards, *Train Robbers and Tragedies*, pp. 55-56; "An Outlaw and His Family," p. 90.
2. *Visalia Weekly Delta*, November 8, 1892.
3. "An Outlaw and His Family," p. 91.
4. *Visalia Weekly Delta*, September 15, 1892; *Los Angeles Times*, September 14, 1892; *San Francisco Chronicle*, September 14, 1892.
5. Secrest, *California Desperadoes*, p.199.
6. "An Outlaw and His Family," pp. 91-92.
7. *San Francisco Examiner,* October 7, 1892.
8. "An Outlaw and His Family," p. 93.
9. *San Francisco Examiner*, June 9, 1893.
10. *San Francisco Examiner*, September 20, 1892; *San Francisco Chronicle*, September 18, 1892.
11. "An Outlaw and His Family," pp. 94-95.
12. *Visalia Daily Times*, September 17, 1892; *San Francisco Examiner*, September 17, 1892.
13. *San Francisco Examiner*, September 20, 1892.
14. John K. Winkler, *W. R. Hearst, American Phenomenon* (New York: Simon & Schuster, 1928), p. 73; John Bruce, *Gaudy Century: The Story of San Francisco's Hundred Years of Robust Journalism* (New York: Random House, 1949), p. 213.
15. *San Francisco Examiner*, 1896.
16. San *Francisco Examiner*, March 14, 1893; "An Outlaw and His Family," p. 145.

17. This supposes that when Eva wrote that it was at George's trial that she first met Bigelow ("An Outlaw and His Family," p. 109), she actually meant his arraignment hearing. This would have to have been the case if she met him before they helped arrange the interview because George's actual trial did not start until three weeks after the interview appeared. This was an understandable error in memory, and there is no reason to think she intentionally tried to obfuscate the issue. This also makes clear Bigelow befriended the Evans family primarily to further his journalistic ambitions.

18. *San Francisco Examiner,* October 7, 1892.

19. *San Francisco Examiner*, October 6, 1892.

20. *San Francisco Examiner*, October 8, 1892.

21. "An Outlaw and His Family," p. 106.

22. *Los Angeles Times*, October 21, 1892; *San Francisco Examiner*, October 12, 1892.

23. *San Francisco Examiner*, October 28, 1892.

24. *San Francisco Examiner*, October 29, 1892.

25. *Los Angeles Times*, October 30, 1892; *San Francisco Examiner*, October 30, 1892.

26. *San Francisco Examiner*, October 30, 1892.

27. "An Outlaw and His Family," p. 102.

28. Ibid., p. 103.

29. *Visalia Daily Morning Delta*, February 10, 1894.

30. "An Outlaw and His Family," pp. 104-5; author's visit to site, led by guide Larry Jordan, May 7, 2005.

31. Smith, *Prodigal Sons*, pp. 148-9.

32. "An Outlaw and His Family," pp. 100-101.

33. Smith, *Prodigal Songs*, p. 204.

34. Glasscock, *Bandits and the Southern Pacific*, p. 164.

35. "An Outlaw and His Family," pp. 97-99.

36. Ibid.

37. Ibid., p. 99.

CHAPTER NINE/AID AND SUPPORT

1. *Stockton Independent*, February 12, 1893.

2. *Fresno Daily Republican*, February 14, 1893.

3. "An Outlaw and His Family," p. 148.

4. Smith, *Prodigal Sons*, p. 227.

5. Winkler, *W. R. Hearst: An American Phenomenon*, pp. 72-73.

6. Evelyn Wells, *Champagne Days of San Francisco* (New York: D. Appleton-Century Co., 1939), pp. 1-5.

7. Wells, *Champagne Days*, p. 32.

8. "An Outlaw and His Family," pp. 150-51.

9. *Los Angeles Times*, December 14, 1892; *San Francisco Chronicle*, March 8, 1893.

10. *San Francisco Chronicle*, March 10, 1893.

11. *San Francisco Examiner*, March 14, 1893.

12. *San Francisco Examiner*, October 7, 8, 1892.

13. *Fresno Daily Expositor*, April 6, 1893; *Visalia Weekly Delta*, April 13, 1893.

14. *San Francisco Chronicle*, April 21, 1893; *Visalia Weekly Delta,* April 20, 1893; *San Francisco Examiner*, April 21, 1893.

15. *San Francisco Chronicle*, April 20, 1893; Edwards, *Train Robbers and Tragedies*, p. 70; *Visalia Weekly Delta*, April 27, 1893.

16. "An Outlaw and His Family," p. 85.

17. *Visalia Weekly Delta,* April 27, 1893. Although the *Delta* doesn't credit it as a reprint, the exact same paragraph appeared in the *San Francisco Examiner* on April 21, 1893.

18. *San Francisco Chronicle*, April 21, 1893.

19. *San Francisco Examiner*, April 21, 1893; *San Francisco Chronicle*, April 22, 1893.

20. *San Francisco Examiner*, April 22, 1893.

21. Smith, *Prodigal Sons*, p. 263.

22. *San Francisco Examiner,* May 3, 1893.

23. *Visalia Delta*, June 1, 1893.

24. Ibid.

25. Glasscock, *Bandits and the Southern Pacific*, p. 189; Smith, *Prodigal Sons,* p. 266. Eva makes no mention of this in her memoir, but both Glasscock and Smith interviewed her for their books.

26. *San Francisco Examiner*, May 28, 1893.

27. *Visalia Delta*, June 1, 1893.

28. *San Francisco Examiner,* May 28, 1893.

29. Benjamin Lawson, *Joaquin Miller* (Boise, Idaho: Boise State University Western Writer Series, No. 43, 1980), pp. 11, 18.

30. *Tulare County Times*, May 25, 1893; *Los Angeles Times*, May 28, 1893.

31. Warner, *Pardoned Lifer*, p. 111.

32. William B. Secrest, *Perilous Trails; Dangerous Men* (Sanger, Calif.: Word Dancer Press, 2000), p. 232.

33. *San Francisco Examiner*, July 1, 1893.

34. "An Outlaw and His Family," p. 123.

35. *San Francisco Examiner*, July 1, 1893.

36. Bruce, *Gaudy Century*, p. 215.

37. *San Francisco Examiner*, June 4, 1893.

38. *San Francisco Examiner*, June 9, 1893.

39. *San Francisco Examiner*, June 10, 1893.

40. Edwards, *Train Robbers and Tragedies*, p. 79; William B. Secrest, *Lawmen and Desperadoes: A Compendium of Noted, Early California Peace Officers, Badmen and Outlaws, 1850-1900* (Spokane, Wash.: The Arthur H. Clark Co., 1994), pp. 142-43.

41. *San Francisco Chronicle*, June 13, 1893.

42. Ibid.

43. Smith, *Prodigal Sons*, p. 120; "An Outlaw and His Family," p. 111.

44. *San Francisco Chronicle*, June 13, 1893.

45. *San Francisco Examiner*, June 4, 1893.

CHAPTER TEN/STONE CORRAL

1. *San Francisco Chronicle,* June 12, 1892.

2. *Visalia Weekly Delta*, June 15, 1893.

3. *Tulare County Times*, June 15, 1893.

4. *Visalia Weekly Delta*, June 15, 1893.

5. Edwards, *Train Robbers and Tragedies*, p. 80.

6. *Visalia Weekly Delta*, June 15, 1893.

7. Ibid..

8. Ibid.

9. *San Francisco Examiner*, June 13, 1893.

10. Ibid.

11. Glasscock, *Bandits and the Southern Pacific*, p. 201.

12. "An Outlaw and His Family," p. 114.

13. *San Francisco Chronicle*, June 14, 1893.

14. "An Outlaw and His Family," p. 114.

15. *San Francisco Chronicle*, June 14, 1893.

16. *San Francisco Examiner*, June 14, 1893.

17. "An Outlaw and His Family," p. 115.

18. Transcript of Testimony in the Trial of Chris Evans, Indicted for Murder of Vernon Coke Wilson, in the Superior Court of Fresno County, Calif., Dec. 6-11, 1893, Vol. II. (Bancroft Library, Berkeley, Calif.), p. 1224; Latta, *Dalton Gang Days*, pp. 137, 163.

19. "An Outlaw and His Family," p. 115.

20. Ibid., p. 124.

21. Ibid., p. 126.

22. Ibid., pp. 126-27.

23. Ibid., p. 117.

24. Ibid., p. 116.

25. *Visalia Weekly Delta*, June 13, 1893.

26. "An Outlaw and His Family," p. 118.

27. *San Francisco Examiner*, June 22, 25,1893.

28. *San Francisco Examiner*, June 28, 1893.

29. Edwards, *Train Robbers and Tragedies*, p. 98; *San Francisco Examiner*, June 28, 1893.

30. Koblas, *Robbers and the Rails*, p. 210.

31. Edwards, *Train Robbers and Tragedies*, pp. 98-99.

32. "An Outlaw and His Family," p. 119.

33. *San Francisco Examiner*, June 29, 1893.

34. *San Francisco Examiner*, July 4, 1893.
35. Warner, *A Pardoned Lifer*, p. 161.
36. "An Outlaw and His Family," p. 129.
37. Ibid.

ACT THREE—INFAMY

Chapter Eleven/Life in the Theatre

1. *Visalia Weekly Delta*, July 6, 1893.
2. U.S. Census records; author's casual conversations with Bob Lilley, great-great grandson of R. C. White.
3. Wells, *Champagne Days*, pp. 30-40.
4. *San Francisco Examiner*, July 29, 1893.
5. *Fresno Republican,* July 11, 1893; *San Francisco Examiner*, July 11, 29, 1893.
6. *San Francisco Examiner*, July 29, 1893; "An Outlaw and His Family," p. 131.
7. *San Francisco Examiner*, July 29, 1893.
8. *San Francisco Call*, January 24, 1894.
9. Will Smith scrapbooks, letter dated November 27, 1893. The unsigned letter was presumably authored by Byrd because of his known detective work and his familiarity with the family. The scrapbooks containing this and a few other letters, but mostly newspaper clippings about cases he had worked, were compiled by Southern Pacific detective Will Smith and are now in the private collection of John Boessenecker.
10. Benjamin McArthur, *Actors and American Culture 1880-1920* (Iowa City: University of Iowa Press, 1992), p. 129.
11. McArthur, *Actors and American Culture*, p. 35.
12. "An Outlaw and His Family," p. 131.
13. *Bakersfield Echo*, July 31, 1893.
14. Wells, *Champagne Days*, p. 248.
15. *San Francisco Examiner*, September 4, 1893.
16. *Sacramento Bee*, December 2, 1893.
17. *San Francisco Examiner,* September 4, 1893.
18. Ibid.
19. *San Francisco Examiner*, July 29, 1893.
20. *San Francisco Examiner*, September 9, 1893.
21. R. C. White papers, handwritten draft of undated letter (Bob Lilley Collection, Tulare County Museum).
22. *San Francisco Examiner*, September 4, 1893.
23. *San Francisco Examiner*, September 9, 1893.
24. "An Outlaw and His Family," p. 131.
25. *San Francisco Examiner*, September 4, 1893.

26. *San Francisco Call*, September 19, 1893; *San Francisco Chronicle*, September 9, 1893.

27. *San Francisco Examiner*, September 19, 1893.

28. *San Francisco Examiner*, "Players Column," September 24, 1893.

29. "An Outlaw and His Family," p. 132.

30. Original handwritten manuscript of R. C. White's "Evans and Sontag, or The Visalia Bandits" (Bob Lilley Collection, Tulare County Museum).

31. *San Francisco Examiner,* September 19, 1893; *San Francisco Chronicle*, September 19, 1893.

32. *San Francisco Examiner*, September 19, 1893.

33. Ibid.

CHAPTER TWELVE/TRIALS AND TRIBULATIONS

1. *San Francisco Examiner*, October 1, 1893.

2. Warner, *A Pardoned Lifer*, p. 174.

3. *San Francisco Examiner*, October 2, 1893.

4. *San Francisco Chronicle*, October 1, 1893.

5. Warner, *A Pardoned Lifer*, pp. 165-66.

6. *Fresno Republican*, October 1, 1893; *Los Angeles Times*, October 1, 1893; *San Francisco Examiner*, October 2, 1893.

7. *San Francisco Examiner*, October 2, 1893.

8. *San Francisco Examiner*, October 1, 1893.

9. R. C. White papers, company stationery (Bob Lilley Collection, Tulare County Museum); McArthur, *Actors and American Culture*, p. 9.

10. McArthur, *Actors and American Culture*, p. 62.

11. "An Outlaw and His Family," p. 163.

12. *Visalia Weekly Delta,* October 26, 1893.

13. *Sacramento Bee*, November 18, 1893.

14. *San Francisco Examiner*, October 24, 1893.

15. *Hanford Journal*, clipping from November 1893, Will Smith scrapbooks.

16. *Fresno Republican*, November 8, 1893.

17. *Hanford Review*, November 11, 1893.

18. R. C. White papers, margin note in original music score sheets (Bob Lilley Collection, Tulare County Museum); *Tulare County Times*, November 19, 1893.

19. County of Tulare, divorce papers, March 30, 1896 (copy via Arleen Anderson).

20. *Tulare County Times*, November 30, 1893; *Fresno Republican*, January 19, 1894.

21. The author's paternal grandparents were first cousins, legally married in California.

22. *Fresno Expositor*, December 2, 1893.

23. *Sacramento Bee*, December 2, 1893.

24. *Sacramento Bee*, December 11, 1893.

25. *San Francisco Examiner*, November 29, 1893.

26. Letter to Tupper, November 27, 1893. An unsigned letter informed the prosecuting attorney that the Evans family felt: "All of there hopes is to git a hang jurry + ware [sic] the case out." Will Smith scrapbooks (John Boessenecker private collection).

27. Will Smith scrapbooks; *Fresno Morning Republican,* November 28, 1893.

28. Will Smith scrapbooks.

29. *Fresno Morning Republican*, November 29, 1893.

30. *San Francisco Call*, December 2, 1893.

31. Koblas, *Robbers of the Rails*, p. 234; "An Outlaw and His Family," p. 157; *San Francisco Call*, December 2, 1893.

32. *Fresno Morning Republican*, December 3, 1893.

33. *Los Angeles Times*, December 8, 1893.

34. *San Francisco Examiner*, December 8, 1893.

CHAPTER THIRTEEN/CONVICTION

1. *San Francisco Examiner*, December 9, 1893.

2. *San Francisco Examiner*, December 9, 1893; *Fresno Morning Republican*, December 9, 1893; *Visalia Weekly Delta*, December 12, 1893.

3. *San Francisco Examiner,* December 9, 1893.

4. Transcript of Testimony in the Trial of Chris Evans, Indicted for Murder of Vernon Coke Wilson, in the Superior Court of Fresno County, California, Dec. 6-11, 1893, Vol. II. (Bancroft Library, Berkeley, Calif.), pp. 1083-84.

5. Ibid., p. 1086.

6. *Visalia Weekly Delta*, December 14, 1893; Trial transcript, p. 1099.

7. Trial transcript, pp. 1103-04.

8. Ibid., p. 1119.

9. Trial transcript, p. 1115.

10. *Los Angeles Times,* December 10, 1893; *San Francisco Chronicle,* December 10, 1893; *San Francisco Morning Call*, December 10, 1893.

11. "An Outlaw and His Family," p. 158.

12. Trial transcript, p. 1169.

13. Ibid., p. 1224.

14. Ibid., pp.1182-83, 1292-93.

15. *San Francisco Examiner*, December 14, 1893.

16. *Visalia Weekly Delta*, December 21, 1893.

17. *Fresno Morning Republican,* December 16, 1893.

18. "An Outlaw and His Family," p. 160.

19. *San Francisco Examiner*, December 2, 1893.

20. *Fresno Morning Republican*, December 15, 1893.

21. "An Outlaw and His Family," p. 160.

22. *San Francisco Examiner*, December 30, 1893.

23. *San Francisco Examiner*, December 15, 1893.

24. *Fresno Morning Republican*, December 31, 1893.

25. "An Outlaw and His Family," p. 169.

26. Ibid.

27. William Secrest, "In the Matter of Edward Morrell," *Fresno Past & Present*, *The Journal of the Fresno City and County Historical Society*, Spring 1997.

28. Secrest, "In the Matter of Ed Morrell."

29. Ed. Morrell, *The Twenty-Fifth Man* (Montclair, N. J.: New Era Publishing Co., 1924), p. 73.

30. *San Francisco Chronicle*, December 30, 1993.

31. *San Francisco Examiner*, December 30, 1893.

32. *San Francisco Chronicle*, December 30, 1893.

33. *Fresno Morning Republican*, December 31, 1893; *San Francisco Examiner*, December 30, 1893.

34. "An Outlaw and His Family," p. 174.

Chapter Fourteen/On Tour Again

1. *Fresno Morning Republican*, December 29, 1893.

2. Edwards, *Train Robbers and Tragedies*, p. 137.

3. "An Outlaw and His Family," p. 170.

4. Smith, *Prodigal Sons*, p. 347.

5. *Los Angeles Times*, December 29, 1893.

6. *San Francisco Chronicle*, December 30, 1893; *San Francisco Examiner*, December 30, 1893.

7. *Visalia Weekly Delta*, January 4, 1894.

8. *Fresno Morning Republican*, December 30, 1893.

9. Smith, *Prodigal Sons,* p. 352.

10. *Fresno Morning Republican*, December 31, 1893; *Visalia Weekly Delta*, January 11, 1894; *San Francisco Examiner*, January 24, 1894.

11. *San Francisco Examiner*, January 23, 1894.

12. Ibid.

13. *San Francisco Examiner*, advertisement for the play, February 9, 1894.

14. *San Francisco Examiner,* January 21, 1894.

15. *San Francisco Examiner*, January 24, 1894.

16. *San Francisco Examiner*, January 25, 1984.

17. R. C. White papers, handwritten draft of his curtain speech (Bob Lilley Collection, Tulare County Museum).

18. *San Francisco Examiner*, January 21, 1894.

19. *Visalia Weekly Delta*, January 25, 1894.

20. Morrell, *The Twenty-Fifth Man*, pp. 118-9.

21. *San Francisco Examiner*, January 2, 3, 5, 9, February 4, 1894.

22. "An Outlaw and His Family," p. 182.

23. Morrell, *The Twenty-Fifth Man*, pp. 211-12.

24. *San Francisco Examiner*, February 9, 1894.
25. "An Outlaw and His Family," p. 183.
26. *San Francisco Examiner*, February 9, 1894.
27. Morrell, *The Twenty-Fifth Man*, p. 220.
28. *San Francisco Examiner,* February 10, 1894.
29. "An Outlaw and His Family," p. 183.
30. *San Francisco Examiner*, February 14, 1894.
31. *Fresno Morning Republican,* February 9, 1894.
32. Harold L. Edwards, "The Man Who Tricked Chris Evans," *Los Tulares*, June 1999.
33. *Visalia Weekly Delta,* February 22, 1894.
34. "An Outlaw and His Family," p. 184.
35. *San Francisco Examiner*, February 20, 23, 1894.
36. Morrell, *The Twenty-Fifth Man*, p. 229.
37. "An Outlaw and His Family," p. 185.
38. *San Francisco Examiner,* February 20, 1894.
39. Morrell, *The Twenty-Fifth Man*, p. 231.
40. *San Francisco Examiner*, February 20, 1894.
41. *San Francisco Examiner*, February 21, 1894.
42. *San Francisco Examiner*, February 20, 1894.
43. Ibid.
44. "An Outlaw and His Family," p. 188.

Chapter Fifteen/Hard Times

1. *Visalia Weekly Delta*, February 22, 1894.
2. Secrest, "In the Matter of Ed Morrell."
3. "An Outlaw and His Family," p. 189.
4. Ibid., p. 190.
5. Ibid., p. 188.
6. *Fresno Daily Expositor*, March 14, 1894.
7. Secrest, "In the Matter of Ed Morrell"; Morrell, *The Twenty-Fifth Man*, pp. 251, 257.
8. "An Outlaw and His Family," p. 198.
9. *San Francisco Examiner*, March 24, 1894; *Fresno Daily Republican*, March 24, 1894.
10. *Fresno Daily Republican*, March 24, 1894.
11. "An Outlaw and His Family," p. 127.
12. *Fresno Daily Republican*, March 24, 1894.
13. "An Outlaw and His Family," p. 203.
14. *San Francisco Examiner*, April 3, 1894.
15. *Los Angeles Times,* February 12, 1894.
16. *Visalia Weekly Delta*, February 15, 1894.
17. *Visalia Morning Delta*, April 17, 1894.

18. R. C. White papers, original musical score (Bob Lilley Collection, Tulare County Museum); *The Astorian*, May 10, 1894.

19. *Columbia Encyclopedia*, 6th Ed. (Columbia University Press, via internet).

20. *Heppner Gazette*, June 19, 1894.

21. *Heppner Gazette*, July 17, 1894.

22. *Heppner Gazette*, July 31, August 3, 14, 28, 1894

23. "An Outlaw and His Family," pp. 193-94.

24. *San Francisco Examiner*, August 19, 1894.

25. *Heppner Gazette*, August 24, 1894.

26. *Fresno Weekly Republican*, September 28, 1894.

27. "An Outlaw and His Family," p. 199.

28. *Tulare County Times*, May 1895; *San Francisco Chronicle*, May 1895.

29. Copy of divorce complaint, Eva Evans, Plaintiff vs. James U. Evans, Defendant, March 30, 1896 (Tulare County Clerk's Office, Visalia, Calif.); *Fresno Weekly Republican,* June 19, 1896.

30. Charles Michelson, *San Francisco Examiner,* July 27, 1895.

31. Secrest, "In the Matter of Ed Morrell."

32. *Fresno Weekly Republican*, May 17, 1895; Secrest, *Lawmen and Desperadoes,* p. 125.

33. *San Francisco Examiner*, June 29, 1893.

34. "An Outlaw and His Family," p. 203.

35. Ibid., pp. 208-9.

ACT FOUR—MOVING ON

CHAPTER SIXTEEN/OREGON PORTRAITS

1. Switzer family genealogy, Byrd family genealogy. Citing death certificate and marriage record (copies provided to author courtesy Barbara Baker and Arleen Anderson and online as "Baker-Byrd-Logan Tree," Ancestry.com, World Tree Project).

2. "An Outlaw and His Family," p. 223

3. *The Arena*, March 1895.

4. "An Outlaw and His Family," p. 215; *The Arena,* March, 1895; *Frank Leslie's Popular Monthly*, December 1891.

5. Clipping from *San Francisco Call*, August 21, 1892, (Joaquin Miller papers, Claremont College, Calif.).

6. John Young, *Journalism in California* (San Francisco: Chronicle Publishing Company, 1915); John Winkler; *W. R. Hearst: An American Phenomenon* (New York: Simon & Schuster, 1928); www.littlejimclub.org/history.

7. "An Outlaw and His Family," pp. 216-17.

8. Harr Wagner, *Joaquin Miller and His Other Self* (San Francisco: Harr Wagner Publishing Company, 1929).

9. Tulare County Recorder, Indentures, January 1900; June 1900 (copies furnished to author courtesy of Rich Kangas).

10. "An Outlaw and His Family," p. 223.

11. Ibid., p.197.

12. Byrd family genealogy.

13. Department of Corrections, File #F2745:113, re: Chris Evans, California State Archives (copy on file in Annie Mitchell History Room, Tulare County Library, Visalia, Calif.).

14. Department of Corrections, re: Chris Evans.

15. *Visalia Delta*, March 8, 1909.

16. "An Outlaw and His Family," dedication page.

17. Peter Palmquist, *A Bibliography of Writings By and About Women in Photography 1850-1950* (Borgo Press, 1994); "An Outlaw and His Family," p. 221.

18. "An Outlaw and His Family," p. 222.

19. Warner, *A Pardoned Lifer*.

20. Koblas, *Robbers of the Rails*, pp. 264-69.

21. Secrest, "In the Matter of Edward Morrell," *Fresno Past and Present*; California State Archives, Ed Morrell parole files (Fresno County Library historical files).

22. *Coos Bay Times*, May 12, 1908.

23. Original photos (Kinkela/Keil Collection, Tulare County Museum); *Coos Bay Times*, May 27, 1908.

24. "An Outlaw and His Family," p. 223.

25. *Sunset Magazine*, June 1907.

26. *Coos Bay Times*, December 28, 1908.

CHAPTER SEVENTEEN/UTOPIAN DREAMS

1. "An Outlaw and His Family," p. 243.

2. Edwards, *Train Robbers and Tragedies*, p. 176.

3. William Deverell, *Railroad Crossing: Californians and the Railroad, 1850-1910* (Berkeley: University of California Press, 1994), p. 171; www. McDougalLittle.com; www.californiahistory.net.

4. Department of Corrections, re: Chris Evans, correspondence: R. T. McKisick to his Excellency the Governor, January 25, 1911.

5. Edwards, *Train Robbers and Tragedies*, p. 176.

6. Chris Evans letter to Eva, April 15, 1911 (Kinkela/Keil Collection, Tulare County Museum).

7. *San Francisco Examiner*, April 16, 1911.

8. *Sacramento Star*, May 2, 1911.

9. Original scrapbook with clippings (Kinkela/Keil Collection).

10. *Sacramento Star* clipping, original scrapbook (Kinkela/Keil Collection).

11. Edwards, *Train Robbers and Tragedies*, p. 176. Citing from Board of Prison Directors minutes, April 14, 1911.

12. Scrapbook clippings from *The Star*, May 20, 1911 and the *Times* (presumably "Los Angeles") dated May 2, 1911, (Kinkela/Keil Collection).

13. "An Outlaw and His Family," pp. 243-44.

14. Ibid., p. 253.

15. Ibid., p. 244.

16. Emma Goldman, *Living My Life* (two volumes, Dover Publications, 1970, originally published by Alfred Knopf, New York, 1931), back cover of Volume One.

17. Emma Goldman Papers, a Chronology (http://sunsite3.berkeley.edu/goldman).

18. "An Outlaw and His Family," p. 244.

19. Ibid., p. 245.

20. Ibid., p. 246.

21. Ibid., p. 245.

22. Emma Goldman, *A Sketch of Alexander Berkman*, 1922 (via www.dwardmac.pitzer.edu /Anarchist archives).

23. "An Outlaw and His Family," pp. 249-50.

24. *Visalia Delta*, March 25, 1909.

25. *Mankato Daily Review*, October 12, 1910.

26. Secrest, "In the Matter of Ed Morrell."

27. For the complete Kaweah story, see the author's *Co-Operative Dreams: A History of the Kaweah Colony* (Van Nuys, Calif.: Raven River Press, 1999).

28. O'Connell, *Co-Operative Dreams*, p. 89.

29. Christopher Evans, *Eurasia*, (online via The Gutenberg Project, originally published by the James Barry Company, San Francisco, 1912). The author knows of only two extant copies of the actual book: one at the California State Library in Sacramento; another copy, which is inscribed by Chris Evans, is in the personal collection of Robert McCubbin and was on loan to the Tulare County Museum for their Evans and Sontag Exhibit.

30. Handbill copy, Emma Goldman Papers, images accessible online.

31. "An Outlaw and His Family," p. 251.

32. Ibid., p. 255.

33. Ibid., p. 257.

34. Ibid., pp. 258-59.

Chapter Eighteen/Writing a Legacy

1. Carey McWilliams, *Southern California Country, an Island on the Land* (New York: Duell, Sloan & Pearce, 1946), p. 242.

2. "An Outlaw and His Family," p. 266.

3. *Oxnard Courier*, July 5, 1907.

4. Glasscock, *Bandits and the Southern Pacific*, pp. 76-77.

5. *Los Angeles Times*, February 17, 1929, in scrapbook (Kinkela/Keil Collection, Tulare County Museum).

6. Glasscock, *Bandits and the Southern Pacific*, p. 291.

7. Laguna Beach City Directories (Laguna Beach Public Library).

8. Emma Goldman letter to Eva Evans McCullough, September 17, 1929 (Emma Goldman Papers, http://sunsite3.berkeley.edu/goldman).

9. Emma Goldman letter to Perry McCullough, November 29, 1929, (Emma Goldman Papers).

10. Goldman, *Living My Life* (volume 1), p. *vi*.

11. Eva Evans McCullough letter to Saxe Commins, March 12, 1937 (Kinkela/Keil Collection).

12. Ynez Jensen letter to Eva Evans McCullough, November 3, 1933 (Kinkela/Keil Collection).

13. "An Outlaw and His Family," p. 271.

14. Ibid., pp. 271-78.

15. Eva Evans McCullough letter to editor of *Colliers*, February 12, 1937 (Kinkela/Keil Collection).

16. Eva Evans McCullough letter to Houghton Mifflin, January 28, 1937 with handwritten margin list of other publishers to which same letter was sent; Joel Satz letter to Eva Evans McCullough, undated; Saxe Commins letter to Eva Evans McCullough, February 17, 1937 (Kinkela/Keil Collection).

17. Perry McCullough letter to Ruth Boyd, August 9, 1937; Ruth Boyd letter to Perry McCullough, July 29, 1937; misc. letters to publishers, 1938 (Kinkela/Keil Collection).

18. Eva Evans McCullough letter to *Writers Digest*, March 4, 1938 (Kinkela/Keil Collection).

19. Eva Evans, "Polar Bear Rug," "The Basement Door," and "No Death is Untimely," unpublished manuscripts (Kinkela/Keil Collection).

20. Eva Evans, "Grat Dalton's Ride," unpublished manuscript (Kinkela/Keil Collection).

Chapter Nineteen/Laguna Beach Passings

1. City Directories (Laguna Beach Public Library); Byrd family genealogy.

2. Smith, *Prodigal Sons*, p. 7.

3. Remlow Harris, *South Coast News*, May 13, 1941.

4. *South Coast News*, September 13, 1938.

5. Remlow Harris, *South Coast News*, May 13, 1941.

6. *South Coast News*, July 7, 1942.

7. Bill Secrest, interview with the author. As a young man, Secrest took a college history class from Wallace Smith.

8. Death certificate, County of Orange, Byrd family genealogy.

9. Lillian Kinkela Keil (stepdaughter of Eva Evans McCullough Kinkela) interviews with the author, June 29, 2004, October 2004, January 2005.

10. Adrianne Whitmore (granddaughter of Andy Kinkela), interview with the author, August 2005.

11. Bill Garvey and Elizabeth Kay McCall, "Extraordinary Service," *Hemispheres, the Magazine of United Airlines,* April 2001; author's correspondence with Adrianne Whitmore.

12. "Captain Lillian Kinkela Keil," *Air Force Link* (official website of the United States Air Force, http://www.af.mil/history/personnel).

13. *Los Angeles Times* (obituary), July 10, 2005.

14. Based on interviews with Lillian Keil, although the specific dialogue is pure conjecture, Lillian's comments provided the basis for the essence of the exchange.

15. Author interviews with Lillian Keil.

16. Ibid.

17. Author interview with Adrianne Whitmore: The author asked her about her grandfather remarrying after Eva died, because Lee Edwards once conveyed that he had tracked down Andy Kinkela in the late 1970s and that Andy was not forthcoming with information about Eva, being far too busy caring for a frail and elderly wife. Adrianne confirmed that her grandfather, Andy Kinkela, had indeed remarried. The obvious armchair analysis was pondered: that Andy had become a compulsive caregiver to compensate for the guilt he felt after abandoning his first family.

18. Author interviews with Lillian Keil and Adrianne Whitmore; Orange County death certificate, Byrd family genealogy.

BIBLIOGRAPHY

PUBLISHED BOOKS

Aldrich, Mark. *Safety First: Technology, Labor, and Business in the Building of American Work Safety, 1870-1939.* Baltimore: Johns Hopkins University Press, 1997.

Arax, Mark and Rick Wartzman. *The King of California: J. G. Boswell and the Making of a Secret American Empire.* New York: Public Affairs, Perseus Book Group, 2003.

Beckman, Alexander. *Prison Memoirs of an Anarchist.* New York: Mother Earth Press, 1912.

Bellamy, Edward. *Looking Backward 2000-1887.* R. C. Elliott Publishing, 1966. (Originally published in 1888).

Bordman, Gerald. *American Theatre: A Chronicle of Comedy and Drama, 1869-1914.* Oxford University Press, 1994.

Boessenecker, John. *Badge and Buckshot: Lawlessness in Old California.* University of Oklahoma Press, 1988.

Brown, J. L. *The Mussel Slough Tragedy.* 1958.

Bruce, John. *Gaudy Century: The Story of San Francisco's Hundred Years of Robust Journalism.* New York: Random House, 1948.

California Interstate Telephone Co. *Romantic Heritage of Inyo and Mono Counties.* 1960.

Chalfant, W. A. *The Story of Inyo.* 1933.

Deverell, William. *Railroad Crossing: Californians and the Railroad, 1850-1910.* Berkeley: University of California Press, 1994.

Dobie, Charles Caldwell. *San Francisco: A Pageant.* New York: D. Appleton-Century Company, 1939.

Edwards, Harold L. *Train Robbers and Tragedies: The Complete Story of Christopher Evans, California Outlaw.* Visalia, Calif.: Tulare County Historical Society, 2003.

Evans, Christopher. *Eurasisa.* San Francisco: The James H. Barry Co., 1908.

Elliott, W. W. *History of Tulare County*. San Francisco: Wallace W. Elliott & Co., 1883.

Gist, Brooks D. *Empire Out of the Tules: A True Story of the San Joaquin Valley in California*. Tulare, Calif., 1976.

Glasscock, C. B. *Bandits and the Southern Pacific*. New York: Frederick A. Stokes Co., 1929.

Goldman, Emma. *Living My Life.* 2 vols. Dover Publications, 1970. (Originally published by Alfred Knopf, New York, 1931.)

Griggs, Monroe C. *Wheelers, Pointers and Leaders,* Joseph Doctor and Annie Mitchell, eds. Visalia, Calif.: Valley Press, 1985.

Hearst, William Randolph. *A Portrait in His Own Words*, edited by Edmond D. Coblentz. New York: Simon & Schuster, 1952.

Johnston, Hank. *They Felled The Redwoods: A Saga of Flumes and Rails in the High Sierra*. Fish Camp, Calif.: Stauffer Publishing, 1996.

Koblas, John J. *Robbers of the Rails: The Sontag Boys of Minnesota*. St. Cloud, Minn.: North Star Press, 2003.

Latta, Frank F. *Dalton Gang Days.* Santa Cruz, Calif.: Bear State Books, 1976.

Lawson, Benjamin S. *Joaquin Miller*. Boise, Idaho: Boise State University Western Writer Series, No. 43, 1980.

Lee, Hector. *Tales of California*. Date/publisher unknown, Visalia Public Library History Room.

Lewis, Oscar. *High Sierra Country*. New York: Duell, Sloan and Pearch, 1955.

Lowrie, Donald. *My Life in Prison*. New York and London: Mitchell Kennerley, 1912.

Marberry, M. M. *Splendid Poseur: Joaquin Miller—American Poet.* New York: Thomas Y. Crowell Company, 1953.

Maxwell, Hu. *Evans and Sontag: The Famous Bandits of California*, revised edition. Fresno, Calif.: Panorama West Books, 1981.

McArthur, Benjamin. *Actors and American Culture, 1880-1920*. Philadelphia: Temple University Press, 1984.

McConachie, Bruce A. *Melodramatic Formations: American Theatre and Society, 1820-1870*. Iowa City: University of Iowa Press, 1992.

McWilliams, Carey. *Southern California Country, an Island on the Land.* New York: Duell, Sloan & Pearce, 1946.

Mitchell, Annie R. *Visalia: Her First Fifty Years*. Exeter, Calif., 1963.

____. *The Way It Was: The Colorful History of Tulare County*. Fresno, Calif.: Valley Publishers, 1976.

____. *Land of the Tules*. Fresno, Calif.: Valley Publishers, 1972.

Morrell, Ed. *The Twenty-Fifth Man*, Montclair, New Jersey: New Era Publishing Co., 1924.

Nasaw, David. *The Chief: The Life of William Randolph Hearst.* Boston and New York: Houghton Mifflin, 2000.

Norris, Frank. *The Octopus: A Story of California.* New York: Doubleday, Page and Co., 1901.

O'Brien, Robert. *This is San Francisco.* New York and Toronto: Whittlesey House, McGraw-Hill Book Co., 1948.

O'Connell, Jay. *Co-Operative Dreams: A History of the Kaweah Colony.* Van Nuys, Calif.: Raven River Press, 1999.

Palmquist, Peter. *A Bibliography of Writings By and About Women in Photography 1850-1950.* Borgo Press, 1994

Patterson, Richard. *The Train Robbery Era: An Encyclopedic History.* Boulder, Colo.: Pruett Publishing.

Secrest, William B. *Lawmen and Desperadoes.* Spokane, Wash.: Arthur C. Clarke Co., 1994.

____. *California Desperadoes: Stories of Early California Outlaws in Their Own Words.* Clovis, Calif.: Word Dancer Press, 2000.

____. *Perilous Trails, Dangerous Men.* Sanger, Calif.: Word Dancer Press, 2000.

Small, Kathleen. *History of Tulare County.* Chicago: S. J. Clarke Company, 1926.

Smith, Wallace. *Prodigal Sons: The Adventures of Christopher Evans and John Sontag.* Boston: The Christopher Publishing House, 1951.

____. *Garden of the Sun.* Los Angeles: Lymanhouse, 1939.

Wagner, Harr. *Joaquin Miller and His Other Self.* San Francisco: Harr Wagner Publishing Company, 1929.

Warner, Opie L. *A Pardoned Lifer: Life of George Sontag.* San Bernardino, Calif.: The Index Print Company, 1909.

Wells, Evelyn. *Champagne Days of San Francisco.* New York: D. Appleton-Century Company, 1939.

Winkler, John K. *W. R. Hearst: An American Phenomenon.* New York: Simon & Schuster, 1928.

Young, John P. *Journalism in California.* San Francisco: Chronicle Publishing Company, 1915.

PUBLISHED ARTICLES IN MAGAZINES, JOURNALS AND QUARTERLIES

Clarke, Francis H. "Coos Bay's North Bend." *Sunset Magazine,* June 1907.

Edwards, Harold L. "Chris Evans: The Ready Killer." *Quarterly for the National Association and Center for Outlaw and Lawman History,* Vol XI, No. 1 (Summer 1986).

_____. "Odyssey of George C. Contant." *Outlaw and Lawman History*, Vol. X, No. 4 (Spring 1986).

_____. "Come In Sheriff Kay, and Welcome." *Los Tulares* (Quarterly of the Tulare County Historical Society), No. 159 (March 1988).

_____. "Whatever Became of Jo P. Carroll?" *Los Tulares*, issue unknown.

_____. "Deputy George Witty's Last Shot." *Los Tulares*, No. 177.

_____. "Chris Evans' Early Troubles." *Los Tulares*, No. 204.

_____. "The Man Who Tricked Chris Evans." *Los Tulares* (June 1999).

_____. "Will Smith, A Study in Controversy." *Outlaw and Lawman History*, date unknown.

Fox, Stephen. "Chris Evans Could Always Be Relied On to Pull a Fast One." *Smithsonian,* May 1995.

Garvey, Bill and Elizabeth Kay McCall. "Extraordinary Service." *Hemispheres* (The Magazine of United Airlines), April 2001.

Gregory-Flesher, Helen. "A Day with Joaquin Miller." *The Arena*, No. LXIV (March 1895).

Huddleston, Charles. "A California Story: Evans and Sontag and Uncle Oscar." *Valley Voice*, June 1992.

Leslie, Frank, editor. "Joaquin Miller's Home on the Heights." *Popular Monthly*, December 1891.

McKee, Irving. "Notable Memorials to Mussel Slough." *Pacific Historical Review*, No. 17 (February 1948).

Miller, Joaquin. "Tales of Bad Men and Frontiersmen." *Pacific Monthly*, Vol. XIX (January 1908).

O'Connell, Daniel. "Sontag and Evans." *Police and Peace Officers' Journal*, August 1936.

O'Neal, Harold. "The San Joaquin Train Holdups." *Golden West* magazine, date unknown.

Orsi, Richard J. "The Octopus Reconsidered: The Southern Pacific and Agricultural Modernization in California." *California Historical Quarterly*, No. 54 (Fall 1975).

Secrest, William B. "Four Lawmen Ambush Two California Outlaws." *Outlaw and Lawman History*, Vol. III, No. 1 (Summer 1977).

_____. "In the Matter of Edward Morrell," *Fresno Past and Present* (The Journal of the Fresno City and County Historical Society), Spring 1997.

Steckmesser, Kent. "Sontag and Evans: Outlaws or Outraged?" *The Californians*, Vol. 1, No. 1 (January/February 1983).

Williams, Sam B. (as told to William B. Secrest). "He Saw the Posse Die." *Frontier Times*, July 1966.

MANUSCRIPTS, LETTERS, MISCELLANEOUS DOCUMENTS, AND INTERVIEWS

California State Archives. File# F2745:113 Department of Corrections, re: Chris Evans. Annie Mitchell History Room, Tulare County Library, Visalia, Calif.

_____. Ed Morrell parole files. Fresno County Library historical files.

Canadian Census Reports: Public Archives of Canada, Ottawa.

Transcript of Testimony in the Trial of Chris Evans, Indicted for Murder of Vernon Coke Wilson, in the Superior Court of Fresno County, California, Dec. 6-11, 1893, Vol. II. Bancroft Library, Berkeley Calif.

Evans, Eva (Evelyn McCullough). "Grat Dalton's Ride." Unpublished manuscript, Tulare County Museum, Kinkela/Keil Collection.

_____. "An Outlaw and His Family." Unpublished manuscript. Tulare County Museum, Kinkela/Keil Collection.

_____. Miscellaneous unpublished short stories: "No Death is Untimely," "An Old Cowhand," "Basement Door," and "Polar Bear Rug." Kinkela/Keil Collection, Tulare County Museum, Kinkela/Keil Collection.

Goldman, Emma. Correspondence: EG to Billee McCullough, 9/17/1929; Perry and Billee McCullough to EG, 9/29; EG to Perry McCullough, 11/29. The Emma Goldman Papers.

Keil, Lillian Kinkela (stepdaughter of Eva Evans McCullough Kinkela). Interviews with the author, June 29, 2004; October 2004; January 2005.

Kinkela, Evelyn Evans McCullough. "An Outlaw and His Family." Unpublished manuscript, The Huntington Library, San Marino, Calif.

Kinkela, Evelyn and Lillian Keil Collection. Correspondence, scrapbooks and miscellaneous personal documents kept by Eva Evans McCullough Kinkela. Tulare County Museum, Kinkela/Keil Collection.

Pugh, Jack. "Sontag and Evans: As Told to Me by Frank Maxwell." Original manuscript, Bill Secrest private collection.

Small, Kathleen, "Sontag and Evans," from *History of Tulare County* (manuscript form). Annie Mitchell History Room, Tulare County Library, Visalia, Calif.

Smith, Will. Original scrapbooks, two volumes of clippings and correspondence. John Boessenecker private collection.

Tulare County Clerk's Office, Visalia. Copy of divorce complaint, Eva Evans, Plaintiff vs. James U. Evans, Defendant, March 30, 1896.

United States Census Reports, various.

White, Richard Cullen. "Evans and Sontag: The Visalia Bandits." Original handwritten manuscript of the play, 1893. Tulare County Museum, Bob Lilley Collection.

____. "Evans and Sontag: The Home of Sontag." Original handwritten manuscript (unfinished) of play, date unknown (circa 1909). Tulare County Museum, Bob Lilley Collection.

____. Curtain Speech. Original handwritten draft, 1894. Tulare County Museum, Bob Lilley Collection

Whitmore, Adrianne (granddaughter of Andy Kinkela, Eva's last husband). Interview with the author, August 2005.

NEWSPAPERS

Bakersfield Californian
Bakersfield Echo
Chicago Tribune
Cutler-Orosi Courier
Coos Bay (Oregon) *Times*
Fresno Daily Republican
Fresno Expositor
Fresno Weekly Democrat
Hanford Journal
Heppner (Oregon) *Gazette*
Laguna Beach Post News
Los Angeles Times
Los Angeles Evening Express
Los Angeles Record
Mankato (Minnesota) *Free Press*
Mankato (Minnesota) *Daily Review*
Milwaukee (Wisconsin) *Journal*
Modesto Daily News
New York Times
Portland (Oregon) *Journal*
Portland (Oregon) *Morning Oregonian*
Sacramento Evening Bee
San Diego Union
San Francisco Call
San Francisco Chronicle
San Francisco Examiner
South Coast (Laguna Beach) *News*
Stockton Independent
Tulare County Times
Tulare Daily Evening Register
Visalia Daily Times
Visalia Weekly Delta

ACKNOWLEDGMENTS

I DISCOVERED A LONG TIME AGO that writing a book can be an experiment in cooperation and takes the strength born of giants. Well, it also requires a sizeable posse and I offer thanks to the following individuals.

Arleen Anderson and Barbara Baker, for sharing their genealogical research; Hawley Anderson; David Atherton, who shared my efforts in putting this story in a different format and will certainly be involved when Eva makes her screen debut; Jesse Babb, grandson of Ranger Jess Waller; Paul Bryant; Bill Deverell; Maxine Story Dougan; Jessica Gordon; Crystal Greene; Jane Janz; Paul R. Jones and Steve LaMar for bringing the melodrama to life; Larry Jordan; Rich Kangas, Jack Koblas, the "Minnesota Connection"; Lillian Keil; Bob Lilley; Bob Mathias; Bob McCubbin; Kathy McGowan; Brooke Minters; Gertrude Paul of the Colfax Area Historical Society; Bob Salas, Ray Silva, Jami Spittler, and Adrianne Whitmore.

I couldn't even contemplate writing a book about Eva Evans without the support of the following band of "outlaws." We've all traipsed the territory covered by Evans and Sontag together, both figuratively and literally. Thanks to Troy Tuggle, who always made sure I was invited to those memorable bull sessions at the Raddison; Lee Edwards, who wrote the book on Chris and first told me where to locate Eva's memoir; Terry Ommen, Visalia's historian extraordinaire and the driving force behind the Evans and Sontag Project; John Boessenecker, who offered his expert support and actually grew to like Eva...really like her; and Bill Secrest, who has been a generous champion of this project since I first knocked on his door.

A number of institutions made the research for this biography possible. Among the libraries that provided materials and/or a clean, well lighted place to work were the Los Angeles Public Library (especially the beautiful main branch downtown); the Burbank Public Library; the

Claremont College Library; the California State Library in Sacramento; the Laguna Beach Public Library; the Oviatt Library at California State University at Northridge; the Huntington Library in San Marino; the Fresno Public Library and its wonderful California Room; and the Tulare County Public Library in Visalia, especially the Annie Mitchell History Room. I heartily thank the librarians, volunteers and custodial staffs of all those libraries.

Several institutions made possible inclusion of the illustrations in this book. I would like to thank Bill Franks, Jennifer Watts and Peter Blodgett at the Huntington Library; Chris Brewer and Bear State Books in Exeter, California; the Tulare County Library; the Ohio State University, Library of Cartoon Art; and Kathy McGowan and the Tulare County Museum, which now houses the Kinkela/Keil Collection and the Bob Lilley Collection and boasts the wonderful permanent exhibit "From Headlines to Footlights: The Sensational Saga of Evans and Sontag."

I've mentioned many of them already, but one can't thank those who read and edit their work enough. A good reader is never afraid to tell a writer what they really think, and the following were all courageous and insightful in their comments, notes and suggestions: Hawley Anderson, John Boessenecker, Jessica Gordon, Brooke Minters, and Bill Secrest. Sarah Barton Elliott has edited just about everything I've ever published, and I can't thank her enough for her exceptional work on this project. I also owe a debt of gratitude to her and John Elliott and the *Kaweah Commonwealth* for publishing my first meager attempts at telling the story of Evans and Sontag.

This book is ultimately a story of family love, and with that in mind I must take the opportunity to thank my own family for their love and support. I thank my parents for fostering my creativity and curiosity. And finally, thanks to my wife, Susie, and our boys, J. P. and Colin, for everything because they are everything to me.

Index

Abbott, Charles, 132
acting profession, 141, 156
Adelaide (San Luis Obispo County), California, 15
anarchist movement, 230, 232
Astoria, Oregon, 199
Aucland, California, 7, 14
Aull, Charles, 117, 153-55, 193-94, 198

Bacon, Billy, 120, 123
Bakersfield Echo, 142
Bandits and the Southern Pacific (Glasscock), 91, 105, 240-41
Barton, Hudson, 3
Beaver, Oscar, 74, 75-76
Bellamy, Edward, 234-35
Bells Corners, Ontario, 4
Belshaw, Mortimer, 14
Bentley, Ed, 33-34
Bequette, Frank, 64, 67, 163
Berkman, Alexander, 231-32
Bessie Brady (steamer), 14
Bierce, Ambrose, 87, 108
Bigelow, A. D., 10
Bigelow, Constance, 109
Bigelow, Henry D. "Petey," 97-99, 107-10, 110-11, 113, 126, 176,
big trees. *see* giant sequoias
Black, Samuel, 114-15
Bonanza wheat farms. *see* wheat production in Central Valley
Brighton, Jonas V., 187-89, 190
Brighton, Mrs., 187, 190
Broder, John, 92-93, 99
Brophy, Eddie, 108-9
Burke, Frank, 84, 91, 92-95
Burns, Tom, 114-15, 123-25
Burrell, Walter, 216

Burrell, William "Billy," 231
Burrell, Winifred. *see* Evans, Winifred
Byrd, Edith (cousin of Eva), 171
Byrd, Frank (uncle of Eva), 79
Byrd, George (uncle of Eva), 191
Byrd, Isabella "Grannie" (Saunders; maternal grandmother of Eva), 7, 9, 12, 13, 18, 140, 166, 187, 190, 229
Byrd, Jesse (maternal grandfather of Eva), 6, 7-8, 10, 18
Byrd, Louis (uncle of Eva), 10, 13
Byrd, Perry (uncle of Eva), 55, 57, 122, 127, 128, 140, 162, 171-72, 177

Camlin, Jack, 90, 170
Camp Badger, 113-14
Camp Manzanita. *see* hideouts
Carroll, Jo P., 97, 125
cattle industry in Central Valley, 7
Cerro Gordo mines (Inyo Co.), 13
Champagne Days of San Francisco (Wells), 138
Claypool, Jacob, death of, in livery stable fire, 43-44
Cochran, Bennie, 179
Coffee, John, 98
Coffeyville (Kansas) bank robbery, 99-100
Collis, California (Kerman), 65
Columbia River, flooding of, 199-200
combinations, touring, 156
Comstock, Smith, 7, 265
Contant, George. *see* Sontag, George
Contant, Jacob (father of John and George Sontag), 25
Contant, John. *see* Sontag, John

Contant, Maria. *see* Sontag, Maria
    Contant (nee Bohn)
Coos Bay (Daily) Times, 219
Cribbs, Albert F. (husband of Eva),
    211-12
Cribbs and Mason (photography
    studio), 219-20, 221, 223
Cribbs, Eva. *see* Evans, Eva
Crow, Walter J., 16, 30-31
Cunningham, Thomas, 54
curtain speech (White), 183

Dalton, Bill, 51, 56
Dalton, Bob, 51, 100
Dalton, Emmett, 51, 100
Dalton Gang Days (Latta), 55
Dalton, Gratton (Grat), 51, 53, 55,
    57, 100, 251
Dalton, Lewis, 51
Dalton, Littleton (Lit), 51, 52
Davidson, E. M., 125
Deck, Edward, 178, 180-81
Deep Creek Cemetery, 244
Delany, Martin. *see* Morrell, Ed
DeMasters, Newton, 6
Deverell, William, 225
Downing, Bill, 7, 85, 91, 96, 185,
    188-89
Downing, Jane, 96
Downing ranch, 104
Dry Creek, 186

Edwards, Harold L., 88, 263
Egan, Jack, 5
Ellis, Arthur. *see* Ellis, John (Jack)
Ellis, John (Jack), 200, 201, 202,
    203-4
Ellis, Samuel, 89-90, 92
English, William, 125
Eurasia (Evans), 234-35
*Evans and Sontag: The Bandits of
    Visalia* (melodrama), *xii-xiii*, 138
    excerpts of, 147, 148-151
    negative reaction to, 142, 144,
        157-59, 182
    opening night of, 146

    reviews of, 146, 148, 151-52, 159,
        199
    Up to Date (revision after jail-
        break), 181, 187
Evans and Sontag (touring) Combi-
    nation, 156, 158, 161, 172-73,
    198
Evans, Carl (brother of Eva), 52, 189,
    205-6, 213-14, 252, 254-55
Evans, Chris (father of Eva):
    abuse of Mrs. Brighton by, 190
    acquires livery stable, 39
    amputation (arm) of, 130-31
    appeal, hopes of, 174
    army experiences of, 4-5
    arrest at Perkins house, 126-28
    arrival in Visalia, 5-6
    attends Goldman lecture, 236
    baptism (Catholic) of, 133
    beating of A. D. Bigelow by, 10-11
    birth of, 4
    as character in melodrama, 181
    as Charles Naughton, 61-62
    code of ethics of, 20, 203
    Collis robbery and, 66-67, 102
    confederates (gang) of, 178
    Dalton (Grat) and, 52, 55, 57, 251
    Dalton trial and, 53, 58
    death of, 237-38
    defense of, 81-82, 148, 154-55,
        164, 170, 233
    and Ellis (Samuel), 89-90
    encounter with Smith and Witty,
        71-73, 81-82
    escape from jail by, 179-81
    on Eva appearing in play, 141
    final capture of, 188-91
    at Folsom Prison, 193-94
    horses, fondness of, 41-42, 44, 76
    Indian yarns of, 19
    interviewed by Bigelow, 99
    jailhouse autobiography of, 5
    Kaweah Colony and, 234
    leaves parents' home, 4
    letter to White from, 140

Evans, Chris (*continued*):
  literary appreciation/education of, 21, 22, 100
  loses money on bean crop, 22-23
  in Mankato (Minnesota), 61
  meets Molly Byrd, 6-8
  Miller (Joaquin) and, 227-28
  Morrell (Ed) and, 184-87, 189
  moves to Portland, 227
  nickname (Bolivar) of, 116
  obituaries of, 241
  parole of, 217-18, 225-26
  predicts citrus prevalence, 244
  profiled in press, 85-86, 87
  property transactions of, 49, 56-57
  prosthetic arm of, 186-87
  question of guilt, *xiv,* 50, 54-55
  relationship with Eva, 43, 97, 194
  shootout with Beaver (Oscar), 75-76
  shot at Stone Corral, 122-24
  Smith (Will) and, 68, 95
  snow plant gift from, 120
  Sontag (George) and, 63-64
  Sontag (John) and, 30-31, 36, 116, 124
  teamster career of, 8
  trial of, 162-65, 166-72
  visits Eva in Los Angeles, 236-37
  visits to family during manhunt by, 80, 105-6; 111-13
  wedding day of, 3-9
  work at grain warehouses, 29, 52
  work on Owens Lake, 14
  writes *Eurasia*, 234-35
  at Young's cabin shootout, 94-96
Evans, Elmer (brother of Eva), 14, 15, 244
Evans, Eugene (brother of Eva), 10, 244
Evans, (Evelina Isabella) Eva (Mrs. Albert Cribbs, Mrs. Perry McCullough, Mrs. Andrew Kinkela):
  acting ability of, 143, 145, 152, 158, 166, 182
  additional acting roles of, 202
  admission of father's guilt by, *xiv,* 82, 260
  appearance in melodrama by, 138-41, 144, 153, 158
  attempted rape of, 201
  attempts to publish memoir, 247-48, 253
  attendance of Catholic services by, 205
  attendance of George's trial by, 84, 100-102
  on betrayal by Perry Byrd, 128, 171-72
  Bigelow (Petey) and, 97, 107-10
  birth of, 12
  as caretaker, 254
  as character in melodrama, 148-151
  comments on death of John by, 134, 154
  consciousness of criminal activity, 37, 38, 42-43, 50, 60, 65, 82, 100, 180
  contracts diphtheria, 15
  on Dalton's jailbreak, 57, 251
  death of, 261-62
  on death of Elmer, 15
  on death of father, 237-38
  depression and drug use of, 206, 211
  describes melodrama, 147, 181
  divorces of, 204, 223
  donation of memoir by, *xii,* 259-60
  engagement of John Sontag and, 86, 126, 176
  equestrian skills of, 198
  failure as an actress of, 202
  at father's baptism, 133
  on father's final capture, 188-89
  father's jailbreak and, 178-80
  on father's Los Angeles visit, 236-37
  first visit to theatre by, 109
  Fredericks (William) and, 129-30, 176, 195-97
  George's confession, reaction to, 153, 155

Evans, Eva (*continued*):
Goldman (Emma) and, 229-31, 241-43
guns, use of and procurement by, 67, 119, 129-30, 155, 174
hears news of Stone Corral, 123
illness of, 200
illness of Perry and, 228
injured on stage, 157-58, 200
in Inyo County, 13
Jim Evans and, 140-41, 160-61, 174, 183-84, 203
Keil (Lillian) and, 258-59
Kinkela (Andy) and, 256, 260-61
maintains father's innocence, 233, 241, 247
marriages of, 160, 176, 183-84, 203-4, 211-12, 223, 256
marriages (rumored) of, 107, 203-4
meets Perry McCullough, 222
memories of Redwood Ranch, 19, 40
as messenger to fugitives, 103-4, 113
Miller (Joaquin) and, 117, 221
at Moore's (Clark) trial, 110-11
Morrell (Ed) and, 177, 178
as mother figure to Carl, 255
moves to Laguna Beach, 241
moves to Los Angeles, 225
news coverage, interest in, 85, 96, 184
nickname (Billee) of, 229
in nursing home, 260-61
obituary of, *ix*
parole of father and, 226
photography career of, 219-20, 228
physical description of, 13, 32, 36, 44-45, 86, 101, 117, 159, 166, 255-56
press coverage/public notoriaty of, 86, 107, 118, 151-52, 158, 161, 183-84, 197-98
propensity for older men of, 211
protest of play, reaction to, 182
reaction to birth of sisters, 17

recounts Beaver shooting, 75
recounts start of troubles, 69-73
respect for Sheriff Kay by, 191-92
riding ability of, 144
in San Francisco, 40-41, 108-9, 181
school attendance/education of, 21-22, 58, 249
seaside vacation, memories of, 53-54
sex appeal of, 142-43, 156, 161, 175-76
on shooting of Deputy Black, 114-15
short stories of, 250-51
Smith (Will) and, 70-71, 118
Sontag (George) and, 67
Sontag (John) and, *xiv,* 32, 43, 60-61, 64, 74, 105, 126, 130-31, 133
sues Smith (Wallace) for plagiarism, 254
suicide attempt of, 206
testimony at father's trial by, 161, 167-72
as touring actress, 156, 187, 199-200
verdict, reaction to, 173
visits father at Folsom Prison, 194, 203
visits father in jail, 131
visits father in Portland, 228-29
visits from father during manhunt, recollections of, 81, 88, 105-6, 112-13
warns father of Wilson's threat, 91, 97
Wilson (Vic) and, 90, 170
writes memoir, 243-247
writing ambitions of, 248-51
on Young's cabin shootout, 94
Evans, James (husband of Eva), 140-41, 159-60, 174, 176, 183-84, 203-4
Evans, John Christopher (brother of Eva), 37, 206
Evans, Joseph (brother of Eva), *ix*, 21, 105, 191, 206, 259
Evans, Louis (brother of Eva), 30, 105, 206-7, 229, 239-40, 250

Evans, Mary Ann (nee Switzer) (paternal grandmother of Eva), 4
Evans, Molly (Mary Jane) Byrd (mother of Eva), 6, 14
  appearance in melodrama of, 138-41, 145, 152, 159
  attendance of George's trial by, 84, 100-102
  in auto accident with Louis, 239-40
  boards Joaquin Miller's children, 214
  Brightons and, 188
  consciousness of criminal activity, 36, 64, 178
  death of, 254
  delicate nature/fainting of, 76, 112-13, 118, 174, 179-80
  emotional state of, 120
  Eva's marriage to Jim Evans, reaction to, 160, 183-84
  George's confession, reaction to, 153, 155
  in Inyo County, 13-14
  Kay (Sheriff Eugene) and, 79-80
  as laundress, 205
  on melodrama tour, 200
  at Moore's (Clark) trial, 110-11
  moves to Portland, 215-16
  ownership of Redwood Ranch by, 57
  pregnancy and childbirth, 9, 17, 21, 30, 37, 52
  public humiliation of, 104-5, 107
  reaction to Smith/Witty encounter, 73, 75
  sale of Redwood Ranch by, 215
  Sontag (Maria) and, 133, 154
  wedding day of, 3-9
Evans, Thomas Galway (paternal grandfather of Eva), 4
Evans, Tom (uncle of Eva, twin brother of Chris), 10, 13
Evans, Winifred (Mrs. Walter Burrell, Mrs. Albert Gutierrez), 105, 129, 165, 206
  birth of, 17-18

  brings Carl to The Hights, 214
  at Convent school, 205
  efforts toward father's parole, 217, 224-26
  marries Burrell, 216
  marries Gutierrez, 224
  Miller (Joaquin) and, 212-13
  moves to Portland, 216
  moves to Sacramento, 216
  testimony at father's trial of, 169
Evans, Ynez (Mrs. Mason, Mrs. Norris Jensen), *ix*, 105, 126, 240, 243
  birth of, 17
  at Convent school, 205
  death of, 259
  as jealous octogenarian, 256
  marries Jensen (Norris), 222
  marries Mason, 216
  moves to Laguna Beach, 252
  Miller (Joaquin) and, 212-13, 221
  moves to Portland, 216
  rents room to Andy Kinkela, 255
express companies/agents, 37

Farmersville, California, 7, 244
Farrelly, Father, 131, 133, 205, 206
Fitzgerald, Mary, 232
Flight Nurse (motion picture), 257
Folsom Prison, 116, 132, 193-94, 195
Ford, John, 259
Fort Defiance. *see* hideouts
Fredericks, William, 116, 129-30, 132, 155, 175-76, 195-97, 204
Fresno, California, 63, 66, 84, 97, 100, 110, 133, 145, 161, 166, 175-77
Fresno Expositor, 24, 80, 161, 195
Fresno jail, 132, 133, 174, 177, 179-81, 187, 193
Fresno Republican, 37, 139, 158, 164, 177, 179, 180, 187

Gard, George, 119-20, 123-25, 189
General Grant (giant sequoia) Tree, 117

Glasscock, C. B. (Carl), 26-27, 91, 105, 240-41
giant sequoias, 53, 265
Goldman, Emma, 229-31, 232, 236, 241-43
Goshen, California, 26
Goucher, G. G., 167
Grat Dalton's Ride (Evans), 251
Great Railroad Strike, The (play by H. Knox), 202
Gutierrez, Albert, 222, 224
Gutierrez, Winifred. *see* Evans, Winifred

Hall, Charles, 74
Hall, Fred, 68
Hall, Luke, 125
Hall, William, 126-28, 191
Hanford, California, 15, 31, 158
Hanford Journal, 158
Harris, M. K., 163-65, 170, 195
Haskell, Burnette, 234-35
Haswell, Charles, 50
Hearst, George, 27
Hearst, William Randolph, *x*, 27-28, 85, 108, 115, 142
Heppner Gazette, 199, 202
Heppner, Oregon, 199, 216
Herrick, William, 196-97
hideouts, 103
    Camp Manzanita, 104, 185
    Fort Defiance, 104
Hights, The (estate of Joaquin Miller), 212-13
Hill, Warren, 92, 99
Hinds, Samuel J., 163-65, 172
Hirst, Reverend Dr., 182-83
horse racing in Central Valley, 51-52
horses, stage trained, 156
Hubley, Grace, 218-19
Hume, James, 68, 80, 84, 153-54
Huntington, Arabella, 260
Huntington, Collis P., 65, 260
Huntington, Henry E., 260
Huntington Library (San Marino, California), *xii,* 259-60, 263

Hutchinson, Grace Lee, 175
Hutchinson, Henry, 180-81
Hutchinson, Jim, 175, 178, 180-81
Hutchinson, Rose Lee, 175, 180-81
Hutchinson, Will, 180-81
Hyde sawmill, 9

Indian trackers, 92, 95, 99
Inyo County, California, 13
IWW (Industrial Workers of the World), 231

Jackson, Fred, 122, 123-25
James, Jesse, *x*, 35-36
James and Younger gang, 36, 51, 100
Jensen, Norris, 222
Jensen, Ynez. *see* Evans, Ynez
Johnson, (California governor) Hiram, 224-25, 236
Jungmeyer, Jack, 226

Kaweah Colony, 234-35
Kay, (Sheriff) Eugene, 73, 80, 90
    Alila robbery and, 50-51
    botches capture at Evans house, 111-12
    Dalton jailbreak and, 57
    Evans surrender and, 189-91
    gratitude by Eva to, 192
    horses of, 76
    hunt for Daltons, 52
    kindness to Evans family by, 79
    political difficulties of, 80, 113
    rumors of Evans sightings and, 118
    suspects Evans and Sontag, 50-51, 54-56, 68
Keil, Lillian Kinkela, *xiii,* 256-59, 260-61
Keil, Walter, 257
Kings River, California, 185
Kinkela, Andrew (husband of Eva), *xiii,* 255-56, 258, 260
Kinkela, Evelyn (Eva). *see* Evans, Eva
Kirkland, Walter, 185

Laguna Beach, California, *ix*, 241,
    249, 252-53
Latta, Frank, 55
Laurie, Annie. *see* Sweet, Winifred
Lee, Milton Harvey, 175
Lewis, Bill, 66
Lilley, Bob, *xii,* 263
Little Jim Hospital (San Francisco),
    213-14
livery stable (Sontag & Evans,
    Modesto), 39, 43-44, 49, 53
Living My Life (Goldman), 243
"Locksley Hall" (Tennyson), 21, 238
logging in southern Sierra, 7, 234,
    265
London, Jack, 109, 233
Looking Backward (Bellamy), 234-35
loot (swag), search for by officers,
    78, 84
Los Angeles, California, 25, 119, 225,
    239
*Los Angeles Time*s, *xiii,* 65, 87, 93,
    101, 115
Los Angeles River, flooding of, 25
Lovern, Si, 129-30
lynching, threat of, 132

Maddox, Ben, 85
Mainwaring, Ed, 94
Mankato House (hotel), 25
Mankato, Minnesota, 25, 35-36, 232
Markham, (California governor)
    George, 108, 154
Marshfield (Coos Bay), Oregon, 219
Martin, Ed. *see* Morrell, Ed
Mason, Ynez. *see* Evans, Ynez
McCullough, Bret, 222, 223
McCullough, Eva "Billee." *see* Evans,
    Eva
McCullough, Perry, 222-23, 224, 228-
    32, 239, 241, 244-45, 248, 252-54
McEwan, Arthur, 108
McEwen, Mildred, 233
McGinnis, Andrew, 92-96
McGowan, Kathy, *xii,* 263
McKeon, Mr. (school janitor), 22, 90

McSwords, Dr. (Heppner, Ore.), 200,
    216
McWilliams, Carey, 239
melodrama, "blood and thunder,"
    146-47
Methodist Church, South (Visalia),
    81, 104
Methodist ministers, protest by,
    182-83
Michelson, Charles, 97, 204
Miller, Joaquin, 115-16,120, 145
    appeal for Evans' parole by, 217
    helps Evans family, 212-15
    interview with Chris Evans, 117-18
    photographed with Chris Evans,
    227-28
    visit to Marshfield by, 221
M'Liss, or the Waif of the Sierras
    (play by Bret Harte), 200
Modesto, California, 38-39, 54
Modesto Daily News, 43
Moore, Clark, 98, 109-10
Morrell, Ed, 162, 175-77, 178-181,
    184-87, 191, 195, 205, 220-21,
    233, 242-43
Muldoon's Picnic (play), 202
Mussel Slough, tragedy at, *x*, 15-16,
    30-31
    referred to in melodrama, 150, 158

Nationalist movement, 239-35
Naughton, Charles (alias of Chris
    Evans), 61-62
New York World, 28
No Fence Law of 1874, 17
Norris, Frank, 17, 109

Oakland, California, 156-57
Octopus, The (Norris), 17, 242
Ommen, Terry, *xiii,* 263
"Outlaw and His Family, An" (mem-
    oir by Eva) *xii, xv,* 247, 249, 254
Overall, Dan, 50, 74, 76, 80
Owen, Pike Bill, 6
Owens Lake, 14

Page, Dr., 206, 211-12
Palace Hotel, (Visalia), 67, 124
Pardee, (California governor) George, 218
Pascoe, Sheriff (Nevada Co.), 196
Patnot, Arthur, 79
Perkins, Elijah, 9, 127-29
Perkins, Lije (character in melo-drama), 147
Perkins Ranch (Wilcox Canyon), 126-28
Phipps, Al, 66, 163
photography, 218-19
Poodle Dog Cafe (San Francisco), 40-41, 109
Portland, Oregon, 199, 211, 215-16, 227, 236
posses, 80, 87, 92, 111, 186-87
Prison Memories of an Anarchist (Berkman), 232
Prodigal Sons (Smith), 19, 22-23, 254
Pulitzer, Joseph, 28

Radcliffe, George, 50
railroads:
    arrival of in Central Valley, 17
    worker safety and, 24
Rapelje, Hi, 122-25, 128, 133
Rattlesnake Ranch, 7, 8, 245
Redwood Mountain, 246-47
Redwood Ranch, 9, 18, 20, 57, 215, 244-45
redwoods. *see* giant sequoia trees
Reedley, California, 253
Reitman, Ben, 230-31
reward for capture of Evans and Sontag, 34, 68, 91
Riley, Dean, 56
Roberts, George, 65, 163
rumored sightings of Evans and Sontag, 79, 87, 89, 118-19

Sacramento Bee, 143
Sacramento Star, 226
Sampson's Flat, 60, 93-94, 111, 115
San Bernardino, California, 157, 175

San Francisco Call, 140, 163
San Francisco Chronicle, 28, 54, 59, 72, 84, 89, 96, 122, 146, 148, 177, 180, 203, 219
San Francisco (city of), 108-9, 181
    Midwinter Fair at, 187
    Mission District of, 142
    popularity of theatre in, 138
San Francisco Examiner, x, 5, 66, 72, 73, 79, 96, 127, 133, 137, 153, 155, 158, 177, 180, 189-90, 197, 202
    Bigelow interview in, 98-99
    contribution to Robin Hood myth by, 114
    coverage of Evans trial by, 165, 166-68
    coverage of melodrama by, 183
    editorializing on Evans and Sontag by, 83, 87, 114
    extent of coverage by, 77, 85, 115, 142, 146
    headline use by, 77, 134, 143, 184
    Hearst takes control of, 28
    Market Street offices of, 108
    purple prose of, 82, 139
    reviews of melodrama by, 145-46, 148, 151-52, 182
    sensational style of, 85
San Francisco Star, 227-28
Sanger, Margaret, 231
San Jose Mercury, 142
San Quentin (prison), 220-21
sawmills. *see* logging in southern Sierra
Scott, Ben, 179, 181
Scott, Jay, 128, 187, 218
Secrest, William, 233
Sequoia Mills, 113
Sequoia National Forest, 215-16
Sequoia National Park, 216, 234
Smith, Wallace, 19, 22-23, 91, 113, 181, 253, 254
Smith, Will, 68, 69, 99
    background and professional history of, 71

Smith, Will (*continued*):
  characterized as Wily Smooth, 144
  Daltons and, 52, 56
  encounters with Chris Evans, 68,
    70-73
  Eva Evans and, 70-71, 118, 167-70
  Morrell (Ed) and, 176
  personality of, 56, 71
  ridicule faced by, 80
  at Young's cabin, 92-96
Smooth, Wily (character in melo-
    drama), 144, 148-51
Snow, Alva, 217
snow plants, 120
Songs of the Sierras, (Miller), 115
Sontag, George (Contant), 25, 36, 83,
    134
  attempted breakout at Folsom,
    132-33
  Chris Evans and, 59-62, 63-64
  Collis robbery and, 66-67, 69, 81,
    84
  confession of, 153-55
  death of son and wife, 220
  early crimes of, 58
  at Folsom Prison, 116
  on lecture circuit, 232-33
  paroled, 220
  Racine robbery and, 59
  testifies at Evans trial, 163-64,
    171-72
  trial of, 101-2
Sontag Hotel, 25, 35
Sontag, John, *xiv,* 163, 167-69, 183
  arrival in California of, 25
  birth of, 25
  broken ankle of, 60, 62, 76
  character in melodrama, 149, 203
  Chris Evans and, 31, 36, 63, 116,
    124
  Collis robbery and, 64, 66-67, 102
  death of, 133-34
  discharge from hospital, 29
  Eva Evans and, 86, 105, 130-31,
    133, 176, 203
  grave of, 145

  horse expertise of, 38
  injured working on railroad, 24-25
  moves in with Evans family, 32
  persecution by SPRR of, 81-82
  physical description of, 43, 118
  property transaction by, 56-57
  reminiscence of James gang by,
    35-36
  return to Minnesota of, 52, 54, 58
  shootout with Beaver, 76
  at Stone Corral, 123-25
  at Young's cabin shootout, 94-96
Sontag, Maria Contant (nee Bohn),
    (mother of John and George
    Sontag), 25, 133, 134, 154
  as character in melodrama, 147
Sontag, Mathias Josef (stepfather of
    John and George Sontag), 25
Sontag Tragedy, The (melodrama),
    138. see also *Evans and Sontag:
    The Visalia Bandits*
Southern Pacific Railroad, *x*, 101,
    225, 260
  Kaweah Colony and, 234
  main line bypasses Visalia, 25
  monopoly on transporting goods, 23
  Mussel Slough and, 15
  Porterville branch line, 178
  reward offered by, 91
Star Rover, The (London), 233
Stewart, George W., 85
Stokes Mountain (Tulare County), 88,
    120, 123
Stone Corral, 245
  cabin from, 137, 182
  landmark of, 120
  location of, 123
  photo taken at, 125-26, 137
  shootout at, 122-25
Stuart, Harry, 125
Sweet and Company, mercantile
    (Visalia), 38, 64, 78, 104
Sweet, Sol, 38, 55-56
Sweet, Winifred (Annie Laurie), 108,
    214, 247-48

teamsters, 7
Tennyson, Alfred Lord, 21, 100
Thacker, John, 68, 74, 80, 84, 99, 119
theatres:
  Armory Hall (Bakersfield), 157
  Avon Theatre (Stockton), 160
  Baldwin Theatre (San Francisco), 139
  Barton Opera House (Fresno), 157
  Grand Opera House (San Francisco), 138
  Hazzard Pavillon (Los Angeles), 156
  National Theatre (San Francisco), 142, 146, 155
  Oakland Theatre, 187
  Orpheum (San Francisco), 138
  Tivoli Opera House (San Francisco), 109, 138
touring theatrical productions. *see* combinations (theatrical), touring
train robberies:
  Alila (Earlimart), 49-50
  Ceres, 54
  Collis, as depicted in melodrama, 149, 158
  Collis (Kerman), 65-66
  by Dalton gang in Oklahoma, 64
  Goshen, 37, 55
  Kasota, Minnesota, 61
  Pixley, 33-35
  Racine, Wisconsin, 59
  Train Robbers and Tragedies (Edwards), 88
Train Wreckers, The (melodrama), 137
Traver, California, 30
Tulare (city of), California, 26, 30
Tulare County Museum, *xiii, xiv,* 263
Tupper, W. D., 140, 162-63, 171

Twenty-Fifth Man, The (Morrell), 176, 233

Vasquez, Tiburcio, 14
Visalia, California, 6, 14, 17, 53, 57, 83, 85, 92, 115, 120, 123-26, 129, 177, 180, 187, 212, 244-45
Visalia Daily Times (*Tulare County Times*), 85, 86, 87, 115, 159, 203
Visalia Delta, 6, 16, 34, 37, 53, 84, 85, 89,115, 124, 157, 198
Visalia jail, 132, 193, 251

Wagner, Harr, 214
Waller, (Ranger) Jess, 245-47
Wells, Evelyn, 138
Wells Fargo (Co.), 84, 91
wheat production in Central Valley, 17, 29
White, Laura, 161, 200
White, Nora, 201
White, R. C. (Richard Cullen), *xii,* 138, 139-43, 153, 156, 159, 173, 181, 183, 199-200
Whitmore, Adrianne, *xiii*
Wilcox Canyon, 120, 123
Williams, Frank, 116, 132
Wilson, Vernon Coke "Vic," 82-84, 90, 92-96, 170
Wilty, Jud (character in melodrama), 149
Witty, Al, 92-96
Witty, George, 50, 55, 68, 69, 72-73, 81-82, 125, 167
Wolf, Dan, 201

Younger, Adeline Lee, 51
Younger, Cole, 35, 51
Young's cabin, shootout at, 93-96

ABOUT THE AUTHOR

JAY O'CONNELL is the author of *Co-Operative Dreams: A History of the Kaweah Colony,* the co-author of *A Strength Born of Giants: The Life and Times of Dr. Forest Grunigen,* and has written numerous newspaper and magazine articles on regional history. He served as Executive Director of the EVANS & SONTAG PROJECT, producing a permanent museum exhibit for the Tulare County Museum and bringing to the stage, for the first time in over a century, *Evans and Sontag: The Visalia Bandits* at the historic Fox Theatre in Visalia, California.

O'Connell, who works in the television industry as a production manager, is researching his next book, a narrative history entitled *The Battle Over Mineral King: Walt Disney, the Sierra Club, and a Small California Town.* He lives in the Los Angeles area with his wife and two sons.